GOVERNING
GLOBALIZATION

GOVERNING GLOBALIZATION

Challenges for Democracy and Global Society

Edward A. Kolodziej

ROWMAN & LITTLEFIELD
INTERNATIONAL

London • New York

Published by Rowman & Littlefield International Ltd
Unit A, Whitacre Mews, 26-34 Stannary Street, London SE11 4AB
www.rowmaninternational.com

Rowman & Littlefield International Ltd. is an affiliate of Rowman & Littlefield
4501 Forbes Boulevard, Suite 200, Lanham, Maryland 20706, USA
With additional offices in Boulder, New York, Toronto (Canada), and Plymouth (UK)
www.rowman.com

British Library Cataloguing in Publication Data
A catalogue record for this book is available from the British Library

ISBN: HB 978-1-78348-762-2
      PB 978-1-78348-763-9

Library of Congress Cataloging-in-Publication Data

Names: Kolodziej, Edward A., author.
Title: Governing globalization : challenges for democracy and global society
   / Edward A. Kolodziej.
Description: London ; New York : Rowman & Littlefield International, 2016. |
   Includes bibliographical references and index.
Identifiers: LCCN 2015049755 (print) | LCCN 2016008693 (ebook) | ISBN
   9781783487622 (cloth : alk. paper) | ISBN 9781783487639 (pbk. : alk.
   paper) | ISBN 9781783487646 (electronic)
Subjects: LCSH: Globalization—Political aspects. | Globalization—Economic
   aspects. | International cooperation. | Democracy—International
   cooperation. | Legitimacy of governments.
Classification: LCC JZ1318 .K6516 2016 (print) | LCC JZ1318 (ebook) | DDC
   303.48/2—dc23
LC record available at http://lccn.loc.gov/2015049755

∞™ The paper used in this publication meets the minimum requirements of
American National Standard for Information Sciences—Permanence of Paper
for Printed Library Materials, ANSI/NISO Z39.48-1992.

Printed in the United States of America

To my wife, Antje

Contents

Illustrations

Figures

Tables

Acknowledgments

M Y SINCERE THANKS TO MY GRADUATE STUDENTS in "Global Studies 500: Governing Globalization: The Pursuit of Order, Welfare, and Legitimacy." Student feedback and criticism perfected this volume's argument. Yaacov Vertzberger of Hebrew University and Roger Kanet of Miami University read earlier versions of the manuscript. Professors Hadi Esfahani, Larry Neal, and Mahdi Rastad critiqued the economic chapters. All made valuable suggestions that strengthened the manuscript.

Tom Ewing, John Laich, and Harold Chang were unfailingly excellent research assistants. Lynn Charters, the office manager for the Center for Global Studies during my tenure as director, and Kathleen Anderson-Conner, who occupied the same post when I was director of the Program in Arms Control, Disarmament, and International Security, provided timely and flawless logistical support through the many revisions of the volume.

The Center's global studies librarian, Lynne Rudasill, was always at the ready in replying to my seemingly endless requests for access to materials.

I am also indebted to Anna Reeve, senior commissioning editor of Rowman & Littlefield International, for guiding the manuscript through the publication process and for soliciting critiques of the volume by two anonymous reviewers, who recommended publication.

My son, Professor Matthew Eliot Kolodziej, graciously permitted use of one of his arresting paintings as the cover for the volume. In this case the reader is, indeed, prompted to judge the book by its cover.

The final editing, formatting, and permissions for citations in the volume are the amazing work of Merrily Shaw. I quiet my embarrassment for disturbing her merited retirement to assume these onerous tasks because I know that the volume would have been delayed months more and have included countless errors in form and substance absent her invaluable contributions and those of Doug, her spouse.

As she has for over fifty years, my wife, Antje Heberle Kolodziej, provided the steady and unconditional encouragement and familial support needed to pursue a scholarly career, raise four sons, and enjoy nine grandchildren. I likewise need to salute the enormous contributions she has made over the years in tirelessly reading, editing, and correcting my inevitably flawed manuscripts.

Responsibility for errors of form and substance remain mine.

Edward A. Kolodziej
Emeritus Research Professor Political Science
Champaign, Illinois

Introduction

THIS VOLUME EVALUATES THE effectiveness and legitimacy of democratic solutions to governance of the global society. Specifically, it assesses the strengths and weaknesses of the responses of the democratic peoples and states to three imperatives of governance—Order, Welfare, and Legitimacy (OWL imperatives)—and identifies reforms to bolster this governing model.

The contesting power structures, rival processes of decision-making, and competing incentives for actor choices and action with regard to OWL imperatives, developed throughout the volume, are foundation stones for the governance of all human societies. Absent workable solutions to OWL imperatives, no human society can replicate itself through time, space, and changing environmental circumstances, social and physical. Governance is the glue that holds a society together. It also protects it from external threats to its human and material composition. This volume raises the key question of whether democratic solutions to OWL imperatives can prevail within a resistant global society, to counter and contain powerful antidemocratic forces.

A global society has emerged for the first time in the evolution of the human species. It is the evolving and ever-enlarging product of the ongoing, relentless, multiplying, and reinforcing processes of globalization. From the broadest possible perspective, this volume views globalization *as* the rise of a global society. The principal properties of this morphological change in the human condition are the *connectedness* and *interdependence* of the world's diverse and divided populations. Multiple forms of instant social and commercial media and ease of transportation increasingly connect the seven billion members of the human species—nine to ten billion by 2050. The rapid transfer of the Ebola virus from Liberia to Dallas, Texas, in the fall of 2014 by an errant traveler, and the subsequent transmission of the virus to health care professionals, broadcast instantly to a global audience by social and public media sources, illustrates these connections.

More significant than the expanding and deepening connectedness of the world's populations is their mutual dependence on each other to get what they want. Members of the global society increasingly depend on the decisions, actions, and deployment of power of other, largely anonymous actors in their pursuit of what they care about. Their physical security, the provision of their material needs, and the validation of their identities and most profound values hinge on the cooperation, however achieved, of other actors—individuals, groups, national populations, states, multilateral corporations, and social movements as well as hosts of private and state-based international organizations. The instances of interdependence of particular concern to this volume are those that cut across state boundaries to form a global society. Particular attention is directed to those nodes of interdependence in which the democracies and their populations are enmeshed.

To grasp, sententiously and immediately, the dimensions and dynamism of the global society, imagine a seemingly limitless and expanding number of cooperative, competitive, and conflict games between mutually dependent actors. The outcomes of these exchanges decide who gets what, when, and why across all these game domains; whether some win or lose; whether both lose or gain; or whether some differential distribution of winning and losing outcomes results from these continuous and relentless interdependent exchanges. The sum of these multiplying games is, at any fixed point, a snapshot of the global society.

Who governs these transactions of the global society has much to say about whose values, time-bound interests, and contingent preferences in these games will be realized. Governance, whether consciously understood or instinctively grasped, then becomes, objectively, an overriding aim of the contesting members of the global society, whether or not they fully grasp the significance of their participation in these entangling webs.

Globalization is clearly producing a tight-knit system, though the members of the global society have scarcely achieved a shared consciousness of this new condition. What has not been achieved, and in many ways is precluded by the diverse and divergent social paths that humans have taken, is the creation of a common sense of purpose and convergence of values of the world's populations. If increasingly many progressively recognize their entanglement in a "global system," as William McNeill suggests,[1] they decidedly reject subordinating themselves to any one governing system other than the one they prefer.

Conversely, what remains as an inescapable fact is the shared dilemma of the mutual and multiplying interdependencies of the world's peoples while they differ—profoundly—on how they should govern their dependence on each other. Democratic populations no less confront this conundrum. Since they do not have the collective power, soft or hard, to convince or compel others to adopt their value system, their challenge is to use their vast, but still limited, power to ensure that their model for global governance flourishes to contain and defeat their formidable adversaries.

The Democracies at Bay

The litany of challenges confronting the democracies today and extending to the foreseeable future belies this sanguine vision of an American or, more broadly, a liberal democratic dominant future.[2] There are visible signs of democracy in retreat on all continents.[3] Russia and China have pointedly derided President George W. Bush's reference to them as "great powers . . . increasingly united by common values."[4] Russia forcibly annexed Crimea and maintains a protectorate over Moldova and half of Georgia, while pressing to extend its sway, politically and territorially, over parts of the former Soviet Union, with eastern Ukraine the latest target. Moscow's military intervention in the Syrian civil war undermines American power and interests in the region and its efforts to oust the Bashir al-Assad regime. China progressively modernizes its military forces to offset American power. Rebutting the claims of its neighbors and the entreaties of the United States, Beijing exercises its muscle in the South China Sea to assert its exclusive right to vast, oil-laden, contested stretches of ocean. Neither the United States nor the other democratic states are able to restrain either regime from violating the civil liberties and human rights of its citizens—so much for converging norms and interests of the great powers.

The failed Arab Spring of 2010, initially spurred by democratic impulses, ushered instead a new era of authoritarian rule, incited widespread civil wars, and gave rise to such terrorist groups as the Islamic State of Iraq and Syria (ISIS). Venezuela, Bolivia, and Ecuador remain in the grip of illiberal democratic regimes. Widespread corruption and powerful criminal elements undermine Mexican democracy. The global Muslim awakening, a struggle that portends to be as long lasting, bloody, and disruptive as the Protestant Reformation, shows little inclination to adopt liberal democratic practices, norms, and regime constraints.[5] However much Muslims may be at odds with each other, many still share an abiding distrust of the liberal democracies, reject their secular principles of legitimate rule, and resist, some by force of arms and terrorism, the spread of the democratic solution to global governance.

The democracies, as this volume recounts, also undermine their own moral and material power.[6] Money corrupts electoral processes. Special interests rig legislation and regulations in their favor at the expense of the public good. Democratic majorities, manipulated by these special interests, fail to address collective issues, such as environmentally damaging climate change or the husbanding of scarce land, mineral, and water resources. The growing inequality of wealth and income, the gradual erosion of upward social mobility, and persistent, chronic poverty within the richest democratic states, notably the United States,[7] foster class divisions. Also engendered is growing cynicism about the effectiveness and even legitimacy of democratic rule to cope with these shortcomings. Public opinion polls evidence deep skepticism and distrust of governing institutions. Conversely, China has made spectacular progress in raising hundreds of millions out of poverty. The Communist government offers the success of the authoritarian model to foster economic growth more effectively than its democratic competitors.[8]

The challenges confronting the democracies go well beyond responding to this or that specific threat. The uncharted dimensions of the democratic enterprise are defined increasingly by the fundamental transformation of the still-evolving human condition. Every significant element of human concern is being progressively invested in enlarging and entangling webs of interdependencies. These envelop both the democratic and nondemocratic populations of the globe. Growing exponentially in scope, depth, and thickness,[9] these globalizing webs encompass security (nuclear proliferation, terrorism, enduring regional conflict), all manner of economic exchanges (monetary, financial, investment, and labor flows across state borders), rapid and disruptive technological innovation, and profound and deadly conflicts between enduring rival religious, cultural, and secular ideologies as well as national, ethnic, and tribal value systems.

How can the democracies counter the formidable global and local forces arrayed against them? They will either hang together or hang separately; their survival and flourishing hinges on their ability and willingness to pool their resources and power to ensure that their solutions to global governance contain and frustrate their adversaries. There is little likelihood that their rivals will be decisively defeated. Under these parlous and perilous conditions, preserving and expanding the power of the democratic peoples through their institutions of governance is a prerequisite if open societies are to prevail in a resistant global society.

Organization of the Volume

Part I anchors the discussion. Chapter 1 argues that the webs of connectedness and interdependencies of the world's populations across all areas of human concern, growing in scope, depth, and accumulating thickness, are transforming the human condition.

Chapter 2 identifies globalization with the rise of a global society for the first time in the evolution of the species. It develops key properties of the global society that distinguish this fundamental change in the human condition from previous eras.

Chapter 3 lays the groundwork for a theory of governance applicable to all human societies. It argues that every human society, and now the global society, must address three contending imperatives of governance: Order, Welfare, and Legitimacy (OWL). In the modern period, OWL solutions are clearly differentiated. The nation-state is the preferred solution of the world's populations for Order. The open market system has gained ascendancy as the dominant solution for the Welfare imperative. Finally, contesting value systems—cultural, religious, and ideological—vie with each other to impose their conceptions of the Legitimacy imperative on their rivals.

Currently, each solution to an OWL imperative involves an autonomous structure of power with distinct processes of decision-making and actor incentives for choices and action. Only under utopian conditions, in which there is a harmony of wills among all members of a society, could one envision a convergence of OWL solutions. These will be shown to be in fundamental conflict with each other in theory and in practice over time until the present. The prospect of harmony today, in the early twenty-first century, is ruled out in a world of billions of diverse and deeply divided peoples. They form a fragile global society, but clash radically over what form of governance should regulate their relations.

Part II develops the democratic solution to OWL imperatives. Chapter 4 reviews the response of the democracies to global order. As much by ad hoc adjustments as by design, democratic peoples have been principally responsible for the creation of the global state. It encompasses but goes beyond what is known as the Westphalian state system, initiated by the Treaty of Westphalia in 1648, which is the foundation stone for the current state system and its later national transformation. Like its Westphalian competitor, the democratic global state expands the state's coercive power. Conversely, free peoples have also constrained state power while invoking its authority to promote the material welfare of its populations and to foster civil liberties and human rights. The central conclusion of this chapter is that the democratic global state must either expand its power within the global society or risk being progressively weakened and marginalized in governing the global society, a vacuum that its opponents can be readily expected to fill.

Chapter 5 credits the democracies for having created a global market system to respond to the Welfare imperative of governance. This institutional innovation has facilitated the unprecedented creation of wealth and technological innovation. Its success has also induced nondemocratic states like

China to adapt to the democratic solution of the Welfare imperative, while turning the institution to its own advantage. Conversely, the failure of the democracies to regulate the behavior of economic actors, notably large corporations and banking institutions, led to the almost total dissolution of the global financial system in the first decade of the twenty-first century, a threat still hanging menacingly over both the democracies and their opponents.

Chapter 6 exposes the additional systemic weaknesses of democratic solutions to the Welfare imperative. The democracies have fully addressed neither chronic poverty in their midst or around the globe nor the unequal and inequitable distribution of income and wealth. The challenge goes beyond improving the performance of the market for both democratic peoples and nondemocratic populations. The expansion of the democratic global state depends on meeting these challenges.

Chapter 7 summarizes the case of the moral superiority of the democratic solution to the imperative of Legitimacy. That solution is grounded in the Rousseaunean conjecture that all humans are free and equal. No other contesting ideology can make that claim. The great religions—Islam, Christianity, Hinduism, Buddhism, Judaism—are necessarily exclusive. Citizens are accorded privileged status primarily on the basis of their religious identities. Similarly, national sentiment, which fuses the loyalty of populations to their states, is also necessarily exclusive. Conversely, the moral claim of the democratic states and peoples that they observe the norms that generate legitimacy—freedom and equality—is undermined by the widespread gap between the moral ideal of democratic rule and its actual practice.

In light of the shortcomings of the democratic solution to global governance, sketched in the preceding chapters, the final chapter calls for creation of a concert of democratic peoples to address the shortcomings of their OWL solutions and, through their collective power, to frustrate the formidable countervailing challenges of nondemocratic actors and their rival solutions to global governance.

What we wish to assess is how sturdy and robust are the democratic solutions to OWL imperatives. Whether the democracies will prevail will depend decisively on how resilient and resourceful their response to global governance is and how well-accepted democratic solutions are viewed as legitimate by the world's populations. Meeting these challenges involves more than the destiny of just the American people. These obligations also extend to all peoples dedicated to the principles of freedom and equality and popular rule.

Notes

1. W. H. McNeill (1992).

2. Fukuyama (1992) argues this case, belied by formidable antidemocratic actors since its publication and by the failure of the second Bush administration to impose American rule on Iraq in the wake of the US military intervention in 2003. See Kolodziej & Kanet (2008) for an extended critique.

3. Kurlantzick (2013); Zakaria (1997). See also Micklethwait & Wooldridge (2014).

4. Ibid.

5. There are some optimists who would dispute this harsh conclusion; see Aslan (2005). For a contrary view, which is more persuasive, see Juergensmeyer (2003, 2005, and 2008).

6. Michael Mann (2005) traces the dark side of democracy.

7. Piketty (2014). See also chapter 6 of this volume.

8. Micklethwait & Wooldridge (2014, pp. 133–69).

9. The image of expanding webs of human connectedness and interdependence culminating in this era of globalization is drawn from the prescient scholarship of William McNeill: McNeill & McNeill (2003); McNeill (1992, 1998).

I

THE RISE OF A GLOBAL SOCIETY

1

Globalization as
the Rise of a Global Society

So oft in theologic wars,
The disputants, I ween,
Rail on in utter ignorance
Of what each other mean,
And prate about an Elephant
Not one of them has seen!

> —John Godfrey Saxe, "The Blind Men and the Elephant,"
> *The Poems of John Godfrey Saxe*, 1868

HOW CAN, AND SHOULD, GLOBALIZATION, a contested notion, be understood? There exists no shared notion of what globalization is, what its
principal properties might be, or the implications for humankind of what
forces, themselves in dispute, are driving its complex social processes. Observers tend to seize on one, albeit important, dimension of globalization
rather than view globalization as a whole—that is, as enlarging webs of *connections* and *interdependencie*s of humans and human communities across
the full range of their most significant and salient concerns.[1]

These social webs, abstracted from the actors and agents ensnared and entangled in them—what Jean-Jacques Rousseau terms *chains*[2]—are what interest this discussion. These social chains, paradoxically, empower individuals
to act and, simultaneously, to limit the possibilities of their choices and the
prospects of their self-realization.[3] These layers of ever enlarging and increasingly denser tissues of social exchanges create a global society. To avoid the

"blind men and the elephant" problem, it is the elephant, as a metaphor of the global society, that we wish to view as a whole.

It is important to keep in mind that the democracies are suspended within larger and more confining webs of connectedness and interdependence comprising the global society. These webs embrace powerful antidemocratic states and peoples as well as criminal and terrorist organizations. These diverse actors, themselves divided against themselves, reject, some violently, the democratic solutions to OWL imperatives for global governance. Their multiple forms of pushback are delineated in succeeding chapters.

Connectedness: The Emergence of a Global Society

To anchor the priority of global governance as a central concern of democratic populations, we need to show that a global society exists. Since connectedness and interdependence are properties of all human societies, they are no less so with the emergence of a global society. What has fundamentally changed is the scope of these properties, entangling inhabitants of the globe in greater or lesser measure. These properties are deeply embedded in the ceaseless interactions of the world's states and populations today. The totality of these countless and expanding interactions between and among democratic and nondemocratic peoples *are* the global society.

This conception of society departs from textbook or conventional understandings of society. For many scholars and observers, a society implies a community of like-minded, directed individuals. A typical textbook definition of society is a "group of individuals living as members of a community."[4] They are assumed to have developed over time "common ideas, interests, and techniques for living and working together. It is the sense of living together as a community that makes up a society."[5]

This widespread notion of society, loaded with normative baggage, does not readily fit the reality of a global society more divided against itself than united around common purposes. To fit the notion of society to a global society, I mean a lot less and also a lot more by "global society" than the notion of a society as a tight, morally integrated community. At a global level, humans, as social evolution and historical processes have served them up to us, can scarcely be said to have "common ideas, interests and techniques for living and working together."[6] Fundamental, insurmountable differences abound. These are woven deeply into the web of humanly constructed social relations.

The connections and interdependencies engendered by globalization reinforce rather than reduce or diminish these clashes.[7] The result is a global society of billions of people woven into a crazy-quilt of divergent and disputing identities, riven by tribal, ethnic, and national loyalties and contending cultural or religious values, and split even finer into clashing attributes of language, class, status, gender, and race. Yet, paradoxically, all are increasingly connected and interdependent in the pursuit of their divergent goals.

So when I use the term "global society," I mean a lot less than prevailing notions of communal cohesion. Nor do I assume an eventual convergence of cultural and religious beliefs and practices of the world's peoples. Much less, too, does this discussion assume some shared end point toward which humans are inexorably directed, yet to be discovered.

A Global Society: A Lot Less than a Traditional Society

The conception of a global society advanced here does not require meeting a test of internal coherence or cohesion.[8] Connectedness and interdependence will do. In the extreme, a Hobbesian war of all against all is no less a society than the utopian societies that dotted western expansion in the United States, wherein the members of these societies shared the same values and adhered to the norms of the group. In the limiting case of a Hobbesian world, developed in chapter 3, the very survival of its members hinges not only on their wits and resourcefulness but also on the responsive actions of their rivals, and vice versa. At both extremes, the property of interdependence, radically different in form and outcome, makes for a global society divided against itself.

The conception of society used here includes and revolves around all human interactions taken as a whole. In its fullest representation, "society," as Martin Shaw suggests, "is the totality or complex of social relations. Since social relations of all kinds are increasingly global, and all forms of social relations everywhere in the world are, at least in some indirect sense bound into global networks, society in this sense is now necessarily global."[9] In adopting Shaw's perspective, our concern is focused primarily on that subset of "global networks" that are fashioned by free peoples. These webs are ensnared, in turn, within a more encompassing global society comprised of resistant antidemocratic webs of actors profoundly opposed to the democratic model of governance and its extension.

A global society can be characterized as a dense, intricately layered, and expanding matrix of enmeshed spider webs. The actors spinning these webs include empowered individuals,[10] nation-states, tightly knit ethnic or tribal communities, multinational corporations, organized religions, social movements, terrorist organizations, and vast criminal enterprises. Included, too, are thousands of nongovernmental (NGOs), international nongovernmental (INGOs), and intergovernmental organizations (IGOs).

The diversity of the actors of the global society suggests that the point of departure in analyzing governance should be, as chapter 3 delineates, on the fractured and contesting OWL power structures that tenuously hold the global society together. This departure point also has the added merit of not entangling or reducing the analysis to the particular aims, interests, and values that might be attributed to the actors. A focus on power, as Michael Mann has shown,[11] frees the analysis of the social forces driving societies from the particular circumstances of time and place in which communities and whole civilizations are nested.

A Global Society: A Lot More than Traditional Notions of Society

I also mean a lot more by *society* than shared norms within an integrated community. The multiplying forces unleashed by a global society, however refracted in their multifarious effects, exert a causal impact on human behavior that is far broader in scope, more compelling, and a lot less predictable than ever before on the lives of the world's populations. Social outcomes of interdependence are attributable both to purpose and to process, a mix of causes and causal explanation that is not linear in its direction but subject to a bewildering array of yet to be fully understood circular feedback loops.[12]

The members comprising the global society, linked by widening, deepening, and accumulating connections and interdependencies, are unique among the animal kingdom. Among their distinctive properties are the endowments they share of unmatched conceptual and linguistic capacities relative to other species, superior and increasingly more powerful and innovative tool-making skills, and a remarkable capacity for social cooperation, whether consensually or coercively elicited.

In these senses, then, I mean a lot more about society, and specifically a global society, than the notion, held widely abroad, notably in much of contemporary economic theory, of a world of autonomous, rational actors, disconnected from the social bounds defining them. This perspective views only individuals as real. Social relations are viewed as radically conventional, fragile, and subject to individual preferences, defined by the relative moral values humans create and limited, objectively, by the cost, gains, and risks in the pursuit of their preferences.[13] Notwithstanding these constraints, the capacity of individuals to achieve their preferences, trivial and profound, depends decisively on the preexistence of a supportive society and the social power actors can draw from this social setting to get what they want their way.

The notion of a global society we will be relying upon extends to humankind as a whole. It is the existence of this fluid system of actor relations that is the object of analysis. This whole is postulated not only conceptually but also as causally distinct from the actors comprising the global society. Specifically, as the discussion below adumbrates, the concern will be with a subset of this whole—namely, those social relations of free people that depend on their mutual cooperation, however achieved, to survive and thrive in a larger and resistant global society. The aim of the discussion is to show the causal connection between humans as social animals with what they have wrought—namely, a global society.

Connectedness, an indispensable and irreducible component of all human societies, does not by itself make a society. At the simplest level, it refers to an awareness of the existence of individuals and groups of each other but with whom there is not necessarily any direct experience, continuing exchanges, or material and moral interdependence. An example is a media report of a physical catastrophe—a tsunami or earthquake—visited on anonymous peoples thousands of miles away. Media connections bombard us on all fronts. Information about the despair of others connects us within a global society. When we are moved by emotion or moral obligation to help affected populations or to cooperate with other peoples to prevent natural and human disasters from happening, connectedness morphs into interdependence.

The missing link in the connectedness required of a society is mutual dependence. If groups or individuals appear to be self-sufficient—materially—or self-referential—unmindful of the evaluations of others (that is, their social identities)—they may well be connected with each other, but they do not form a society in the sense meant here. A seemingly discrete self-sufficient group, like an aboriginal tribe in the Amazon valley, may well appear to form an intact society, but its particular society still falls within the set of the global society once that societal grouping and its members depend on others for their survival, welfare, or validation of who they are or what they believe they are.[14]

Until the period of the great European explorations, beginning in the fifteenth century, large bodies of peoples and their civilizations knew little or nothing of each other. Recall how stunned sixteenth-century Spanish conquistadors were in falling upon highly developed and sophisticated Inca and Aztec civilizations. Isolated from each other for centuries over the long period of the human diaspora out of Africa, Europeans, Incas, Aztecs, Chinese, and Indians, among others, were able to erect great civilizations and complex societies—indeed, tightly woven communities—without interacting with each other or depending on each other for their security, economic development, or the validation of their identities and value systems.

That was then, and this is now. Humans have never been so connected in real time as they are today. Billions everywhere are now acutely aware of each other, although most will never have direct contact with each other. They are daily flooded with news about anonymous others. News of the global melt-downs of financial markets in 1997 and those of a decade later are reported on a continuous 24/7 news cycle. Natural and human disasters—the 9/11 New York twin towers terrorist attack in 2001, the Southeast Asian tsunami in 2004, the flooding of New Orleans by Hurricane Katrina in 2005, or the earthquakes of China and Haiti in May 2008 and January 2010, respectively—are instantly communicated around the globe. Members of developed and developing states now increasingly find it quite unexceptional that they are connected by instant media communication: newsprint, radio and TV, Inter-net, e-mail, and multiplying forms of social media.

While humans are virtually being drawn ever tighter into a web of global connectedness in real time, they continue to identify primarily with their im-mediate social milieu and their kith and kin.[15] That is hardly surprising. That is what appears natural to most people in contrast to the no less real entangle-ments of a global society. What humans are also experiencing are the cease-less intrusions of events and the invasion of other peoples and social agents into their lives. Nor do many wish, or try, to preserve their privacy at all costs, as they actively become actors in the global drama of connectedness. The in-centive of instant world fame (or infamy) through worldwide communication makes everyone potentially a celebrity if they can gain the notice of millions of TV watchers or thousands of followers on Facebook or Twitter. The line between directly experienced and virtual reality becomes increasingly blurred and indistinct in human consciousness.

What is of interest for humankind are the implications of sustained and widening connectedness, compressed in time and space. What narrative of human social evolution best fits the processes of globalization? What mental pictures afford some reliable conceptualization of globalization as a whole? Which mental pictures reconcile the daily experience of its impacts on hu-mans everywhere and on the diverse subjective states of mind of the multiple and conflicting identities, largely locally shaped, that make up humankind in spite of growing connectedness and interdependence?

There is a growing disconnect between discrete tribal, ethnic, national, re-ligious, and cultural groupings, and the consciousness holding their members together, on the one hand, and the objective connectedness and interdepen-dence of the world's populations, on the other. Surmounting this gap is more than a question or issue of conceptual and perceptual accuracy. It requires of individuals and communities profound and unsettling psychological adapta-tion and extraordinary moral courage to acknowledge, as William McNeill suggests, "that every people and polity is forced to recognize its subordination to and participation in a global system."[16] If humans limit themselves to their local identities or, more broadly and abstractly, to discrete loyalties, they cannot be expected to be mentally, morally, or psychologically equipped to view their particular problems in a more encompassing global context—that is, as instances of issues confronting the world's populations as a whole.

Public choices in addressing the shared problems of the world's populations are likely to be made, as Peter Singer argues, from a narrow and self-serving perspective, absent a transformation in the self-identity of the peoples of the globe as members of a global society. This process of change will be long in coming and scarcely assured, however pressing and urgent the collective issues to be addressed.[17] Among the more than seven billion inhabitants of the world, only a few appear to be able or prepared to transcend the loyalties, values, and identities associated with their socialization and commitments to their particular religious and cultural beliefs or national, ethnic, or tribal loyalties. Few, like a Mother Teresa or Albert Schweitzer, would substitute humanity as the touchstone of their personal values. Few would give their lives to save humanity, while millions are ready to do so for their ethnic or linguistic communities, nations, or religions.

The dilemma of the human condition is that the viability of these vital but necessarily particular cares and concerns will depend on humans deliberately casting their lots with the actors who comprise their global social webs, which they, collectively and largely unconsciously, have woven. However much the world's populations may be split, there is no escape from the struggle over what rules and institutions should—or should not—govern how they resolve their mutual dependency on each other. That ceaseless struggle is itself negative testimony to their membership in a global society whose existence cannot be reduced to any of its actors or their particular concerns.

It is this phenomenon of the whole of these exchanges that poses unprecedented challenges for the species and, pointedly, for democratic states and peoples. The task before them is to try to understand the composition and workings of this web of the whole, a global society. How is it transforming the human condition? How is it shaping the life chances of all of us ensnared in its countless tangled webs? How does the human creation of a global society serve and support the conflicting, competing, and convergent interests and values of its members? For this reason, its survival, its replication, and the direction of its evolution and transforming power are the concern, as an objective imperative, of all its members, whether that dependency is acknowledged or not by those who are implicated in its doings. The valences and trajectories of these contingent trends will depend decisively on the quality and composition of global governance, however chaotic it may appear.

Interdependence: The Entangling Webs of the Global Society

This brings the discussion to interdependence as *the* core property of globalization. The interdependent webs generated by globalization across all areas of primary human concern are both the source and driver of the global society. Viewed from this circular perspective, the processes of globalization are both the product and the principal cause of its expansion. Globalization and the scope and depth of the global society are of ever-enlarging significance in the lives of the world's populations. Even before the term *globalization* entered into circulation, C. Wright Mills captured the mutual contingency between societal forces and individual biographies at a global level: "Neither the life of an individual nor the history of a society can be understood without understanding both."[18] Mills's insight applies now to a global society in which the futures of the world's populations are inextricably entwined and their shared fates joined with the emergence of a global society.

In following Wright's lead, the approach adopted here in no way diminishes the moral worth of the individual or the central role that individuals should play in deciding what social system best suits them. Chapters 3 and 7 explicitly affirm Rousseau's stipulation of the universal moral unity of humans as free and equal—criteria by which the governing rules and institutions of democratic regimes are evaluated as legitimate. Privileging the normative status of individuals still depends on supportive governing structures for the realization of individual freedom and equality.[19]

What is to be avoided is to rely solely on the moral ideal of human freedom and equality as if it could suffice to explain either individual behavior or the dependency of individuals on some form of social power in pursuing their interests and moral worth. Good intentions that privilege individuals and their rights without reference to the social power supports necessary for the exercise of those rights does little to ensure the exercise of those rights. That half-move hinders understanding of multiple forms of social power that determine the prospects of individual pursuits. As Roy Bhaskar sententiously stipulates, "Societies are irreducible to people."[20] The preexistence of these forms of social power "establishes their *autonomy* as possible objects of scientific investigation and their *causal power* establishes their *reality*."[21] Society, itself, is the most inclusive and enabling social form. It "expresses the sum of the relations within which individuals stand."[22]

If it can be shown that a global society exists, that its pervasive and intricate webs of social power inform, orient, constrain, and enable actor choices and action, then the claim is established that the prospects of humankind under conditions of a global society depend on the replication and perfection of this new and transformational societal form and on the effectiveness and legitimacy of its governing arrangements. More to the point of this discussion, democracies must rely on their solutions to OWL imperatives if they are to expand their reach and power and deter and defeat their opponents.

Humans, as we experience them and ourselves, are the evolutionary end point thus far of the workings of natural selection. Viewed from a longer time horizon, from the origins of the universe and the big bang upward of fifteen billion years ago, humankind's physical and mental makeup is in no small way the unsettling result of chance, a disquieting psychological realization for some. Conversely, human societies are the product of social choices, actions, and network interdependencies. They are not only possessed of causal power in socializing individuals to their communities and identities but also capable of surmounting some of the constraints posed either by the physical environment or by confining social bonds resistant to beneficial reform.[23] Humans, unlike animals, can mount a "jailbreak," as James Rosenau suggests,[24] and rend their social chains. In re-creating themselves, they must still fabricate new chains—that is, social institutions of power that bind and loose.

As Immanuel Kant observes,[25] human intelligence has grown over time as the product of a collective cooperative effort: "In man (as the only rational creature) *those natural capacities which are directed towards the use of his reason are such that they could be fully developed only in the species, but not in the individual.*"[26] While this social evolutionary process may have begun without conscious deliberation, humans today are certainly capable of reevaluating their social conditions and of redefining themselves, their values, and their conceptions of legitimate and effective governance.

Echoing Kant, William McNeill explains that "groups receiving and acting on information about best practice tended to enlarge their share of world resources, while those who rejected change or received information belatedly fell behind and sooner or later ceased to be able to protect what they already had."[27] The rapid rise of China as an economic giant in the wake of the ruling regime's adaptation of the Chinese economy to the competitive constraints of global markets illustrates McNeill's explanation of how the historical processes of increased communication, connectedness, and interdependencies work to facilitate human control over nature and self-imposed social limits. The pull of best practices of a global market system induced the Chinese Communist regime to modify its socialist ideology for the sake of economic growth and, not incidentally, for the survival of the regime, too.

The conventional belief that all humans are connected by only "six degrees of separation" may stretch the imagination. Rather, what is implicitly captured in John Guare's play is the immensely expanding and increasingly dense webs of social bonds comprising the totality of interdependent exchanges forming the global society.[28] Somewhere in this mix individuals find themselves joined, whether or not they are fully aware of their mutual dependency. The stakes of these countless exchanges need not be the same for the actors. They may well be fundamentally at odds. What is important to recognize is that they are mutually contingent, whatever the valences of the outcomes of these interdependent exchanges may be.

Big power politics between the Napoleonic Wars and World War I illustrates the positive and negative interdependence of the European empires. For over a century, as Paul Schroeder explains, the great European powers depended for their security on their cooperation despite the diverse, disparate, and conflicting aims and interests each pursued.[29] Their profound conflicts over outcomes in the relations between these allied-rivals reveal their entangling interdependencies precisely because of their opposed aims and the clashing interests dividing them, their cultural affinities to the contrary notwithstanding. The preferred outcome of each rival depended on the cooperation of the engaged parties and how that cooperation would be supplied, whether consensually elicited or coercively compelled.

The unwitting decisions of the European empires to rely solely on force to generate their adversaries' compliance with their preferences proved mutually destructive. World War I shattered the German, Austrian, and Russian empires. The French, English, and Dutch empires temporarily survived, but the war ultimately dealt them a fatal blow. Their serial collapse after World War II largely destroyed what remained of the Eurocentric system. Among the most important developments of the emergence of a nation-state system is not only the collapse of empires as the historically rejected solution to OWL imperatives but also the spread of democratic regimes and peoples. The latter trend has led to the creation of the global state. It has the potential of eventually transforming the Westphalian nation-state system. That transformative change would recast security within a theory of OWL governance beyond the narrow view, promoted by many, which stipulates security simply as a function of military power.[30]

What actors seek, as individuals or as members of discrete groups or communities, depends for their realization on exacting the cooperation of all relevant actors in these social exchanges, whether friend or foe. There are only three possible strategies (or a mix of these) to exact cooperation from other actors: mutual consent to aims and means to produce desired (if not necessarily congruent and convergent) outcomes; agreed-upon rules of exchange (customary or formally prescribed as in governing rules, institutions, or market practices, bound by shared notions of contracts and property) to foster cooperation or to resolve differences about the outcomes of these transactions; or the imposition of sheer power and force to compel cooperation.

The film *The Godfather* captures this latter mode of induced cooperation. The godson of Don Vito Corleone pleads for the Mafia boss to intervene on his behalf to compel a film studio to offer him a key part in a film to save his waning career. Corleone instructs an aide—his consigliere—to speak to the resistant studio head and "make him an offer he can't refuse"—that is, accede to the Godfather's preferred outcome (a movie role for the godson) or forfeit his life. The threat works.

Where outcomes of these exchanges converge on values and interests or where outcomes, however different, are mutually rewarding and compatible, consent on the terms of cooperation—the means and the ends—is the obvious and most efficient choice of the cooperating parties or social agents. This is a central assumption of liberal economic theory. It predicts the greatest amount of material good for the greatest number, assuming that decisions about allocating scarce human and material resources or in settling conflicts are based on consent, not coercion,[31] modulated by self-interest. In game-theory language, these are variable, not zero sum, games with differing but positive outcomes for the players.

Where preferences clash but the partners remain committed to an agreed upon system of rules of engagement and resolution—rules of law and governing institutions capable of issuing commands—then differing gains as outcomes can be accepted by the competing parties. They are disposed to accept the outcomes dictated by customary modes of exchange or by the authority of arbitrating officials or international bodies. They accede to a decision or outcome that the contesting parties adjudge as workable and legitimate. Retaining a working system of rules and institutions assumes a privileged value among actors since the pursuit and realization of other, substantive interests depend on their willingness to regulate their exchanges for their mutual, if differently realized, interests. Rules and institutions, potentially, have the advantages of transparency; mutual gains for cooperating parties (however dissimilar), including maintenance of a system of order as a prized value; and lowered transaction costs in the long run for all.[32] Actor cooperation for mutual gain through reliance on agreed-upon rules is another way of posing the issue of the governance of the global society.

Failing these two voluntary solutions—that is, agreement on rules or consensual cooperation—coercive threats and violence, which have a long and costly history in social evolution,[33] may be invoked by one or all mutually dependent parties to impose a preferred outcome and compel the cooperation of the reluctant or resistant party or parties. That decision, if it conforms to rational calculation, rests on a cost-benefit-risk estimate that force will produce a probabilistically determinable positive outcome for at least one of the contesting parties.

The evolution of a precarious nuclear deterrence regime between the United States and the Soviet Union during the Cold War illustrates how the concept of cooperation in interdependent exchanges extends to armed rivals capable of destroying each other in a matter of hours. Through trial and error, both states developed a strategy of deterrence to protect their vital interests, territories, and populations. With partial success, they also extended their deterrents to protect allies and clients. The resultant and evolving global deterrent regime—including communication strategies, rules of engagement, technological innovations in nuclear striking power, shifting levels and dispersal of nuclear forces, and arms control agreements—required cooperation between the adversaries to make the regime work (that is, to avoid a mutually destructive nuclear exchange).[34] Cooperation in interdependent relationships, as used here, applies not only to mutual consent and conformity to agreed-upon rules but also to coercive exchanges, marked by threats or actual use of force, to ensure preferred outcomes between the engaged rivals. Cooperation in these three modes of action holds all human societies together, no less so for a global society.

A simple example may illustrate how these nodes of interdependence work simultaneously at two levels of power relations: (1) the exchange focused on a defined and desired outcome by the engaged actors and (2) the underlying rules and institutions—the power structures—through which the exchange is mediated. Assume that a family represents a social power structure. The individuals who make up the family negotiate and work out their personal and individual wants and needs within the processes of decision and action defined and enabled by the power structure of the family as a social unit. How this dual process operates can be illustrated by the case of a teenager who wants use of the family car for a date. The teen's parents must approve the request. They own the car keys and underwrite the car's insurance, maintenance, and fuel. How does the teenager get a "yes" within this closed system of governance?

Where the interests of the teenager and parents are parallel (but not necessarily congruent), he or she very likely gets the car. Despite the disparity of social power between the parents and the teenager, all of the actors are essentially in alignment in terms of their differing but mutually contingent purposes, shared loving regard, and largely unqualified support for each other's wishes and wants. The parents have implicit trust in their teenage child and wish the best for the child's welfare, though they may harbor reservations about his or her safety and possible damage to the car. Their calculated risk is discounted to the level of permission because their progeny has earned their respect and confidence in countless previous exchanges over his or her long upbringing, up to the moment of the request for the car.

Conversely, the preferences of the parents and the teenager may not be the same. They may well be irreconcilable. The parents perhaps fear that their child will wreck the car or get into trouble by driving too fast or recklessly, a fear either rooted in experience or imagined as likelihood based on the teenager's past misbehavior on other fronts. The teenager is desperate to get the car. He or she may be able to bribe both parents by cutting the lawn for a month or actually turning in homework on time for once. Or the teen may be able to play one parent against the other, working on the parent who favors the request to wear down the resisting spouse. The latter prefers to refuse the car but may eventually relent to his or her more pliable spouse either because that spouse can impose a loss on some other of the resistant one's preferences or because the latter simply wishes to be spared more grief. And so on. Each of the actors has different and varying amounts of social power. Their deployment of that power is still bounded by the marriage bond, the context of social power, and the final arbitrating institution—composed of rules and customary practices—within which the family power struggle ensues.

In these two contrasting narratives, each new mode of interdependent transaction involves not one but two exchanges. The first is the surface and visible exchange of the moment with respect to the transaction itself—access to the family car. The narrative plays out within the existing distribution of social power of the principals. All implicitly accept the rules of the game—that is, the family's rule of law. The second, and more significant, exchange is a test of the institutional architecture and its social power support or capacity to arbitrate the surface exchange. What may appear to be a trivial matter, access to the family car, may be the end game of a long series of mutually frustrating exchanges among the principals over a host of other issues that have nothing to do with the car case. Cumulatively, these may finally trigger a rupture of family governance. Actor frustration with a particular outcome may incite an assault on the very structure of family social power itself. A shattered family—divorce, the child's running away from home, or both—may ensue, dissolving the social power that previously held the family together, however tenuously.

If all of the exchanges operative at a point in time could be frozen (which they cannot in dynamic and ceaselessly evolving social relations with countless moving parts), the total number of interdependent transactions would constitute the skeletal structure of the world society at that imagined static moment. Revealed would be a bewildering and seemingly incalculable number of actors entangled in webs of interdependence comprising the global society at that instant. The challenges confronting the world's populations, sketched in the following chapters, provide some hint of the complexity of social exchanges and interdependencies compromising the global society, the innumerable unbalanced and unequal actor power plays at work, and the multiplicity of trade-offs and dilemmas of choice and action constraining all actors in differing ways as they seek to elicit their preferences from other actors or to impose them on others.

Governance is no less crucial for the world's populations than for the family disputing access to the family car. The workings of the ceaseless social dynamics of global interdependencies underscore how essential effective and legitimate governance is as a precondition for the perpetuation and replication of the global society, notably one congenial to free peoples. Governance is a precondition to achieve at least a modicum of the conflicting preferences of the world's populations in the numberless exchanges and to foster, paradoxically, their mutually incompatible interests and values, short of the collapse of the global society.

This volume focuses on the OWL solutions to global governance advanced by democratic regimes. Are they sufficiently robust, powerful, and legitimate to address the security and welfare needs of their populations? Can the global states, erected by democratic populations through their variable but compatible social contracts, withstand formidable antidemocratic actors and forces working to undo popular rule? Do democratic regimes, resting on the principles of freedom and equality of all persons, offer a superior moral response to the Legitimacy imperative than competing value systems based on tradition, culture, religion, rival secular ideologies, or national sentiment? Whether democratic solutions to OWL solutions will prevail in this resistant, hostile environment is by no means certain.

These questions, while daunting, are of urgent moment. The interdependencies of the world populations and their governance are obviously far more complex than those of a family. They entail considerably more uncertainty about outcomes both with respect to the marginal issue in play and to the governing structure of power within which the actors decide the marginal issue. Involved and engaged are countless actors working on multiple levels, all striving for simultaneous and synchronous cooperative responses from millions, even billions, of other actors over a multitude of global issues. What are also readily apparent are the massive disparities in social power that the actors bring to bear in these interdependent exchanges to effect their preferred outcomes. Asymmetries in material power—coercive, economic, and technological—or in access to authoritative institutional and personal decisional power create systematic imbalances in whose preferences are being served. Power to get one's way will vary then across different interdependent exchanges within an expanding global society.

Before we turn to the questions animating this volume, there is still the challenge of presenting evidence that a global society actually exists. That is the job of the next chapter.

Notes

1. The image of globalization as ensnaring webs is drawn from the insights of William McNeill. See McNeill & McNeill (2003); McNeill (1963, 1992).

2. Rousseau (1978).

3. The dilemma of free choice and social constraint raises the unresolved agent-structure issue, a problem beyond the scope of this analysis. For an extensive discussion of this issue, see Dessler (1989); Wendt (1987).

4. Hunt & Colander (2008, p. 80).

5. Ibid., p. 81.

6. Mark Juergensmeyer (2005, 2008) masterfully traces the rejection of Western secularism by a wide spectrum of religions, which themselves are also profoundly at odds with each other. The likely convergence of value systems of the world's populations is beyond imagination.

7. From clashing perspectives—religious, economic, and political—the processes of globalization have elicited a backlash that itself is an intrinsic component of globalization. See Aslan (2005); Broad (2002); Lewis (2003); Rodrik (1998).

8. Shaw (1994).

9. Ibid., p. 5.

10. Rosenau (1990) was among the first to recognize this property of globalization.

11. Mann (1986, 1993).

12. See the works cited in this chapter by Jared Diamond, William McNeill, and Friedrich von Hayek. However much they differ, they agree that both process and purpose must be causally linked to explain social evolution.

13. Elster (1989); Hayek (1948, 1960, 1982).

14. Jared Diamond (1992) observes that the Amazon tribes were the last first tribes to be encountered.

15. Peter Singer (2011) develops the argument that, while kith and kin remain the primordial touchstones of empathy for humans, the circle has progressively enlarged, as humans have progressively recognized their mutual dependency.

16. McNeill (1992, pp. x–xi).

17. Singer (2002).

18. Mills (1959, p. 3).

19. Barnes (1995) develops a balanced view of the relation of humans as social animals and their individual contributions to the human condition.

20. Bhaskar (1998, p. 25).

21. Ibid.

22. Ibid.

23. Rosenau (1990).

24. Ibid.

25. Kant (1991 [*Kant*], pp. 41–53 [italics in the original]).

26. Ibid., p. 42.

27. McNeill (1998, p. 218).

28. Guare (2004).

29. Schroeder (1994).

30. Kenneth Waltz and his partisans cling to this limited conception of security. See Mearsheimer (2001); Walt (1991); Waltz (1979). For a critique, see Kolodziej (1992; 2005, pp. 127–74).

31. Coase (1988, esp. pp. 159–85, "Notes on the Coase Theorem").

32. North (1990).

33. Tilly (1985, 1990).

34. Freedman (1989); Morgan (1983, 2003); Schelling (1960, 1966). See also Kanet & Kolodziej (1991).

2

Properties of the Global Society

Globalization ... is not simply about how governments, business, and people communicate, not just about how organizations interact, but is about the emergence of completely new social, political, and business models. It's about things that impact some of the deepest most ingrained aspects of society right down to the nature of the social contract.

—Gary Hytek and Kristine M. Zentgraf, *America Transformed: Globalization, Inequality, and Power*

WHEN WAS THE LAST TIME YOU HAD LUNCH with the United States ... or interviewed the United Nations ... or asked the stock market about its health? Have you ever exchanged e-mails with the Chinese or the Iranians?

We have no trouble using shorthand to reify bodies, like the United States, United Nations, markets, Chinese, Iranians, corporations, or nongovernmental organizations (NGOs). It should be easy then to stipulate the existence of a global society as no less real than these collective shorthands, a view shared from various perspectives by a growing number of informed observers.[1]

Viewing globalization as the rise of a global society is a more concise, cogent, and comprehensive way to conceive globalization than other widely circulating but narrower and more circumscribed conceptions. These alternative perspectives, such as equating globalization with increased economic integration or with culture clash,[2] have their place and uses. I will draw upon them throughout this discussion, incorporating them into a larger and inclusive understanding of globalization, but my view of globalization will be limited neither to them nor by them.

The notion of a global society is a handy way to quickly and sententiously characterize globalization as transformational in the human condition. There is no turning back to a simpler, less complex time in human social evolution. Even if the current trend toward ever more interdependence among peoples across the major sources of human concern were to be reversed and the world society were to implode, we would know that outcome by reference to our experience of the world society of which we are all members.

Establishing the existence of an expanding global society is also a highly practical matter—a challenge—for the species. The readers' acknowledgment of their engagement in a global society should convince them that their life chances as well as those of the world's populations and their multiple and multiplying agents—states, markets, corporations, churches, communities, NGOs, and so forth—depend on their collective efforts to ensure that the global society survives and thrives. The imperative of cooperation among the world's democracies is especially critical if their conceptions of how the global society should be governed are to shape the future of their populations and those of the nondemocratic world.

This chapter identifies key properties that distinguish the global society from earlier human societies. This discussion owes much to a growing body of scholarship about how and why this society emerged.[3] What is lacking is a better understanding of how the moving parts of the global society work to form a human society. How does this society compare with any previous era in human history in its daily doings? And how well is it governed?

The properties of the world society may be viewed, metaphorically, as so many prisms through which we can faintly discern how and why a global society works. As we peer through the refracted light of each prism, it should become apparent that these selected viewpoints will gradually merge to form in the reader's mind's eye a larger panorama that is the global society—as a whole rather than segmented and disaggregated parts—and our membership in this expanding, but still dimly understood, social universe.

Social change today moves at a fast and bewildering pace. Incessant change is among the most distinguishing characteristics of the global society when compared, say, with the static feudal orders of Europe of the thirteenth century or Tokugawa Japan of the seventeenth century. Emerging from World War II, a once seemingly bipolar world, which appeared to many scholars and informed observers as stable and immutable,[4] disappeared overnight only to reappear as a fractured multipolar world of state and powerful non-state actors. The 2010 Arab Spring uprising, driven by populations seeking greater freedom and material well-being, has since either regressed to bolster authoritarian regimes, like Egypt, or collapsed into multiple civil wars, as in Syria, Iraq, Libya, and Yemen. The fear that the world might run out of oil has been replaced by the heady optimism prompted by fracking technology that releases previously unreachable oil and gas reserves—but to what purpose? Fossil fuels both drive economic growth and accelerate climate change, which threatens ill-conceived material gains.

What, then, have humans wrought in creating a global society? What are the key properties of the global society, and who are the actors both spinning and caught in these webs?

Let's begin with eight prominent but scarcely exhaustive properties of the global society. Three others, which are central to this evaluation of the democratic solution to global governance—the state and market systems and democratic rule—are reserved for succeeding chapters. Keep in mind, as we move through this disaggregated inventory, that what we are really observing is a global society as a work in progress—enlarging and entangling webs of human interdependencies with no clear end game in sight.

The Multiplication of Actors

Never before have so many actors composed a human society. Among the most powerful are *nation-states*. The nation-state has become the preferred unit of populations to organize their political affairs. The United Nations began in 1945 with fifty-one members. That number increased almost three-fold to 144 thirty years later, principally as a result of the dissolution of Europe's empires and the successful efforts of indigenous populations to gain independence and realize their goal of national self-determination.

The implosion of the Soviet Union and Yugoslavia in the 1990s added still more states to UN membership. The United Nations totals 193 states at this writing in 2016. New states are emerging or in the wings. Kosovo, while recognized by most Western governments, awaits entry into the United Nations, subject to surmounting opposition to its membership by the Russian Federation, Serbia (which formerly ruled the Albanian population), and a scattering of other UN members. East Timor gained independence from Indonesia in 2002, and South Sudan was split from Sudan in 2011. Both are now UN members. There is also the possibility that some states—for example, Iraq, Afghanistan, Syria, or the Congo Republic—may implode, if not into separate states, then into ungovernable parts as a consequence of incessant civil strife.

The rise of powerful and resourceful *nonstate actors* is a particularly unique aspect of globalization. Threatened are not only existing regimes and their populations but also the very states themselves and their boundaries. The attack on the World Trade Center and the Pentagon by nineteen Al Qaeda operatives galvanized US-led international military interventions into Iraq and Afghanistan. Military and civilian casualties in dead and injured have mounted into the tens of thousands. Attacks by the Islamic State of Iraq and Syria (ISIS) and Al Qaeda have also been launched against targets in Britain, France, Spain, Yemen, Libya, Iraq, Syria, and Mali. Self-organizing terrorist cells, operating without central direction, stretch across central Asia, the Middle East, Africa, and the Western states. In the midst of this chaos, ISIS is attempting to redefine the state boundaries of the Middle East in a quest to create a new Islamic caliphate.

Attention to threats posed by Al Qaeda, ISIS, and their franchises obscures the globalization of terrorist attacks across the globe.[5] The Global Terrorism Database (GTD) lists 104,000 terrorist attacks between 1970 and 2010.[6] Deadly terrorist assaults have been launched by individuals and groups against vulnerable civilian populations in countries on every continent. The six leading countries incurring such attacks include Colombia (7,180), Iraq (6,475), India (6,114), Peru (6,045), El Salvador (5,347), and Pakistan (4,436). In this period, the United States registered 2,347 terrorist incidents.

The explosion in the number of *intergovernmental organizations* (IGOs), *nongovernmental organizations* (NGOs), and *international nongovernmental organizations* (INGOs) parallels and is symbiotically related to the creation of a global nation-state system. IGOs advance member state interests. They promote their security and economic interests and preserve their status as recognized sovereign entities and members of the nation-state system.[7] The United Nations, the European Union, the World Bank, the International Monetary Fund (IMF), and the World Trade Organization (WTO) illustrate the expansion of IGOs as extensions of state power and, conversely, as constraints on state power as a function of the authority delegated to these international actors by their member states.

The increase in INGOs has been even more dramatic and extensive than those of IGOs. The origins of INGOs, possessed of a global reach, go deep into the history of globalization. The British and the Dutch East India companies, chartered in the early seventeenth century, evidence a close association between the overseas expansion of European states and the rise of nongovernmental organizations. Even before these state-created corporations were formed, institutionalized religious bodies—Catholic, Protestant, Buddhist, and Muslim—sought converts around the globe. They were complemented later by secular organizations with an equally humanitarian purpose animating their founders and adherents. Among the most notable were the Anti-Slavery Society, formed in 1839, and the International Red Cross, formed twenty-five years later. Charles Chatfield lists almost 1,100 such organizations at the outbreak of World War I in 1914.[8]

Both IGOs and, especially, INGOs grew at an accelerating rate after World War II, principally among democratic and open market states. The Union of International Organizations in its *Yearbook of International Organizations Online* lists over sixty thousand INGOs, of which thirty-five thousand are considered still actively engaged.[9] John Keane notes that there are an estimated five thousand INGO world congresses, which involve a myriad of professional associations; bridge, chess, and sports clubs; and an expanding array of business and trade shows. Operating in all regions of the world, they employ or enlist the voluntary support of millions of people.[10] INGOs are synonymous with globalization, given their increasing scope and reach, the range and complexity of their missions, the millions comprising their leadership and membership, the huge budgets they collectively control—amounting to billions of dollars—and their impact on the daily lives of the world's populations.[11] The expanding universe of NGOs, INGOs, IGOs, and social movements are the principal actors forming a global civil society.

The creation of thousands of *multinational corporations* (MNCs), particularly important INGOs organized for profit, has been no less dramatic in multiplying the number of global actors today. As *Forbes 2000* observes, "business . . . needs a civil society to survive."[12] There is a mutually supportive relationship between the expansion of global civil society, providing a space not otherwise occupied by the state, and the rise of these corporate behemoths. Measured along four metrics—sales, profits, assets, and market value—*Forbes* identifies over two thousand "business titans" worldwide—North America (821), Pacific Rim (544), Western Europe (527), and other regions around the globe (117).

MNCs form the skeletal structure of the world economy. Their growth has been nothing less than astonishing over the last twenty years. From a base of three thousand in 1990, the number of multinationals grew to 63,000 by 2003. Their 821,000 subsidiaries girdle the earth. They employ ninety million people, almost a quarter of whom are in the developing world. They produce a quarter of gross world product (GWP). The leading one thousand MNCs account for 80 percent of the world's industrial output.[13] Their accumulated net worth exceeds that of most countries in the world.

The enterprise, scope of action, and impact of *individuals* have also been enlarged through globalization. Celebrities in the arts, sports, and political life can assume a global profile. Opportunities for individuals to attain global celebrity status have never been as available as today, thanks to the facilitating support of social media and the Internet. The Rolling Stones, Michael Jackson, and Lady Gaga attracted fans globally. Michael Jordan and Kobe Bryant were followed by basketball fans around the globe from China to Brazil. Other personalities traded on their celebrity status to address global issues. Jody

Williams, an American teacher, gained global prominence by winning the Nobel Peace Prize in 1997 for her work to ban land mines, a campaign also championed by ex-Beatle Paul McCartney. Defeated presidential candidate Al Gore gained worldwide fame as a leader in the fight against global warming. Bono of U2 teamed up with Jeffrey Sachs, a leading global economist, to lobby before the United Nations for implementation of the UN Millennium Development Goals to cut global poverty by half. Mohammad Yunus, a Bangladeshi banker, won the Nobel Peace Prize in 2006 for founding the Grameen Bank, emulated around the globe, as a vehicle to furnish microloans to the poor, notably women, to enable them to enter local market economies.

The resulting polyarchy of power among global actors furnishes new and enlarged spaces for individual action and resistance to established authority. Whereas authority was more clearly delineated before, "a vast network of waxing and waning groups and strategies"[14] now makes authority along an expanding polyarchy of collective actors more problematic. Adding to this confusion is the increased stress on performance by publics to justify a regime's legitimacy and authority.[15] The capacity of individuals to join with other like-minded individuals across and within state borders through the World Wide Web and social media has created a new politics of the public square. Note the impact of public protest to initiate the ill-fated Middle East Spring as well as the successful European protests that led to the end of the Cold War. As James Rosenau observes, the implications of these changes in the relation of individuals to authority at all levels of state and civil societal interaction is "that the arrangements underlying the prevailing order (or orders) are endlessly subject to revision, to fluctuations somewhat erratically as new issues and challenges surface on the global agenda and arrest the attention of mobilized publics."[16] Illustrating Rosenau's insight, there is the example of Edward Snowden's release of thousands of sensitive American documents, which seriously disrupted US relations with other countries by revealing US programs to hack into private and public computers as well as to spy on allied leaders such as German chancellor Angela Merkel.

The world's population itself, which might be termed an accidental international actor, should not be overlooked. Currently at seven billion, it is estimated to balloon to eight billion by 2030 and reach nine to ten billion by 2050. Most of the increase will be in the developing world. The pressures exerted by population growth on the carrying capacity of the world is unprecedented in the evolution of the species and is among the most pressing challenges of the twenty-first century. The rising demand of underdeveloped populations for economic growth, to approach, if not match, the levels of material wealth of the peoples of the Western states, will inevitably accelerate the rate of the world's environmental and ecological degradation. Much of this growth may well be undone. The burning of fossil fuels, principally coal and oil, is already having major adverse effects on climate change and global warming.[17]

The carrying capacity of the earth is also threatened by rapid deforestation, loss of agricultural land, decreased freshwater supplies, desertification, depressed marine fisheries, the spread of toxic wastes, and the accelerated decline of biodiversity.[18] Competition for scarce energy and water resources is also likely to increase, potentially resulting in heightened armed confrontations. The civil wars in the Congo and Sierra Leone are also harbingers of future conflicts over mineral resources.[19]

The Emergence of a Borderless
Global Society: Civil and Uncivil Global Society

The global society has also generated two fundamentally opposed, irreconcilable subsocieties: one civil and one uncivil. They are inextricably entangled in their organization and workings as well as in the interactions of their members. The actors and associations arising from each owe much, as preconditions for the globalization of these subsocieties, to the synergisms generated by these systemic forces: the revolution in communications and transportation, the emergence of a nation-state system, the progressive integration of the world economy, the spread of open, liberal democratic regimes, and these regimes' transnational promotion and protection of civil liberties and human rights on behalf of all peoples.

The political processes by which the rule of law, domestic and international, are created and applied today are no longer the exclusive province of the state system. Not only are NGOs, INGOs, and IGOs, as well as transnational movements (the Catholic Church, etc.), actively engaged in defining state and market rules, significantly shaping their institutional development, but they also perform countless indispensable political, socioeconomic, and governmental functions.[20] As an ensemble, they form a rich and textured subsystem of global governance, nestled within the interstices of the state and market systems.

Civil Global Society

INGOs are of particular interest to the governance of a global society because of their number, power, financial reserves, expertise, and impact on the lives of the world's populations across borders.[21] Most arise initially from within the democratic regimes in which they operate. Often overlooked is the fact that among the greatest contributions to the theory and practice of government is the right, inspired and implemented principally by democratic regimes, of citizens to join freely in association with others to pursue their particular aims and interests and to check the state's capacity to limit this right. In the exercise of this basic right, democratic regimes have extended their regional and global reach to create a global civil society.[22]

Illustrative of the many significant transnational governmental roles these INGOs play in laying down rules and building governing institutions are: profit making (transnational corporations), humanitarian assistance (Red Cross, Doctors without Borders), advocacy of member interests to shape state and market practices to their liking (Amnesty International, AFL-CIO, chambers of commerce), global spread and institutionalization of religious norms (World Council of Churches), advancement of professional and union interests (Service Employees International Union), and education (International Studies Association). INGOs also regulate international sports, including the winter and summer quadrennial Olympics as well as tennis, soccer, cycling, boxing, bridge, and chess competitions; and the tracking of regional and global security issues (International Institute for Strategic Studies).

INGOs are enmeshed in global governance in several key ways. First, members accord these associations, corporations, and social movements the authority to issue rules for member behavior, which enjoy both their support and legitimacy. Many of these associations can also levy significant sanctions to control or penalize members who do not abide by their bylaws, protocols, standard operating procedures, or constitutions. In exercising considerable power over their members,[23] these associations and their leadership, taken together, represent a vast complex of private authorities. They are no less essential to global governance than the state and market systems and political regimes, notably democratic polities, in which they are implicated.[24] The Olympic Committee disciplines athletes who fail to meet Committee standards, notably those athletes who use prohibited performance-enhancing drugs.

Second, these associations are also engaged in pursuing their interests by opposing and frustrating rival associations bent on imposing their preferences and rules of law for governance on the larger global society of which they are members. Illustrative is the conflict between the Catholic Church and women's groups, like NOW, over the right to abortion and family planning, or INGOs pressing for corporate codes to check global warming and to maintain clean, safe working environments for workers around the world. Still others work to support and sustain a healthy global ecology for plants, wildlife, and humans as symbiotically and mutually dependent. INGOs comprise a complex kaleidoscope of shifting alliances between and among them to enhance their collective power to foster shared interests or to counter rivals.

If the actors included in global civil society are restricted only to those which employ nonviolent means to impress their preferences on other actors, it is still readily apparent that the rise of a global civil society does not imply a convergence of interests and values across these associations. Many enlist the power of states to intervene on their behalf to impose their preferences within and across states and by that token frustrate and control their opponents. In a word, NGOs and INGOs have a powerful say over who gets what, how, when, and why,[25] the stuff of political power. Private associations working within a global civil society provide a transnational process "aimed at publicizing and reducing the incidence of such disparate phenomena as murder and rape, genocide and nuclear war, the violence of disciplinary institutions, cruelty to animals, child abuse, and capital punishment."[26]

From the perspective and workings of global civil society, the patterns and outcomes of the interdependencies of actors in global politics can no longer be reduced simply either to the relations between states or to the interrelations of states and their domestic populations. Relying solely on the state system to portray global socioeconomic and political interdependencies disregards the permeability of state boundaries, the weakened capacity of states to control their own populations, borders, and global markets, or their failures to discharge the multiple functions and obligations of what is now a global state, a view developed in chapter 4. Absent reference to the power and authority of these nongovernmental and transnational associations, it is scarcely possible to explain the organization and workings of global governance.

Conversely, these nongovernmental bodies depend for their birth, survival, and growth on the power structures of the state and market systems as well as on that of open, economically liberal, democratic regimes that rest on broad, popular support. These institutions and the public support of popular regimes generate the power, opportunities, and incentives for civil associations to play their important roles as sources of private authority in global governance.

One implication of the emergence of a global civil society is that there is a hollow ring to the claim of authoritarian regimes that by fiat they can preserve the classic structure of power and authority of the Westphalian state system. The Chinese Communist government continues to voice this restrictive notion of a civil society as bounded by state power and sovereignty. It claims to support civil society under the aegis of its restricted notions of the rule of law. This self-serving rationale of public order is used to justify the jailing of dissidents, to control global Internet communications, and to build a firewall between its citizens and their access to information abroad. In justifying its censorship of Internet access and e-mail messaging of its citizens, a Chinese foreign ministry spokesman insisted, "that online services in China must be conducted in accord with the law."[27] It is precisely this constrained notion of the rule of law, as defined and bounded solely by the state, that no longer squares with the existence of a global civil society as a derivative of the power and authority of private, nongovernmental associations.

The proliferation of private authorities through NGOs and INGOs however pales before the power and influence of multinational corporations (MNCs). Between 1970 and 2002, the number of MNC parent companies grew from 700 to 65,000—greater than a ninefold increase. The number of affiliates also exploded to 850,000, covering all regions of the globe.[28] Saskia Sassen estimates that at the turn of this century, much of the wealth of MNCs was concentrated in the northern transatlantic economic system, linking the European Union and the United States. "This region accounted for 66 percent of world-wide stock market capitalization, 60 percent of inward foreign investment stock and 76 percent of outward foreign investment stock, 60 percent of worldwide sales in mergers and acquisitions, and 80 percent of purchases in mergers and acquisitions."[29] The balance of these proportions is gradually shifting toward the states of Asia, as China has now surpassed Japan to become the second largest national economy after the United States.

Corporate authority structures are largely hierarchical, with affiliates responsible to central headquarters. These centralized entities also control the outsourcing of financial, accounting, advertising, investment, and trade functions.[30] The result is a globalized MNC complex forming a vast system of private authority girdling the globe that largely escapes state control. Constituted is an immense, sprawling reservoir of private wealth, authority, and power capable of resisting state oversight and regulation and of co-opting segments of state power for its advantage. These corporations command the heights as a consequence of the human, material, and technological resources at their disposal.[31]

MNCs are actively involved in defining domestic and international policies in areas of their interest to ward off controls and to blunt NGO and INGO opponents in policy areas ranging from environmental, energy, financial, investment, labor, and trade regulations to product and service standards. They prefer voluntary agreements and insist on fashioning industrial codes of their own to suit their interests. For example, some 49,000 firms in 118 countries subscribe to the environmental standards developed by the International Organization for Standardization, titled ISO 14000. Whether these standards are being observed is problematic. For example, the international construction industry is reportedly sufficiently powerful and insular to have written the standards for this industry and to have elicited state acquiescence in these protocols.[32]

Central to the development of a global civil society has been the increasing locus of populations and resources in cities. These form, as analysts increasingly recognize,[33] nodes of connections that, while embedded in nation-states, are increasingly autonomous in their mutual relations. Created is a new global geography of socioeconomic and political activity in which the state is passed over or passed by on many fronts, although its material power remains largely predominant if activated.

Illustrative of the new global geography of politics, pivoting on the global city, is the agreement reached between former president Bill Clinton and ex–New York mayor Michael Bloomberg to develop a single global program aimed at leading the major cities of the world to confront global climate change. The paralysis of states to confront environmental risks to the planet, notably global warming, invites cities, like the organization of the forty largest cities of the world, to assume leadership in controlling harmful emissions by relying on their own authority and resources. As the *New York Times* report of this initiative noted, "Cities now house more than half of the world's population, and while they occupy 2 percent of the globe's land mass, cities emit 70 percent of greenhouse gas emissions."[34]

If states fail to provide the collective good of controlling greenhouse gas (GHG) emissions, cities are prepared to fill this vacuum. "We are putting a stake in the ground around the idea that national and international governments have failed, possibly quite permanently, or at least in a way that they will not make any serious progress before it's too late," noted Kevin Sheekey, a political adviser to Bloomberg. "If you address the problems of the cities, there will be no need for China and India to sign onto some international accord. And thank God, because that's not going to get done. It's time to say it."[35] Michael Bloomberg, upon leaving office, announced the creation of a global advisory service to help cities around the world to cope with their problems, which many of their host states are incapable of addressing.[36] Cities, and not just states, are the site of civil and uncivil society and increasingly significant centers for the production of the global society and its governance.[37]

To sum up, the global civil society shares several properties. They are voluntary, self-organizing, outside the boundaries of state agencies, law-abiding, peaceful, decentralized, and heterogeneous. Most have bylaws governing membership and member behavior, establish rules for the election of officers, and pursue complex strategies to ensure their preservation, replication, financial integrity, and growth. INGOs, in promoting power-sharing across state borders, challenge state and market actors through a broad spectrum of means, including exposure in the global media and pressures for changes in domestic, international, and global institutional laws, norms, and practices. Illustrative are successful INGO pressures to affect, if not fully control, the lending policies of the IMF and World Bank or to induce the WTO and NAFTA (North American Free Trade Agreement) partners to promote fair labor practices and to protect the environment.[38]

Global Uncivil Society: The Globalization of Transnational Crime

The globalization of transnational crime and ipso facto the creation of an uncivil subsociety nestled within a larger global society has formidable supports throughout the globe: a decentralized and anarchical global state system; an expanding and increasingly integrated global market system; the freedom and permissiveness provided by open democratic regimes; the corruption associated with authoritarian and semiauthoritarian regimes, like Russia; and the widespread collapse of state power, resulting in failed or failing states. The uncivil society principally refers to the emergence of complex, dense transnational networks of illegal/criminal activities associated with millions of transnational actors.[39] These profit from the material riches, economic and political power, and significant asocial status afforded them by their exploitation of a larger, richer civil society in which these criminal elements are nested. Actors in the uncivil society operate freely, if illegally, in violating state and international laws. The physical harm they visit on the world populations— death, bodily injury, rape, kidnapping, extortion, and intimidation—and their enormous destruction and theft of private and public property constitute a global network of illegal rule imposed on vulnerable populations.

Like civil INGOs, these criminal elements act outside and across the boundaries of the state. They are also heterogeneous, varying in their organizational structures, mechanisms of control over their members and targeted elements of civil society, in the modalities of their criminal activities, and in the forms of force and coercion they use. In contrast to their civil counterparts and victims, these self-organizing, unlawful actors principally rely on violence, real or menacing, to survive and extend their power, to defy the rule of law, to corrupt or co-opt legitimate private and public governmental institutions, and to direct targeted members of the civil society for illegal and immoral gain.

Transnational criminal organizations and fraudulent practices across state boundaries have been around for a long time.[40] There are more of them and their power and cross-border reach is greater than ever before. They have a particular affinity and association with the rise of a global market system. Transnational criminal organizations provide illicit commodities for sale— drugs, arms, slave labor, and prostitution—principally through actual or implicit violence as the preferred method of ensuring delivery of their products and services. Increasingly, these activities, products, and services have been de-territorialized. As Phil Williams observes, "Transnational organized crime is, then, criminal business that, in one way or another, crosses national borders. The border crossing can involve the perpetrators, their illicit products, people (either illegal migrants or women and children being trafficked illegally), their profits, or digital signals (a virtual border crossing)."[41]

Figure 2.1 outlines the principal forms of transnational crime impacting on the United States and, by extension, to all regions of the world. [42] Threats to Americans and their communities include smuggling of alien contraband, materials or devices associated with weapons of mass destruction, financial fraud, money laundering, high-tech crime (stealing social-security and credit-card numbers), and environmental crime. Threats to American business and financial interests involve theft of intellectual property rights, economic espionage, and the corruption of governmental officials and businessmen. These depredations are globalized further in arms trafficking, sanction violations,

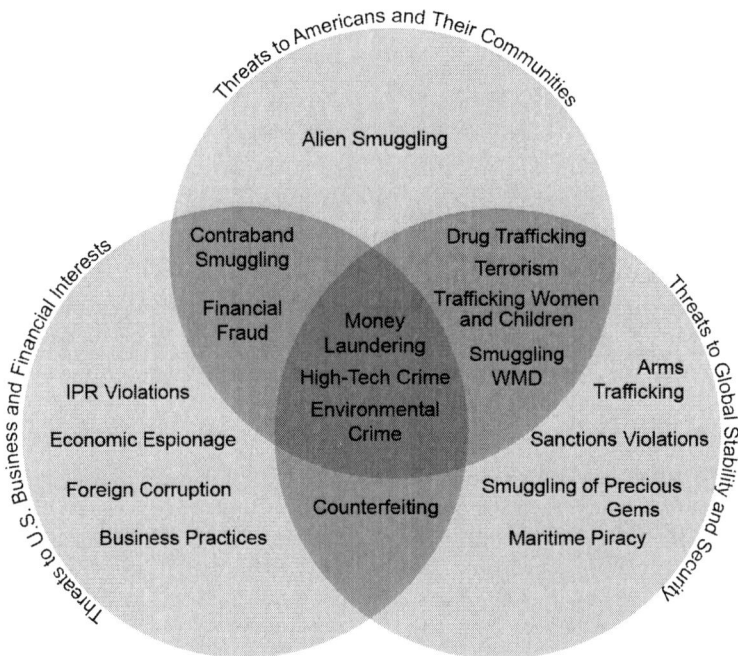

FIGURE 2.1
Global Crime against the United States (This graphic depiction of how international crimes affect US interests should not be interpreted as suggesting any level of threat magnitude; crimes intersecting all three circles of threats to US interests are not necessarily a greater threat than those intersecting two or only one.)
Source: CIA. https://www.ncjrs.gov/App/Publications/abstract.aspx?ID=189403.

smuggling of conflict diamonds and precious minerals, and increasingly more costly and deadly maritime piracy, notably off the east coast of Africa.

Illegal trafficking in all forms from drugs to migrant labor and prostitution are global enterprises. Afghanistan is the world's largest producer of opium. In 2013, the United Nations estimated that the drug trade contributed $21 billion to the Afghan economy or 4 percent of its gross national product (GNP).[43] The leading supplier of cocaine is Colombia, which accounts for 55 percent of global production. Together illicit trafficking in all types of controlled substances approaches $1 trillion in annual revenues or more than 1 percent of gross world product (GWP). The IMF estimates that money laundering annually amounted to somewhere between $590 billion and $1.5 trillion or approximately 2–5 percent of GWP. These illicit gains are in addition to those arising from tens of millions of crimes committed within the borders of each state, many of which are linked to transnational crime organizations.[44] The impact of these illicit revenues extends to legitimate business and financial activities, funded by these criminally generated resources. This symbiosis suggests that it would be misleading to think of civil and uncivil transnational societies as autonomous and insulated from each other. While it is difficult to accurately estimate the revenue derived from all forms of illicit drug trafficking, the important point to keep in mind is that it represents an enormous economic activity even when lower figures are relied upon.[45]

All regions of the world are implicated in human trafficking. This conclusion is echoed both in the US annual report on global trafficking[46] and the United Nations 2008 report on trafficking.[47] If UN and International Labour Organization (ILO) figures are to be relied upon, the number of victims may be as high as 10 million.[48] Eighty percent of the victims face sexual exploitation. The remaining 20 percent are herded into forced labor. Of these totals, 20 percent are estimated to be children.

The crossover between civil and uncivil global society is perhaps clearest when illicit gains are used specifically for legal business purposes. With money and power, criminal groups are able to assume governmental functions, to arbitrate conflicts within the communities in which they are embedded, or to elicit public support through payoffs or paternalistic practices and clientelism. Together the two entangled subsocieties generate rules, norms, and sanctions for enforcement that are enmeshed in the larger state, market, and regime systems on which they depend. It comes then as no surprise that individuals bridge both subsocieties. Witness HSBC, a top British bank, which admitted to money laundering of crime proceeds, or the rigging by the Royal Bank of Scotland of interest rates, itself a felony on its face.[49] JP Morgan Chase was also fined over $2 billion for its lack of due diligence. The bank failed to alert authorities of evidence of fraud in overseeing Bernard Madoff's accounts, essentially assisting him in executing his $17 billion Ponzi scheme.

One of the ironies of globalization and modernization is the capacity of transnational crime both to exploit the assets of state sovereignty and the decentralization of the nation-state system and to challenge the power and authority of the state and the state system. States provide a range of assets for criminal elements. Among these are home, host, transshipment, and service for criminal operations.[50] Williams summarizes the ironic "strengths" of state weakness in providing useful services for transnational crime to flourish: "[W]eak states share certain characteristics: There is a low level of state legitimacy; border controls are weak; rules are ineffective; the institutions and people who represent the state put other goals above the public interest; there is little economic or social provision for the citizenry; business is not legally regulated or protected; social control through a fair and efficient criminal justice system is lacking; and other typical state functions are not carried out with either efficiency or effectiveness."[51] There arises a natural iron triangle of criminals, political leaders, and law enforcement personnel. These alliances institutionalize transnational crime in a country, whether Russia, South Africa, or Afghanistan. Crime syndicates can engage in not only highly effective risk management of their dangerous and volatile environments but also preemptive management by basing their operations on these reliable alliances, bound together by mutual gain and a culture of violence.

This brief review of the illicit global trade underscores not only the globalization of these criminal behaviors but also the scale of the cooperation required of states to effectively address international crime. The actors engaged, whether perpetrators, victims, or law enforcement agencies, reinforce the image and reality of a global uncivil society that transcends local, national, and regional networks to form an integral, if illicit, component of the global society. Exposed, too, are the weaknesses of the decentralized, anarchical nation-state system and its governmental institutions to eradicate or control the spread of these illicit activities. These weaknesses, conversely, implicitly support and facilitate the extension of the global uncivil society.

Webs of Governance without a Global Government

World order and global governance can be summarily represented as a multilayered, expanding system of intertwined webs of rules and institutions, spun by the global society's multiple, empowered actors who pursue their converging and diverging preferences within five entangling webs of governance. The first three refer to the OWL institutions of the state, markets, and domestic regimes, most prominently those based on popular rule. The latter two refer to the rule-making power of actors, individuals, and agents, thriving in the civil and uncivil subsocieties of the global society. This dynamic and ceaselessly changing system of a five-layered polyarchy, under the pressure of opposing and converging actor preferences and the deployment by actors of their power, hard and soft, to get the world order they want, can be summarily characterized as *governance without a global government*.[52] The rules of law and institutions that would be apt to resolve differences or to coordinate pooled preferences are themselves sources of intractable conflict between and among clashing global actors, posing insurmountable obstacles to the creation of a universal, integrated world government.

The existing condition of global governance without a government presents the members and agents of a global society with a bewildering and conflicting array of choices about what system of governance they want or choose to obey. Each of their interdependent transactions, as chapter 1 suggested,[53] is also, implicitly, an occasion for them to affirm or challenge the rules and institutions—and supporting power structures—that advance or frustrate their preferences, impede the realization of their opponents' interests, or arbitrate these conflicts of interest. The very complexity of the globalization process precludes the feasibility that a universal state would be equipped and capable of addressing the needs and diverse interests of more than seven billion people. Governance without government implicitly becomes the preferred choice of billions more by default than by conscious deliberation.

Governance without government responds to global social and cultural diversity and complexity and reflects the diffusion of power across peoples and states. Global governance is, accordingly, a perpetual process of strategies, negotiations, and exercises of power by actors of different capabilities to create ipso facto their preferred world government, a fundamentally unachievable objective under conditions of widely varying power and competing value systems among the multiple and growing number of actors in play in global society. The composite of rules and institutions of global governance, precariously at risk at any point in time and space, is itself the product of the competing interests, aims, and values of countless actors. Under these circumstances the future trajectory of world order and global governance cannot be confidently predicted. Too many uncertainties surround the outcomes of the struggles for ascendancy of the billions of actors engaged in the three webs of governance of the global society and those of the civil and uncivil subsocieties. Global governance—governance without government—is one of the great challenges of the twenty-first century.

Global Power as Protean

A significant property of the global society is the protean nature of power among its members. Four key dimensions warrant attention: (1) the inability of any actor to shape the global society to fully suit its interests and values; (2) the rapid and unanticipated shifts in relative power balances of the actors across their clashing concerns and preferences for security, material welfare, and legitimacy; (3) the uncertainty endemic to the actual rather than the expected outcomes of the decisions of actors and the deployment of their limited power to realize their preferences in their interdependent exchanges; and (4) power as an expanding universe both in its availability to a growing number of actors of the world society and in the multiplicity of its novel hard and soft forms.

A Global Society without Superpowers

In either addressing or resolving the global issues impacting on the world's populations, including most especially global governance, no actor fully gets its way—at least not for very long. Many observers precipitously proclaimed the rise of a unipolar world in the wake of the ascendancy of the United States as an outcome of the Soviet Union's implosion.[54] That expectation has no currency today in light of a beset United States at home and abroad.[55] No one actor possesses either the vision to induce or the power to impose its preferences on other actors, much less to surmount the many formidable obstacles posed by a rapidly changing geopolitical, economic, and technological environment. French foreign minister Laurent Fabius poses the challenge clearly: "Today we live in a zero-polar, or a-polar, world. No one power or group of powers can solve all the problems."[56]

Policy experts and decision-makers differ widely in explaining the sources of power diffusion that yield so large a spectrum of unexpected results. Some accent economic power despite the unpredictability and fragility of global financial markets, reflected in their meltdown in the first decade of the twenty-first century.[57] Others stress the anarchy of the nation-state system.[58] Still others pose culture and culture clashes as driving global politics.[59] No actor, however much endowed with material power—military, economic, or technological—can fully and unconditionally dictate, coercively, its preferences to other actors about how outcomes of their interdependent exchanges should be ordered. Scholarship devoted narrowly to a theory of hegemonic politics of state power and to the rise and fall of hegemons, focused narrowly on states and on the interstate system, has lost much of its relevance in a world with a bewildering number of actors capable of frustrating what other actors want, including states, while exercising partial control over the preferences they pursue.[60]

44Chapter 2

With the rise of a global society, populated by a multiplying number of actors deploying a vast array of power forms, the notion of superpowers also warrants serious reformulation, even abandonment.[61] A largely unrecognized implication of the paradox of unprecedented state material power, particularly attributable to big states (the United States or China), and of a state's impotence to command other actors to accede to its preferences is that there are no superpowers within the kind of global society that has evolved to this day. The sense in which a superpower is understood to be able to get what it wants—its way—in its interdependent exchanges with other states and actors has little purchase in explaining big or small state or nonstate actor behavior and power exchange outcomes.

If a demanding standard of what qualifies as a superpower is applied to the United States or China, neither qualifies now or in the foreseeable future as a superpower.[62] It certainly does not apply any longer, as it once was ascribed to a seemingly invincible Soviet Union and to a stable, enduring bipolar system.[63] In retrospect, most informed observers and policy-makers were ill informed about the underlying weaknesses of the Soviet state and its susceptibility to dissolve into its warring, ethnic, nationalist, and religious parts, and about the power of the actors working within the Soviet state, including state officials, ironically, most dependent for their power on its survival. The same criticisms hold for characterizing China or a rising India today as aspiring superpowers. None of these states, however large or endowed its human and material resources, meets a rigorous test of a superpower.

The United States is still viewed as a superpower, mistakenly in many quarters, as a function of its status, measured as the world's leading military and economic power with a gross domestic product (GDP) roughly balanced at $17 trillion at the end of 2013.[64] These absolute measures of material power have not translated into a capacity of the United States to attain its principal announced foreign policy objectives or to shape the global society to suit its values and interests since the end of the Cold War. The frustrations of the Iraq and Afghan wars and Syrian civil war illustrate the waning influence that the United States has had over other actors and events vital to its security and economic interests in the Middle East. Its influence in Iraq is tenuous, ceded to some degree to Iran as a result of its accelerated troop withdrawal in 2011. American efforts to create a unified Iraqi state and government have foundered on the shoals of an Iraqi society divided against itself into irreconcilable religious and secular communities—Shi'ites versus Sunnis, Sunnis versus Sunnis, Kurds versus both, and the emergence of the radical ISIS, whose aim is to proclaim an Islamic caliphate by imposing its military power on these contending actors.[65]

The Taliban insurgencies in Afghanistan and Pakistan also threaten US interests and those of its allies. The Afghan government's legitimacy, staying power, and popular support remain problematic. A beleaguered Pakistan, beset by civil strife and widespread terrorist attacks, borders on a failed state. The Taliban and Al Qaeda enjoy sanctuary in western Pakistan and are resurgent in Afghanistan. North Korea defies US and allied efforts to dissuade them from developing nuclear weapons. Foreign investors, with China in the lead, own a fifth of US foreign debt. In relying on China to purchase US securities, amounting to about one-quarter of foreign holdings, Washington is weakened in its ability to induce China to join in effective sanctions against North Korea, to revalue upward the Chinese yuan in accord with China's economic prowess, or to coordinate with Beijing on an effective strategy either to lessen global unemployment or to combat global warming or other economic and environmental issues,[66] much less to compel China to let up on its suppression of dissidents or to relax its censorship of all forms of digital communication. In every region of the world, the United States has been frustrated in achieving its announced aims. In many instances weaker powers and nonstate actors, like Hezbollah in Lebanon and Hamas in Palestine, are amply capable of resisting US entreaties. From the vantage point of an expanding global society and the diffusion of power among its members, no state qualifies any longer as a superpower in the sense of a hegemon that gets its way.

Certainly states will differ in their relative power and in the leverage they have in influencing other actors to their liking and to do their bidding. What is a conceptual and empirical stretch is to assign overweening power to a particular state as a superpower and, thereby, to raise unfounded expectations about the likelihood of its success in its negotiations with actors at home or abroad. The notion of a superpower also has the unwitting effect of implicitly viewing power as absolute rather than relative in the capacity of a state to shape the outcomes of its interdependent transactions with other actors to its liking. Assessing state power depends on the stakes at issue, their salience, and the number and power distributions of the actors in play.

Viewing power in this fluid and flexible way guards against surprise when an alleged superpower fails or falters. It orients the observer and analyst to assess the relative power balances between actors. Note that the global state, developed in chapter 4, is expected to perform multiple and competing functions and to deploy a wide spectrum of power forms, whether military power, economic resources, technological prowess, diplomatic agility, or superior claims to legitimacy. Prevailing use of the notion of hegemony scarcely covers these power sources and the significant outcomes they produce within an expanding global society.

The Changing Map of Power

Rapid and unforeseen shifts in the relative power of global actors are also a distinguishing feature of global politics.[67] A cursory review of the changes in the territorial boundaries of states during the twentieth century to the present (2016) supports this contention. Before the collapse of the Eurocentric system after World War II, the European powers cast their rule over most of the world populations outside the Western Hemisphere. Controlling Europe was tantamount to ruling over the billions of peoples within the Eurocentric system. World Wars I and II can be explained to no small degree in terms of the failed efforts of the warring European states to achieve an uncontested hegemonic position. After World War II the Eurocentric system gradually descended into an anarchical nation-state system as former colonies gained independence and joined the United Nations.

The Cold War between the United States and the Soviet Union divided Europe into two spheres of influence. The European states were organized around two security alliances under the leadership of Washington and Moscow. The North Atlantic Treaty Organization (NATO) alliance initially comprised the United States and eleven other West European states, later including Turkey and Greece at its perimeter, versus the Warsaw Pact of the Soviet Union and seven other East European states. Germany and Berlin were also divided into West and East components. Between these two rival alliances were grouped a neutral belt of countries, ranging from Sweden and Finland in the north to Austria and Switzerland in the center of Europe.

This division held until the implosion of the Soviet Union in 1991, leading to the reemergence of fifteen nation-states out of the former Soviet empire. Subsequently, the European Union, formed from among the Western states, expanded to include the states of the former Warsaw Pact and some of the neutral states, growing to a membership of twenty-eight states. Whether the European Union will hold together remains an open question under the pressure of economic downturns, political rivalries, and the reemergence of nationalism across Europe. These divisions have been dramatized by Greek insolvency and its threat to the Euro (which is supported institutionally by only nineteen of the twenty-eight members of the European Union), as well as by the EU's chronic economic underperformance since the turn of the century, marked by double-digit unemployment. The proposed British referendum in 2017 over whether the United Kingdom should remain within the Union also bodes ill for the Union.

Conversely, the Russian Federation, which arose from the ashes of the Soviet Union, reasserted its territorial claims to some of the states of its lost empire where, for the most part, Russians were a minority and where Moscow sought to exercise its influence. That led to the Ukraine's loss of Crimea and, at this writing, its rule over its eastern provinces where the majority of the population is Russian-speaking. Moscow also exercises control over half of Georgia with Russian troops supporting the breakaway provinces of South Ossetia and Abkhazia in western Georgia. It also exercises influence over Moldova. How far the Russian Federation under President Vladimir Putin will pursue its territorial ambitions, notably in the Baltic region, remains unclear. The map of Eastern Europe remains unstable and subject to continuing change.

The Balkans also experienced a breakup of its former cohesion with the dissolution of Yugoslavia. The communal divisions within the states of the former Yugoslavia produced seven states, including Kosovo, which remains to be recognized by Serbia and the Russian Federation and a number of other states. The state lines that were drawn largely followed communal lines of national sentiment; the exception is Bosnia, which is split among Muslim, Christian, and Christian Orthodox communities.[68]

East Asia and Africa have not been spared significant changes in their state territorial boundaries. East Timor successfully gained its independence from Indonesia. Sudan split into two with the creation of South Sudan in 2010. China claims rule over a recalcitrant Tibetan population. It has regained control over Macau from Portugal and Hong Kong from the United Kingdom. It also seeks the integration of Taiwan as part of the mainland. Meanwhile, it asserts claims to vast reaches of the South China Sea against those pursued by its neighbors in the region. A formerly integrated Korea appears permanently divided into North and South, although the implosion of the authoritarian government of North Korea—possibly as sudden as the dissolution of the Soviet Union—cannot be ruled out.

The most dramatic changes in state boundaries are presently occurring in the Middle East. The dissolution of the Ottoman Empire and caliphate in the wake of World War I was the first major reorganization of the region. The Middle East state borders, which emerged from World War II, largely arose as a consequence of British-French dictation in the Sykes-Picot agreement of 1916. These have been since significantly redefined by the creation of the state of Israel out of Palestine. The Jewish state has subsequently expanded as a consequence of the 1967 war and the spread of Jewish settlements into the West Bank and Jerusalem.[69]

The rise of Muslim extremism in the Middle East as well as the deep and enduring communal division in the region have effectively effaced the state boundaries created by the European powers. The transnational movement that emerged under the leadership of the self-proclaimed ISIS now controls vast swaths of Syrian and Iraqi territory and exercises harsh rule over the inhabitants caught in its maw. Figure 2.2 depicts the extent of its rule in the

FIGURE 2.2
Operating Areas of ISIS or ISIL (Islamic State of Iraq and the Levant) as of April 2015
Source: US Department of Defense. http://www.defense.gov/Portals/1/features/2014/0814_iraq/20150410_
    ISIL_Map_Unclass_Approved.pdf.

fall of 2015. Civil war reigns over this vast region, engulfing Sunnis, Shi'ites, other Muslim offshoots, Christians, and sundry minorities, with no clear end in sight. ISIS seeks to organize all Muslims, their religious divisions notwith-standing, under the rule of a resurrected caliphate. Its appeal to Muslims, notably Muslim youth, connected by the sophisticated use of the Internet and social media, extends beyond the Middle East to North Africa, the northern tier of Afghanistan and Pakistan, Western Europe, and the United States.

What this brief tour of shifts in state boundaries and the power among the states and peoples in the twentieth and early twenty-first centuries reveals is that there is little certainty that the state composition of Europe, Asia, Africa, or the Middle East will remain in its present form in the future. Nor is there much certainty that the material and human forces that have produced these dramatic changes in the distribution of power of states and populations have been arrested and harnessed by the actors in play today—or that these actors will succeed anytime soon.

The power of the weak state and nonstate actors is also one of the most paradoxical properties of the global society. Already noted were the dismem-berments of the Eurocentric system, the Soviet empire, and the Yugoslav state as a consequence of the resistance and resilience of the populations under their control, who demanded national self-determination and independence. Both the Soviet Union and the United States were defeated, respectively, in Afghanistan and Vietnam by social movements and armed forces vastly less powerful than the militaries of these two occupying states. Whether the United States and the Western states will prevail against the Taliban insurgency in Afghanistan and Pakistan or against the rising threat posed by ISIS remains uncertain. These nonstate, transnational actors pose entirely new challenges to local, regional, and global security as well as to the current boundaries of states. Meanwhile, states like North Korea—among the most impoverished nations of the world—defy the great powers over nuclear weapons.

With a population of less than eight million, Israel is able to resist international pressures, including those from the United States, its principal protector and aid benefactor, to stop the expansion of Jewish settlements into the occupied territories. In turn, social movements, like Hamas and Hezbollah, thwart a militarily more powerful Israel that seeks to ensure the security of its population. The corrupt government of Robert Mugabe in Zimbabwe holds onto power despite widespread condemnation as a predator regime. The United States has also been singularly incapable of overturning the Castro regime in Cuba, although it allegedly lies within Washington's sphere of influence. So much for the power of the Monroe Doctrine and the Roosevelt Corollary that previously justified US intervention into the states of the Caribbean and Latin America.

Enduring insurgencies puncture the security fabric of the global society. The list is long and mostly exhibits little sign of diminishing: Colombia (the Revolutionary Armed Forces of Colombia or FARC [Fuerzas Armadas Revolucionarias de Colombia]), the Russian Federation (Chechnya), China (Tibetan resistance and Uyghur uprising), Palestine (Hamas), Lebanon (Hezbollah), India (Pakistani subversion in Kashmir; Maoist rebels), Pakistan and Afghanistan (Taliban), the Philippines (Aby Sayyaf), Nigeria (Boko Haram), Kenya and Somalia (Al-Shebab), Sudan (Darfur insurgents), the Congo Republic (multiple tribal conflicts and militias), and multiple insurgent groups in Syria and Iraq (ISIS, Al Qaeda affiliates, Free Syrian Army, etc.), and Yemen (Shi'ite and Al Qaeda groups). The insurgency in Northern Ireland and the more deadly movements in Sri Lanka, led by the Tamil community, have only recently been brought under control after decades of fighting, the first through negotiations, the second by defeat of the rebels.

Ethnic cleansing and genocide, marked throughout human history, still survive as blights.[70] What is different from past atrocities is that regional and global security organizations had been created with the express purpose of providing for local and world security. They are supposed, presumably, to have the means and will to preclude these gross crimes against humanity.

The impotence of the United Nations' regional organizations—the Organization of African Unity (OAU), NATO, or the Association of Southeast Asian
Nations (ASEAN)—and failed states to check predator gangs or other states
from murdering and maiming millions of victims is very much in evidence
in the modern era.

Neither the UN nor ASEAN played a role in arresting the killing fields of
Cambodia where the Khmer Rouge murdered millions with impunity. The
United States and China turned a blind eye to the slaughter and compounded
their indifference by opposing Vietnamese intervention to end Khmer Rouge
rule. The United Nations and the great powers also stood by as upward of one
million Tutsis and Hutus were massacred in three short months by rampag-
ing mobs in Rwanda.[71] Violence continues in the Congo more than a decade
after the fall of the Mobutu Sese Seko regime in Zaire. Over the past decade
an estimated five million people have died in the civil wars still raging today
throughout the Republic of the Congo, whether local insurgencies or interventions by the military forces of the Great Lakes states and of states as far
away as Zimbabwe.

The Sudanese civil war has added significantly to the number of victims.
The fighting in Darfur has claimed tens of thousands of lives, many at the
hands of roving bands of Janjaweed militia, which enjoy the patronage of the
Sudanese government. NATO and the European states were equally slow to
check the ethnic cleansing in the Balkan wars of the 1990s. Thousands of Bosnian Muslims were massacred at Srebrenica in 1995 before the United States
finally intervened to broker the Dayton accords. After some delay, NATO did
eventually intervene by bombing Serbian forces to arrest a campaign of ethnic
cleansing launched by the Milosevic regime in Belgrade, leading subsequently
to the creation of the state of Kosovo, carved from the territory once ruled
by Serbia.

On the other hand, there has been a strong flow of power within the global
society resistant to the trends sketched above, particularly with respect to
providing security for threatened populations and promoting their human
rights. However feeble may be the responses of states and regional security
organizations to ensure the security of individuals or to protect and promote
democratic reforms and human rights, there has been substantial progress
in these domains. The European Union, grouping twenty-eight states into
a formidable economic system, essentially ended four hundred years of
civil war among Europe's contentious peoples. The recent approval of reform measures of the EU's constitution opened the way for the election of a
president of the European Union and the strengthening of the powers of the
European Parliament—changes that offer some promise to enhance the voice
and influence of the EU in global policy and establish a closer bond between

the Parliament, the EU, and the European electorate, as well as institutional supports for civil liberties and human rights.

The demand of populations for popular rule and human rights spread throughout the world over the twentieth century,[72] engulfing, however fleetingly, even a once authoritarian-ruled Arab Middle East. Power is no less necessary for good as it is for evil.[73] A complex collaborative network of individuals, groups, NGOs, INGOs, IGOs, and self-selected states form a loose coalition that sustains and extends democratic practices and human rights claims around the globe. Chapter 7 extends this discussion of the spread of democratic regimes and the transnational reinforcement of human rights protections.

Which of these two rival power coalitions—oppressors or free peoples—will prevail cannot be predicted with any certainty. Authoritarian states, terrorist organizations, and global criminal syndicates comprising uncivil global society are daunting barriers to freeing subject populations. Local, national, or regional struggles for freedom or its denial are incidences of a global contest, analogous to the clash between the partisans of community versus society, posited by Ferdinand Tönnies.[74] Working for a peaceful order and for legitimate government, based on democracy and human rights, is more than simply an ideational or an ideological quest. It is also a struggle for power that now envelops the lives of all peoples whether they recognize their implication in this global contest or not. Nothing so marks the global society as this struggle and the transformation of human social power that is implied when compared to previous eras and other humanly created and crafted societies.[75]

All Politics Is Global Politics

The conventional wisdom that all politics is local loses much of its currency under the relentless expansion of globalization. Its processes progressively invest all areas of significant human concern. Local politics is increasingly globalized.[76] Issues that might previously have been confined and resolved at a local, sectional, national, or regional level are now subject to a global test and stress. All issues of major concern to humans must progressively be addressed *simultaneously, systemically, and synchronously* at these levels *and* at a global level. Introduced into the global decisional process are millions of actors, most unknown to each other, whose decisions and power implicate all of them in the outcomes of their interdependent exchanges. They increasingly play decisive roles in shaping and shoving global politics and policies. If the global society is viewed *as a whole*, encompassing all its actors, it becomes readily apparent that humans have reached a transformational stage in their development. They are members, scarcely citizens, of a global society for the first time in the social evolution of the species.

Three issues illustrate the blurring of domestic and global politics. Take, for example, health care in the United States. The cost of ensuring that most Americans have access to health insurance will inevitably increase the size of the national deficit. That deficit had already been significantly increased as the Obama administration sought to bolster financial institutions at risk, to stimulate demand and employment to prevent a depression, to fight two wars, and to sustain entitlement programs besides health. By 2015, the deficit ballooned to over $18 trillion, roughly equal to the GDP of the United States.

The financing of the American debt requires continued purchases by investors and banks, notably from Chinese and Japanese sources, to sustain these deficits. The value of the dollar as a reserve currency is, in turn, weakened, with potentially adverse effects on the American and the world economy. Unless governmental fiscal policy can be put on a trajectory of diminishing these deficits and their drag on the American economy, investors whose assets are monetized in dollars have incentive to stop or slow their purchase of US Treasuries or, what is more likely, to demand higher interest rates for their loans. What begins as the local politics of health reform translates into the end game of global politics, revolving around the financing of public debt by foreign investors. These have an increasing, if largely implicit, impact on US policies, such as tempering American human rights pressures on China. American health programs translate into issues of global financial management as well as trade-offs in pursuing other desirable policy objectives as hostage to the public debt. These issue synergisms are real and palpable. Globalization blurs the distinction between domestic and foreign policy. Internal and external policies become increasingly different sides of the same coin.

The challenge of full employment of the world's population illustrates further the globalization of what is still largely, but misleadingly, framed as a national issue. After World War II, the coalition of democratic market states confronted the issue of restoring their economies, principally in devastated Europe, and of laying the foundation of a transcontinental global economic system to foster sustained growth.[77] Adopted was a strategy of "embedded liberalism."[78] States agreed to abide by a global system of fixed exchange rates monitored by the IMF and could secure loans from the World Bank to tide them over in periods of disequilibrium. Within this international regime, states could tailor their welfare policies of health, education, social security, and the like, to their particular economic and political needs and the constraints of their domestic politics. The system of embedded liberalism, underwritten by US Marshall Plan assistance, provided a comprehensive and flexible financial scheme to promote economic growth and to approach the goal of full employment.

None of these converging interests is present today to support a global policy of full employment. This challenge has not abated, but enlarged and deepened, with the expansion of open markets to an increasing number of states and peoples. Absent is the cultural and political cohesion of the Western states after World War II. Gone, too, is the convergence of their security, economic, and political interests of that period. The number of global actors has enlarged to seven billion people and their local, national, and regional provisional solutions to full employment require a global response that, like the experiment in embedded liberalism restricted to Western states, creates a stable and reliable global financial and economic system flexibly responsive to the different needs of states and the world's populations.

There is today a growing gap between the domestic economic and political policies of each state to combat unemployment and the global dimensions of this challenge. There currently exist no reliable global institutions or mechanisms to address this issue. The default mode to meet this challenge, more to exacerbate than alleviate the issue, are the uncoordinated, competitive policies of each state. Among the democracies the latter are shaped in turn by the struggle for power among groups to impose their preferences on public policies. A narrow, nation-state approach to promoting full employment, currently informing what passes as global economic policy, fails to make a substantial purchase on unemployment. The experience of the 1930s is obviously not a guide. States then pursued their domestic interests through beggar-thy-neighbor trade, investment, labor, and monetary policies. The unintended outcome of these defective anarchic strategies was to increase unemployment and deepen the global depression. The results were collective and individual state economic damage, a variant of the tragedy of the commons mentality.

A third example of the fusion of domestic and global politics is stanching the proliferation of nuclear weapons. That objective requires not only the cooperation of increasing numbers of affected states but also the harmonizing of their foreign and domestic aims and interests as well as the dynamics of their domestic political processes. The accord reached between the five members of the UN Security Council and Germany with Iran to arrest its development of a nuclear weapon illustrates the blurring of domestic and global politics within and across these states. Within the United States, the accord deeply split public opinion as well as the Congress, the president, and his administration. The accord also created a deep partisan division between the two political parties. Republican members of the House of Representatives and the Senate as well as the candidates vying for the party's nomination for the presidency opposed the accord. Into this mix the Israeli government under Prime Minister Benjamin Netanyahu galvanized American domestic opponents of the Iranian agreement, notably the American Israeli Public Affairs Committee (AIPAC), to fight the accord in Congress. Other otherwise pro-Israeli groups lobbied for the accord. The struggle within the Jewish community to put a solid stamp of approval (or disapproval) on the Iranian accord paralleled the split within the nation. The incessant struggle for domestic political power merged with the global politics of Israel and Iran, the Middle East states immediately affected by the Iranian nuclear program, and the permanent members of the UN Security Council and Germany. Local politics morphed into global politics and vice versa.

The Permeability, Interpenetration, and Reflexive Causality of Global Issues

The famous story of the Indian blind men, referenced at the beginning of chapter 1, captures and caricatures the human proclivity to compartmentalize thinking about problems. The segmented and narrowly defined disciplinary and professional paradigms that largely define university and college academic agendas also fall into this practice in portraying the collective challenges facing the world's populations today. The erection of precise and constrained disciplinary and professional boundaries to foster in-depth, rigorous study and to apply relevant methods to focused analysis has unquestionably yielded significant, empirically tested knowledge in the social and natural sciences. But is this enough?[79]

The issues confronting the world's populations do not comfortably admit to the inherited and traditional categorizations of the disciplinary and professional programs dotting the academic landscape. They cut across these scholarly domains. Cybercrime, for example, involves not only digital forensics and sophisticated capabilities to identify Internet thieves and hackers but also reliance on national and international law and the cooperation of transnational law enforcement to identify, capture, and convict malefactors. Disciplines and professional degree programs deconstruct globalization and the challenges of a global society into sequestered conceptual compartments. Obscured are the permeability of the boundaries of global issues when viewed from the march of armies of actors and the multiple interests and power sources in play in addressing these issues, often without the conscious understanding of many of those engaged in pursuing their particular aims and values.

There is much force in the argument advanced by one informed observer of the disarray of academic departments in confronting global issues. "There can be no adequate understanding of the most important issues we face when disciplines are cloistered from one another and operate on their own premises. . . . It would be far more effective to bring together people working on questions of religion, politics, history, economics, anthropology, sociology, literature, art, religion, and philosophy to engage in comparative analysis of common problems."[80] Yale professor Edward Tufte made much the same point, though more sententiously: "The world is much more interesting than any one discipline."[81] The conservative inertia of the academy, sustained by the decentralized authority of disciplinary and professional units, a bewildering number of degree programs, and unit budgetary and administrative autonomy, will not be surmounted any time soon.

The shortcomings of academic understanding of globalization and the problems it poses for humankind are mirrored in policy communities across the state system.[82] Once the interconnected parts of global issues are dissected, their intercausal relations are exposed as well as the diffusion of power among competing actors in which no one actor is in charge. Once the complexity and decentralized distribution of power of a global society is grasped, it follows logically that no state or people has the power to impose its preferences on all other world actors or to fully neutralize their resistant power.[83] A casual examination of the foreign policy debates and regime pronouncements of rival states—for example, the United States versus North Korea—reveals, on the other hand, an irresistible temptation among decision-makers to assert their nations' omnipotence and their nations' capacity to impose their preferences on adversaries (or allies) despite the obvious workings of a mountainous number of constraints, limiting all actors to get their way in a chaotic global society.

Two sets of global issues, affecting the United States and China, illustrate the boundary permeability and the blurred and refracted lines of control available to actors to determine their preferred outcomes in exchanges with other actors when the realization of what the former want across a range of interdependent issues depends on the cooperation, however achieved, of the latter. As issues "bleed" into each other, the limits of actor control to dictate preferred outcomes of exchanges with allies and adversaries become abundantly clear. There is an intimate, synergistic, and countervailing causal relation between popular demands for increased economic growth, access to energy sources—principally dependent on fossil fuels for the foreseeable future—and the generation of greenhouse gases that produce global warming.[84] The trade-offs that China and the United States are willing to make between these competitive objectives do not presently converge, nor can harmony be expected in the foreseeable future, given the differences in socioeconomic and political development, histories, cultural values, and political interests of both states and peoples, and of their populations' radically contrasting demand curves and expectations. Whatever optimism might be placed in realizing the November 2014 agreement between the United States and China to limit greenhouse gases is sobered by the long timeline, extending decades, to reach agreed-upon goals. Meanwhile, China continues to rely principally on coal-burning power plants to fuel its economic development.

A second set of issues turns on progress in ensuring populations everywhere of their human rights and opportunities for self-rule and the imperative of stable and confident economic relations between states and peoples, concerning trade, investment, technological innovation, and labor standards. To press for human rights and demand the democratization of autocratic regimes that are powerful economic actors, such as China, imperils the cooperation required to support a working global economic system and hinders the search for compromises needed to halt global warming or cooperatively address security issues like weapons of mass destruction and terrorism.

What should not be overlooked is the imperative that the permeability of global issues and their collective and comprehensive solutions must be understood as challenges not only to an individual state and its people but also to the preservation of a global society and just government on which actor preferences depend for their realization. If all actors act as "free riders," pass the buck, or hide, each ignoring its systemic dependence on and responsibility for the preservation of a global society, all risk losing by putting at risk the system on which they tenuously rely.[85] Chapters 5 and 6 dramatize the permeability of global financial mismanagement, the widening gap between rich and poor, and chronic poverty.

The permeability of global issues is predicable across state policies in all of the regions of the globe. The modalities and substantive outcomes of actor exchanges will naturally vary as will the interest and value priorities of the implicated actors. What can be generalized across the regions of the globe is that the property of permeability of national policies persists under the cloud wherein neither states nor their populations are fully aware of the mutual impacts of their different and divergent policies on each other. It is beyond the current capacity of the world's populations and their agents to conceptualize, much less to confront, their shared problems together—simultaneously, systemically, and synchronously. Hence the global society is permanently at risk.

As William Nordhaus reminds us, "Many issues facing humanity today—global warming and ozone depletion, financial crises and cyber warfare, oil price shocks and nuclear proliferation—resist the control of both markets and national governments."[86] Wrestling with overlapping and crosscutting global issues is not new, but what is perhaps increasingly perilous to this era are the compounding complexities and uncertainties generated by these interrelated issues. Certainty is not on offer. Nordhaus recalls Irving Fisher's observations made over a century ago: "Risk varies inversely with knowledge."[87] The permeability of global issues and their time urgency places severe limits on what knowledge can be accumulated to view the interdependence and impact of discrete global issues on each other and the cooperation and coordination of billions of actors in addressing these complexities. This insight directs us to the following property of the global society.

The Permanent Instability and Uncertainty of Globalization

Flowing from the preceding properties—particularly the expanding number and power of global actors, the encompassing reach of global politics, and the permeability of global issues—are two others: the endemic instability of global politics and the uncertainty of its multiple outcomes and evolutionary trajectories. This should come as no surprise if we reflect on the unexpected systemwide transformational changes and power shifts visited upon the world's populations in recent memory. Who foresaw the end of the Cold War, much less the implosion of the Soviet Union? And who anticipated the return of Russia, under President Vladimir Putin, to traditional big-state power politics, in its seizure of Crimea, expansion into eastern Ukraine, effective creation of a Russian protectorate over western Georgia, and military intervention in Syria to save the Bashar al-Assad government?

Who could have predicted China's adaptation to the rigors of an open market system and the remarkable capacity of an authoritarian regime to best its Western liberal, democratic competitors at their own game? Who foresaw the Middle East Spring of 2010 or the subsequent Arab fall, dashing the hope of more open societies and positive economic and political reform throughout the region? The rise of ISIS and its territorial gains in the quest of re-creating an Islamic caliphate surprised all actors.[88] Why did experts who followed terrorist activities also fail to anticipate 9/11?[89] Genocides and ethnic cleansings associated with the Balkan wars, Rwanda, the Congo, Syria, Iraq, and Sudan persist into the twenty-first century despite the atrocities of the preceding century.[90]

Why, too, were most businesspeople, economists, and financial experts caught off guard by the Asian financial meltdowns of 1997, the dot-com bust at the turn of the century, and the burst of the housing bubble and near collapse of the global financial system of 2007–2008? The failure of informed economists and savvy market analysts to forecast booms and busts was not new to Paul Samuelson, a Nobel laureate in economics. "It is indeed true," Samuelson is quoted as observing, "that the stock market can forecast the business cycle. The stock market has called nine of the last five recessions."[91]

Unforeseen consequences of actor actions are, of course, inherent in politics through time and space. Uncertainty about the outcomes of actor decisions and their power deployments follows from this endemic human condition. What are new are the greater number, scope, complexities, accumulating impacts, and global reach of these unpredictable outcomes on peoples and states. Disconnects between actor decisions, actions, and consequences are not uniquely attributable to any one political leader. They are inherent in the flawed designs of actors, all with limited power to realize their preferences in a resistant environment populated by other actors with pushback power to frustrate the aims of opponents and, often, to undermine the realization of mutually, if differing, collective values and interests.

Political elites may well believe they are pulling on levers of power to effect desired results. Actual outcomes of policy initiatives reveal either that these levers are largely unconnected or insufficiently positively charged with power to achieve expected outcomes or, worse, that those initiatives actually set off a chain of events that leads, ironically, to the very outcomes that the exercise of limited power was intended to preclude. President George W. Bush prided himself, for example, on being the "decider," the end point of a domestic political process that, as President Harry Truman observed, is where "the buck stops." Bush's self-approbation as a decider may well be accurate. What is misleading is his assumption of a causal connection between deciding a course of action, the deployment of national power, and the guarantee of preferred outcomes, such as the creation of a democratic Iraq in the aftermath of the American invasion of 2003 and the overthrow of the Saddam Hussein regime.

The same lack of predicable results despite the best intentions of policy-makers had previously dogged the United States in Vietnam.[92] The Vietnam War, portrayed as vital to the Cold War struggle, prompted the sending of over a half-million troops to defeat Viet Cong insurgents and North Vietnamese forces. Prominent among reasons for the intervention was the fear of Communist gains at a cost to states friendly to the United States, so-called falling dominoes throughout Asia. Instead, the North Vietnamese victory in 1975 and the unification of Vietnam under Hanoi's rule, however regrettable, had no discernible impact on the outcome of the Cold War. The negative effects of the Vietnam War were more lasting in the United States. Civil-military relations were seriously damaged, and divisions within American opinion over the conflict still resonate in American politics.

As for the regional and global implications of the Vietnam War, the American invasion of Cambodia to stop Vietnamese infiltration into South Vietnam contributed to the fall of the pro-Western government to the Khmer Rouge and the subsequent deaths of over a million Cambodians. Vietnamese nationalism proved more significant in explaining the determination and dedication of Vietnamese forces to defeat the United States and its South Vietnamese allies than inspiring appeals to Communist doctrine. Like China, the Vietnamese government is now adapting its economy to a global market system, while the regime retains tight political control over its population—for how long one can't say.

When Soviet party secretary Mikhail Gorbachev launched the reforms of *glasnost, perestroika,* and democratization in the 1980s, few foresaw that these reforms, aimed at modernizing the Soviet economic and political system to keep pace with the West, would eventually lead to the collapse of the Soviet state, the end of Communist Party rule, the breakup of the Warsaw Pact, the reunification of Germany, and the absorption of former Soviet satellites into the European Union and NATO alliance. That was clearly not the intent of Gorbachev's reforms. *Glasnost* and democratization gravely weakened Communist Party control of the Soviet Union and its East European empire. It released the pent-up nationalism of the diverse peoples under tight Soviet rule, including, ironically, the Russian people, many of whom sought to divest themselves of the burdens of global expansion and empire and Soviet Communist control.[93] *Perestroika* totally disrupted the Soviet economy without facilitating the subsequent Russian republic's adaptation to a global market system. None of these outcomes were foreseen by Soviet reformers, many of whom were devoured by the new power centers created by their reforms.[94]

Misapplied power and unanticipated outcomes are not the monopoly of Russian or American policy-makers. The Chinas of Mao Zedong and Deng Xiaoping are instructive. Mao's launching of the so-called Great Leap Forward in the late 1950s to accelerate Chinese economic growth proved disastrous: millions of Chinese starved, scarce natural resources were squandered, the environment was despoiled, and Chinese economic development was retarded for a generation. This ill-begotten policy was then followed by the Cultural Revolution of the mid-1960s, lasting a decade until Mao's death in 1976. In attacking the Communist Party and the governmental bureaucracy, Mao succeeded in sacrificing a generation of China's elite, while inflicting enormous damage to China's social and economic fabric and gravely disrupting its educational system. The return of discredited party elites to power after Mao's death and the ascendancy of Deng Xiaoping led to market reforms that over a generation transformed China into an economic powerhouse. The Communist Party also emerged stronger than ever despite Mao's attempt to recapture control of the party and regime. There is no evidence that Mao foresaw any of these outcomes.

If regime and state "deciders" are unable to predict the outcomes of their policies, one can only imagine the flood of anxieties now unleashed by the adaptations that individuals are compelled to make, and will have to continue to make, as the global environments within which they act rapidly change. The ideal of the rational actor model, so prevalent in social science and, especially, in economic theory, assumes perfect knowledge of the costs, benefits, and risks of options available to an actor and the capacity of markets to accurately price these outcomes to ensure the maximum realization of an actor's economic preferences. These heroic conditions cannot be easily met cost-free under the impact of ceaseless, irremediable, and, as the illustrations just reviewed suggest, fundamental change within the strictures of social power that constrain individual actor choices and, as often as not, frustrate their expectations of gain.

In contrast to the concept of *Economic Man*, and from a sociological perspective, Anthony Giddens allows that individuals are capable of rapid and effective adjustments to social change.[95] Their reflexive capacity purportedly provides them with a flexible and nimble psychological disposition, analytic skills, and conceptual tools to acquire the information they need to adapt to new constraints or exploit opportunities for gain in demonstrating a continuing ability to exercise control over their lives and the outcomes of their innumerable exchanges with other actors. They are also attributed to being endowed with the drive to persistently close the circle of acquirable information and successful adaptation. The assumption of reliable reflexivity is no less problematic than the *rational actor* assumption of individual behavior. It is not just a question of actors seeking information and knowledge about options and outcomes. They do so, and will. Rather, the question is whether they have the means to acquire accurate and reliable data or whether such data are actually and readily available in real time under the conditions of rapid and disorienting change.

The relaxed psychological assumption of the *Satisficing Man*, advanced by economics Nobel laureate Herbert Simon, to challenge the rational actor model, does not fully satisfy, either.[96] That assumption for which there is persuasive empirical evidence,[97] notably in individual and in organizational behavior, still begs the question of what information or knowledge will satisfy actors in their quest for desirable preference outcomes. Actors must still have some basis for identifying what is important or what is just noise in negotiating their multiple environments. How are these significant data to be recognized and, if correctly identified, what confidence can the actor have that these seemingly fixed points in the social and physical environment will remain stable and in place as the social context within which individual actions are acted out and performed? These reservations are equally applicable to Giddens's "Reflexive Man."

While these characterizations of the human capacity to adapt to rapidly changing circumstances, whether as rational, reflexive, satisficing, or psychological actor, have more than a kernel of persuasive force, all fall short of capturing the complexity of decisions confronting individuals and their agents in coping with the challenges of globalization and the consequent enveloping expansion of a global society. Rosenau provides a useful summary of the gap between growing individual analytic capacities and the challenges of the issues confronting them: "To be able better to locate oneself in complex scenarios . . . is not necessarily to be more competent in assessing goals, accumulating relevant information, estimating costs and benefits, choosing the most efficacious course of action, or otherwise engaging in the diverse calculations on which rational action is founded. For all their analytic and cathectic advances, peoples are still subject to abiding by tradition, clinging to habits, yielding to unreasoned passion, screening out unwanted information, and otherwise engaging in the diverse practices through which non-rational conduct is sustained."[98] Throwing off these social chains is not a free good, nor a desirable objective for those committed to their moral value.

Will the security, political, and economic systems on which individuals rely in making personal and professional decisions persist? Millions in the former Soviet Union, Congo, Sudan, Rwanda, the Balkans, Iraq, Afghanistan, Pakistan, Cambodia, Honduras, and Venezuela—and millions more engaged in conflicts across all of the regions of the globe—did not, nor do many still, have a lodestar to guide what they may have believed were their rational, reflexive, satisficing, or psychologically directed decisions. Will I have a job tomorrow if my industry or corporation becomes obsolete or if my skill sets are either no longer marketable or purchasable at lower cost elsewhere by equally proficient laborers or professionals working thousands of miles away? If the predicted adverse effects of global warming—disease, droughts, floods, pollution, reduced food production, starvation, and so forth—become reality, can one depend on the physical environment as stable and unchanging to work out a safe and productive life? This is an especially acute question for the billions in the underdeveloped world who, while already barely eking out an existence, will be the most disadvantaged by adverse impacts of climate change and environmental degradation. More generally, earthquakes, tsunamis, volcanic eruptions, hurricanes, cyclones, and floods—even extraterrestrial bombardment of the earth—and new, more potent and vaccine-resistant viruses will continue to plague the planet and the world's populations.[99]

Threats to Life on the Planet: Human Disasters

Walt Kelly's Pogo, a cartoon character now largely forgotten, still lingers on today in his memorable exclamation: "We have met the enemy and he is us!" The modern period, culminating in the global society, has witnessed more human (non-natural) disasters in number and in the destructiveness of human life and precious wealth than any preceding era. Recall the tens of millions killed in World Wars I and II. Millions more perished in the wars of self-determination in the post–WWII period. The genocides of the twentieth century, including the Turkish suppression of Armenians in 1915, the Nazi Holocaust, and more recent human depredations in the Balkans, Rwanda, Sudan, Syria, Iraq, Afghanistan, and the Congo, add several millions. Professor Rudolph Rummel, who has devoted most of his career to cataloging deaths at the hands of governments, contends that regime killings in the twentieth century—what he terms *domicides*—were several multiples of those inflicted by war.[100] There is also the quite plausible threat that nuclear weapons will be used by a state or that these capabilities will fall into the hands of terrorists bent on destroying civilian populations.

The specter of a human race fouling its nest is also a clear and present danger. Global warming poses a real threat to millions. If CO_2 emissions can be capped, there are still other looming, human threats to the planet that currently go begging. Among these are the overfishing and the mounting pollution of the oceans, the deprivation of clean water from hundreds of millions, and the diminution of water and arable land to support an exploding world population.[101] By 2050, when the world's population is expected to reach at least nine billion, food production will have to increase 70 percent above current levels on receding availability of arable land. The loss of biodiversity, largely due to human exploitation of the world's resources and natural habitat, will continue to grow apace. Figure 2.3 traces a disquieting correlation between global economic growth and the loss of biodiversity. There appears also to be no limit to the human exploitation of scarce natural resources or humans' self-defeating capacity to treat the global environment as an inexhaustible free good to meet the demand for economic growth.

This sketch of some of the key properties of the global society does not nearly exhaust what can be said of this transformational change in the human condition. What can be said with more certainty is that the realization of the particular, parochial, and circumscribed interests of actors everywhere depends increasingly on their cooperation to ensure the replication, in peace and prosperity, of a global society.[102] Humans are far from universally acknowledging this constraint, which, if well addressed, might be turned to an opportunity for human advancement. If global cooperation is elusive and illusory, then it is incumbent to narrow the focus on the capacity of the open, democratic states and peoples to collectively cope with global issues and to ensure that their preferences for the governance of the global society can sustain and enlarge their current dominance.

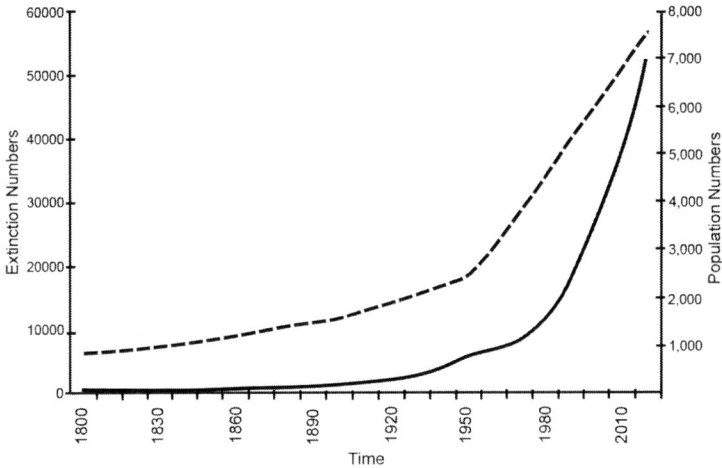

FIGURE 2.3
Species Extinction and Human Population
Source: USGS. http://journowl.com/are-we-ready-to-head-off-the-extinction-trend/. Original in *Threats to Biological Diversity: Global, Continental, Local,* by J. M. Scott, 2008, US Geological Survey, Idaho Cooperative Fish and Wildlife, Research Unit, University of Idaho.

Notes

1. See, for example, Avant, Finnemore, & Sell (2010); Cerny (2010); Held & Koenig-Archibugi (2005); Shaw (2000 [*Theory*]).

2. Bhagwati (2004); Huntington (1996).

3. See Beck (2006, 2007); Diamond (1997); Findlay & O'Rourke (2007); Held, McGrew, Goldblatt, & Perraton (1999); Held & McGrew (2002); Keane (2003); McNeill & McNeill (2003); McNeill (1998); Modelski (2008); Nayan (2007).

4. Waltz (1979); Waltz (1964).

5. Crenshaw (1996); Dekmajian (2007); Hoffman (1998, 2001); Pape (2006); Richardson (2006).

6. The GTD data set is a joint effort of two units at the University of Maryland. They include the Human-Computer Interaction Lab and the National Consortium for the Study of Terrorism and Responses to Terrorism.

7. See Wendt (1992, 1994, 1995). Also relevant is the English school, most notably Barry Buzan (2004) and the late Hedley Bull (1977).

8. Chatfield (1997).

9. See http://www.uia.be/node/163992.

10. Alexis de Tocqueville's ideas about the role of private associations are projected on a global scale in Avant, Finnemore, & Sell (2010) and Cerny (2010).

11. The literature covering NGOs and INGOs is extensive and growing in light of the significance of these associations. See Jacobson (1993); Kaldor (2003); Kaldor, Glasius, & Anheier (2005); Karns & Minget (2004); Keane (1998, 2003); Paolini, Jar-

vis, & Reus-Smit (1998). The Union of International Organizations cites over sixty thousand INGOs, of which approximately twenty-five thousand are currently dormant or inactive. See http://www.uia.be/node/52.

12. See http://www.forbes.com/free_fores/2005/0418/066.html.

13. Data about the dramatic increase in the number of MNCs may be found in *Globalinc*, per Gabel (2003).

14. Quoted in Rosenau (1992, p. 263). See also Rosenau's forward-looking *Turbulence in World Politics* (1990) and his emphasis on the power of the individuals in a post–Cold War era.

15. Rosenau (1992).

16. Ibid., p. 283.

17. See the report of the United Nations Environmental Programme, October 25, 2007. On biodiversity, see figure 2.3.

18. Speth (2008, pp. xx–xxi, 1–13). See also Kolbert (2014).

19. For a brief review of conflicts over oil and mineral resources, see Kaldor (2006); Kaldor, Karl, & Said (2007); Klare (2002, 2004, 2009, and 2012).

20. For example, David Brooks (*New York Times*, January 15, 2010) reports that ten thousand NGOs and INGOs were working in Haiti before the devastating earthquake of January 2010.

21. See http://www.uia.be/node/163992.

22. Alexis de Tocqueville was among the first to recognize the importance of private nongovernmental associations for the effective and legitimate workings of a liberal democracy; see Tocqueville (1945). Philip Cerny (2010) advances a theory of transnational pluralism that essentially draws on Tocqueville and Arthur Bentley.

23. Robert Michels (1966) challenges Tocqueville's optimistic view of the governance of private associations by showing that they can be as authoritarian as their state counterparts.

24. Avant, Finnemore, & Sell (2010); Cerny (2010); Hall & Bierstecker (2002); Keck & Sikkink (1998).

25. For a general description of the differences and impact of transnational movements, NGOs, and INGOs, see Kaldor (2003); Keane (2003). Also useful is Smith, Chatfield, & Pagnucco (1997). Also consult Kriesberg (1997).

26. Keane (1988, p. 119). See also Kaldor (2003).

27. *New York Times*, January 15, 2010, p. A10. For a comprehensive survey of the evolution of the rule of law as a principle of government, see Fukuyama (2011).

28. UNCTAD (2002, pp. xv and 272.

29. Sassen (2007, p. 60).

30. Ibid., pp. 62ff. Illustrative of this point is Daniel Yergin's analysis of the oil industry. See Yergin & Stanislaw (2002).

31. Gill & Law (1993).

32. Sassen (2007, pp. 224ff.).

33. Sassen (2012).

34. *New York Times*, May 29, 2011, p. 19.

35. Ibid.

36. *New York Times*, December 15, 2013.

37. This proposition is developed at length and persuasively by Saskia Sassen in her numerous publications. See Sassen (2006 [*Cities*; *Territory*], 2007).

38. Breen (2013); Clark, Fox, & Treakle (2003); Ebrahim & Herz (2011); Fox & Brown (1998); Scholte (2011 ["Civil Society"]).

39. Terrorism, keyed to overthrow a regime or state, will be addressed in chapter 4. The focus here is on unlawful activities to increase the power and wealth of private criminal groups, notably those working across state boundaries.

40. Sarna (2010).

41. Williams (2002, p. 64). See also Williams (1994).

42. The literature on transnational crime is extensive, consult Berdal & Serrano (2002); Cameron & Newman (2008); Edwards & Gill (2003); Jojarth (2009); Liddick (2004); Schendel & Abraham (2005).

43. UNODC (2013).

44. NationMaster.com lists over sixty-three million criminal acts that were reported by eighty-two countries, fewer than half of the states of the globe. The United States is ranked first with almost twelve million criminal acts, followed by the United Kingdom and Germany, each with about half the US total, http//www.nationamaster.com/graph/cri_tot_cri-crime-total-crimes.

45. Most of the data for the drug trade is drawn from UNODC (2008). See also the following studies that parallel UN findings: Curtis & Karacan (2002); Jojarth (2009); Kelly, Maghan, & Serio (2005); Lumpe (2000); Naim (2005); Schendel & Abraham (2005); Thachuk (2007). For the impact of international crime in all of its principal aspects on US security interests, consult CIA (2002).

46. United States (2009).

47. UNODC (2009).

48. Ibid.

49. *New York Times*, February 7, 2013, financial section. See also chapter 5 for additional discussion of the illegal fixing of interest rates.

50. Williams (2002, pp. 168ff.); Williams (2009).

51. Ibid., p. 170.

52. Rosenau & Czempiel (1992).

53. See chapter 1, which argues that each exchange over a particular outcome desired by an actor is also the occasion to affirm, reject, or amend the rules governing the exchange.

54. See Layne (1993) for a critique of the United States as a unipolar hegemon.

55. The articles in Kolodziej & Kanet (2008) develop the thesis of lost superpower status across the major regions of the globe.

56. Quoted in the *New York Times*, December 16, 2013, p. A4.

57. McDonald (2009); Soros (2000).

58. Brzezinski (1993); Bull (1977).

59. Huntington (1996).

60. The power transitions school of hegemonic politics is evaluated in Kolodziej (2005, pp. 127–74). See also Dicicco & Levy (1999) for a probing but sympathetic critique.

61. This view is shared by an increasing number of informed observers. See, for example, Rosenau & Czempiel (1992).

62. Kolodziej & Kanet (2008) develop this argument from a global perspective. The attribute of superpower is increasingly being extended to China. See Jacques (2009), who predicts that China will create a new world order. Jacques and others confuse influence as hegemony.

63. Neorealists are particularly prone to this reductionist position of state power at the expense of other forms of power to produce significant outcomes in global politics, including the unexpected collapse of states themselves; see Waltz (1964).

64. See Google, Banking.com, and US Treasury, Bureau of Public Debt, http://publicdebt.treas.gov/.

65. Critical evaluations of the American invasions of Afghanistan and Iraq abound. Among the best-argued and documented are Gordon & Trainor (2005); Ricks (2006, 2009); Stiglitz & Bilmes (2008).

66. The two powers did agree in December 2014 to work toward decreasing carbon emissions, but the target dates are set so far in the future that they do not provide effective guidelines for this policy objective.

67. For a stimulating explanation of the ups and downs of nations, see Olson (1982).

68. The states are Bosnia and Herzegovina, Croatia, Serbia, Macedonia, Montenegro, Slovenia, and Kosovo.

69. The literature covering the formation and evolution of Israel is voluminous. Among the most perceptive and informed of its history is Ari Shavit's *My Promised Land: The Triumph and Tragedy of Israel* (2013).

70. Power (2002) provides an overview of mass killings in the twentieth century.

71. For an overall review of the incidence of genocide, see Power (2002); Shaw (2000 [*What Is Genocide?*]). For a critique of the failure of the UN and regional organizations to stop the Rwandan genocide, see Kolodziej (2000).

72. Kolodziej (2003).

73. This is one of the principal themes of President Barack Obama's acceptance speech in receiving the Nobel Peace Prize in 2009: http://www.msnbc.msn.com/id/34360743/ns/politics-white_house/.

74. Tönnies (1957).

75. Ignatieff (2000, 2004); Risse-Kappen (1994, 1995).

76. A useful work supporting this thesis from the perspective of international regulation is Drezner (2008).

77. Acheson (1969).

78. Cooper (1968); Ruggie (1997).

79. Critiques of the narrowness of the academic agenda are multiplying. See Ira Shapiro (2005); Wallerstein (2001).

80. Op-ed recommendations of Mark C. Taylor, chairman of the Religion Department at Columbia University, *New York Times*, April 27, 2009. See also Ira Shapiro (2005) and Wallerstein (2001) for similar views developed at length.

81. *New York Times*, February 19, 2013, p. A23.

82. Ulrich Beck (2007) develops the shortcomings of current thinking to conceptualize and understand the reciprocal impact of global issues on each other, generating systemic risks beyond the capacity of humans to grasp either their scope or causal complexity.

83. This is the conclusion of an in-depth evaluation of the Bush Doctrine that was based on the assumption of US superpower status and ability to impose its preferences for world order on other states and peoples. See Kolodziej & Kanet (2008), especially chapters 1 and 15, pp. 3–30, and 299–336, respectively.

84. See Nordhaus (2013); Speth (2004, 2008).

85. Beck (2007).

86. Nordhaus (2013, p. 18).

87. Nordhaus (2013); see title page for the Fisher quote.

88. See the *Frontline* documentary, first broadcast October 28, 2014, on the rise of ISIS.

89. Clarke (2004) makes this point. Terrorist scholars were no less caught off guard by the audacity of Al Qaeda. See Dekmajian (2007); Hoffman (1998, 2001); Pape (2006); Richardson (2006).

90. Power (2002).

91. *New York Times*, December 14, 2009.

92. The literature covering the American disaster in Vietnam is large and growing. Useful as a start are United States (1971); FitzGerald (1973); Halberstam (1972); Sheehan (1988).

93. Carrère d'Encausse (1993); Kaiser (1994).

94. The volume of literature explaining these unforeseen events seemingly grows exponentially. For an evaluation, consult Kolodziej (2005, pp. 77–126).

95. Giddens (1993, pp. 120ff.).

96. Simon (1975).

97. Kahneman (2011).

98. Rosenau (1992). *Cathectic* generally refers to the emotional investment of an individual or group in a person, proposal, idea, etc.

99. Langwith (2012); Quammen (2012); Wolfe (2011).

100. Rummel (2005) contends that the deaths of 262,000,000 people in the twentieth century were due to domicide; 50 million domicides were the result of colonial developments and another 76.7 million domicides occurred in the People's Republic of China from 1928 through 1987. According to Rummel, domicides were six times greater than his estimate of all of the killings attributable to foreign and internal wars.

101. Speth (2004, 2008).

102. Cohen & Easterly (2009).

3

Toward a Theory of Global Governance

Pursuing Order, Welfare, and Legitimacy Imperatives

THIS CHAPTER LAYS THE GROUNDWORK for a theory of governance, resting on three imperatives: Order, Welfare, and Legitimacy (OWL). These imperatives, applicable to the governance of all human societies, now confront an increasingly interdependent—certainly not integrated—global society of over two hundred states and seven billion diverse and divided peoples.

The deep, presently insurmountable fissures in the social composition of the world's populations preclude any expectation of a universal government for the globe. Simultaneous with the conflicts over the value of clashing social identities and global public issues between and among the states and peoples of the world—climate change, sustainable growth, and so forth—is a profound struggle, punctuated by violent exchanges, over how the global society should be governed.[1]

This volume is particularly interested in the OWL solutions of the democratic states and peoples. These apply only to those states that are ruled by popular consent. Even in this set of states, there are wide variations in how the OWL solutions are understood and implemented. The democratic states do not move in lockstep whether in creating the global state for Order, observing free exchange principles in market behavior for Welfare, or dutifully applying all norms applicable to legitimate democratic governance. Where the democracies largely depart from the OWL solutions of their antidemocratic rivals pivots on their support for a secular democratic state, their toleration of all religions, diverse cultural values, and linguistic practices, their advocacy of human rights, and their allegiance to the principle that all humans are free and equal.

Opposed to the democratic project are several alternatives supported by powerful and resourceful states, nonstate actors, and billions of peoples otherwise divided by religion, culture, or interest. Prominent among these are authoritarian secular states, notably China and the Russian Federation as well as a passel of smaller powers (Cuba, Venezuela, Egypt, North Korea, Myanmar, et al.). These states prefer the traditional Westphalian solution to global order, developed below. This Westphalian system insulates states and their regimes from the criticisms of liberal democratic states and nonstate actors, which expose authoritarian abuse of civil liberties and human rights. Guidelines issued by the Chinese Communist Party—Document 9 of 2013, and Document 30 of 2014—pointedly reject journalistic freedom and unfettered Internet access of its citizens.[2] To legitimate their rule, authoritarian regimes also tend to promote intense nationalism, public solidarity, and unswerving loyalty to the regime—powerful instruments to stifle internal dissent and challenges to the prevailing police state.

There is also the redoubtable challenge of nation-state regimes based on religion and culture. Partisans of religious-cultural foundations for governance reject both the secular Westphalian model and, most decidedly, the democratic paradigm of governance.[3] The epicenter of opposition, but by no means exclusively, is in the Middle East. What is particularly disruptive to the stability of the global society is not only the rejection of the democratic secular model, often pursued by resort to force, but also the deep divisions within religious communities over their preferred model of government. The more than one billion Muslims around the globe are deeply split on this issue. The major division is between Sunnis and Shi'ites and their offshoots. There are also bloody internal conflicts even within this overall division.

These intense and irreconcilable conflicts over governance, marked by wholesale violence as in Syria and Iraq, are further inflamed by the rise of nonstate actors—Al Qaeda, ISIS, and others. These movements call for the creation of a caliphate to rule all Muslims despite the diverse social and religious evolutionary paths that members of the Muslim community have taken across the globe in their interpretation of the "Book" and Shari'a law. However much they disagree on what constitutes effective and legitimate government, these religiously motivated actors converge in their rejection of the liberal secular state and the underlying values of free peoples. To these formidable foes can be added countless self-contained communities, tribes, and regional social movements resistant to globalization and to any form of integration of governance beyond local control.

There are also the multiplying global networks of criminal activity of the global uncivil society. Their leaders resist all forms of governance that they cannot control or co-opt. They form a sprawling array of global illicit behavior that defies governance or limitations on the scope of their activities.

These insoluble conflicts over how the world should be governed pose the principal question of this volume: Will the OWL solutions of the democracies prevail and flourish while entangled within countless constraining webs of resistance to their solutions to governance? Can the democracies, scarcely organized as a closely knit coalition and beset on all sides,[4] prevent the erosion and potential collapse of their power, more decentralized than collective, in a chaotic global society? However much the OWL solutions of the democratic states and peoples may occupy the moral high ground against their opponents, that claim provokes more pushback than elicits approbation and acquiescence. If the aim of a universally and democratically governed global society is ruled out by a global society at sixes and sevens, then the challenge confronting the democracies resolves itself into a long-term, enduring struggle to preserve and increase their material power versus their opponents and to sustain the commitment of their populations to engage in this titanic struggle and to observe rigorously the exacting norms of popular rule.

Before we make the case for a provisional theory of governance of all human societies, the distinction should be kept in mind between the unique power components of each OWL imperative, the object of this chapter, and the actual OWL solutions advanced by populations to govern their societies through time and circumstance. As even a casual look at the rise and demise of human societies and their solutions to OWL imperatives readily reveals, they come and go.[5] There is no reason to believe that democratic OWL solutions, developed in part II, are invulnerable to this fate absent continuing expenditure of blood and treasure to prevail against its rivals. How then are OWL imperatives composed to which the prevailing democratic solutions are contemporary responses?

Toward a Pure Theory of Governance: Introduction to the Method

The quest to develop a theory of governance applicable to a global society does not begin in an empirical or moral vacuum. The conceptual insights about governance advanced by Thomas Hobbes, Karl Marx, Adam Smith, and Jean-Jacques Rousseau develop the core elements of a theory of governance based on OWL imperatives. It is precisely their contesting notions of the principal physical and biological forces as well as the material and nonmaterial incentives driving human choice and behavior that provide the shaky but still serviceable foundation for stipulating OWL imperatives as endemic to an understanding and explanation of governance of all human societies.

What emerges from these fundamental, if conflicting, contributions to OWL theory are (1) the insoluble but potentially pragmatically manageable contradictions underlying human governance as a consequence of competing OWL imperatives and (2) the unavoidable necessity of both addressing the autonomous power claims of each OWL imperative and prudently balancing these competing power capabilities and the conflicting incentives generated by each OWL imperative for actor preferences and decisions. If no OWL imperative is allowed to dominate the others and all have some say in governance, a workable system of institutions and rules can emerge to govern a human society to ensure its functioning, replication, and duration.

Each OWL solution results in a discrete, autonomous structure of power, decisional processes, and incentives for actor choices. These are the analytic components of each imperative. Each is conceived for this analysis as a "pure" or "ideal" force working through actors entangled in the governing process. The pure or ideal models of human behavior stipulated by the theorists on whom this presentation relies are methodological tools. These models of OWL imperatives provide conceptual frameworks, abstracted from the real world, to help move us haltingly toward the goal of not only a provisional theory of governance but also a theory that can be fitted to our time, yet applicable for understanding earlier eras.[6] What is particularly significant about the contributions of our OWL theorists are, paradoxically, their contrasting moral understandings of what it means to be human and their competing conceptions of the pure end points of social behavior if actors pursue any one of the imperatives to the exclusion of the claims and constraints of the others. This proclivity toward the pure or ideal end point is readily apparent in each of the models of human behavior advanced by the theorists on which this attempt to construct a theory of governance relies.[7]

In drawing initially on the pure models of human behavior advanced by these theorists to outline a theory of governance and as the basis for an evaluation of the democratic solution to global governance, the discussion selects only those elements of each theorist's contribution to a rationale for governance that can be usefully applied to the emergence of a global society. There is no attempt, much less interest, in developing a comprehensive appreciation of the writings—including lapses and shortcomings—of each theorist's system of thought. Nor do I propose to dwell on the impact of the historical context within which each theorist developed his ideas about governance. Those important tasks are better left to philosophical analysis or to historians of ideas.

The aim here is narrower, more robust, pragmatic, and problem-solving in orientation: to identify the need for governance of the global society and to evaluate the solutions advanced by the democracies. Based on this evaluation, the volume proposes ways to improve the global state, which the democracies have uniquely created; global markets, developed, again uniquely, by the democracies; and the institutionalization by the democracies of popular rule as the appropriate response to legitimacy and global rule. OWL imperatives focus attention on what is important for the lives and well-being of free peoples and the world's populations. Democratically inspired governing institutions can be reformed, but very likely not to the level of a revolutionary transformation of the global society and its governance in the foreseeable future. Flaws in executing the democratic project by its partisans and the formidable power of those opposed to the democratic paradigm impede progress toward more effective and legitimate global governance. Neither drawback to this enterprise is sufficient to abandon trying to understand the underlying forces of governance and the democratic response to these imperatives. The stakes are too high to quit.

In a way, but not to denigrate the original contributions each of these theorists has made to our knowledge about governance, each is somewhat akin to the blind men's discussion of the elephant. Each has a different problem or imperative of governance to solve; and by deliberate choice each adopts a selective point of view. The task before us is to extract that transhistorical dimension of governance from each theorist that, when combined with those of the others, provides a foundation on which to build a theory of governance. By drawing on their contrasting understandings of human nature—each possessed of a compelling kernel of truth—a clearer, if still complex and perplexing, picture can emerge of the taxing challenges posed by the imperatives of government and the clashing standards that are applicable in evaluating the governing mechanisms of the global society today. Note, too, that each accents a compelling source of power as the driver of each imperative. Thomas Hobbes's conception of the imperative of Order depends on force and awesome physical power; Karl Marx's notion of the imperative of Welfare pivots on revolutionary shifts in technology in response to the material needs of humans and those who control these means of production; Adam Smith stipulates that humans are wired to truck and barter in pursuit of material Welfare; Jean-Jacques Rousseau, echoed today by modernists and constructivists, stresses the capacity of humans to create the moral values that define Legitimate rule as the basis for the social contracts which they strike between themselves and their rulers.

Standing on the Shoulders of Giants

The Contribution of Thomas Hobbes to a Pure Theory of Order

Thomas Hobbes's *Leviathan* is the starting point to understand Order as an imperative of governance and why the issue of Order is so intractable to definitively resolve.[8] No one before or after has so clearly defined the centrality of this imperative from which there is no escape in resolving human conflicts, a primary function of a working government. Nor has anyone been more explicit, coldly objective, and realistic about the incentive driving humans to use force to elicit the cooperative behavior they seek in their interdependent exchanges with other actors. According to Hobbes, this incentive is inherent in the human condition, rendering all social orders inherently fragile and furtive over their life cycles.

Hobbes stipulates that disorder and incipient violence is the underlying natural condition of human social life. "So the nature of War," Hobbes argued, "consisteth not in actuall fighting, but in the known disposition thereto, during all the time there is no assurance to the contrary. All other time is peace."[9] Humans tend, in other words, toward conflict and appeals to force to impose their preferences on others, when all peaceful means and methods prove unavailable to elicit cooperation and consent. To grasp what Hobbes means by "the known disposition [to war]" as endemic to the human condition is to grasp the scope of the challenges posed by the imperative of Order to the competing demands of the other OWL imperatives. A global society, divided against itself, in which the billions of its members and their multiple and multiplying agents are ceaselessly striving to get their way and have their say, is especially disposed toward violence. The result is chronic global disorder. Once invoked to impose a preference for a desired outcome in an interdependent exchange, violence "promiscuously" corrupts all other social interests and values.[10]

From a theoretical perspective, Hobbes demonstrates that the imperative of Order is insoluble. Only provisional, fundamentally contingent solutions are possible. Once violence invests a social exchange, after all other appeals to noncoercive solutions to resolve a conflict have been exhausted—nature, custom, religion, culture, pragmatic compromises, and the like—the exchange moves in a downward spiral of violence, sweeping all other human limits before it. All human values and interests are reduced to a test of wills with violence as the arbiter of the exchange. Either one or the other of the actors is compelled to submit or all are drawn into the thrall of a permanent, potentially mutually destructive, coercive relationship.

Notwithstanding this dilemma, workable solutions for order must still be devised to escape societal self-destruction and the forgoing of personal and group needs and satisfactions. The historical record supports an attitude of conditional optimism: that order will somehow always emerge in some particular, nonuniversally applicable, form to manage, if not resolve, the Hobbesian dilemma. Much like the ocean waves crashing perpetually on the shore, successive political orders have come and gone, each replacing the

other. Waves of order, each different from the other, but each no less a kineti-
cally powerful wave, continue to be created, since all societies and a society
of societies—what is now the global society—depend on some form of provisional order, however fragile or fleeting.[11] Absent order, the life chances of
a society and those of its members—present and future—are put at perilous
risk. Threats stem either from internal implosion or from the coercive intervention of external actors forcing their solution of order on an exposed and
vulnerable population at the cost of the latter's way of life and value systems.

So what are we to make of the paradox that order must be addressed but
cannot be definitively solved; that threats to an existing domestic state order,
such as nineteenth-century China and Japan, are permanently, if not immi-
nently, at risk; and that the dilemmas posed by order can be relaxed for a time,
often for centuries, but not surmounted?

Hobbes took humans as he saw them: disposed to violence to effect their
preferences in their interdependent social relations with their homologues.
That disposition—more an "is" than an "ought"—was what Hobbes understood that it meant to be human. Humans were engaged in the search for an
elusive harmony in which their incompatible preferences—that is, their most
profound values, cherished interests, even their trivial pursuits—would be
realized and their personal identities and self-worth confirmed.

For Hobbes, only on entering an ordered society through the imagined vehicle of a social compact did the issue of right and wrong, good and evil, arise.
Morality arose in the wake of an established order that provisionally solved
the dilemma of violence and the resolution of contesting human preferences.
Hobbes's original contribution to social theory and governance was his abandonment of the Greek question of defining an ideal society or polity as the
guide for political action. Hobbes's understanding of the human condition
made that question unanswerable. All human societies and their governance
were problematic since they had to be founded on force. The persistent,
chronic violent disputes among peoples over their conflicting responses to
this question, rooted with particular intensity and ferocity in irreconcilable
material interests, competition for power, and religious and cultural values,
made the quest of the ideal pointless and self-defeating, until a secure order
could first be put in place.

Hobbes brought the Greek question of an ideal society down to earth,
grounding the prospects of human perfection, moral worth, and rights in the
creation of a working order.[12] Contending religious responses to this ideal
were no answer; they were more an invitation to limitless violence. Only
when order was established could morals, laws, rules, and governing institutions emerge. Hobbes thus broke with traditional notions of natural law as
the solution to the Order imperative. As Leo Strauss observes in contrasting

natural and conventional law, "Such a difference does in fact exist. Traditional natural law is primarily and mainly an objective 'rule and measure,' a binding order prior to, and independent of, the human will, while modern natural law is, or tends to be, primarily and mainly a series of 'rights,' of subjective claims, originating in the human will."[13] As one of its originators, Hobbes placed himself squarely in the modern camp. Rights were human creations and inherently conventional; hence they were vulnerable to change and repudiation—or assertion.

In Hobbes's account of the human condition, the limitless preferences of humans for what they sought through their interdependent exchanges would never converge. The clash of preferences, however conceived and formulated, as a function of human creativity and a relentless striving for power, is central to a pure theory of order. Since humans necessarily rely on others to realize their multiple and, as likely as not, their internally contradictory values, aims, and interests, the preferences of humans in their countless and evolving exchanges can never be fully harmonized. Humans entered society to ensure their survival and security, including the protection and promotion of their self- and social-regard, the enhancement of their personal power, the protection of their property, and state enforcement of their contracts with their brethren. This natural and unenviable condition of perpetual and pervasive conflict derives from the ceaseless and exacting demands of humans on each other to effect their competing preferences. Consensual cooperation was of course always possible—the typical experience of daily life in a peaceful society—but its appearance implicitly relied on the preexistence of a functioning political order, grounded on force.

To get their way humans respond to compelling incentives not only to prevail at the margin over some contested preference in their interdependent exchanges with other actors—say, a dispute over a property line or access to a scarce resource, like water or productive land—but also to impose, if all else fails, their preferred order on others. The latter ensures success in repeated encounters, much like the narrative of family governance sketched in chapter 1. A governing order is the greater aim. It controls for repeated human exchanges. The endless decline and fall into disorder arises from the interminable contest over preferred outcomes of humans engaged in these social exchanges of value to them. All human societies are vulnerable, paradoxically, to the antisocial behavior of their members, what an effective order presumably tames, but cannot fully excise from human affairs, the incipiently tragic condition of being human.

As a translator of Thucydides's *The Peloponnesian War*, Hobbes grasped Thucydides's warning—namely, that when force is invoked to resolve a conflict over irreconcilable values or decide what regime should govern the relations of contesting communities, human interaction is reduced to an unremitting struggle of whose wills and material means would prevail. Thucydides's recounting of Athens's destruction of the Spartan colony of Melos, with which Athens had long had peaceful relations, to preclude its possible alliance with Sparta, illustrates poignantly and pointedly how armed conflict absorbs all other human aims and interests into its maw.[14]

The immediate cause of the Greek war, the outbreak of civil war in Epidamnus, appears as a minor issue confronting the Greek city-states. It mattered little that few of Thucydides's "fellow Greeks would have known where Epidamnus was or anything else about it."[15] The underlying cause of the war did not revolve around resolving a dispute in a faraway place. Rather, the issue was the governance of all of the Greek city-states. Specifically raised into question, as Thucydides recounts, was checking Athens, which was perceived to be bent on imposing its order on the Greek city-states—allies, neutrals, and opponents alike.

As Thucydides observes, "The truest explanation for the war is that Sparta was forced into it because of her apprehensions over the growing power of Athens."[16] Only power pitted against power, informed and propelled by force, could resolve, however briefly, which Greek coalition—under Athenian or Spartan rule—would impose its preferred order on the Greeks.[17] Unforeseen by all sides, was the ruinous and unintended outcome of the struggle for all rivals. A weakened Greek city-state system, the product of the misguided choices and relentless pursuit to a Hobbesian end game, paved the way for the conquest of Greece and its submission to Macedonian rule and, accordingly, the erection of a fragile Hellenistic order over the peoples of the Mediterranean region.

The Godfather film trilogy, which traces the Corleone family's life of crime, also richly exposes the many phases of the Hobbesian dilemma at work. In the opening scene of the first movie, a petitioner asks the head of the Mafia family to mete out justice and restore the reputation of his family and daughter, who was violated by two young men. In honoring that petition, the Mafia boss substitutes his own (and the petitioner's) preferred order for the failure of New York's flawed and feckless order to provide a just remedy for the transgression against the petitioner's daughter.

The Hobbesian end game, not surprisingly, extends also to gangland order. At the end of the first film, and in the wake of an assassination attempt on the senior Corleone, the youngest son, Michael, assumes control of the Corleone family. He launches an all-out war against his father's opponents. In a well-orchestrated attack, Michael's hit men assassinate the five Mafia bosses contesting the Corleone family's rule of the rackets. Michael restores the ascendancy of the Corleone family to unchallenged power and rule among the Mafia families. Note that two orders are created: that prevailing between the Mafia families and that between this uncivil order and the surface order of New York and the United States. Two contesting rules of law are pitted against each other to produce an incipient disorder, obscured by the seemingly peaceful patterns of everyday life in New York.

The logic of Hobbesian violence is also subsequently exposed in Michael's eventual assassination of his older brother, Fredo, for having collaborated with Michael's gang rivals, exposing Michael to an assassination attempt. Even blood and family loyalty, stressed repeatedly throughout the trilogy as putatively overriding values, are transgressed by the Hobbesian imperative of survival and sway over opponents. Familial obligations and brotherly love are sacrificed on the altar of the struggle for power and dominion.

Hobbes's portrayal of the disorder and the war of all against all underlying human conflicts remains cogent and compelling. It describes the continuing threat of the decomposition of all valued human exchanges for mutual benefit into an endless cycle of violence. His end game is not presented as an actual description of the implosion of any particular human society. Rather, it indicates the tendencies to degenerate into a power struggle, unmixed by any noncoercive constraint that might arrest the downward movement toward the mutually destructive limiting case. That recidivist prospect infects all human transactions in society as a consequence of the voracious appetite of coercive power to consume all other forms and values of social exchange. Hobbes observes that

> whatsoever . . . is consequent to a time of Warre, where everyman is Enemy to every man . . . the same is consequent to the time, wherein men live without other security, that what their own strength, and their own invention shall furnish them withal. In such condition, there is no place for Industry; because the fruit thereof is uncertain; and consequently no Culture of the Earth, no Navigation, nor use of the commodities that may be imported by Sea; no commodious Building; no Instruments of moving, and removing such things as require much force; no Knowledge of the face of the Earth; no account of Time, no Arts; no Letters; no *Society*; and which is worst of all, continuall feare, and danger of violent death; and the life of man, solitary, poore, nasty, brutish, and short.[18]

Hobbes's solution to stanch violent conflict was the counterpoise of awesome coercive power. To provisionally solve the chronic problem of disorder, he proposed to locate overwhelming coercive power in a Leviathan, Hobbes's absolute monarch. The Leviathan's subjects would accord to him sufficient material power to arbitrate their conflicts and to protect them against foreign invasion or incursions on their peace and well-being in the pursuit of "Industry," "Culture," "Building," "Knowledge," and so forth. He would provide them the order that they could not provide for themselves. The authority of the Leviathan from which law and morality derived was based on an imagined social contract. His authority and, *ipso facto*, the legitimate exercise of his overweening material power was unquestioned as long as he kept his part of the contract to ensure the security of his subjects.

Hobbes's Leviathan solution is of lesser importance than his presentation of a pure theory of Order as one of the three indispensable imperatives of governance. What each human society must decide is *where* to locate awesome power to arbitrate human conflicts and to legitimate the use of that material power to preclude the tendency toward a Hobbesian end game. The locus of legitimate violence might be a tribal chief, a monarch, an aristocratic elite or party, or the public will expressed through periodic elections of representatives invested with the authority to employ the state's awesome power.

We wish to know whether the solution to the Order imperative advanced by the democratic states is viable within the Westphalian state system. Unique to the peoples of open, free societies is their construction over the past several centuries of the global state, developed in chapter 4. The global state is certainly capable of performing the security functions of the traditional Westphalian state. How else would the democratic peoples have been able to rise to global ascendancy in the wake of the implosion of the Soviet Union and the end of the Cold War?

What is noteworthy about the democratic global state is that it substantially relaxes, if not surmounts, the Hobbesian dilemma in significant ways. Created has been a global civil subsociety within the global society that allows for the free flow of goods, services, ideas, and peoples across state borders. Within this protective shell, a free market system has emerged that is both the product of a global civil society and one of its principal supports. The global state relies on state power not only to ensure popular rule and to protect and promote civil liberties and human rights within its own sovereign borders but also to extend these practices to authoritarian regimes.

As Martin Shaw reminds us, "The key questions of all politics are whether, and how, the power and organization of the state can be brought into harmony with the needs of society—of people in their social relations."[19] Its flaws notwithstanding, the democratic global state, as the succeeding chapters argue, is a superior solution to the imperative of Order than that of its many rivals.

The Contributions of Karl Marx and Adam Smith to a Pure Theory of Welfare

Governance of human societies requires more than the location of awesome power in a tribal chieftain, emperor, king, feudal lord, a self-appointed party elite, military junta, charismatic leader, or an aristocratic, oligarchic, or democratic regime. Karl Marx introduces us to the imperative of Welfare. It includes an autonomous structure of power, multiple decisional processes, and a rich array of actor incentives on which a society must no less depend for its governance, survival, and replication than its ordering power.

No theory of governance or depiction of the immense and expanding webs of interdependencies of the world's populations is complete if it focuses on whatever institutional vehicle is accorded destructive power to the exclusion of other rule-issuing sources of authority and power. The poverty of reducing the governance of a society to destructive power is especially evident in realist and neorealist thought. It mistakenly equates the state's coercive power with global governance. All other forms of power to shape human choices and behavior, deriving from the Welfare or Legitimacy imperatives, are expected to regress to the Order imperative and to be drawn to the Hobbesian end game once force is invoked to resolve conflict preferences.

The realist move creates the misleading and potentially mischievous self-fulfilling prophecy that big power politics is sufficient to understand and explain the evolution of governance of human societies.[20] The interest of the theorist, practitioner, and citizen is deflected from the multicolored tapestry of interdependent exchanges and the rules deciding their outcomes that comprise a global society to narrow concerns about the hegemony of the state system. A fixed focus on the Westphalian state and its material power decomposes the complex rule-making and rule-applying of welfare institutions, not to mention those associated with legitimate rule, that are essential components of the governance of human societies into simplified structures of force and coercive threats.[21]

Obscured by a selective focus on Hobbesian order issues are the boundless scope and unplumbed depths of the complexity of global governance of the global society, its multiple and threatening flaws to the contrary notwithstanding. This is particularly true when the imperative of Welfare is subordinated to the state's material power and monopoly of legitimate violence. Human genius and creativity is marked by its capacity to enter into social compacts and to construct governing institutions to check the downward descent toward war, foreshadowed by Hobbes and fellow realists, absent the awesome power of a Leviathan or, for the state system, a hegemon.[22]

For a century, European statesmen were able to avoid catastrophic war, informed, as Paul Schroeder convincingly argues, that war was the greatest threat to their states, regimes, and peoples, a lesson that was gradually forgotten in the run up to World War I. In the wake of the devastating experience of World Wars I and II, Europeans have succeeded in creating a European Union that has provisionally solved the problem of civil war among European peoples over the past four hundred years. No one expects Germany to attack France any time soon. Nor is it a decisive criticism of the market system as a barrier to war to cite Norman Angell's failure to foresee that the economic interdependence of the Great Powers would be insufficient to prevent World War I. His argument is still compelling that, under conditions of wide and deep economic interdependence, war is Pyrrhic for all rivals.

From radically different points of departure in their contrasting notions of human nature and their conception of human freedom, Karl Marx and Adam Smith advance a pure theory of Welfare. For our purposes, their contributions constitute one of the key legs of a three-legged stool forming the skeletal power structures of the governance of all human societies. The modalities of welfare power structures, decisional processes, and the incentives generated by the Welfare imperative obviously differ widely and fundamentally over time across human societies, largely as a function of environmental conditions,[23] knowledge transfer of best practices and technological development,[24] and cultural value systems.[25] These contextual conditions promote, impede, or preclude increased wealth production.

For Marx and Smith, what has to be unleashed is the creativity of humans in the employment of their inherent freedom. Note that the Welfare imperative rests on an entirely different conception of human freedom than that of Hobbes. If Hobbes, Marx, and Smith agree on freedom as an inherent and overriding human property, Marx and Smith would construct institutions to ensure that humans could exercise their freedom of thought and choice in pursuing their stipulated preferences for wealth and welfare, while Hobbes would check what he views as the self-destructive implications of this distinctly human trait. For Marx, human freedom is associated with the demise of the capitalistic market system; for Smith, it is with the creation of that system. For Marx, the capitalistic market system illegitimately utilizes the coercive power of the state to oppress a global working class. For Smith, the state is actually enlisted to create a global market system and to ensure its security. Freedom to produce wealth is a positive force for Marx and Smith; for Hobbes, freedom must be constrained first before industry and culture can move forward.

Karl Marx and the Welfare Imperative

Beginning with Marx, the creation of a structure of power, associated with the Welfare imperative, is rooted in the bio-sexual composition of humans. Marx makes the seemingly banal but slighted observation "that mankind," as Frederick Engels, Marx's patron and collaborator, explains, "must first eat, drink, have shelter and clothing before it can pursue politics, science, art,

religion . . . that therefore the production of the immediate means of subsistence and consequently the degree of economic development attained . . .
in an epoch form the foundation upon which the state institutions, the legal
conceptions, art, and even the ideas of religion, of the people concerned have
been evolved, and in the light of which they must, therefore, be explained,
instead of vice versa."[26] On this primordial proposition of the inexorable
human pursuit of welfare, with subsistence as the inescapable requirement,
Marx (and notably Smith a century earlier) constructs an indispensable component of a theory of governance. From radically opposed points of view, they
converge on a pure theory of markets as the latest stage of human striving in
response to a Welfare imperative.

If Marxian theory can be shown to overdetermine the causal direction
of the Welfare imperative—economic power promiscuously enveloping all
other forms of human choice and action, making much the same error for
capitalist markets as realists for state violence—Marx can still be credited
with having identified a central element of a pure theory of welfare and governance: that the logic and primal urges of bio-sexual needs move humans,
by fits and starts, to overcome the constraints of coercive power, religious
and cultural prohibitions, and environmental limits toward maximizing their
material welfare and wealth. A century before Marx, Adam Smith and the liberal economists had essentially reached the same conclusion of an overriding
drive toward material welfare.

Given the proven benefits of ceaseless scientific discovery and technological innovations under the aegis of modernization and industrialization to
facilitate and foster the material betterment of the world's populations, states
and regime leaders ignore popular demands for greater economic welfare at
their own peril.[27] The very survival of the state, as the implosion of the Soviet
Union evidences, is at risk. In contrast to the predictions of some realists,[28]
states, or at least their political regimes, risk being "selected out" if they fail to
address the demands of "more now" of their populations. Whereas before, the
state and its awesome power may well have been used with predatory abandon and precluded sustained economic growth and wealth creation while
holding onto power, that is not a winning strategy today. We are, as Richard
Rosecrance reminds us, in the era of the trading state—or as Philip Cerny
prefers, the competitive state.[29] These fundamental transformations of the
Westphalian state imply the preexistence of a global civil society in support
of free exchange across state borders and rule-based governance underwritten
by state power to protect private contracts and property.

Thanks to the efforts of democratic peoples, the coercive power of the
global state protects and promotes free, voluntary, and unfettered economic
exchange. It is expected and held accountable in using its destructive powers

to enhance the economic competitiveness of the population over which it provisionally rules. Witness China's resistance to reevaluating its currency to favor its export strategy for economic growth or President Barack Obama's 2011 State of the Union message that calls for the United States to "Win the Future"—that is, to maintain its competitive position in global trade and finance.[30] Of course, states use their coercive power to favor the material interests of their respective populations through tariffs, import quotas, subsidies, and the like. These distortions in free exchange highlight and reveal, ironically, the creative power of a global market system to generate incentives for wealth and welfare.

How does the logic of welfare work through time and across human societies, culminating in the emergence of a global society and the globalization and institutionalization of a market system? Marx's sententious presentation of this causal process is superior to any summary that I might attempt:

> In the social production of their existence, men enter into definite, necessary relations, which are independent of their will, namely, *relations of production* corresponding to a determinate state of development of their material forces of production. The totality of these relations of production constitutes the economic structure of society, the real foundation on which there arises a legal and political superstructure and to which there correspond definite forms of social consciousness. The mode of production of material life conditions the social, political and intellectual life-process in general. It is not the consciousness of men that determines their being, but on the contrary it is their social being that determines their consciousness. At a certain stage of their development, the *material productive forces* of society come into conflict with the existing *relations of production* or—what is merely a legal expression for the same thing—with the property relations within the framework of which they have hitherto operated. From forms of development of the productive forces these relations turn into their fetters. At that point an era of social revolution begins.[31]

Marx explains how the process of producing wealth—goods and services—works through history and its implications for governance: "The handmill gives you society with the feudal lord; the steam mill, society with industrial capitalism."[32] The handmill, associated with a preindustrialized agricultural economy, represented metaphorically Europe's feudal system of governance. The feudal lord controlled the means of production—land, serfs, and the capital (handmills, etc.) for producing food and consumer products. Serfs, bound to the land, were subservient to the lord's authority. Holding unquestioned property rights over his land and over his serfs, the lord could deploy these assets as he pleased for his own economic gain. Labor was neither fungible nor moveable.

Marx's reference to the "steam mill" symbolizes the replacement of agriculture and the feudal system by industrialization, the mass production of goods, and the rise of a global market system controlled by a capitalist class. To add to Marx's evolutionary depiction of technological development, information technology (IT) now gives rise to a global knowledge society, the latest stage of human economic development. The knowledge industry has now produced a new elite, governmental and nongovernmental, in control of information, the media, and the production and dissemination of knowledge as well as ownership of the property rights over these processes.[33] New forms of global crime are also created: credit card theft, illegal downloading of governmental and private corporate documents, cybersecurity breaches, and cyberwarfare.

In Marx's exegesis of history, "Freeman and slave, patrician and plebeian, lord and serf, guild master and journeyman—in a word oppressor and oppressed— . . . carried on an uninterrupted fight that each time ended in revolutionary reconstitution of society at large, or in the common ruin of the contending classes."[34] For Marx, this struggle culminated in the Industrial Revolution. As a consequence of the alleged flaws of capitalist markets, which, through the unequal distribution of wealth, created two antagonistic classes—capitalist and labor—human history would end in the global utopian victory of the proletariat, uniting all humanity for the first time in human social evolution. Contra Hobbes, human preferences would converge—what is otherwise a definition of utopia.

What is useful to extract from Marx is not his reductionist conception of human social evolution or, much less, his prediction of utopian universal proletariat rule. These cannot be taken seriously if either Hobbes or Adam Smith has any say or if historical experience is invoked to rebut Marxist claims. Nor would Rousseau, as the discussion below of legitimacy develops, find the dismissal of human values and subjective notions of right rule and legitimacy solely a derivative of economic exchange and technological change.

That said, Marx is important for a theory of governance on two grounds: First, there is no escape from the bio-sexual material constraints of life. That imperative creates the incessant drive, however much frustrated by political, social, ideational, or cultural limits, for ever-greater production and distribution of material welfare. The second reason to appeal to Marx is his insight that in the pursuit of the Welfare imperative—food, shelter, clothing—humans will always choose, over time, best practices—that is, technological innovations and associated governmental rules and institutions, which are increasingly more efficient and effective to fuel their drive for material wealth. On this score Marx and Adam Smith agree.[35]

Marx takes the right step in identifying this compelling force—technological innovation and best economic practices—but moves in the wrong direction in limiting the rich and multifarious creativity of humans to a particular period in history—the Industrial Revolution—and to a simplistic bimodal class struggle. Marx explains too much and, therefore, too little about human thought, decision, action, and values and the complex societies that human-kind has imaginatively constructed (and deconstructed and destroyed). Here Max Weber has the better of the argument in demonstrating the material power and autonomy of the state, the abiding importance of religious and cultural values, and the complexity of the global society and its bewildering congeries of status, not just class, differences. Compelling, too, is the concept of nationalism as having a grip on human consciousness and as a powerful driver of social and political change and global war.[36]

What can be usefully extracted from Marx is what was already explicit in Adam Smith and later, notably, in Joseph Schumpeter's work on the creative destruction of technological change.[37] Marx stipulated incessant technologi-cal innovation to explain social change and the rise of new actors and power brokers associated with best practices. Technological change produced sys-temic shifts in the distribution of power to the advantage of those in the pos-session of new means of production. Those wedded to outdated technologies would see their property rights and power progressively decrease in value and be dispatched eventually to the "dust bin of history."

This human disposition to choose best practices of production drives social history unless arrested by countervailing coercive power, notably exercised by the state, or blocked by community mores—guilds or the Luddite move-ment in Britain come to mind. These barriers gradually erode, albeit at great human and material cost and sacrifice, following the trajectory predicted by Marx (and Smith) toward ever-greater global economic growth and innova-tion within the institutional power structure of a free exchange global market system.

If enough time is allotted for "an historical experiment," humans can be expected to choose superior ways of fostering wealth and welfare despite the opposition, often violent, of those whose interests are tied to less effective and efficient property rights and economic practices or who are so ideologically wired that they reject economic change and the loss of power that it would produce. For Marx and for the evolution of the global society, best practices comprised the "steam mill"—the metaphor for the Industrial Revolution and its spread through capitalist markets around the world. Similarly, the IT revo-lution is being embraced by an ever-increasing number of states and peoples around the globe. Humans choose these superior systems since they respond to the logic of the Welfare imperative working over time and changing cir-cumstances. The ascendancy of a superior means of production over its rivals illustrates how human choice, as much by trial and error as by deliberate design, moves toward the ever maximization of wealth, though scarcely in a straight and predictable line.[38]

Obviously the drive toward economic growth and the adoption of best technological and market practices are not inevitable at different, discrete moments in history. The decision of the Ming dynasty to turn inward and abandon naval exploration despite its seafaring superiority to potential competitors, indicates that the Welfare imperative and the Marxian prediction of material pursuits can be temporarily arrested by countervailing state power. Japan also turned inward at the expense of technological progress under Tokugawa rule, only to be forced to enter into global commerce by American naval power in the middle of the nineteenth century. In the long run the Marxian expectation still holds true.

If Hobbes helps us come to grips with the condition of incessant conflicts as a derivative of preference clashes over objects of value to the rivals and their determination to have their way and to impose their will, rule, and governance on opponents, Marx is no less indispensable in insisting on the primordial need and drive of humans, whatever their differences over order and the preference conflicts it generates, to focus on the prerequisite that they "must first eat, drink, have shelter and clothing" before they can do much else, including fighting over their clashing preferences.

The unquenchable strivings that Marx stresses secrete themselves toward creating and adopting best productive practices and the erection of new power structures to support these innovations, however throttled by streams of regime predators, religious and cultural impediments, or, increasingly today, by environmental and ecological constraints—natural and artificial. The results are transformative in governing solutions in response to the Welfare imperative. The power structure erected on these technological innovations is indispensable for understanding and explaining not only the Welfare imperative at work but also the unique solution of a market system as a key component of the governance of the global society.

Adam Smith: Rationale for Global Markets

Now at stage right, Adam Smith enters the human drama to help advance the development of a pure theory of the Welfare imperative without Marxian baggage of class struggles and a utopian end of history. What Marx failed to grasp, but which Adam Smith already understood a century earlier, was that the drive for best practices was lodged in human freedom and creativity rather than in unconscious, materially directed social processes over which humans had no reflexive knowledge (presumably and presumptively until Marx's elucidation of economic growth).[39] Even before Marx comes upon the stage, Smith relegates him to a supporting role in economic theory in the presentation of a pure theory of the market.

Smith also opened the way for liberal economists and for Joseph Schumpeter, in particular, to show that humans had the capacity for achieving, if not always predictably, sustained economic growth and ceaseless technological development in pursuit of their self-interests and, by that token and unintentionally, the material benefit of humankind. If Marx accepted the principle that best practices would always prevail over time, he was curiously unable to envision, contra Smith and Schumpeter, continued economic and technological development that would gradually supplant the capitalist modes of production extant in Marx's era. In a sense, Marx did not avail himself of his own theory of incessant economic change to envision technological innovation beyond mass production and industrialization, where the human species is today. A free market created incentives for innovation. An unexpected effect of these freely floating incentives was the reversal of the aphorism that necessity is the mother of invention. Now invention is the mother of necessity.

What are Smith's principal contributions to a theory of Welfare as an imperative of governance? Smith stipulates that intrinsic to humans is their "propensity to truck, barter, and exchange one thing for another."[40] Humans have an endemic disposition to seek their material well-being by profiting through trade with others of their kind whose environment constraints, skills, endowments, and creativity yield mutual, if differing, material gain. If that propensity were unleashed from the shackles of authoritarian rule, wasteful imperial pursuits, community constraints, and self-limiting ideological notions of what were the constituents of wealth—namely, mass consumption— the result would be a free exchange market system. The propensity to truck and barter, fostered by human freedom, would lead to the global application of the principles of the division of labor as the principal driver of increased wealth and innovation for humankind.

Smith recognized that all humans would profit if this social principle could be applied to all humankind through the creation of new economic institutions of global scope—that is, free markets. That is precisely what a global market system could do: facilitate free and efficient economic exchange between and among humans, a global division of labor. The result of this transforming institutional reform would be increased production of more and increasingly improved goods and services. The market system afforded economic actors the freedom to decide how the scarce resources available to them could most effectively and efficiently be employed in pursuing their selfish interests.[41] All those implicated in a market system would also draw on the comparative advantages of all of its members. Northern climes would specialize in large grains; tropical areas, in fruits and vegetables. The endowment pool of human skills, knowledge, creativity, and entrepreneurship would be made available to all those implicated in a global market system.

Smith had no illusions that his vision of a global market system would be realized in his lifetime. Its ascendancy as a winning idea and as a power structure, challenging the authority of its opponents, would be "very slow and gradual."[42] The widespread global institutionalization of feudal systems, the commitment of Europe's rulers to mercantilist policies, favoring of the accumulation of gold and specie instead of wealth production and widespread public consumption, precluded rapid reform. The spread of European empires, antithetical to free exchange, and the brake that craft guilds exercised over domestic economies impeded the erection of a global market system. But once the wealth-creating incentives of a free exchange system were set in motion, its superior wealth-producing capabilities, as Marx later recognized, would prevail over competing economic systems. These would eventually be opted out. This is not to say that this evolutionary trajectory was inevitable despite the powerful attractive power of a global market system to respond to the imperative of Welfare. Its success would also depend on its support of the global state and state system and the legitimacy accorded the market system by the otherwise contesting populations.[43]

The formidable incentives of a free, open global market system, supported by its own power structure, with its own norms, rules, institutions as well as compelling incentives for actors to pursue their own material interests, would, as Smith foresaw, propel the increased wealth of nations. Writing in 1776, Smith foresaw the global transformation of economic exchanges between actors in civil society and states, even before the Industrial Revolution had appeared in its full development to evidence the superior workings of the principle of the division of labor in the service of "trucking and bartering." If the predatory proclivity of states and their tendency to protect inefficient monopolies and to erect barriers to trade could be eliminated on a global scale, then sustainable economic growth and the increasing *Wealth of Nations* was possible for all mankind.

Smith, aligned with Immanuel Kant, squarely based his understanding of the providential effects of a theory (and practice) of a pure global market system on the capacity of people to rely on "reason and speech" and their utilization of these unique properties among animals to create institutions to promote wealth. This is the first glimmer of the liberal economist's "Rational Actor." Reversing the assumption shared by Hobbes and his partisans, that selfish egoists had to be controlled by awesome power for the sake of peace, for the protection of property, for the enforcement of contracts, for the provision of collective goods, and for perfecting civil society in its industry, buildings, and arts, Smith postulated the voluntary, free transactions of humans in their trucking and bartering for their mutual material benefit. This economic system would result, paradoxically, in the unintended increase of greater wealth for all parties, albeit in unequal but in equitable and just proportions. Each economic actor would, theoretically, extract material gain in proportion to its contributions to wealth formation.

Smith also reversed Marx's causal arrow in assigning beneficial global social change to global capitalistic markets, which promoted self-interest.[44] "In civilized society [man] stands at all times in need of the co-operation and assistance of great multitudes (what this discussion refers to as a global society). . . . It is in vain for him to expect it from their benevolence only. He will be more likely to prevail if he can interest their self-love in his favour, and shew them that it is for their own advantage to do for him what he requires of them. . . . It is not from the benevolence of the butcher, the brewer, or the baker, that we expect our dinner, but from their regard to their own interest. We address ourselves, not to their humanity but to their self-love, and never talk to them of our own necessities but of their advantages."[45]

For Smith, a free market, promoting a global division of labor, will result in "that general opulence to which it gives occasion."[46] Smith's pin factory narrative captures in miniature his expansive grasp of the utility of this principle for the efficient and effective production and distribution of wealth. He opens trucking and bartering to all humans, not just the English to whom he initially addressed his economic theory. What these vehicles for trucking and bartering afford is to pool, potentially, all of humankind's endowments, talents, resources, creativity, and entrepreneurial skill with the result that the wealth of nations is promoted, accelerated, and put on a trajectory that is, cumulatively, ever greater.[47]

The causal links between self-interest and wealth creation, furthered by the division of labor and by the voluntary exchanges between egoists in a global market system, is at the foundation of contemporary liberal economic theory. The division of labor, applied globally and ideally without frictions or impediments to free, voluntary exchange, fosters specialization; reduces costs of production; generates incentives for the more efficient and effective uses of the factors of production; decreases economic transaction costs; facilitates technological development; promotes the ceaseless introduction of new products and services into the market place; fosters the erection of educational programs, engineering, and science to service the market; and elicits the emergence of a class of entrepreneurs and managers to exploit global markets for their advantage and, accordingly, for all those seeking to materially enrich their lives.

Basing an economic system on individual freedom, pushed by self-interest to maximize material gain, results, ironically, in greater societal benefit than what egoists expected or intended: "He intends only his own gain; and he is in this, as in many other cases, led by an invisible hand to promote an end which was no part of his intention. Nor is it always the worse for the society that it was no part of it. By pursuing his own interest he frequently promotes that of the society more effectually than when he really intends to promote it."[48]

Smith understood that humans are the only ones who, subjectively, know and can decide, economically and morally, their preferences and their preference orderings. Governments err if they substitute their economic preferences for those of their subjects. That would result in less efficient and effective responses to citizen demands. All of the countless decisions that have to be made by economic actors are orchestrated better in free global markets than by any other alternative economic system. Within Smith's general theory of the market, nothing could be more damaging to wealth production and human freedom than the merging of the power structures of the imperatives of Order and Welfare—the cataclysmic error of the Soviet Union's solution for the Order and Welfare imperatives. Centralized command economic systems insulate themselves from the discipline of market competition and are inured to the preferences of buyers and sellers and entrepreneurs seeking profits. The coordination and satisfaction of these latter preferences are accomplished (at least theoretically) by the market's generation of common prices for the factors of production and for the exchange of goods and services.

In the same way that the logic of the Hobbesian end game is its descent to unremitting violent conflict unless arrested by an ordering awesome power, so also is the ascent upward toward increased personal and collective wealth and welfare the product of a humanly created social institution—a global market system. In contrast to the actual operation of the market system today and the increasing recognition of its profound structural failures and flaws, the subject of chapters 5 and 6, the logic of pure markets is unassailable on its own assumptions and terms. Free rational actors have incentives to move toward the end game of the pure market. They are expected to acquire the knowledge they require to maximize personal gains, notwithstanding the formidable constraints on that pursuit by economic actors, possessed of unequal economic and political bargaining power.

Free, rational actors are assumed to focus on relative gains in pursuing material wealth through the market system. They expect and applaud its distribution of wealth in unequal portions. The market is, as Charles Lindblom explains, a quid pro quo system.[49] If the market system works in conformity with its theory (and of course it never fully does), actors receive from the market what value they can exchange with other players, while, as an unintended byproduct of their selfish pursuits, fostering the collective public good. Following the logic of liberal economic thought, the global institutionalization of markets is the optimal social framework for acquiring wealth, for ensuring personal welfare, and for fostering *The Wealth of Nations*. Deviations or variances from the disciplined logic of markets in allocating scarce material and human resources will in theory and practice produce less wealth; distribute fewer goods and services to all engaged in the market system; fail to identify profitable and productive investments on a global scale; and frustrate ceaseless technological innovations (that is, best practices).[50]

Now the issue is joined between Hobbes and Smith (and to a degree with Marx). They all agree on human freedom as an essential human property (as does Rousseau, whom we will get to soon). They radically differ in their projection of the social consequences for OWL imperatives of freedom. For Hobbes priority extends to the assignment to the state of overwhelming coercive power to arbitrate rival preferences, generated by human freedom and creativity. Hobbes's singular focus on awesome power to be attributed to the Leviathan—a monarch or a democratic regime—failed to address the adverse economic consequences of fusing the imperatives of Order and Welfare.

Smith implicitly foresaw these damaging effects in his subversion of mercantilism's rationale for wealth creation. Whereas the power of the state was supposed to rest on precious metals and their acquisition through imperial expansion as well as the protection of home industries and restrictions on trade, Smith foresaw that a market system would not only increase the nation's wealth but also redound to the power of the monarch in coping with foreign threats. No matter that a free exchange system was not necessarily dedicated to that purpose. It was no accident that the Dutch principality and the British crown profited most from the creation of a free trade system. The power of the British state grew in the same measure as its economic power in world trade also enlarged to become the dominant naval power and global hegemon of the nineteenth century.[51]

Contra Hobbes, Smith adopts an optimistic notion of human freedom and the capacity of humans, using reason and speech, to reconcile their differences for their mutual and collective welfare short of the intrusion of violence. These two clashing moral visions of humans and their prospects lie at the foundation of two inescapable but adversarial imperatives of governance, both based on clashing and irreconcilable conceptions of the social implications of human freedom. How the contradictory claims of the imperatives of Order and Welfare and the respective power structures on which they draw are balanced and reconciled—one based on the coercion, the other on voluntary and free exchange—will determine whether democratic OWL solutions for global governance will survive and thrive. That balance must also integrate the claims and contend with the power arising from converging and diverging conceptions of legitimacy held by populations, the third leg of the governance of all human societies.

Jean-Jacques Rousseau: Toward a Pure Theory of the Imperative of Legitimacy

Since the Greeks first raised the question of what constituted an ideal society and its governance, a pure theory of Legitimacy—the third imperative of governance—has remained elusive. Countless efforts by untold human societies over millennia, most long gone, have failed to advance a value system as well as a moral ethical code that have enjoyed universal consent and allegiance. Much of the explanation for the proliferation of diverse value systems lies in the global diaspora of the human species since its emergence out of Africa. Each discrete and isolated society, confronted by the particular challenges of its environment—physical and human[52]—created perforce its own OWL solutions to governance. Legitimacy rested on each society's unique explanation of its circumscribed physical, socially constructed, and inspired spiritual world. These explanatory narratives and myths, rooted principally in religion, culture, and tradition, have carried through to the modern era.

The modern era's contribution to the imperative of Legitimacy was its secularization. Added to religious, cultural, and traditional value systems were nationalism, Fascism, Nazism, Communism, and liberal democratic ideology. The partisans of these value systems compete for the allegiance of the world's populations. Some, like Fascism and Nazism, have been largely repudiated. Communism still lingers in some states, but it has been profoundly redefined by the Chinese Communist government, which preserves centralized party rule under the problematic guise of representing the will of the Chinese people while affirming, paradoxically, the regime's engagement in an open, free market system that owes its rationale to liberal democratic thought. Religion and culture remain major, global sources of value commitment for billions of the world's divided populations. Given potentially limitless emotional attachments to sets of religious values and norms and the deep-down personal identities associated with these systems, it is readily apparent that profoundly conflicting and competing value systems present insurmountable obstacles to the creation of a universal set of values and a shared code of conduct to legitimate the governing practices regulating and resolving the interdependent exchanges of the members (though not citizens) of the global society.

Jean-Jacques Rousseau advances a universal solution to the conundrum of the Legitimacy imperative. His conjecture that "men are born free, and everywhere they are in chains" roots the diversity of human value systems in their shared possession of the moral quality of freedom. By that token, too, they must all be equal. They equally share, as a constraint applicable to all humans through time and circumstance, the moral capacity to determine by the sheer exercise of their collective wills whatever they construe as constituting legitimate rule.[53] This dramatic Rousseaunean conjecture establishes freedom and equality as transcending history. In a profound sense, one may trace the diversity of humanity to varying and contradictory solutions humans have devised for legitimacy. However interesting that enterprise, it is not relevant to an intrinsic, transhistorical understanding of legitimacy. Rousseau goes beyond daily and casual observation and beyond human history. The shared human property of freedom to create and will values—Friedrich Nietzsche's friendly amendment to Rousseau's conjecture—has precluded and will continue to preclude the convergence of value systems. Ipso facto, common standards for evaluating the legitimacy of political regimes, of rules and rulers, and of governing institutions will forever remain problematic.[54] Rousseau presents Legitimacy as an imperative of government—more significant than Order and Welfare in his thinking—but also embarks on an elusive quest to unalterably define Legitimacy through time and circumstance.

A century before Marx, Rousseau had already set the stage to reverse the direction of Marx's causal arrow to explain social change. Rousseau's stipulation of the moral composition of humans attributed to them the power, once they grasped their shared properties of being free and equal, to determine what social chains would bind them. Following Rousseau, humans had an unlimited capacity to shape their societies to their liking. Contra Marx, "the consciousness of men . . . determines their being," not their "social being," chains in Rousseau's mind. What they will as their governing values determines their consciousness—that is, their self-regarding and reflexive conceptions of their self-worth and the moral meanings they invest in their physical environments and in their exchanges with their fellow humans. Their freedom to create what values suit them affords them the capacity to determine whether the material conditions of what Order and Welfare imperatives are compatible with their conceptions of legitimate rule. That capacity, when activated, constitutes a structure of power, potentially more compelling than the power structures associated with those of Order and Welfare imperatives.

The profound irony of Rousseau's conjecture should also be recognized. The social truth underlying Rousseau's insight is the potentially infinite capacity of humans to create the values and identities they *will* as the basis for what rules and institutions they will obey. This redefinition of what makes humans *human* lies, ironically, in a reversal of Rousseau's stipulation of the human condition. Humans are necessarily born into chains,[55] but their moral freedom provides them the ability to throw off these chains in creating new constraints of their own design. The implication of Rousseau's moral insight lies, then, more in the future than in the past.

At any time humans can, theoretically, will their chains away once they have grasped the freedom to which they are heir. What rules are legitimate to regulate human social exchanges and who and what humanly created institutions and their agents have a right to issue directives and expect them to be obeyed by targeted populations are profoundly enmeshed in contesting value systems and in the distinct social identities of its adherents. These arise from what people care about deeply. What is unique about humans is their singular ability to free themselves from received, socialized, or imposed social fetters and fashion chains more to their liking. They can will their values and affirm their diverse conceptions of legitimacy, quite apart from the material constraints that may limit their actions and aspirations.[56] The promiscuous power of the Legitimacy imperative can also relax and surmount those limits to create new material conditions submissive to the sanctions of authoritative governmental conduct.

Rousseau's conjecture is important as a start toward a theory of legitimacy for several reasons. The first lies in his stipulation of a moral right inherent to all humans to decide what institutions of government and rulers they wish to invest with authority. Only they have the right to construct a *general will* to bind themselves. Only the ruled, not the rulers in command of material power—political and economic—can determine legitimacy. In a strict sense Rousseau is not describing an observable, empirical reality—humans as free and equal—but stipulating a subjective reality yet to be created wherein humans are universalized as a moral entity who have an absolute and privileged right to rule themselves, because they possess these two irrevocable moral attributes. It is up to them how they will exercise these qualities of human nature.[57]

Second, universally enjoyed freedom and equality, increasingly and progressively affirmed by the world's populations in diverse and contradictory ways, fosters incentives for humans, perpetually, to create new value systems. They are morally equipped to reinvent their identities in ways compatible with their evolving notions of who they are, what they care about, what they wish to be, and in response to the constraints and opportunities of their evolving physical and environmental settings.[58] These divergent and incompatible value systems advance alternative and largely mutually exclusive explanations for the material makeup of the universe and infuse virtue and value into human life and action—on this earth and in what many imagine is an afterlife.

Third, Rousseau's stipulation of legitimacy, as the product of the general will of a community of like-minded individuals, is fungible. It can result in potentially limitless numbers of social contracts defined by discrete political bodies. Rousseau's conjecture initially resonated in the American Declaration of Independence and the French Declaration of the Rights of Man. Coming forward, it is institutionalized in the UN Universal Declaration of Human Rights. It has been extended further in the spread of popular governments since the nineteenth century to become today the preferred regime of many states.[59]

While Rousseau's notion of the social contract has traditionally been associated with liberal democracies, there is nothing to preclude a population from affirming a general will antithetical to a liberal code, whether resting on secular, religious, cultural, or traditional principles. The liberal democratic interpretation of Rousseau's principles of freedom and equality, as one person, one vote, is just that—one form of the general will. Other forms created by nonliberally animated populations, notably religiously founded regimes, compete with a liberal interpretation of Rousseau's conjecture.

Fourth, the darker implications of the Rousseaunean conjecture must also be addressed. However much general wills may differ and conflict, they share the same source of authority for legitimate government. Authority rests in the body politic, in the populace. A charismatic leader—Hitler, Mao, or Castro—can claim legitimacy. In keeping with Rousseau's conception of the social compact, authoritarian leaders assert that they represent the people's authority: the Volk for Hitler, the Communist Party of China for Mao, and the ceaseless revolution for Castro.

Fifth, a disquieting element of Rousseau's conjecture is the leveling of competing moral claims to legitimacy if they meet a general will test. An Osama bin Laden and his Al Qaeda followers can reject the Western liberal secular state as illegitimate on the basis of their understanding of the Prophet's teachings. ISIS leader Abu Bakr al-Baghdadi, opposed to Al Qaeda and the West, can also claim to rule all Muslims and to justify the subjugation or elimination of all who are judged apostates of Islam (Shi'ites), adherents of other religions, or nonbelievers. However heinous the acts of coercion perpetrated by ISIS may be, they are still perversely justified as dictated by Baghdadi's notion of his interpretation of the "Book." In this same vein, authoritarian regimes, based on secular ideologies and bolstered by nationalism, are equally justified in their own understanding of legitimate rule as their interpretation of the general will.

The moral relativism of Rousseau's conjecture poses two immense challenges for the creation of global governance. Each conception of the general will or social contract is obliged to justify its claim to legitimacy as potentially of universal applicability. None of these claims to legitimacy is self-justifying and self-referential. Their justification lies not only with their adherents but also with their opponents. To compete successfully against its rivals, each system and its corresponding conception of legitimate rule must insist on its moral superiority. Chapter 7, drawing on democratic theory, makes the claim of moral superiority for the democratic project. Its competitors are equally put on their mettle to do likewise, to justify their moral positions, attract adherents to their cause, and deploy legitimacy as a source of power.

It is important to recognize that the imperative of Legitimacy is a structure of power, no less capable of directing human choices than the power counterparts of Order and Welfare imperatives. Shared notions of legitimacy empower a populace. That empowerment is an active force working through history and carries beyond the life of any of the members of a community. As a source of power, the imperative of Legitimacy is not to be confused with the notion of "soft power." The latter is little more than an instrument for tactical gain in winning at the margin in the interdependent exchanges comprising a global society. Legitimacy as an imperative is a structure of power and a complex decisional process generating its own unique incentives for human choice in governing a populace. When invoked by a population it can promiscuously invest and transform the structures of power and incentives for choice associated with Order and Welfare imperatives. The Legitimacy imperative prompts adherents to proselytize to increase their number and, faute de mieux, to impose their moral claims on resistant actors. Pushed toward their end point, legitimacy claims are not designed merely to make a point or gain a marginal advantage. They are intended to underwrite a government congenial to the values and interests of its partisans.[60] Human rights advocates, for example, can do no less than press for extension of those rights to all of humanity.

This brings the discussion to the most worrisome implications of Rousseau's conjecture. If social contracts within the contemporaneous global society are irreconcilable, they invite incessant conflicts among the communities tied to their social contracts, whether by consent or coercion. Under the revolutionary condition of the expanding interdependencies of humans around the globe across all areas of vital human concern, the absence of a universally acknowledged value system, in principle and in practice, to arbitrate conflicts casts the governance of the global society into permanent crisis, marked by ceaseless socioeconomic and political instability.

Today, the promiscuous power of the Legitimacy imperative brings into question the nation-state and nation-state system and the viability of an open market solution to Welfare. The former, while a warfare system, provides a fragile, precarious order, an anarchical society of states, if the legitimacy of domestic regimes is not raised in question.[61] The market system, based on the impersonal assumption of universal prices in the exchange of goods and services, is oblivious to value preferences and conflicting identities other than completing a mutually beneficial utilitarian exchange. Rousseau recognized the implications of clashing value systems, competing social contracts, and incompatible principles of legitimate rule. Communities loyal to clashing value systems would be trapped into irremediable conflict and war. At the level of the relations of contesting peoples and states, each pledged to an opposed social contract, there could not be perpetual peace but perpetual war, real and prospective, a fundamentally unstable global society.[62]

It is important to stress the power components of the Legitimacy imperative, not just its qualitative and subjective content. The willingness of millions to give their lives for their values, whether to foster liberal belief in the integrity of individuals or to impose their ideological and religious values on others, testifies to the power of the Legitimacy imperative. The power and promiscuity of the Legitimacy imperative—its capacity to profoundly change human evaluations of authoritative rule and also to fundamentally transform order and welfare systems and power structures—can be illustrated by three cases that reveal the revolutionary potential of radical changes in human value systems and their transformational effect on governance: the Protestant Reformation; the end of slavery in the United States; and the fall of the Eurocentric system, including the implosion of the Soviet Union, as the last of Europe's empires.[63]

The single thread working across these differentiated revolutionary processes is the exposition of legitimacy as a power unto itself as a central element of governance. The view here is that the substantive makeup and form of a particular system of legitimacy is shaped by the power of order and welfare institutions, but, conversely, so also do widely held popular notions of legitimacy constrain these material power structures and discipline them to the subjective, intangible claims of widely shared notions of legitimacy. Realists, inspired by Hobbes, and Marxists, focused on economic development, reduce legitimacy to these material concerns. Slighted and neglected but no less powerful is the human quest for legitimate rule that is a key factor in any explanation of social change and governance.

The Protestant Reformation

The Protestant Reformation destroyed the unity of European Christendom under the moral authority of Rome and the Catholic pope. Secular and religious authority, however contested throughout the Middle Ages, was still assumed in principle to be harmonious and mutually supportive. Even as kings, feudal lords, and cities battled over territories, populations, and resources, the assumption was still widely shared that they owed their right to rule to a singular moral code of a unified Christendom. If conflicts arose over who had legitimate title to assume the throne over a population or territory, these turned less on disputed religious grounds than on blood lineage or on challenged accords between rulers, defining accession to rule. William the Conqueror's defeat of Harold Godwinson at Hastings in 1066 resulted from William's challenge to Harold's right to rule over disputed English and French territories, not because either opposed the moral authority of Rome or viewed the Christian religion as anything other than subject to a singular interpretation, however elusive a convergent understanding of that interpretation might have appeared to them.

Martin Luther's posting of ninety-five theses on the castle church of Wittenberg in 1517, challenging the authority of Rome, fundamentally transformed the moral basis for political legitimacy within the West. Rather than rely on a hierarchy of priests and the authority of the pope in Rome to define what God had revealed by entering history to guide men to salvation, Luther taught that the Bible and scripture, not Rome, was the original source of revelation and, ultimately, the foundation for the legitimacy of political rule. With God's grace as guide, each Christian was capable of hearing and subjecting himself or herself to God's word and will, without the intervention of a pope and priestly hierarchy.

As the resulting wars of religion between Protestants and Catholics and, subsequently, between burgeoning Protestant sects reveal, the Protestant message of individually determined salvation did not automatically translate into social harmony across Christendom. That struggle for the soul of Christendom continues, evidenced in the Irish civil war and carried forward in the intense struggles in the United States over religious beliefs and their implications for public policy. In decisively destroying the moral unity of Christendom, the Protestant Reformation opened the way to enduring religious conflicts between Christian sects to define life and death, citizenship, marriage, childbirth and rearing, the social and sexual roles and obligations of men and women—culture wars within Christianity itself.

Divisions over Christian beliefs ushered in internecine conflict across Europe. A turning point in European governance, spurred by religious strife, was the Thirty Years' War (1518–1548), culminating in the Treaty of Westphalia, the foundation stone on which the nation-state and the nation-state system were eventually constructed. A few years later, the Treaty of Augsburg of 1555 established the principle that the religion of the prince was the religion of his populace—*Cuius regio, eius religio*. Secular and religious authority, while divergent across European states and principalities, converged in each differing unit. The Christian conscience of each ruler (and whatever calculation he may have made to further his interests and power) legitimated his secular rule. However much the material power of these units may have varied, each was to be treated as a moral equal. Neither the Catholic pope in Rome nor any other religious or secular political power had a right to intervene in the territorial rule of a recognized principality or state—a right often recognized more in the breach than in the observance.

The Protestant Reformation also had consequences for the economic modernization of Europe and the United States. The Welfare imperative was gradually, and often with convulsive force, transformed into a global market system. While the spur to the acquisition of wealth and the creation of a global free exchange system cannot be solely attributed to the values and cultural change initiated by Protestantism, as Max Weber argued,[64] the moral centrality of the individual, spurred by the Renaissance and reinforced by the Reformation, validated and promoted individual entrepreneurship to create and accumulate wealth, a sign of God's favor in the eyes of many Christians. Also fostered were the spread and strengthening of social values to support scientific discovery, technological innovation and industrialization, global trade and markets, and the spread of popular regimes. No less significant for the transformation of Europe's Order and Welfare imperatives of governance was the Protestant Reformation's elevation of individuals and their moral worth, and the impact of this transformation of human values, as cause and catalyst, on the spread of popular regimes and adherence to human rights as sources of legitimate rule.[65]

As a cautionary note in this sketch of the impact of values and notions of legitimacy on the imperatives of Order and Welfare, it is important again to emphasize that this is not a one-way street. As Benjamin Friedman reminds us, there is a symbiotic and mutually contingent relation between OWL imperatives and their power structures: "For our society's moral values to nurture the behavior that spurs its economic growth seems especially apt, if . . . rising living standards in turn make our society more open, tolerant, and democratic. Because we value these qualities in moral terms rather than market terms, market forces on their own produce insufficient growth . . . Economic growth not only relies upon moral impetus, it also has positive moral *consequences*. That we may depend at least in part on moral means to our moral ends, even when the link that connects the two is economic, has a particularly satisfying resonance."[66]

The Abolition of Slavery and the Collapse of the Southern Feudal Plantation System

The tumultuous creation and evolution of the history of the American republic also dramatizes the power and promiscuity of legitimacy. A tension that has yet to be resolved was struck at the outset of the regime. There is a fundamental contradiction between the principle of legitimacy of the Declaration of Independence and the uneasy and flawed compromises struck by the Founders to ensure adoption of the Constitution of the United States, creating the federal government. The Declaration of Independence is clear and universal in its stipulation of the source of legitimate government: "We hold these Truths to be self-evident, that all Men are created equal, that they are endowed by their Creator with certain unalienable Rights, that among these are Life, Liberty, and the Pursuit of Happiness. That to secure these Rights, Governments are instituted among Men, deriving their just Power from the Consent of the Governed."

Conversely, the Constitution limited human freedom and embedded inequality of influence and say over public policy into citizenship. It divided the consent of the American people between a federal government and unequally populated state governments. It then divided the federal government into three branches, each exercising some control over the others. The authority invested in the Congress was again divided by place and time, with the election of the House every two years and the Senate every six years, while the president was to be elected by the people as a whole for a four-year term, but their votes were to be filtered through electors whose number were unequally (and inequitably) assigned to each state. On at least two occasions (1876 and 2000), a presidential candidate winning a majority or plurality of the popular vote ceded his victory to a runner-up with more electoral votes.

Finally, the federal judicial branch, whose members are initially determined by the president and the Senate and sit for life, is insulated from popular pressures and, to an appreciable degree, the control of the other two branches. The Preamble of the Constitution proclaims the aim of a more perfect Union, while the institutional organization of the Constitution ensures that the Union will be fractured and fractionalized as a consequence of the federal system, the separation of powers, the spaced election of governmental officials over time and changing circumstances, and an unelected judiciary. Cobbling together a cohesive and continuing ruling majority coalition is all but ruled out by these institutional barriers that reinforce the social and ideological divisions of the American people.

To these structural inequalities in electoral and citizen power must be added slavery, a disparity in the application of the principles of freedom and equality that most directly joined the issue between the Declaration of Independence and the Constitution. In abstruse language, the original Constitution sanctioned slavery and denied the Declaration's self-evident truth that "all Men are created equal." Article 1 of the Constitution declares, "Representatives . . . shall be apportioned among the several States . . . according to their respective Numbers, which shall be determined by adding to the whole Number of free Persons, *including those bound to Service for a Term of Years, and excluding Indians not taxed, three fifths of all other Persons."*[67] Negro slaves are counted as three-fifth persons. Indians, as aliens, did not count at all. Neither group could vote, nor could women until the passage of the Nineteenth Amendment to the Constitution.

The Civil War posed two incompatible systems of governance and two contesting principles of legitimacy. For the North, the locus of ultimate and legitimate coercive power rested with the federal government and the American people. For the South, that locus was invested in each of the several states and their discrete populations. Robert E. Lee, commander of the Army of Northern Virginia, underscored the difference in rejecting the offered command of the Union's troops. In resigning his federal commission, Lee announced his refusal to draw his sword against his beloved state of Virginia, which, incidentally, had the most slaves of any Confederate state.[68] For the rebellious South, the American order, as understood in this discussion of governance, resided in the states. Secession from the federal Constitution was always a residual right of each state and was not renounced in entering the Union. For the North, states could not secede, based on the principle that authority was invested in the people of the United States, in whom the legitimate order of the United States resided.

At issue, too, was the Welfare imperative of governance that would direct the nation's economic development. The South tied its economic well-being to the preservation and extension of the feudal plantation system. The ruling coalitions in each of the Confederate states relied for their material welfare and social status on slave labor, evaluated as property, much like land, machinery, feed, and fertilizer. Slaves were "bound to Service for a Term of Years" (typically a lifetime), much as serfs were during the European feudal period. The North, while still largely agricultural, hitched its future to free farmers and labor, not slavery, and to the modernization and industrialization of the nation's economy to promote economic growth and technological innovation. Its rapid industrialization and the development of an integrated, national railroad and communication system heralded an entirely new economic system than what was inherited at the formation of the republic.

Slavery posed the challenge of reconciling the Declaration of Independence and the Constitution, as well as, more broadly, the choice between two OWL solutions to govern the American people. The western expansion of the United States raised the question of whether slavery would be eventually eliminated or be permitted to extend westward to all of the states of the Union as a constitutional right, as the Supreme Court's decision in the Dred Scott case allowed. Abraham Lincoln's speech to the Republican convention in 1858 explicitly rejected the proposition that these two conflicting principles of citizenship—free and slave—could be reconciled. "A house divided against

itself cannot stand," argued Lincoln. "I believe this government cannot en-
dure, permanently, half slave and half free. . . . Either the opponents of slavery
will arrest the further spread of it and place it where the public mind shall rest
in the belief that it is the course of ultimate extinction, or its advocates will
push it forward till it shall become alike lawful in all the states, old as well as
new, North as well as South."[69]

Multiple factors and forces account for the defeat of the Southern model
for the future of governance of the nation—a feudal plantation system imped-
ing industrialization and technological innovation, and slavery as the inefficient basis for economic growth versus the opening of the West to nonslave
development, promoted by the authority of the federal government in the
service of an expanding American population. In a profound way, best practices, as Adam Smith and Karl Marx argued, won out, accelerated by the force
of arms rather than by the more gradual but inexorable process of eliminating
an economic system dependent on the coercive exploitation of slave labor.

These factors notwithstanding, slavery and discriminatory definitions of
citizenship as the basis for legitimate rule still account in no small part for the
failure of the Southern OWL model. Not negligible in the mix of factors and
forces working against the Southern OWL model was the receding hold of
slavery as a legitimate basis for democratic government and citizenship. As a
consequence of the North's victory, legitimate rule was nationalized and a citizen's identity, heretofore defined by state or locale, was incorporated in the
pursuit of a more perfect Union.[70] The Preamble of the Constitution signified
more than a hollow rhetorical pronouncement. The Civil War actualized the
Preamble as the authoritative source of the Constitution's legitimacy. Widely
shared values do not float freely in space. It would take another century of
struggle to invest African Americans with legal equality as citizens, a project
yet to be fully realized.[71]

Nationalism, Self-Determination, and the Demise of the Eurocentric System

This final illustration of the significance of legitimacy, as a promiscuous
social force, a structure of human power in its own right, and an imperative
of governance, is traced in the rise and fall of the Eurocentric system.[72] This
is a particularly apt example. It sets the stage for stocktaking today of the unlikely prospect of the world's populations agreeing any time soon to shared
notions of legitimacy or a world government. The European powers were the
first to organize the world's populations into a global system of rule. Their
superior war-making and economic capabilities, first displayed in the Spanish and Portuguese conquests of Latin America, eventually subjugated most

of the world's populations to their collective material power—military and economic—and to their differing national imperial rule.

Spain and Portugal were subsequently joined by even more powerful imperial powers, led by Britain and France, which were joined by the Netherlands, Germany, Russia, and Belgium. These colonial empires were bolstered further by the unequal treaties imposed on China and Japan, respectively, by Britain and the United States. The Eurocentric system, as the provisional solution to the imperative of global order, was eventually destroyed by two world wars and the Cold War.

Equally decisive in the formation of the Eurocentric system was the creation by the European powers of an increasingly integrated global economic system. Among the European imperial powers, increased free trade developed in the latter half of the nineteenth century.[73] Meanwhile, and in counterpoint to the globalization of free market exchange, most states typically retained a privileged position for their citizens in governing their colonial empires or in exploiting their extraterritorial advantages in China and for a time in Japan. Japan's rapid modernization, industrialization, and construction of a modern navy, capable of defeating a European power for the first time in the Russo-Japanese War, facilitated its entry as a subordinate member of the Eurocentric system. The Eurocentric system depended upon the preservation of an imperial economic system, bolstered by large conscript armies not only to govern the colonies of each European imperial state but also to exploit the indigenous labor and resources of these holdings.

The Eurocentric system also rested uneasily on widely, if differently defined, notions of European cultural and religious superiority, Britain's rationale, dramatized in Rudyard Kipling's voluminous literary output in defense of the British Empire, was the fostering of "the White Man's Burden."[74] For France, "empire" entailed the assimilation of foreign populations to French culture in pursuit of France's *mission civilatrice*. For Germany, whose emperor believed the German people were "the salt of the earth," rule by Germany was a benefit, not a burden, for foreign populations. Russia added the obligation to defend and extend Orthodox Christian beliefs, including the protection of foreign populations, like Serbia, loyal to the Orthodox Church. These differing notions of European superior moral authority and legitimate rule also resonated in small states, like Belgium's rule over its African subjects. Granted the Congo by the Berlin Conference of 1870, Belgium under King Leopold ruled the Congo, Rwanda, and Burundi as personal fiefdoms, comfortable in the conceit that its African subjects were morally below their European betters whose rule was sanctioned by religion, culture, and national superiority.[75]

These contesting European claims of moral superiority crystallized into national rivalries that resulted in World War I. Nationalism, an "imagined community," in Benedict Anderson's phrase,[76] created the modern, secular nation-state, foreshadowed in the Treaty of Westphalia two centuries earlier.[77] Europe's populations were molded into discrete, competing, relatively cohesive political entities with shared identities. With the help of historians,[78] individuals were progressively defined, not as members of a united Christendom or by the feudal order or locale into which they were born—Brittany, Normandy, Wales, Hanover, Saxony, or Florence—but as citizens of a nation-state to which they owed their political loyalty and in terms of which their moral worth and identities were cast. The subsequent emergence of a Eurocentric system, composed of a constellation of European empires, served, paradoxically, as the transition belt for the globalization of nationalism that united Europeans into largely integrated political entities, many ready to fight and die for the emotionally charged abstractions of national unity and self-perceived superiority.[79]

The fall of the Eurocentric system ushered in an entirely new system of OWL governance of the European peoples and the world's populations at large. In this process, the principle of national self-determination, as the basis for legitimate rule, played a decisive role in the collapse of the Eurocentric system.[80] It became the rallying cry of oppressed populations to mobilize and nationalize local populations to overthrow European rule—European nationalism created Europe's undoing.[81] Between the end of World War II and the implosion of the Soviet Union into fifteen national republics and the end of white rule in South Africa, most of the world's peoples established their own nation-states. The European export of the principle of self-determination, yet to be fully realized among Kurds, Palestinians, Tibetans, or other insurgent groups, has been internalized by most peoples around the globe. Kosovo and South Sudan, the latest entrants into the nation-state system, exemplify the continuing force of national sentiment and the promiscuous power of legitimacy across the globe's populations. Conversely, where states are internally flawed by contesting religious and ideologically motivated groups, as in Syria and Iraq, nationalism as an integrating force has not taken root. The principal source of violence and civil war is precisely due to the absence of a shared view of legitimate rule.

The Way Forward

This chapter has presented a provisional theory of governance. It pivots on the contesting imperatives of Order, Welfare, and Legitimacy. Each posits an autonomous structure of power, competing processes of decision-making, and conflicting incentives for actor choices. The democratic states and peoples of the world society have responded to these imperatives. For Order, they have erected the global state; for Welfare, they have installed a global market system; for Legitimacy, they advance popular rule and human rights, based on the principles of the freedom and equality of all humans. How well have they responded to OWL imperatives? The following chapters address this question.

Notes

1. These dual tensions between policy outcomes and the governance of those outcomes are developed in chapter 1 through the analogy of conflict within a family.

2. *New York Times*, January 5, 2015, p. 1.

3. The voluminous scholarship of Mark Juergensmeyer (2003, 2005, 2008) details the rejection by religious communities—Muslim, Hindi, Buddhist, Christian, and Jewish—of the secular liberal state. See also Bozeman (1960, 1984) as well as Huntington (1996) for earlier works sounding the same themes.

4. Phillips (1996).

5. See Finer (1999) for an overall review of the rise and demise of governments. Relevant, too, is Mann (1986, 1993).

6. Relying on pure models is a method of thought as old as the Greek dialogues. These pure or ideal models animate social science and humanistic research. OWL imperatives are presented here as three autonomous, but irreconcilable, structures of power that are the *analytic* components of the governance of all human societies, each with its own processes of decision-making and discrete incentives for actor choices.

7. For a more detailed discussion of relying on pure or ideal models, see "A Brief Note on Method" at the end of the volume.

8. See Hobbes (1997). I have principally relied on the Richard Flathman edition of *Leviathan.* It also includes a useful introduction to the text.

9. Hobbes (1997, p. 70).

10. The term "promiscuously" is drawn from the magisterial work on social change of Michael Mann. The notion of violence moving to an endpoint or pure form in defining social relations is also found in Karl von Clausewitz's theory of war. See Clausewitz (1976).

11. Mann (1986, 1993, 1990); McNeill (1998); Tilly (1975 ["Reflections"], 1990, 1975 [*Formation*]).

12. My reading of Leo Strauss, both his works and as a former student, leads me to this assessment. See Strauss (1953, 1963).

13. Strauss (1963, pp. vii–viii).

14. Thucydides (1998, pp. 227–31).

15. Kagan (2003, p. 25).

16. Thucydides (1998, pp. 11–12).

17. Thucydides (1998). Also useful is Kagan (2003), who recounts the overexten-sion of Athenian power and Athens's final collapse, suggesting that democracies by majority vote, no less than authoritarian systems, are quite prepared to self-destruct.

18. Hobbes (1997, p. 70 [italics added]).

19. Shaw (2000 [*Theory*], p. 259). See also Shaw (1994).

20. See Mearsheimer (2001); Waltz (1979, 1999) for examples of this deconstruc-tion process.

21. Waltz (1979) dismisses Marx's contribution to governance. The poverty of this move is defensible only if the Welfare and Legitimacy imperatives and their coun-tervailing structures of power, as limits to the Order imperative, are assumed away as indispensable instruments of governance—a dubious academic ploy that misleads more than informs.

22. See Schroeder (1994) for the Vienna system and Dinan (2010) for the EU.

23. Diamond (1997).

24. McNeill & McNeill (2003).

25. Landes (1998).

26. Quoted in Elliott (1981, p. 334).

27. Allan & Goldmann (1992); Edelheit & Edelheit (1992); Eden (1993).

28. See notes 20 and 21. For a critique, see Kolodziej (2005, pp. 77–174).

29. Rosecrance (1986); Cerny (2010).

30. http://www.huffingtonpost.com/2011/01/25/obama-state-of-the-union-_1_n_813478.html.

31. Marx (1970, pp. 3–4). See Elster (1985) for a comprehensive analysis and ref-erences cited there. For a brief review of Marxist theory, consult Singer (2000). For a critique of Marxism from a libertarian perspective, see Hayek (1948, 1960, 1988).

32. Quoted in Singer (2000, p. 49).

33. Peters (2009); Peters & Besley (2006); Peters, Marginson, & Murphy (2009).

34. Quoted in Elliott (1981, p. 212).

35. William McNeill shares their view with a twist—namely, that humans con-tinually exploit and leverage that knowledge in developing best economic and social practices, which are circulated through the species to shape their mutually contingent lives and their environment. McNeill & McNeill (2003); McNeill (1963, 1983, 1986, 1992, 2010).

36. The enormous corpus of Max Weber's work, following closely on Marx, both af-firms the critical significance of economic exchange and institutions in shaping human societies and insists on the power of the state and ideas, notably religion and culture, as indispensable to explain and understand how societies emerge and evolve and govern themselves. See, inter alia, Weber (1958 [*From Max Weber*; "Politics"], 1968, 1992).

37. Cox & Alm (2007); Schumpeter (1942, pp. 82–85).

38. Friedrich von Hayek argues that economic progress, while unpredictable, is still inevitable in the long run as a consequence of human freedom, provided that the coercive power of the state can be limited to defense of liberty. See Hayek (1948, 1954, 1967).

39. Giddens (1993, especially pp. 120ff.) makes this point.

40. Smith (1937, p. 13).

41. For a very accessible, nontechnical overview of the workings of the market system and its dependence on a global civil society, see Charles Lindblom (1977, 1988, 2001).

42. Smith (1937, p. 13).

43. Eric Jones develops these themes in his influential works; see Jones (1987, 1988).

44. Cameron (1993, especially pp. 130–222). Also see Roncaglia (2001, pp. 115–54).

45. Smith (1937, p. 14).

46. Ibid., p. 13.

47. The genius and prescience of Adam Smith's *The Wealth of Nations* is its global perspective, unique for his era.

48. Smith (1937, p. 423).

49. Lindblom (2001).

50. Michael Sandel (2012) exposes the pervasive and negative influence of economic thinking on social values. His discussion illustrates through multiple anecdotes the promiscuous force of the Welfare imperative once unleashed.

51. Eric Jones makes this case (1988). See also Smith (1976, Book IV). The power of the English crown as a result of its liberal economic policy is also explored in Findlay & O'Rourke (2007, pp. 311–65).

52. For a general description of the impact of the environment on the technological development and power of societies through time, consult Diamond (1997). For a counterproposal that stresses culture as the principal source of technological development, see Landes (1969, 1998). Supporting Landes but probing deeper into the moral dimensions of economic development is Benjamin Friedman (2005).

53. Rousseau (1950, p. 3).

54. I was first introduced to these issues by Leo Strauss as a student at the University of Chicago. Critical, too, are the works of Friedrich Nietzsche, notably *Thus Spake Zarathustra* (1905). Rousseau still seems to me to have defined the problem of legitimacy as the foundation of governance, if not the solution, as well as anyone; hence he is the staff on which this discussion of legitimacy leans.

55. Maryanski & Turner (1992).

56. Ibid.

57. Roger Masters, who translated *The Social Contract*, elaborates on Rousseau's conception of human nature (1997).

58. This theme is developed in Donnelly (1984, 1989, 1993). See also Kolodziej (2003).

59. Beaud (2000); Bendix (1964 [*Nation-Building*], 1978).

60. See Mann (1986, 1993) for a discussion of the promiscuity of the legitimating imperative. Chapter 7 develops the imperative of Legitimacy as a key component of all human governance.

61. See Hedley Bull (1977) and the English school of international relations theory. See also Buzan (1993, 2004).

62. See Hassner (1997); Hoffmann & Fidler (1991); and Waltz (1959) for a more extended discussion of Rousseau's pessimistic view of inescapable and ceaseless armed conflict between states,

63. The power of the imperative of Legitimacy is developed in chapter 7.

64. Weber (1958 [*The Protestant Ethic*]). Weber's thesis that the Protestant Reformation was a key factor explaining the rise of capitalism has come under sharp criticism, since, for example, it does not seem to explain economic growth in Catholic communities. It seems reasonable to argue that the coefficient before the factor of religious ideology and economic growth is not zero.

65. Tracing the history of the nation-state and the many factors contributing to its ascendancy is beyond the scope of this discussion. Relevant citations include Mann (1993); McGrew & Lewis (1992); Shaw (2000 [*Theory*]). Charles Tilly (1975 ["Reflections"; *Formation*]) is especially important for the evolution of the European nation-state. That this unit, as a response of the world's populations to the imperative of Order, was not inevitable is covered in Spruyt (1994). The spread of the nation-state system is traced in Watson (1984).

66. Friedman (2005, p. 19). For supportive evidence, see Landes (1998).

67. Italics added.

68. Ellis (2002, p. 102). Virginia had almost three hundred thousand slaves in 1860, three times as many as North and South Carolina, each with about one hundred thousand slaves.

69. See http://www.pbs.org/wgbh/aia/part4/4h2934t.html. For contrasting interpretations of the moral dilemma confronting the American people, leading to the Civil War, see Burt (2013); Jaffa (2009).

70. Constitution of the United States.

71. Burt (2013). John Burt makes the case for Lincoln's conception of his role and mission in leading the Union in the Civil War as a moral responsibility, quite apart from the political and economic interests prompting and driving the American Civil War. A persuasive explanation for the conflict loses much of its force if this moral dimension of it is marginalized or dismissed.

72. Hobsbawm (1990, 1969, 1975, 1989); Watson (1992).

73. Cameron (1993, pp. 191–248); Findlay & O'Rourke (2007, 365–427).

74. Rudyard Kipling's *Kim*, a remarkable exercise in syncretic religious exposition, still elevates European and English culture above Hindu, Muslim, and Buddhist religious doctrine and practices.

75. Hochschild (1998) details the depredations inflicted on vulnerable Congolese populations by Belgian rule, justified by these invidious cultural dismissals of the value of subject populations.

76. Anderson (1992).

77. Some historians go back even further into the medieval period to find the origins of the modern state. See Strayer (2005).

78. William McNeill calls on historians to instill in their students and the public their membership in a global system; see McNeill (1992).

79. The scholarly literature on nationalism is vast. Representative examples are Anderson (1992); Bloom (1993); Breuilly (1994); Deutsch (1956); Deutsch & Merritt (1970); Gellner (1983, 1994); Hayes (1926, 1968); Hobsbawm (1990); Smith (1971).

80. Ibid.

81. See http://www.youtube.com/watch?v=RGLrdjkcLdM&NR=1 for an instructive YouTube presentation of the failure of French forces to defeat Algerian insurgents despite wholesale terror inflicted on the native population.

II

CRITIQUE OF THE DEMOCRATIC SOLUTIONS TO GLOBAL GOVERNANCE

4

The Global State and Its Rivals

If politics are about social relations in the broadest sense . . . they are also about power, and especially about state power. The key question of all politics are whether, and how, the power and organization of the state can be brought into harmony with the needs of society—of people in their social relations.

—Martin Shaw, *Theory of the Global State:*
Globality As an Unfinished Revolution

THIS CHAPTER EVALUATES THE democratic global state. Unlike the West-phalian/Hobbesian/Weberian state (WHW), focused narrowly on the imperative of Order, the democracies fuse the Order imperative to the Welfare and Legitimacy imperatives to fashion their preferred model for effective and legitimate global governance. The democracies balance the conflicting claims of these three contesting power structures, rival decisional processes, and competing incentives for actor choices to govern the interdependent exchanges of their populations. The governance model of the democracies is also advanced as their candidate for the rule of all of the world's populations and states.

What distinguishes the global state from its opponents, described below, is the larger, more encompassing responsibilities that it has assumed rather than alternative, antidemocratic models of global governance. The greater reach and power of the global states are the consequence of the demands made on the states by the converging social contracts of the diverse democracies of the global society. The global state is no less a security state than its

WHW rival, but it is a lot more. The global state differs fundamentally from the reductionist and recidivist model of the WHW warfare state. Moreover, and in response to the Welfare imperative, the global state is also a *market, trading, competitive,* and *entrepreneurial* state. To these welfare functions, it has also become the *science and technology, research and development,* and *innovative* product state. No less is the state expected to provide for the transportation and communications networks, which undergird its welfare obligations. Backing all these functions, finally, is the state assumption of the role as *investor* of last resort and guarantor of the state's financial system.

Building on these assets, the global state commands the resources needed to assume the mantle of the *safety net* state. It provides for the education, health, relaxation, and recreation of its populations. It is also obliged to afford them a supportive environment not only presently but also for future generations. The supply of these multiple and competing obligations under conditions of scarce resources must also be funneled through the deliberative processes of decision and legitimacy of a popular democracy. To these burdens of the global state must be added the responsibility to foster civil liberties and human rights and to extend the benefits of democratic rule and these freedoms to nondemocratic states and peoples. The global state is thus a *democratic* and *human rights* state.

The gradual assumption of these obligations over two centuries, marked by the American and French Revolutions, dramatize the emergence of the global state as the instrument of popular rule. Whether the global state can prevail in a global society, populated by formidable opponents of the democratic promise, remains an open question. There is always the lurking danger that the global state will relapse again to its earlier WHW form as it did in World Wars I and II.

As the vehicle for the transformation of the WHW state system, the global state confronts three challenges: diminishing the warfare proclivities of the WHW system, whether in the guise of the antidemocratic secular or religious state; addressing the immediate challenges of climate change, terrorist threats to vulnerable populations, and containment of the infectiously damaging spread of failed states; and providing collective goods to sustain economic growth and combat inequality and poverty (covered in chapters 5 and 6).

This chapter contends that the global state meets Martin Shaw's challenge more decisively and comprehensively than do its rivals. The global state brings "the power and organization of the state . . . into harmony with the needs of society—of people in their social relations." Whatever the shortcomings of the global state, and they are many and significant, it surpasses its competitors in fulfilling the multiple needs of not only democratic peoples but also nondemocratic peoples.

Properties of the Global State versus the WHW Leviathan

The global state is both a principal driver and a resulting evolutionary outcome of globalization and modernization. In this self-reinforcing causal loop, it is both a perpetrator and a product of globalizing forces. The global state is constantly reinventing itself to cope with new challenges and to exploit opportunities for public benefit. It is a flexible institutional instrument capable of addressing the evolving challenges confronting the populations of a global state and those of the global society more generally. In contrast to the global state, the WHW state is fixed, static, and functionally circumscribed in its responsibilities. The WHW state is the beginning, not the end point, of the state's evolutionary development in its present form as a global state in the service of the evolving *general wills* of its subjects.

Unlike its competitors for global governance, the legitimacy of the global state rests on periodic free and unfettered election of officials invested with authority to rule and make laws that also bind them. The social compacts of the democracies also protect minorities from what James Madison termed "majority factions" bent on their oppression. From the moral perspective of the global state, all states and political regimes are now expected to adhere to the protocols of democratic rule, civil liberties, and human rights. A state's legitimacy extends not only to the rule of law of its subjects but also to noncitizens crossing its borders as members of a global civil society. Global states are obliged to foster the free movement of people, ideas, goods, and services. That these rights are often recognized more in the breach than in the observance in no way diminishes the moral obligations of the global democratic states from commitment to these ideals. For example, the shortcomings of European and American immigration policies in highlighting the gap between promise and realization of human rights protections underscore the vitality of these ideals, which are absent from the practices of WHW states or those which establish a religious test for citizenship. Over the course of several centuries, the expansion of political space occupied by the global state has transformed the global society by installing these ideals in the practices of global states and, by that token, these ideals are touchstones to expose the depredations of authoritarian states and regimes.

Absent both the power of the global state and the creation of global civil society, the erection of a global market system would not have been possible. The global state fulfills Adam Smith's vision of the state as a market state. Smith envisioned the emergence and extension of a system of free exchange to facilitate trade and barter to encompass all of humanity. That vision, as Karl Polanyi has shown, was brought to life by the intervention of state power and not simply by self-executing market mechanisms: "The road to the free market was opened and kept open by an enormous increase in continuous, centrally organized and controlled interventionism."[1] It would take two world wars, tens of millions dead and maimed, as well as wholesale destruction of the treasure of implicated states and peoples to bring the market system to fruition. Even authoritarian states—like China, which resists the expansion of the global state—have been compelled to either join the market system as an engine of economic growth or, like the Soviet Union, be "opted out" of the state system.

Adam Smith's trading state, as Richard Rosecrance affirms, responds to the Welfare imperative, creating an autonomous structure of power as a central component of global governance. The trading state depends on the state system but, through feedback and blowback, it shapes state policies and behavior.[2] The progressive and unprecedented growth in the wealth of nations is attributable in no small part to the trading state. The upward climb of global world product (GWP) of the world economy since World War II would never have been achieved in the absence of a global trading system. The World Bank estimates that approximately half of the over $70 trillion in GWP in 2011 was attributable to merchandise trade.[3] The economic impact of the movement of labor across state boundaries can be measured in the rise of worker remittances. These grew from less than $300 million in 1977 to over $140 billion in 2011.[4] Annual large-scale human migration, largely driven by labor movements, is now embedded as a continuing feature of global society. Not counting millions more in refugees, *World Development Indicators* of the International Monetary Fund (IMF) show an annual increase in world labor migration from 75.5 million in 1960 to 213.5 million in 2010 with no indication that increasing numbers will be arrested any time soon.

As a trading state to which the creation of the World Trade Organization owes its founding, the global state has also become a competitive state to ensure the welfare of its populations by striving to level the playing field of states participating in the global trading system.[5] These economic webs of interdependencies, entangling the world's global and WHW states and peoples, have had significant impacts on global order. Tempered by the expected loss of material gains are armed disputes that might disrupt trade, investment, and labor flows. Over two centuries ago, Immanuel Kant anticipated these cross-pressured incentives facilitating peace: "The spirit of commerce sooner or later takes hold of every people, and it cannot exist side by side with war. And of all of the powers (or means) at the disposal of the power of the state, financial power can probably be relied on most. Thus states find themselves compelled to promote the noble cause of peace, though not exactly from motives of morality."[6]

Trading among democratic states fulfills Kant's prediction, although there is always the possibility that the Welfare imperative may, as in World Wars I and II, be overwhelmed by the power of the Order imperative and the WHW state. Kant's optimism to the contrary notwithstanding, the possibility of armed conflict between trading states is always present. The chaos rampant across the Middle East among the states of the region, turning the Arab Spring of 2010 into the winter of 2015, and the Russian intervention in Georgia, Ukraine, and Syria reveal the WHW state as the key component of the warfare system. While the likelihood of war between democratic global states has appreciably diminished,[7] as the number of these states has grown to approximately 120 today,[8] the probability of war between WHW states and between trading global and WHW states remains a clear and present danger. The classic example of the weakness of economic interdependence to forestall interstate war is Norman Angell's untimely prediction on the eve of World War I that war among the European states would not break out because they were too dependent on each other for continued economic growth. To these threats to security must be added the rising conflicts between nonstate actors and global and WHW states over the legitimacy of state rule and by implication a profound conflict over the terms of global governance.

Slighted in the public discourse of open societies, notably in the United States, is the critical role played by the global state in advancing scientific discovery, technological innovation, and economic growth, prerequisites if the global state is to supply safety nets for health, aging, recreation, and education of its population. A growing body of scholarship challenges the popular belief that venture capitalists and market incentives have been the principal drivers of technological innovations and the commercialization of new products and services. Fred Block observes, "The Federal government has dramatically expanded its capacity to finance and support efforts of the private sector to commercialize new technologies. But the partisan logic of U.S. politics has worked to make these efforts invisible to mainstream public debate."[9] United States governmental support for new innovations in electronics, medicine, energy, and transportation has been largely justified by the needs of national security or public health rather than simply by interest in the development of public goods and economic growth. Below the surface of the dominant narrative that the free market and venture capitalists know best where to invest in innovation is, as Block notes, a vast "hidden developmental state" that must be credited with having been the principal instigator of innovation and the creation of new markets.[10] Global states Canada, Japan, South Korea, and members of the European Union have also become entrepreneurial states.[11]

The development of the Internet illustrates the central role of the global state in research and development, in inventing new technologies, and in creating global markets.[12] The initial impetus for the Internet was prompted by the need for a decentralized communication system to support the American nuclear deterrent system. In case of a Soviet nuclear strike against the United States, it was imperative that the command and control system that directed American nuclear land, sea, and air forces would survive to direct a counterblow against Moscow. The Pentagon's Defense Advanced Research Project Agency (DARPA) organized a network of federal agencies and governmental laboratories, academic research groups, and private corporate experts to develop a unique social system of networking professionals—corporate, academic, and governmental—to spur scientific knowledge and its rapid transformation into technological innovations and marketable products. With the agencies of the federal government having prepared the scientific and technical foundation for the Internet, its stunning commercialization followed rapidly. The Internet's viral spread around the globe as a motor of the global economy and social media is typically attributed to Silicon Valley and venture capital. This remains the dominant narrative to explain the Internet's success. Lost from sight, as S. W. Leslie shows, "Silicon Valley owes its present configuration to patterns of federal spending, corporate strategies, industry-university relationships, and technological innovation shaped by the assumptions and priorities of Cold War defense policies."[13]

The DARPA model erected a public-private expert network of knowledge, easily transmitted to interested parties, to address national and, by implication, global needs. This proactive developmental model was applied to computers, jet planes, civilian nuclear energy, lasers, and biotechnology. Apple's innovations in computers and electronics, which vaulted the corporation to the top of the multinational corporate world in capital holdings, drew heavily from the scientific and technological breakthroughs produced by the DARPA model.[14] Similarly, big pharmaceuticals profited freely from the discovery of new molecular entities supported by governmental research and development funding and management leadership. These are the underpinnings of many new and profitable drugs.[15] The rapid development of nanotechnology also owes much to governmental initiative during the Clinton presidency and thereafter.[16]

The global states of Europe and Asia have not been left out as entrepreneurial states. Some, like Japan and France, have also developed expert professional networks to advance innovation. Japan has led in television display panels as well as in battery and automobile technology.[17] France, taking a page from DARPA, promoted the development and commercialization of advanced weapons systems as well as military aircraft and missiles.[18] European cooperation among global states launched the Airbus to challenge US dominance in commercial airline production. European states also created the European Organization for Nuclear Research (CERN). It operates the largest particle physics laboratory in the world with a staff of over 2500 and hosts over 12,000 nuclear researchers from around the globe. China has also taken a lead in nanotechnology, begun in the United States, and along with Germany and Denmark is innovating in green technologies.[19]

Several factors help to explain the rise of the entrepreneurial state, extending piecemeal to WHW states like China. Global state response to the Welfare imperative is a primary motivation, as populations demand "more now." The uncertainties associated with developing new products based on new scientific discoveries and technological advances deter large-scale private investment. Venture capitalists require more certainty of a return on investment for the kinds of initiatives undertaken by states. States become the investors of last resort, a function that they perform in stabilizing global financial markets. States can also wait longer for a payoff than private investors, assuming high risk that deters private investors. States also provide the public goods, which supply the resources not only to advance scientific discoveries and technological innovation but also to distribute these benefits widely, rapidly, and freely—functions that profit-making corporations have little incentive to furnish.

That many states may have not yet reached the fulsome status of a global state does not negate identifying the global state as a transformational reformulation of the state system.[20] A key part of the explanation of its continued extension through global civil society can be attributed to the global state as a superior solution to OWL imperatives of global governance than its rivals.[21] What is important to recognize is the tendency of divergent peoples to move their states toward the acquisition of the properties defining the global state. As a work in progress, the global state both cooperates and competes with other actors in their mutually contingent negotiations and power struggles to define the evolving global society and its governance.

Conceptually isolating the state from the economic, religious, cultural, and ideational forces and social movements that shape and shove globalization, grievously misconstrues and unduly minimizes the central role of the state, notably the global state, as a strategic site for the processes of globalization. State power contributes more to global economic development than simply as arbiter of last resort in enforcing contracts or in defining property rights, key determinants of a stable and productive global market system.[22] Saskia Sassen captures the dynamics of the contemporary global state *in* and *of* the global society as a strategic site for the processes of globalization and as both driver of and driven by these processes: "The state is one of the strategic institutional domains in which critical work on the development of globalization takes place. . . . The state becomes the site for foundational transformations in the relationship between the private and public domains, in the state's internal balance of power, and in the larger field of both national and global forces within which the state now has to function."[23]

This is an especially pertinent point with respect to global states. Having defeated formidable competitors—Fascist, Nazi, or Communist centralized economic WHW states—the global trading and entrepreneurial state contributes mightily to a global order congenial and supportive of an increasing number of democratic states and a free market exchange system.[24] The human and material costs to institutionalize this system have scarcely been free. Nor is the maintenance and extension of these institutions without continuing high human and material costs. Like the creation of the state and the state system itself, the slow expansion of the market system, as a solution to the Welfare imperative has over the last several centuries entailed tens of millions of deaths and wholesale destruction of traditional societies to effect this transformational change of the world's economy.[25]

No less costly in blood and treasure has been the rise of the open, liberal democratic state. Democratic regimes share a set of common principles and institutions: the rule of law, sanctioned by popular will; the encouragement, protection, and proliferation of nonstate actors; the expansion of private authority; and support for an increasingly transnational global civil society.[26] The global state is expected, too, to ensure the extension of popular, democratic rule and the extension and protection of human rights.[27] These are primary objectives of US foreign policy. Membership in the European Union also requires state commitment to these ideals, exemplified in its absorption of the East European states of the Soviet Union's Warsaw Pact into the democratic fold. The global state's effectiveness and legitimacy in providing for global order and welfare entails discharge of a host of challenging and competing missions. Absent global state power, engaged in a complex process of cooperation, competition, and conflict with WHW states in defining and negotiating the evolution of the global society, the state system might well have remained confined to its dismal WHW role, with the conditions of life of the world's populations reduced to a Hobbesian end game—or the tendency thereto.

If we now view the state and the nation-state system from the perspective of the global state, the question before us is to assess whether the global state and a globalized state system comprise an effective and legitimate response to the governance of a world society and to the needs of the world's population. The state has never been stronger in terms of its material, coercive, economic, and regulatory power. This is especially true of the democratic global states, which emerged ascendant from the Cold War struggle with the WHW Soviet state.

Nor, paradoxically, has the global state ever been weaker as a consequence of the expanding universe of its enlarging obligations. The material and non-material power available to the state, while unprecedented, still falls progressively short of the capacities required to realize the enlarged scope of the aims, interests, and values assigned to it by the world's populations. State power has certainly increased but so also has the power of a proliferating number of nonstate actors, notably transnational corporations, within an expanding global society to constrain the effectiveness of the state. The reach of the state, defined by its increased functions in responding to the imperative of global order, is well beyond its present grasp.

The challenge confronting democratic global states is whether their solution to OWL imperatives and global governance will prevail over their formidable rivals, notably those secular and religious states committed to the WHW state system. Whether the democratic model will expand in power and influence in shaping global governance will depend, as noted earlier, on the collective capacity of the global states to forestall resort to war in resolving conflicts, to protect the world environment, notably stanching global warming, and to contain the spread of terrorism, crime, and failed states.

As the assessment below suggests, the democracies have a long way to go to effectively address these issues. The road is no less steep and daunting in their striving to gain the adherence of nondemocratic states and peoples to their model for global governance.

The Nation-State System as a Warfare System: The Globalization of the Security Dilemma

The United Nations Charter extends the Hobbesian security dilemma to the nation-state system. Article 2 bases the authority of the United Nations on states, not peoples. It stipulates that "the Organization is based on the principle of the sovereign equality of all its Members." Neither the United Nations nor its member states are authorized "to intervene in matters which are essentially within the domestic jurisdiction of any state." While this prohibition has often been transgressed in the history of the United Nations—note the United Nations received the Nobel Peace Prize in 2005 for its promotion of human rights, challenging the sovereignty of targeted states that oppress their populations—the United Nations largely remains an agent of the states comprising its membership. It can do little to circumvent the big powers that dominate through their veto power in the Security Council. Nor has the United Nations been able to discipline small, recalcitrant states. They have successfully resisted UN sanctions or resolutions to abide by the demands of a majority of its members, including the consensus of the permanent members of the Security Council. The list of UN-defying states is long and promises to get longer, as the record of sanctions imposed on North Korea suggests. Exposed is the impotence of the United Nations as an independent actor to impose its will on intransigent states.

The member states form a fragile and unstable global security system,[28] extending their differential reach, if not their complete control, over most of the world's populations. That system of states, abstracted from all other transactions between states and peoples, has several self-defeating properties. In a decentralized system of states, each claiming to be sovereign and possessed as the final authority to use or threaten force to arbitrate domestic and foreign conflicts, states are induced, as realists contend, to make their security one of their principal, if not exclusive, preoccupations. This is especially the case with the WHW state. The structure of incentives generated by this decentralized system obliges them to be vitally interested in the distribution of violent capabilities across states and peoples. These concerns now extend to powerful nonstate criminal or terrorist actors, which are capable of capturing or co-opting a state.

States are particularly concerned with any change in the overall distribution of physical power or in the capabilities of other states. These changing power configurations threaten to undermine the security regime on which each state relies for its physical security and its ability to arbitrate conflicts in which it is engaged, in its favor. Note, for example, the concern of the Israeli government about the prospect that Iran might develop nuclear weapons, while it arms itself with large arsenals of these weapons to bolster its security.[29]

The widespread worry currently expressed in Western capitals and Japan regarding what is perceived as rising Chinese military power, encompassing the development of a blue water navy, a nuclear arsenal capable of being lethally projected across continents, and a sophisticated space program, including tested killer satellites, illustrates the latest instance of state concern with the relative power of potential rivals. This sense of insecurity in Western-Chinese security relations begins to replicate the naval rivalry between Britain and Germany at the turn of the twentieth century,[30] the French-German remilitarization before World Wars I and II,[31] and the titanic nuclear competition between the United States and the Soviet Union during the Cold War.[32]

With the explosion of nonstate actors in possession of armed capabilities, the security of the state extends beyond other states to nonstate actors, like terrorist organizations and insurgent groups. The threat posed by drug gangs to the Mexican state or the FARC insurgency against the Colombian state exemplify the fragility of state power in combating criminal elements. The spread of militant Islamic groups from Syria, Iraq, Yemen, Afghanistan,

Pakistan, Mali, Nigeria, and Somalia also constitutes a continuing threat to the state and its capacity to ensure public order. These threats are not confined to the state borders in which they arise but extend to other states and populations, as the depredations of the terrorist group Boko Haram illustrate. Its forces threaten both Nigeria and all of its neighboring states.

In a nutshell, a nation-state system is a warfare system. Appeal to force or coercive threats to impose a state's preferences on other actors is embedded in state transactions. The security dilemma can be relaxed through long experience of peaceful relations with another state (say the United States and Canada), through confidence-building measures, or agreed-upon levels of armaments and war preparations that reflect a determination of the cooperating states to mutually define an arms control and security regime on which they can reasonably rely in pursuing their particular interests.

That fragile regime can quickly erode under the assault of repeated blows to its reliability, real or perceived, as the disastrous run-ups to World War I evidence.[33] By 1914 the major European powers had defected from the Congress of Vienna regime, instituted in 1815, because they were unable to reconcile their increasingly clashing security interests, their enlarging global imperial ambitions, and the self-destructive national fervor for war that the leadership of these states fueled. Nor were the European states despite their shared history and culture able to escape being prisoners of their unbridled arms races and the high-risk military strategies directing their forces. They preferred to rely on their own material power, in league with allies, to impose their preferences on their rivals.

Witness, too, the successive breakdowns and armed hostilities between Israel and the Arab states and Palestinians as well as those between India and Pakistan. The tenuous tissue of mutual trust that supports a security regime can be readily torn and shredded, given the underlying distrust that is inherent in a universally shared, if differentially salient, security dilemma by the members of the state system. The anarchical structure of military power and legitimacy of a nation-state system disposes its members to armed hostilities quite apart from the specific, immediate provocations that might engender war.

A relation between two or more actors pivoting primarily on force or coercive threats is the epitome of a negative interdependent relationship. Each mutually holds the other hostage to its security interests. They are necessarily in what can be understood as a negatively cooperative relationship in the sense that the security of one is a function of the loss or degradation of the security relation of the other. This pure zero-sum game models the security dilemma confronting actual or potential rivals within the global society. They advance their security interests if they can defeat, deter, and defend against their rival(s). Or, as in the case of arms control, rivals may have incentive to cooperate in underwriting a security regime that provides more benefits than open hostilities or a precipitous erosion of cooperation that might result in an armed exchange costly to one or the other or both rivals.

Unlike the WHW state, the global state must balance the value of using force to support its security interests against other highly valued preferences, including sustainable economic growth and the fostering of civil liberties and human rights, objectives that compete with the incentives associated with security. Determining the urgency and scope of a security threat or assessing what armed force should be used to address it or, alternatively, to employ noncoercive instruments (diplomacy, compromise, sanctions, etc.) to cope with the threat are scarcely easy and clear-cut decisions to make. WHW states, which within this context are not as hard pressed to make trade-off decisions as global states, either tend to ignore the welfare and legitimacy costs of using force or dismiss them as irrelevant in confronting a security issue. Illustrative is Vladimir Putin's Russia in its military interventions in the Middle East and in the states of the former Soviet Union, which have large Russian-speaking populations, the so-called near abroad, which the Russian state seeks to reclaim within its sphere of influence.

The United Nations has attempted to relax the security dilemma by expanding its role in peace operations. Its efforts have been largely piecemeal rather than comprehensive in developing a global security system on which all of the states and populations of the globe could rely. Both states and peoples must still depend on their own self-help efforts or on provisionally aligned like-minded states. The United Nations has never been able to implement the military clauses of the UN Charter. That would have entailed the creation of a UN security force. In coping with threats to regional and global peace, the United Nations depends on the unreliable ad hoc, time-urgent contributions of member states to cope with each peacekeeping and peacemaking operation. The genocide in Rwanda in the 1990s, resulting in the loss of upward of a million lives, exemplifies the impotence of the United Nations to deal with these human disasters.[34]

The terms "peacekeeping" and "peacemaking" are highly complex and flexible. They do not admit to a simple listing that covers the multiple activities that march under these banners. There is not sufficient space to describe the many discrete activities associated with each term or the disputes arising over their use and applicability to global security threats.[35] These entail, for example, the stationing of neutral troops between combatants to preclude the re-eruption of hostilities, observation and verification of cease-fires and arms control accords, investigation of human rights violations, the monitoring of elections, the conduct of small-scale military operations—large in the overthrow of the Khaddafi regime in Libya—to protect vulnerable populations, the provision of humanitarian assistance, or modest assistance in state-building. In 2009, the United Nations Department of Peacekeeping Operations (UNDPKO) listed sixty-three peacekeeping operations since 1948. Seventeen operations were being supported by UNDPKO. Africa led with eight sites, followed by the Middle East and Cyprus with five, and the remainder in Asia. An estimated 115,231 civilian and military personnel from 118 countries served or were serving in these operations.

The cost of these operations from June 2007 to June 2008 was $7.75 billion. Since the inception of UN peacekeeping operations through the first decade of the twenty-first century, approximately $61 billion has been spent on peacekeeping operations by the UN. While this level of expenditure may appear impressive, it pales before the annual defense budget of the United States, which annually tops one-half trillion dollars. The UN peacekeeping budget, moreover, is spread thinly across the globe, highlighting the gap between the number and complexity of the conflicts that the United Nations is required to address and the limited means available to cope with them, a gap created by an anarchical state system that generates negative incentives for selfish states to shirk their obligations to assist vulnerable populations (say Rwandans, Syrians, or Nigerians).

To supplement the security and foreign policy missions of the United Nations and to circumvent its failings, states have relied on regional organizations and intergovernmental organizations to advance their interests. Article 51 of the UN Charter sanctions regional security organizations. The Atlantic Alliance and its NATO military arm joined the United States and most of the European states into a military alliance that has survived the Cold War and its aftermath. The European Union also purports to be developing its own, independent security and foreign policy for its twenty-eight members. The Organization for Security and Co-operation in Europe (OSCE) groups, in turn, most of the states of the European Union, Russia and its former republics; the United States and thirty-five countries of North and South America are organized into the Organization of American States. In Asia, ten Southeast Asian countries are grouped within the Association of Southeast Asian Nations (ASEAN). ASEAN subsequently spawned the ASEAN Regional Forum (ARF) that extends to twenty-one states, including the United States. ARF provides an informal forum to discuss security issues of interest to its members. It is not organized to directly address them. Chinese leadership has added to this array of Asian organizations concerned with security issues with the creation of the Shanghai Cooperation Organization (SCO). China and Russia are its principal members, and it includes several Central Asian countries that were former republics of the Soviet Union.

Rounding out these regional security organizations are the Arab League and the African Union (AU). The Arab League, comprising twenty-two states (with Syria, Iraq, and Yemen imploding), was formed as a means for asserting a united Arab voice in regional and global security and foreign policy issues. It has primarily functioned as a mechanism to oppose the State of Israel. On either dimension, the cultural, religious, and political divisions among the Arab member states are so deep that it has not developed much beyond a forum for the expression of typically divergent Arab sentiments on policy issues.

The AU, encompassing fifty-two African states, has been marginally more successful as a security organization than the Arab League. It has been held together since its inception by adherence to three principles: the stipulation that all states are equal; that no state is to interfere in the domestic affairs of AU members; and that territorial boundaries are permanent. The states of the AU have participated in peacekeeping operations in Africa, though the AU as an organization, like the Arab League, is too divided to act as a united organization in the same way that NATO has been able to achieve cooperation among its member states, particularly during the Cold War era.

In assessing the security record of UN peacekeeping operations and the activities of regional security organizations, it is important to keep in mind that the states still largely determine what security is afforded the global society. These supplements to the nation-state system are neither designed nor equipped to surmount the weaknesses of the anarchy of the nation-state system. Their limited success in providing security to vulnerable states and peoples has been more to diminish the scope and intensity of violence rather than to transform a warfare system.

The Nation-State System as a Warfare System: A Statistical Profile

The outbreak of wars in the modern period provides ample evidence of the global security interdependence of the peoples and states comprising the nation-state system. The Correlates of War (COW) project, covering several different categories of war between 1815 and 1997, provides data reflecting the inclination of nation-states to resort to armed hostilities to induce the cooperation of rivals and allies. The nation-state system, viewed in its entirety as an interdependent network of state relations, provides a provisional, if precarious, global political order for the world's populations.[36] The system itself, as many theorists argue, also generates incentives for disputing state and non-state rivals within the system to seek a coercive solution to their conflicts.[37]

COW data group wars into three broad categories:[38] interstate; extra-systemic (colonial or imperial); and intrastate or civil. To qualify as an *interstate* war, there must be sustained combat between states, involving the armed forces of all participants, and all of the combatants must have incurred at least one thousand battle fatalities. These rules yielded seventy-nine wars from 1815 to 1997, including World Wars I and II, which dwarfed the others in the number of killed, not to say wounded and disabled.

An *extra-systemic* war refers primarily to a war between a state and dependent or independent nonstate actors. The first refers largely to war between an imperial power and a subordinate population ruled as a colony, protectorate, mandate, or other entity under the control of the dominant power. The second involves a dominant state and some nonstate entity that does not qualify in terms of prevailing international criteria as a state because of "limitations on its independence, a population insufficiency, or a failure of other states to recognize it as a legitimate member."[39] Extra-systemic wars accounted for 108 incidents over the period of COW data. To qualify as an extra-systemic war, at least one of the participants was not a member of the state system and at least one thousand battle deaths were registered "*for every year* for all state participants."[40] In these cases, either the dominant or the imperial power was asserting its control over an alien population that was rebelling against the ruling state or seeking a state of its own to become a member of the state system, or the controlling state was asserting its authority and power within the state system wherein its claim to sovereignty was being challenged.

World Wars I and II underscore the nation-state system as a warfare system. In both world wars, most of the world's populations were directly or indirectly impacted by these struggles for global hegemony. In round numbers, an estimated 15.2 million deaths resulted from World War I, divided between 8.5 million military and 6.6 million civilian deaths. World War II extended the scope and depth of armed hostilities across the globe. Military and civilian deaths increased threefold. Approximately forty-three million people perished in World War II. This included eighteen million battle and twenty-five million civilian deaths. Untold millions of casualties and trillions of dollars in material losses across the globe are not included in these statistics. What is also interesting is the increased number of civilian over battlefield deaths in World War II when compared with World War I. In World War I, battlefield deaths accounted for approximately 56 percent of deaths. This percentage declined to about 42 percent in World War II. The Second World War inflicted greater death and destruction on a larger number of civilians across the globe than World War I, capped by well over one hundred thousand deaths in the atomic bombings of Hiroshima and Nagasaki.

Despite these horrific numbers, the dominant form of violent conflict since 1815 has been *intrastate* or *civil* war. For a civil war to be included in the COW data set requires the existence of an active and recognized state within the system and effective resistance that resulted in at least one thousand battle deaths between the belligerents. This category of wars produced the most incidents, 424 between 1816 and 1997. Figure 4.1 charts the number of civil wars from 1946 to 1997. These peaked at over fifty in the early 1990s and plateaued between thirty-five and thirty-eight in the first decade of the twenty-first century. These included well over five million dead in the Congo and tens of thousands more in the Balkans, Iraq, Afghanistan, and Sudan, not to mention tens of thousands of women raped and populations plundered.[41]

Civil wars will likely remain endemic to the global society's security threats. A toxic mix of additional factors and forces will reinforce the trend toward an upward increase in internal violent conflict: rising ethnic and religious strife, poverty, inequitable state distribution of wealth, corruption, and competition over access to scarce resources and prized minerals (water, arable land, gold, coltan, etc.).[42] These incidents can be expected to occur principally in the developing world. The world's population is expected to increase in the poorest and in the most economically underdeveloped regions of the globe.

While most interstate, extra-systemic, and intrastate wars have not risen to the level of a global war, they still qualify as observations consistent with the notion of a state system inclined toward armed hostilities and incapable of ensuring the security of millions of the world's seven billion inhabitants. Viewed from the perspective of the global society, these different categories

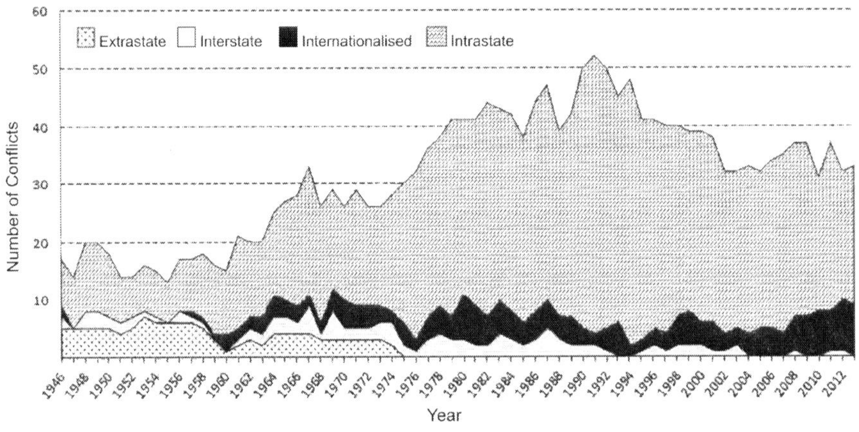

FIGURE 4.1
Number of Armed Conflicts by Type, 1946–2013
Source: Lotta Themnér and Peter Wallensteen, *Journal of Peace Research* 51: 541–54. © 2014. Reprinted by Permission of SAGE Publications, Ltd.

of war are observed incidents of what Quincy Wright might have described in his magisterial study of war as aberrant deviations from what he posited as international law (understood in behavioral terms as expected actor behavior rather than enforceable legal prescriptions).[43] Absent a world state, interstate wars arise from the insecurity between and within states, experienced differentially, as a consequence of an anarchical state system. Put another way, wars arise between disputants who cannot otherwise reconcile their differences other than by a trial by arms because there is no entity or state capable of preventing the conflict.

Adapting to the state system, insurgents seek their own state and its recognition as an equal to other states. The default mode for best practices in coping with the concerns of populations for their security remains the state. The state system sets boundaries to the political aspirations of the rebels. Once they capture a state and install their preferred regime, these new states, like the older powers, are compelled to worry about their survival and self-interests within an insecure state system. The numerous insurgents in civil wars have accepted the nation-state as a constraint on their political ambitions. In overthrowing a regime, new rulers have been quick to conform to the state system and to assume the trappings of state power, authority, and sovereignty on a moral footing equal to other states.

Transnational movements, like Al Qaeda and the Islamic State of Iraq and Syria (ISIS), do not substantially deviate from these norms in seeking the creation of a caliphate that would rule all Muslims and exclude from their territory all foreign powers and nationals.[44] The caliphate, if successfully instituted, would join the system of nation-states, but with a pronounced religious and communal regime orientation, presumably animated by a millennial mission to dominate the system. The religious, national, cultural, and tribal divisions within the Muslim community, stretching from North Africa to Southeast Asia, currently impede the creation of a single ruling body over these contesting and contentious peoples. That this ambitious vision of a unified Muslim state may never be realized in no way diminishes the globalization of this threat to Muslim and non-Muslim populations around the globe. Social movements like Al Qaeda and ISIS must first capture a state to be in a position to fully advance their transnational objectives.

As the civilian populations of the global society become increasingly interdependent, including their mutually contingent concerns about their physical security, the distinction between a state's military forces and civilian populations has become progressively blurred. The breakdown of the firewall between military combatants and civilian populations is already apparent in the strategic bombing of cities in World War II. Mao Zedong's strategy of protracted conflict to win control of China and of the Chinese population by defeating Nationalist forces and eliminating foreign influence over the Chinese people and government effaced the traditional distinction between the military and civilian populations.[45] The object of armed struggle was, indeed, control of the civilian population,[46] whether by insurgents or by the alien forces occupying a foreign territory. This challenge confronted the Soviet Union in its failed effort in Afghanistan and still confronts the United States in central Asia and in the Middle East where US forces are stationed. The World Trade Center attack in 2001 is a metaphor of this transformation of wars in which the distinction between military and civilian populations has been largely effaced.

The Special Threat Posed by Nuclear Weapons to the Security of the Global Society

Wholesale slaughter of civilian populations in war is now a distinct threat to the security of the global society and its clashing peoples. The emergence of weapons of mass destruction, notably nuclear weapons, and their proliferation to nine states, including Israel (an unannounced nuclear power),[47] escalates the threat to populations around the world. The threat has now become more menacing, since nonstate actors may be able to acquire fissionable materials and even a nuclear device to visit on vulnerable civilian populations.

Over the course of the Cold War from 1945 to 1991, the United States and the Soviet Union created what Herman Kahn aptly, if mordantly, characterized as two doomsday machines.[48] Figure 4.2 charts the global nuclear stockpiles of the current members of the nuclear weapons club. The United States and the Soviet Union/Russia clearly outdistanced all other states in warhead capabilities. These forces increased over a generation to reach an apex of approximately 64,000 strategic and nonstrategic warheads for the United States and the Soviet Union in the 1980s.[49] At the end of the Cold War in 1991, the United States and the Soviet Union possessed, respectively, 9,154 and 10,672 strategic, long-range warheads, capable of reaching opponent targets thousands of miles away with accuracies measured in hundreds of meters. These stockpiles further declined to 4,650 and 4,480 for the United States and the Russian Federation, respectively, in the first decade of the twenty-first century.

Paralleling the increasing destructive power of nuclear warheads, the Cold War antagonists deployed a mix of long-range delivery vehicles. The Soviet Union's complex included long-range bombers, intercontinental ballistic missiles (ICBMs), and submarine-launched ballistic missiles (SLBMs). These totaled approximately 2,500 between 1970 and 1990. The United States

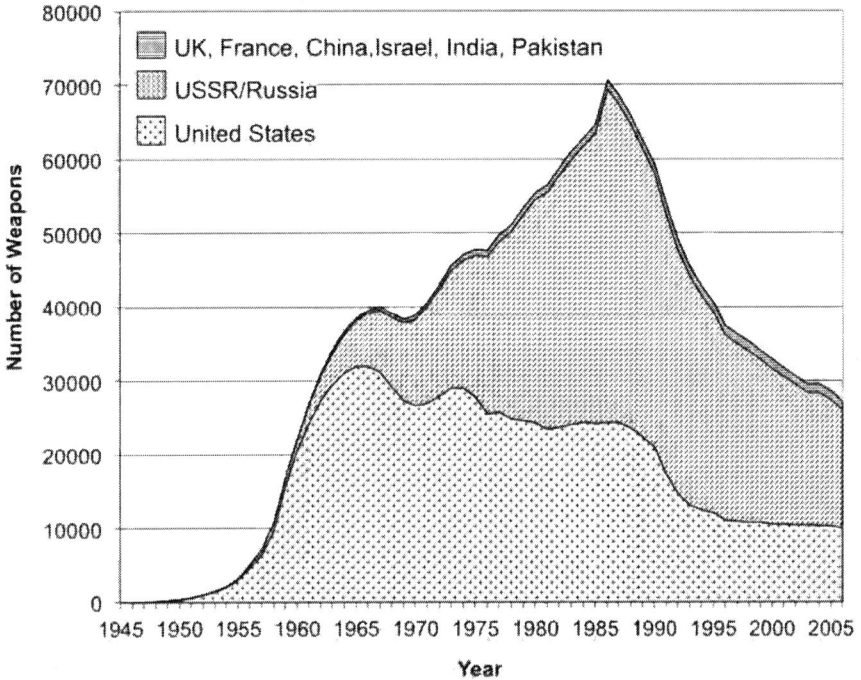

FIGURE 4.2
Global Nuclear Stockpiles, 1945–2006
Source: Robert S. Norris and Hans M. Kristensen, "Global Nuclear Stockpiles, 1945–2006," *Bulletin of Atomic Scientists* 62:4 (July/August 2006): 64–66.

placed greater emphasis on SLBMs and bombers. Its totals hovered around 2,200 launchers during this period. The principal technological breakthrough during this period was in warhead design with the introduction of multiple independently targetable reentry vehicles (MIRVs). This innovation permitted a single ICBM or SLBM to carry eight or more warheads on a "bus" that was capable of dispersing its warheads to hit multiple targets.

The operational nuclear strategy directing the force structures of the two countries evolved through two modes. The first was characterized in the United States as a strategy of mutual assured destruction (MAD). MAD was initially designed to survive a Soviet attack, yet retain sufficient nuclear capabilities to destroy one-quarter to one-third of the Soviet population and at least 50–60 percent of its economic infrastructure in the prompt and delayed effects of nuclear weapons.[50] At the end of the Eisenhower administration in 1961, nuclear planning was poised, if necessary, for a preemptive strike aimed at 2,600 sites composed of 4,100 targets using 1,050 nuclear ground zero explosions affecting 151 Soviet cities, equal to roughly half of the Soviet population.[51] Both powers gradually replaced MAD with a counterforce strategy. This strategic reformulation strove to surmount the dilemma of a mutually damaging nuclear exchange, intolerably destructive to populations and material infrastructures of both nations, not to say severely damaging to distant populations exposed to the radiation clouds created by the nuclear spasm.

Military strategists on both sides pursued the elusive goal of developing a first-strike force that would effectively disarm or destroy an opponent's nuclear forces. The latter were configured to be as invulnerable as possible (hence SLBMs and bombers were preferred over fixed and exposed land-based ICBMs). Programs were also launched on both sides to increase the speed and accuracy of weapons, dedicated to rapidly destroy the nuclear forces of the rival. Targeting under a counterforce strategy shifted from cities and mass populations to nuclear delivery sites in a futile effort to disarm an adversary's nuclear capabilities. That proved an impossible requirement to meet. All conceivable scenarios of counterforce targeting would still have inflicted unacceptable human and material losses on exposed populations and urban centers without having completely destroyed the opponent's second-strike capacity to inflict unacceptable retaliatory damage on the attacker.

Underscoring the negative interdependence of the security of the United States and the Soviet Union was their negotiated decision to cooperate in maintaining an uneasy stability of the nuclear balance and the deterrence systems erected by both sides. These moves were undertaken even as the rivals continued to search for strategic advantage, principally by multiplying their offensive nuclear forces or, as in the case of the United States, by simultaneously embarking on a quixotic antiballistic missile program.

The cooperation between the nuclear antagonists assumed two forms to support a continually changing deterrence regime between them and with other announced and aspiring nuclear powers. The first involved a series of arms control agreements to increase the confidence on both sides to maintain a stable nuclear deterrent regime despite the threat of nuclear annihilation hanging over both states.[52] Initially, the two sides agreed to end testing in the atmosphere that posed a serious threat to global health. They also installed hotlines to keep communications open during a crisis. These moves were aimed at minimizing miscalculations or accidents, which might be construed as imminent nuclear attacks, on both sides, and at precluding regional conflicts, like those in the Middle East, from escalating to the point that they might generate incentives for decision-makers in Moscow or Washington to threaten or use nuclear weapons.

These confidence building measures and arms control accords were then followed by the Strategic Arms Limitation Talks (SALT) I and II treaties. These focused on limiting the number of launchers each side would be permitted to deploy. SALT II restricted both sides to 2,250 launchers, and neither the US nor the USSR could MIRV more than 1,320 of the launchers. Of these no more than 1,200 ICBMs could be MIRVed, and of that total no more than 820 could be ground-based ICBMs. SALT II was never ratified because of the Russian invasion of Afghanistan in 1979. It was superseded by the Strategic Arms Reduction Treaty (START) that shifted the focus from containing launchers to limiting strategic, long-range warheads. START limited both sides to 2,200 warheads.

In 2002 the Bush administration signed a treaty with the Russian Federation to reduce their strategic nuclear weapons to between 1,700 and 2,200 by 2012. No action was taken to implement this treaty until the Obama administration reached an agreement with the Russian Federation in 2010 to eventually reduce their deployed, long-range strategic nuclear weapons to 1,500 each from 2,200. Table 4.1 notes that the United States has 2,150 strategic nuclear weapons deployed and 4,650 as backup, with approximately 3,000 retired or dismantled.[53] The Russian Federation is credited with 1,800 deployed warheads, 4,480 stockpiled, and approximately 4,000 retired from service.[54]

TABLE 4.1
Estimated Worldwide Nuclear Warheads, 2013

Country	Deployed Warheads[a]	Stockpiled Warheads	Retired Warheads	Total Inventory
Russia	1,800	4,480	~4,000	~8,500
United States	2,150[b]	4,650	~3,000	~7,700
France	290[c]	300	—	300
China	—	250	Few	250
United Kingdom	160[d]	225	—	225
Israel	—	80	—	80
Pakistan	—	120	—	120
India	—	110	—	110
North Korea	—	n/a	—	n/a
TOTAL	~4,400	~10,200	~7,000	~17,200

Source: Hans M. Kristensen and Robert S. Norris, "Global Nuclear Weapons Inventories, 1945–2013," *Bulletin of the Atomic Scientists* 69, no. 5 (2013): 75–81.

[a] Deployed warheads are defined as warheads that are on missiles or at bases with operational launchers.

[b] This includes nearly two hundred non-strategic bombs deployed in Europe.

[c] Of these, one or two submarines with about eighty warheads are normally deployed at sea.

[d] Of these 160 "operationally available" warheads, 48 are normally deployed on one nuclear submarine at sea.

In 1968, under the leadership of the United States and the Soviet Union, the first five nuclear powers, permanent members of the UN Security Council, successfully negotiated a global treaty to staunch nuclear proliferation. Under the terms of the Non-Proliferation Treaty (NPT), non-nuclear signatories were obliged not to develop nuclear weapons programs and were required to submit their nuclear facilities to international inspection under the auspices of the International Atomic Energy Agency. Nuclear powers were forbidden to assist the nuclear weapons programs of other states, but were pledged to help them develop the civilian use of nuclear energy.

Table 4.1 suggests that the effort to stop global nuclear proliferation, through the device of what is a discriminatory treaty, has been less than optimal, a shortfall that threatens regional and global security. Both the United States and Russia have yet to meet START limits of 1,500 warheads, although under the NPT there was the expectation that reductions in their nuclear arsenals would encourage other states to resist the temptation to go nuclear. At this writing there is little likelihood that these lower levels will be reached because of the differences between the United States and the Russian Federation over Moscow's military interventions in the Ukraine, Georgia, and Syria. Thousands of tactical nuclear weapons of Hiroshima size or more have been left out of the treaty; operational strategic warheads, while limited to 1,500, do not take account of those in storage. To secure US Senate consent to the nuclear treaty with Russia, the Obama administration was obliged to agree to increased spending for the American nuclear arsenal. The three other permanent members of the Security Council add approximately 1,000 warheads to the world's totals. These states also continue to modernize their nuclear forces.[55]

Meanwhile, India, Pakistan, and Israel, nonsignatories of the proliferation treaty, acquired nuclear weapons and long-range delivery systems. Currently they are alleged to have, respectively, 110, 120, and 80 nuclear warheads in their arsenals. They also continue to improve their nuclear weapon systems in kill and destruction power, reliability, and deliverable range and accuracy. Particularly disturbing are reports that Pakistan is increasing its stockpile of tactical nuclear warheads as a response to Indian military power.[56]

North Korea withdrew from the NPT, has exploded several nuclear devices, and is developing long-range missile delivery capacity. Iran, an NPT signatory, has agreed to curtail its nuclear program below weapons grade levels in an agreement with members of the UN Security Council and Germany. Tehran will also accept full-scope inspection of its nuclear facilities by the International Atomic Energy Agency (IAEA). Iran has also agreed not to install any new centrifuges, which would be required to enrich uranium to weapons grade levels. Iran will stop enriching uranium beyond 5 percent and will dilute or convert stockpiles of enriched uranium at 20 percent into oxide to preclude their rapid accelerated enrichment to bomb grade levels. It also agreed to stop work on building a plutonium plant to complement its enrichment capabilities as an alternate avenue to development of nuclear weapons.[57]

Efforts to keep nuclear materials and know-how out of the hands of terrorists have made little progress. There are two formidable barriers to the making of a nuclear weapon: obtaining either adequate supplies of highly enriched uranium (HEU) or plutonium and creating a spherical implosion of the fissile material to create a critical mass. Both obstacles are potentially surmountable. There are large supplies of HEU and plutonium available around the globe, and the know-how to build a nuclear device is widely available. Almost fifty states now possess fissile materials. These supplies total several thousand tons. This mountain of material is capable of being used to produce thousands of nuclear weapons. Graham Allison estimates that there were 200 sites around the world in 2004 where fissile material could be accessed by rogue elements. In addition, there were 130 operating research reactors fueled by HEU. He also reported hundreds of foiled smuggling attempts to sell fissile materials since the breakup of the Soviet Union.[58]

In 2004, UN Resolution 1540 required governments to "adopt and enforce appropriate effective laws which prohibit a non-state actor from making or possessing nuclear, chemical, or biological weapons, their delivery systems, or related materials." Compliance with UN Resolution 1540 has been fragmentary. Researchers who reviewed compliance with the UN resolution conclude that "unless the international community is willing to make significantly greater investments in international export control assistance . . . the goal of achieving widespread effective compliance with UNSCR 1540 is unlikely to be realized in the near future."[59] These voluntary commitments do not cover plutonium. The threat hangs heavy that terrorists might gain access to fissile materials, know-how, and means to make a bomb.

Other Security Challenges:
A Global Arms Transfers and Production System

An anarchical nation-state system and the underlying security dilemma shared in varying measure by all states drive licit (and illicit) arms production and trade between states and nonstate actors across state boundaries. Between 1998 and 2007 global spending for arms rose from $834 billion to $1.214 trillion. The Middle East, South Asia, and East Asia all registered increases of 50 percent or more in this period. East Asia was among the highest. China increased spending by 202 percent followed by Indonesia and Malaysia by 100 and 153 percent, respectively.

Between 2004 and 2011[60] the United States was the principal supplier of arms. It reached arms agreements that were twice as large as those reached by Russia, its next competitor. These two suppliers accounted, respectively, for 42 and 21 percent of arms transferred during this period. Additional suppliers include France, the United Kingdom, and China. The estimated value of all arms transferred was approximately $544 billion.[61] The bulk of current arms transfers are to the developing states. Principal recipients include Saudi Arabia, India, United Arab Emirates, Egypt, and Pakistan.[62] If the populations of sellers and buyers are totaled, arms transfers affect well over half of the world's populations. What emerges from this sketch is the existence of a self-sustaining global subsystem of arms production and transfers.[63] While this global arms system presumably serves the security interests of the states that sponsor them, it also has its own corporate and bureaucratic interests in their survival and growth, quite apart from the announced security objectives of the actors these services support. Where state security interests and those of the arms production and sales system begin or end is a difficult line to draw.

Below the radar of these production forces lies another global production subsystem of small arms and lethal weapons. The *Small Arms Survey*, an annual review of the production and distribution of small arms and lethal weapons (SALWs), notes that ninety states and several hundred firms are capable of producing these weapons.[64] Craftspersons in developing states, for example, in Ghana, Pakistan, and Colombia, are capable of producing small arms for local use by copying international designs. The production of SALWs is particularly significant because of increasingly greater firepower and destructive capabilities. These include antitank guided weapons, rocket and grenade launchers, and mortars. Many nonstate actors can produce SALWs, including improvised explosive devices (IEDs), which have been widely used in Iraq and Afghanistan. The *Survey* estimates that fifty countries are currently producing SALWs. Trade in these weapons is estimated to be annually at around $4 billion.

Approximately 300,000 people are killed by these means of armed violence each year, roughly two-thirds in criminal or nonconflict contexts and the remainder in wars.[65] A UN press release cites a survey estimate that 650,000 civilian firearms leak out of lawful holdings into illicit circuits. Efforts to dispose of surplus stocks have not proven very effective, since annual production exceeds what has been destroyed.[66]

The commercially driven nuclear proliferation activities of Abdul Qadeer Khan of Pakistan further illustrate the blurred line between licit and illicit arms production and trade and its deleterious implications for regional and global security. The Pakistani military and civilian leadership and bureau-cracy were complicit in selling nuclear know-how and materials to several countries, including Libya, Iran, and North Korea.[67] The global military-industrial-arms sales and transfer complex expands and reinforces the an-archy of the nation-state system. Broadened and deepened, accordingly, is the tangle of negative security interdependencies of states and populations implicated in a volatile and unstable global insecurity system.

Failure of the Nation-State System to Provide for Essential Public Goods for the Global Society

The nation-state system conditions each state to pursue its own self-interests and those of its population. These self-regarding incentives seriously impede cooperation to provide for the collective goods indispensable for the survival and welfare of the global society and its members. Absent the provision of these goods, the global society and large segments of the world's populations are placed at serious risk.[68] Through unanticipated blowback so also are the particular security interests and aims of each state made more vulnerable, since their realization depends on the preexistence of a stable, robust, and flourishing global society that the focused pursuit of their parochial security policies place at risk.

The structural and institutional defects of the nation-state system and the incentives for self-destruction generated by the system are evident across the full spectrum of principal human concerns. The danger of out-of-control, self-propelled vicious circles with regard to these policy domains lurks within the system. In many ways, as a consequence of the widening scope, depth, and accumulating interdependencies of the states and peoples, the dangers to the global society have never been greater. By generating incentives for states to defect, free ride, or hide in response to collective goods imperatives, the capacity of the system to support and replicate itself is further eroded.

Illustrative of the collective goods deficiencies of the nation-state system is the failure of states to effectively develop cooperative policies to cope with global climate change, notably global warming, or to mount abatement pro-grams to lessen its damaging effects on the global environment and on human habitation.

Climate Change and Global Warming

The damaging effects of global warming are gravely and permanently threaten-ing the welfare of the world's populations. In concert with the market system and world public demand for ever-increasing economic growth, states, including democratic global states, are failing to address human-induced greenhouse gas (GHG) emissions. The converging and reinforcing incentives generated by OWL institutions and power structures for peoples and states to forestall effective, universal, and coordinated efforts to abate GHG emissions and to mitigate their adverse impacts promise to produce "a perfect storm." The absence of state provision of an indispensable public good—a supportive human environment—epitomizes the profound breakdown of global governance.

In contrast to the constricted scope of responsibility of the WHW model, the global state is obliged to add global warming to its central obligations. As one of the world's renowned environmental economists reminds us, states over several centuries have acted to "insulate their populations for all kinds of adverse shocks." These extend to "public and private health, agricultural shocks, environmental disasters and degradations, and violence. We would expect that adaptation to the dangers of future climate change would be added to this list of risks of the modern state."[69] That expectation currently goes begging.

What is the range of challenges posed by global warming to the welfare of the world's populations? What is the factual and scientific basis for assigning a high priority to these challenges? If the dangers are real and clear, imminent and urgent as well as long term and potentially catastrophic, what can be done to prevent damage to the world's environment and ecological support systems? And why is that not happening?

Estimating the damaging effects of increasing global warming of the earth, sea, and atmosphere, and its variable impacts on regions around the globe, is an uncertain science, but it is an uncertainty that is not unbounded.[70] The reports of the United Nations' Intergovernmental Panel on Climate Change (IPCC), the work of hundreds of scientists around the globe, provides accumulating evidence of significant human contributions to the likely increase of temperature from one to five degrees Celsius during this century if steps are not taken to arrest this trend.[71] The IPCC reports are certain that, however much scientific results might differ, "warming of the climate system is *unequivocal*, as is now evident from observations of an increase in global average air and ocean temperatures, widespread melting of snow and ice and rising global average sea level."[72] The 2007 report notes that this conclusion rests squarely on more than twenty-nine thousand observational data series, from seventy-five cross-nationally based studies, that show at a probability of greater than 89 percent significant changes in physical and biological systems as the expected response to warming.[73]

The principal sources of global warming are the increased "atmospheric concentrations of carbon dioxide, methane, and nitrous oxide," which have "increased to levels unprecedented in at least the last 800,000 years."[74] In 2005 there were approximately 379 ppm of CO_2 in the atmosphere. This level of concentration is tracked by the so-called Keeling Curve that is depicted in figure 4.3. The 2005 level exceeds the natural range over the past 650,000 years.[75]

That level of CO_2 concentration has now exceeded four hundred ppm and is expected to rise to over five hundred ppm by the end of the century if present trends in population increases and rising demands for economic growth continue to push GHG emissions upward. The volume of carbon emissions has also climbed steeply since World War II from a slower starting point with the emergence of the Industrial Revolution to an explosion in GHG emissions after World War II. In 1946, human activity generated approximately one million tons of CO_2. By the end of the century emissions rose sharply to seven times that amount.[76] What is particularly alarming is that China, the world's largest emitter of greenhouse gases, issued data in November 2015 indicating chronic underreporting of its emissions since the turn of the century. Jan Ivar

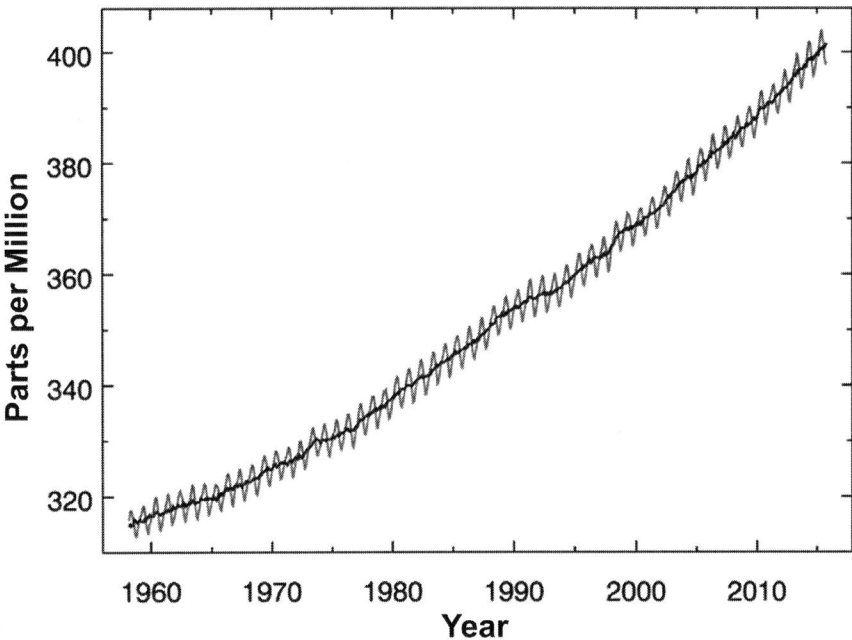

FIGURE 4.3
Keeling Curve: Mauna Loa Monthly Mean CO_2 Concentration, 1958–2015 (The zigzag curve represents the monthly mean values, while the solid black curve represents the seasonally corrected data.)
Source: Dr. Pieter Tans, NOAA/ESRL (www.esrl.noaa.gov/gmd/ccgg/trends/) and Dr. Ralph Keeling, Scripps Institution of Oceanography (scrippsco2.ucsd.edu/); http://www.esrl.noaa.gov/gmd/ccgg/trends/#mlo_full.

Korsbakken, a senior researcher at the Center for International Climate and Environmental Research in Oslo, estimated that from 2011[77] to 2013 China had released approximately 600 million metric tons more of CO_2 than had been previously reported. It is safe to say that today the world's emissions of CO_2 in metric tons exceed the ten thousand limit of figure 4.4 for 2001.

The increase in global warming is expected to have a high probability of a wide range of damaging effects, some irreversible. Ecosystems will be under grave stress. An increase of two degrees Celsius (3.6°F) will put up to 30 percent of species at risk for extinction. At a rise of three degrees Celsius (5.2°F) food production will be decreased, sea levels will rise as a consequence of the melting of the Greenland and the Antarctic ice sheets, and a substantial burden will be placed on health systems.

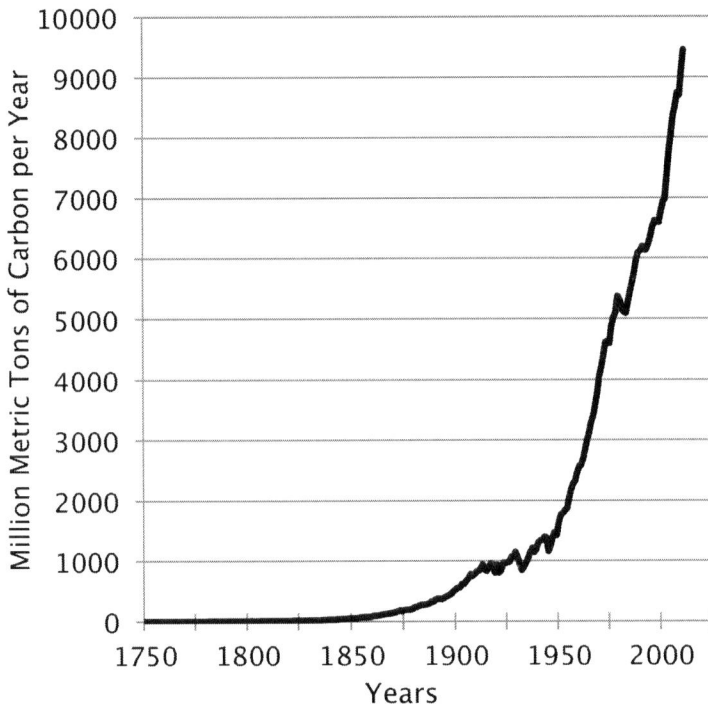

FIGURE 4.4
Global CO_2 Emissions from Fossil-Fuel Burning, Cement Manufacture, and Gas Flaring (1751–2011)
Source: T. A. Boden, G. Marland, and R. J. Andres. *Global, Regional, and National Fossil-Fuel CO_2 Emissions.* Carbon Dioxide Information Analysis Center, Oak Ridge National Laboratory, US Department of Energy, Oak Ridge, TN, 2015, doi: 10.3334/CDIAC/00001_V2015.

As species shift their habitable ranges, some, like polar bears, are threatened with extinction. Wildfires are also expected to become more prevalent and intense. The melting of snow, glaciers, and the polar caps and the Greenland shelf will raise water levels, producing floods and storms. Threatened are hundreds of millions of populations living near or on low-level coastal areas. Millions in Bangladesh are threatened with disaster. And the United States will not be spared. A recent study estimated that a two-foot sea level rise would increase the sea level of New York by 2.3 feet; Hampton Roads, Virginia, by 2.9 feet; Galveston, Texas, by 3.5 feet; and Neah Bay, Washington State, by one foot.[78] A composite of the scientific studies projects risks to hundreds of millions of coastal inhabitants.[79] Sandy, the super-hurricane that flooded New York and New Jersey in 2012, is estimated to have cost more than $40 billion.[80]

Small, subsistence farmers and fishermen will be especially adversely impacted. Cereal production, while it may increase at the two-degree level of change at mid to high latitudes, will decrease in low latitudes where population increase is projected to be the greatest through this century. There will be decreasing water availability and increasing droughts in mid-latitudes and semiarid latitudes, phenomena that are already being increasingly experienced around the globe. Hundreds of millions of people will be exposed to water stress and decreased food availability even as the world's population mounts. As new studies now confirm, global warming will increase widespread malnutrition, as well as diarrheal, cardiorespiratory, and infectious diseases.[81] Increased morbidity and mortality from heat waves caused by global warming are expected in the very near future. The World Health Organization estimated that 150,000 people died from global warming in 2002.[82] In 2003 over 20,000 Europeans died from a devastating heat wave. Added to these miseries will be increased floods and droughts.

While global effects will have variable impacts at regional levels, some greater, some less, depending on the region, there is real danger to some key systems on which humans depend, particularly those which are not managed (sea levels, ocean acidification, etc.). Damaging changes here may be irreversible. Among these, in addition to the rapid and potentially precipitous melting of the Greenland and Antarctic ice sheets, are the reversing of the Gulf Stream, feedback effects of warming that produce a vicious circle of increasing heat; long-term, enhanced warming; and increased violent weather in the form of hurricanes, tornadoes, and cyclones.

There is widespread agreement among economists that timely action now to abate GHG emissions will yield large benefits in the future. One informed estimate, based on a series of runs on a standard model of evaluation, projects a cost of approximately 1.5 percent of GWP to keep emissions at approximately a 2.5 degree Celsius increase in temperature in this century.[83] This expenditure is tantamount to purchasing an insurance policy against the multiple adverse impacts of global warming.[84]

Those who produce GHG emissions have little incentive to stop their activities, while those adversely affected by these carbon spillovers are not compensated for their losses. There are market mechanisms to control GHG emissions. The state, first of all, can tax carbon emissions by developing a "cap and trade" system, similar to what was adopted to arrest the spread of sulfur dioxide emissions. States would issue allowances to major GHG emitters (utilities, energy producers, etc.). These property rights could be traded within a regime defining the maximum amount of carbon emissions that would be globally permitted. Or states can agree to set limits on the quantity of emissions that would be permitted. These two market-based instruments would work if one or the other or a hybrid were universally adopted by all countries and if effective policies of mitigation were implemented. Partial participation would not work. Costs of mitigation at different temperature levels would be substantially increased absent total or near total participation. The heroic requirement for successful mitigation, say at the two degrees Celsius level, would be to "equalize the incremental or marginal costs of reducing emissions in every sector and every country."[85]

Why, then, has there been no progress in mitigating GHG emissions under either the Kyoto Protocol or the subsequent Copenhagen Accord? First, there are no feasible economic alternatives to relying on coal, oil, and gas to furnish enough energy to spur economic growth. Wind, solar, and nuclear energy are currently unable to play that role. Increases in population and rising demand for economic growth drive the global economic system and, in turn, accelerate the rate of GHG emissions. This circle is especially vicious if coal, the leading contributor to CO_2 emissions at approximately 42 percent of the total, continues to be relied upon. Coal emits eleven tons of CO_2 per \$1,000 in fuel versus 0.9 tons for petroleum and two tons for natural gas.[86] Notwithstanding these sobering constraints, more than 1,200 new coal-burning power plants are planned across fifty-nine countries. Three-quarters of them are earmarked for China and India.[87] A *New York Times* article reports that global demand for coal is expected to grow to 8.9 billion tons by 2016, exceeding the total for 2012 by more than a billion tons or slightly more than 10 percent.[88]

The Chinese Communist Party confronts the dilemma of an authoritarian regime, which is vulnerable to attack for its oppressive practices and human rights violations yet is obliged to gain legitimacy by meeting the expectations for greater material welfare from its burgeoning population of 1.3 billion. Two analysts who have reviewed China's climate change policies pose the dilemma confronting the Chinese people and their leadership: "How can a huge country such as China greatly reduce its consumption of fossil fuels when its economy, and indeed the political legitimacy of its ruling party, depend on processes which currently require their large-scale consumption?"[89] If China today is the largest emitter, the problem of global warming and the failure of states to address its multiple threats can scarcely be charged solely to China or to developing states. However much developed states may be responsible for the current climate change problem, these states, notably the United States, the largest emitter after China, are adamant in resisting proposals that would assign them the lead and the principal burden of coping with this issue. Leaders in developed states are scarcely in a position to credibly deny China what they have afforded their own populations over the past two centuries.

So why has not more been done to arrest what appears to be the ineluctable expansion of GHG and, specifically, of CO_2 emissions? First, the nation-state system generates negative incentives to frustrate collective efforts to control GHG emissions. If the Copenhagen Accord now includes both developed and developing states in its protocol, there still remains little incentive for these and other states to restrain GHG emissions if other states fail to do likewise. Absent state use of its coercive powers to collectively set quantitative limits of CO_2 emissions or install carbon taxes or a "cap and trade" system, the market system alone is incapable of arresting GHG emissions.

Second, populations refuse to accept limitations of economic growth by paying a risk premium to address the risks of global warming. The United States, the largest CO_2 polluter on a per capita basis, illustrates the resistance of democratic populations to incur the costs of coping with climate change. There is also surprisingly widespread rejection of scientific knowledge as a basis for policymaking. In surveys, less than 50 percent of Americans were able to correctly explain the theories of evolution or the big bang. In tandem with these findings about American scientific knowledge, only slightly more than 50 percent of those canvassed agreed that global warming was occurring.[90]

Even if many were willing to acknowledge global warming and its damaging effects, they have ample incentives to ignore its warnings. The near-term costs of efforts to arrest global warming and the uncertain long-term benefits of these efforts, stretching beyond the individual life cycles of individual voters, dampen incentives to pay these substantial near-term costs. Reluctance persists despite the certainty that these costs will increase by failing to act now. The implications of this steadfast refusal to pay upfront costs are to shift the burden of costs and damages to future generations. For developed states and their populations, notably among the states and peoples of the democracies, the failure of effective global warming policies also signifies a choice to impose the costs of global warming on those states and peoples who have contributed least to the danger.

Third, there will be losers and winners in the implementation of effective global warming policies. This creates incentives for pushback by those actors that will be expected to carry a larger share of the burden of these costs. Those actors include energy producing industries, car manufacturers, and utilities. They have mounted large-scale disinformation programs to convince a disposed public to deny that global warming is a problem or that it is an issue that needs to be confronted in the immediate future. Free speech and open debate do not necessarily produce good policies, especially when the incentives for effective action are costly and these burdens can be shifted to others while free riding.

From the perspective of this volume, the fourth source of inaction lies in the flawed solutions to global governance of the democracies. Specifically, the democracies, the richest and most powerful states of the system, have failed to provide the collective public goods their populations and those of the globe require for the health of the global society. Prevailing irresistible popular pressures for economic growth across the globe contributed significantly to the failure of the UN Climate Change Conference at Kyoto, a failure that hovers over the weak Copenhagen Accord to gain cooperation from polluting states to cut emissions. The Copenhagen meeting was supposed to move the Kyoto Protocol beyond its 2012 deadline of reaching a global agreement to cut emissions. It has failed to do so.

A decade earlier, analysts had already declared the Kyoto Protocol dead on arrival. "The appearance of a solution in Kyoto . . . is not evidence that diplomats can devise a politically durable scheme for allocating trillions of dollars through international law," as one critic of the Kyoto Protocol argued. "Rather it is evidence that diplomats are skilled at deferring decisions on difficult questions."[91] Diplomats are, of course, the instruments of states and officers of the nation-state system. They are induced to accede to the demands of their populations for more, not less, economic growth.

What is also becoming increasingly clear is that these climatic threats raise grave security threats to individual states and to the nation-system itself. In 2010, the US Defense Department's *Quadrennial Defense Review* assigned a high priority to addressing security threats posed by climate change. Linking climate change to energy and economic security and to increased conflict around the globe, the *Review* concluded, "Assessments conducted by the intelligence community indicate that climate change could have significant geopolitical impacts around the world, contributing to poverty, environmental degradation, and the further weakening of fragile governments. Climate change will contribute to food and water scarcity, will increase the spread of disease, and may spur or exacerbate mass migration. While climate change alone does not cause conflict, it may act as an accelerant of instability and conflict, placing a burden on civilian institutions and militaries around the world."[92]

Research is now suggesting that climate change impacts may be more than "an accelerant of instability and conflict." A recent publication in *Nature* reported a significant statistical relationship between climate change induced by El Niño/Southern Oscillations (ENSO) and conflicts, particularly in Africa. While the research explicitly cautioned that these findings were "no proxy for long-term climate change,"[93] there is the strong likelihood that extreme economic hardships will induce desperate behavioral responses. As the experience with droughts and famine in Africa suggests, these incidents of adverse climate change result in grave security threats to the affected populations. Stressed populations may also be vulnerable to increased bloody conflict in a struggle for survival and access to vital scarce resources of food and water.[94] The December 2015 Paris Agreement on climate change prompts guarded optimism that the 195 participating states finally acknowledge the threats posed to the planet by GHG emissions. That the agreement will go beyond the failure of Copenhagen remains to be seen. Even if the voluntary Paris goals are implemented, they will still be about half of what is needed to preclude a rise in temperature of two degrees Celsius. Nor is there a binding agreement to provide $100 billion dollars annually to developing states to mitigate the harmful effects of climate change. The resistance of a large body of American public opinion to the agreement, centered in the ruling coalition of the Republican Party, threatens to undermine this positive response of the nation-state system, particularly its democratic members, to the challenge of climate change.[95]

The Nation-State System, Terrorism, and Failed States

States have also failed to stanch mushrooming terrorist organizations around the world. The International Institute for Strategic Studies (IISS) identifies 343 nonstate armed groups on all continents that threaten states, their regimes, and civilian populations.[96] Many of these terrorist groups extend their activities across borders. Some, like Al Qaeda and ISIS, can claim to have a global reach through local affiliates. Terrorist attacks have been launched against the United States, several European states, Afghanistan, Syria, Iraq, Libya, Kenya, Tanzania, Mali, Yemen, and Nigeria. Mexico and the United States cope with drug gangs, including the 18th Street gang with over twenty thousand members. FARC in Colombia has threatened that country's security for a generation. The Janjaweed Militias, estimated to be twenty thousand strong, align with the Sudanese government to quell a long-smoldering insurgency in Darfur. Iraq, Syria, and Afghanistan have several terrorist groups operating on their soil either in conflict with each other or opposed to the regimes in power. Africa south of the Sahara has multiple armed groups operating throughout the continent. Included are Al-Shabab in Somalia, Al Qaeda offshoots in the Sahel (and northern Africa), and Boko Haram in Nigeria. Nor is Asia spared with armed groups operating in Nepal, Indonesia, Pakistan, and India.

State-sponsored or supported terrorism reinforces the war-making incentives of the nation-state system. The United States has accused Pakistan, its ostensible ally in the fight against the Taliban, of aiding the Haqqani terrorist organization based in Pakistan that has attacked Afghan and NATO troops in Afghanistan and mounted numerous assaults on civilian sites.[97] Pakistan's intelligence service, Inter-Services Intelligence (ISI), was singled out as providing material support and intelligence to the Haqqani agents operating in Kabul. The ISI has also been implicated in using the extremist Muslim group Lashkar-e-Taiba to launch terrorist attacks against India in Mumbai and to foment disorder in Kashmir. Syria and Iran have been accused of assisting Hezbollah in Lebanon to assassinate political leaders and to mount rocket assaults against Israel. Iran is also charged with aiding Hezbollah in Lebanon and Hamas in the Gaza Strip to conduct terrorist attacks on Israel. States are tempted to use terrorism as an effective strategy of the weak against superior military forces to advance their political objectives.

The failure of the states to agree on what terrorism is and who its perpetrators are seriously weakens the fabric of global security. What is a terrorist group to victims of terrorism is a freedom fighter to those using these elements for their own strategic purposes. This thin fabric is shredded further by the increasing impact of global crime, alluded to earlier. Piracy, which once appeared to have been contained, has reemerged as big business at a cost of tens of billions of dollars to shippers off the coasts of Somalia or Southeast Asia.[98] Corruption of political regimes and even takeover of a state by criminal elements, as formerly in Panama, is especially cancerous. In varying degrees all states of the globe are vulnerable to corruption. Transparency International annually publishes a Corruption Perceptions Index. Of the 178 countries surveyed in 2010, three-quarters scored below 5 on a scale of 10 (highly clean) to 0 (highly corrupt). Among the latter was Somalia with a score of 1.1, slightly below Myanmar and Afghanistan at 1.4 and Iraq at 1.5.[99] Corruption includes bribery, extortion, cronyism, nepotism, patronage, graft, and embezzlement. Fostered, too, are drug and human trafficking and money laundering.

It is useful to distinguish between the threats to global order posed by terrorism and lawlessness in its many and multiplying forms. Terrorism is keyed to disrupt, destroy, and unravel social order without necessarily replacing it with an alternative order. The nihilistic forms practiced by Al Qaeda, which randomly killed or maimed thousands of anonymous victims in the attack on the Twin Towers, for example, are bent on mayhem and ruination. Curiously enough, international and transnational crime thrives best and most profitably under conditions of a global order and vibrant economic growth. As a predatory activity, global crime has no productive or legitimate service function. When the state itself criminally exploits its population, kleptocracies, like Zaire under Mobutu Sese Seko, remain poor since what material wealth and growth potential exists in their civil societies is stolen by the state. The incentive of state leaders to use their power for their personal advantage has prompted one prominent scholar to argue that war-making and state-making are forms of organized crime.[100]

Adding further complications to the multiple and accumulating crises convulsing the global state system from the threats outlined above is the spreading contagion of the failed state. This is a particularly ironic and perplexing challenge to the state system. From its beginnings the state was supposed to provide for the security of its populations. For this service it was accorded sovereignty and a monopoly over the legitimate use of force. Chester Crocker captures these entangling and mutually supporting crises, arguing that failed states pose the greatest challenge to the state system: "Much of the contemporary international state system is crumbling beneath the burdens of warfare, stagnant or declining per capita growth, pandemic disease, rampant official corruption and autocracy. . . . For every South Africa, there are dozens of struggling or failing entities such as Zambia and the Central African Republic. India may be heading in an exciting direction, but much of the rest of South and Central Asia is a mess. . . . In this vast zone of transition and turbulence, the greatest problem is . . . the absence of states with the legitimacy and authority to manage their affairs."[101]

Lacking effective enforcement capabilities, failed states are unable to protect their populations or to arbitrate group conflicts on the basis of a rule of law. In the wake of the collapse of the Eurocentric system and the bipolar Cold War, which tended to dampen and contain local conflicts and underpin fragile regimes and states, an epidemic of failed states has erupted. In 1993, a million Tutsis and Hutus were murdered in a genocide orchestrated initially by a Hutu government but quickly overtaken by a resulting social chaos until the regime was overturned by a Tutsi-led insurgency. The Republic of the Congo has been plunged into a Hobbesian end game with an estimated loss of civilian life of over five million since the overthrow of the Mobutu Sese Seko regime in 1997. Somalia and the Darfur region of Sudan similarly suffer from chronic chaos and large-scale violence visited on vulnerable populations. Somalia has not had an effective government for a generation. Adding to Somalia's distress is widespread drought and starvation, a humanitarian disaster exacerbated by Muslim insurgents who either exploit or prevent aid from reaching affected populations. Warlords and Taliban rebels embattle a weak and corrupt Kabul government whose survival depends on foreign troops that have failed to institute peace and order since the American invasion in 2001.

The internal turmoil and turbulence of state failure cannot be confined to the boundaries of these states. The systemic repercussions of state insecurity are their damaging impacts on neighbors, their regions, and even the security of the state system. Failure results in civil war; religious, cultural, ethnic, and tribal strife; devastation of the local economy; weapons proliferation; drug and human trafficking; and piracy. Except on an ad hoc basis, and then ineffectively, the states of the international community, notably the global democratic states, have been either unable or unwilling to cope with these disasters or contain their contagious effects. In Rwanda UN forces were ordered to abandon populations under their protection to genocide.[102] The Security Council, charged with the responsibility for global security, resisted intervention to stop the bloodshed. In Srebrenica, a UN force under Dutch command allowed invading Serbian forces to kill thousands of Bosnian Muslims. These depredations also expose these states to takeover by rogue and terrorist organizations.

Raised is the unprecedented threat that weak or failing states, like Afghanistan, Yemen, Syria, Iraq, or a collapsing Pakistan, could be hijacked by nonstate actors who could then trade on the dubious legitimacy accorded the targeted state by the WHW system to launch attacks against other states and peoples. The 9/11 attack is a cautionary tale. The danger that a nonstate actor, like Al Qaeda, ISIS, or the Haqqani group, might gain access to nuclear weapons poses an especially serious threat not only to their designated enemies but also to the survival of the system in the wake of a nuclear attack against a major population center.[103]

Conclusion

This delineation of the security threats impacting on states and the state system is daunting as an agenda for action and remedy for the democracies. What makes coping with these challenges unprecedented is the expansion of the state beyond its early WHW composition and characteristics. The rise of the global state, the product of the liberal democratic states, challenges the dominance of the WHW state and state system. The global state has created a wide spectrum of contesting OWL incentives; they weaken those who spur WHW states to resort to coercive threats or force to impose their will on other states and peoples. Democratic liberal states are less likely to become involved in armed hostilities with each other than with WHW states. Global states, however, are only a segment of the state system within the global society. The WHW system remains a warfare system to which the global states are no less inclined to go to war in confronting hostile nondemocratic states and nonstate actors. Once global states revert to WHW status, they are no less susceptible to fall under the thrall of the Hobbesian dilemma than their nondemocratic rivals.

The ruling majorities of the democracies, no less than their competitors, have to provide global public goods that advance both their values and interests and those of the world's populations. While the lack of progress in arresting and containing GHG emissions is a collective failure of all states, culpability rests particularly with the developed democratic global states. They have been the largest polluters before the emergence to statehood of developing states. The latter pursue the same growth strategies as their forbearers in relying on fossil fuels. The global states have also been derelict in developing effective coping strategies to address terrorist organizations and religiously motivated social movements uncompromisingly opposed to the secular liberal democracies and their solutions to global governance.

Whether the global liberal state and its preferred responses to OWL imperatives will survive and flourish in a hostile environment will depend on the collective ability of the democracies to weaken incentives for armed conflict in an anarchical state system, to provide for public goods for their own populations and nondemocratic states and peoples, and to cope with terrorists and failed or failing states that are terrorist bases. Greater cooperation than presently exists among the democracies is needed to meet these challenges and to expand the sphere of influence and power congenial to democratic solutions for global governance.

The struggle for global governance can no longer be (if it ever could have been) reduced to a struggle exclusively between and among states. Nor can the order required for effective governance be equated solely with the threat to use force. The global state has enlarged our understanding of the scope and complexity of creating a stable and just global Order. Putting that learning experience into practice remains among the most important challenges of the global state. Among these, too, are effective responses to the imperatives of Welfare and Legitimacy, to which we now turn.

Notes

1. Quoted by Mariana Mazzucato (2013, p. 30). See Polanyi (1944). The central significance of the global state as a precondition for the institutionalization of the

market system is developed in Evans (1995, 1997); Evans, Rueschemeyer, & Skocpol (1985); Evans & Rauch (1999).

2. Rosecrance (1986).
3. World Bank, *World Development Indicators Database*.
4. Ibid.
5. Cerny (2010).
6. Kant (1991 [*Kant*], p. 114).
7. Bruce Russett summarizes the rich scholarly literature that supports the proposition that democracies do not fight. See Russett & Starr (2000); Russett & Oneal (2001).
8. See figures 7.1 and 7.2 of this book (pp. 234–35).
9. Block (2008, p. 1).
10. Block (2008).
11. Block & Keller (2011 [*State of Innovation*; "Where Do Innovations Come From?"]); Eisinger (1988); Janeway (2014); Mazzucato (2013); Osborne & Gaebler (1992).
12. Abbate (1999).
13. Leslie (2000, p. 49).
14. McCrary (2009).
15. Lazonick & Tulum (2011); Mazzucato & Dosi (2006).
16. Motoyama, Appelbaum, & Parker (2011).
17. Block (2008); Mazzucato (2013).
18. Kolodziej (1987).
19. Appelbaum et al. (2011); Mazzucato, 2013) Not all state ventures have been successful. Critics point to the bankruptcy of Solyndra, which received substantial federal funding. Ireland also has had mixed success as a developmental state.
20. See chapters 2, 3, and, especially, 7.
21. Held (1991, 1995); Ignatieff (2000); Singer (2002).
22. North (1990). Chapters 5 and 6 cover the role of the state in economic and technological development.
23. Sassen (2007, p. 46).
24. For the debate on whether globalization has transformed the nation-state system, see Held & McGrew (2002, especially pp. 1–40); Hirst, Thompson, & Bromley (2009).
25. Gilpin (1987, 2000, 2001); Kindleberger (1974, 1981, 1993); Rosecrance (1986). Among the first to recognize the destructive nature of building a global market economy was Karl Polanyi (1944).
26. See note 20.
27. Held (1991, 1995); Ignatieff (2000); Singer (2002).
28. This is the principal point of Kenneth Waltz's theory of international relations, which enjoys considerable support among security theorists and analysts.
29. The Israeli nuclear weapons program is extensively discussed in Cohen (1998).
30. Kehr (1973); Kennedy (1980).
31. Kier (1996); Weinberg (1995).
32. See figure 4.2.

33. The contested literature surrounding explanations for the breakup of the European concert is voluminous. For a start, see Joll (1984); Koch (1972); Mayer (1969); Van Evera (1984).

34. Power (2002).

35. For a general review of UN peacekeeping and for a clarification of the multiple activities associated with these operations, see Diehl (2008).

36. Bull (1977); Buzan (1991); Buzan, Little, & Jones (1993).

37. Mearsheimer (1994, 2001); Waltz (1979).

38. Sarkees (2000).

39. Ibid., p. 129.

40. Ibid.

41. Figure 4.1 is based on different counting rules than COW data are. However civil wars are counted, they exceed interstate wars and represent the principal threat to populations today.

42. Klare (2012). See also Amnesty International Home Page for conflicts over diamonds and other valuable minerals: http://www.amnestyusa.org/.

43. Wright (1965).

44. Pape (2006) argues that a Muslim caliphate, informed by a fundamentalist Sunni theology, is the political vision animating Al Qaeda as a social and religious movement.

45. Boorman (1969).

46. Ibid.

47. See figure 4.2 and table 4.1.

48. Kahn (1960).

49. The National Resources Defense Council's inventories are the most comprehensive and authoritative in this period. See http://www.nrdc.org.

50. Ball (1980); Craig & Jungerman (1986); Kaufman (1964); Lewis (1979).

51. Rosenberg (1983).

52. Schelling (1960); Schelling & Halperin (1958) develop the theory of cooperation between adversaries.

53. *New York Times*, March 12, 2012.

54. A later estimate by the Arms Control Association of deployed and stockpiled nuclear weapons by nuclear powers cites 1,642 strategic nuclear warheads for the United States and 1,643 for Russia. Those for China, the United Kingdom, and France approximate those of the *Bulletin of Atomic Scientists*, cited in table 4.1. See Arms Control Association report of February 2015.

55. Schultz et al. (2007). The call for the elimination of nuclear stockpiles by four prominent American political officials and strategists has obviously fallen on deaf ears.

56. *New York Times*, January 27, 2014.

57. *Washington Post*, November 14, 2015.

58. Allison (2004). Allison's grim prognosis did not diminish six years later. See Allison (2010).

59. Stinnett et al. (2011, p. 326).

60. Report of Richard Grimmett, *Conventional Arms Transfers to Developing Nations: 2004–2011*, Congressional Research Service, Washington, DC, August 24, 2012.
61. Ibid.
62. Ibid.
63. This self-sustaining subsystem of arms production and sales is scarcely new. See Kolodziej (1980).
64. Check the website of the Small Arms Survey: www.smallarmssurvey.org.
65. Krause (2007) provides a useful overview of SALWs as a significant international security issue as well as citations to other documentation and commentary.
66. http://www.un.org/News/briefings/docs/2008/080714_Small_Arms_Survey.doc.htm.
67. The Khan nuclear sales network is described in Franz & Collins (2007).
68. This theme is developed at length in Beck (2007).
69. Nordhaus (2013, p. 104).
70. The scientific findings and policy reports of the United Nations' Intergovernmental Panel on Climate Change (IPCC), issued in 2007 and updated and extended in 2013, are the foundations for the science of climate change and global warming. See UN IPCC reports (2007, 2013). Indispensable is William Nordhaus's *Climate Casino* (2013). See also Pittock (2010) for a brief discussion.
71. UN IPCC (2007).
72. UN IPCC (2007, p. 2 [italics added]).
73. Ibid.
74. UN IPCC (2013, p. 9).
75. UN IPCC (2007, p. 5).
76. Carbon Dioxide Information Analysis Center, Oak Ridge National Laboratory, Oak Ridge, TN, http://cdiac.ornl.gov/trends/co2/sio-keel.html.
77. *New York Times*, November 4, 2015.
78. Karl, Melillo, & Paterson (2009).
79. Nordhaus (2013, pp. 110ff.).
80. Several reports of the *Huffington Post* recount the cost and destruction of Sandy at www.huffingtonpost.com/news/hurricane-sandy-cost/.
81. Epstein & Ferber (2011).
82. The WTO estimates that between 2030 and 2050, climate change is expected to cause approximately 250,000 additional deaths per year from malnutrition, malaria, diarrhea, and heat stress (see http://www.who.int/mediacentre/factsheets/fs266/en/).
83. Nordhaus (2013).
84. UN IPCC panel reports for 2007 and 2013 extensively estimate the physical and biological damaging effects of GHG as well as their likely differential regional and global effects.
85. Ibid.; see part IV, pp. 197–292, for an extensive discussion and evaluation of using the market system to cope with global warming.
86. Ibid., p. 159.
87. Report of the World Resources Institute, published in the *Guardian*, November 19, 2012.
88. *New York Times*, November 14, 2012.

89. Lang & Miao (2010, p. 405) and Song & Woo (2008). Pan & Chen (2009) develop the Chinese case for special treatment.

90. Nordhaus (2013, pp. 304–5).

91. Ibid., p. 54.

92. See the *Quadrennial Defense Review* 2010: Overview and Implications for National Security Planning, http://www.defense.gov/qdr/images/QDR_as_of_12Feb10_1000.pdf, pp. 84ff.

93. Hsiang, Meng, & Cane (2011); Solow (2011).

94. Michael Klare provides data regarding conflicts over resources. See Klare (2012).

95. Coral Davenport, "Nations Approve Landmark Climate Accord in Paris," *New York Times*, December 12, 2015. See also "UN Framework Convention on Climate Change," December 12, 2015.

96. IISS (2007, pp. 422–38).

97. *New York Times*, September 22, 2011, and *Washington Post*, September 22, 2011.

98. For piracy and maritime terrorism, see Marley (2011); Murphy (2007).

99. See the Corruptions Perception Index, https://www.transparency.org/cpi 2014/results.

100. Tilly (1985).

101. Crocker (2003).

102. Kolodziej (2000); Power (2002).

103. Interest in the causes and consequences of failing and failed states is growing as a research area. See, for example, Brock et al. (2012); Kostovicova & Bojicic-Dzelilovic (2009); Power (2002); Taylor (2013).

5

The Market System I

The Disposition to Implode

The decadent international but individualistic capitalism, in the hands of which we found ourselves after the war, is not a success. It is not intelligent, it is not beautiful, it is not just, it is not virtuous—and it doesn't deliver the goods. In short we dislike it, and we are beginning to despise it. But when we wonder what to put in its place we are extremely perplexed.

—John Maynard Keynes, *National Self-Sufficiency*

SINCE THE PUBLICATION OF ADAM SMITH'S *The Wealth of Nations* over two centuries ago, the peoples and states of the emerging global society have experimented with several, competing solutions to the challenge of global welfare. Among the principal models, since discredited, were the creation of empires, principally in the form of the Eurocentric system, state-based autarchic systems, and command economic regimes, exemplified by the Soviet Union, Mao Zedong's Communist China, North Korea, Vietnam, and Cuba. Slowly, gradually, in fits and starts, with advances and retreats, the peoples and states of the globe have settled upon a free exchange system—a global market system—to respond to the Welfare imperative of global governance.[1]

The institutionalization of a market system, however much it may deviate, theoretically, from a pure, free exchange system today, as outlined in chapter 3, has not been a free good. At an expense of hundreds of millions of dead and wounded and incalculable loss of human treasure, parallel to the costs of installing a global state system to respond to the imperative of Order, a global market system has prevailed over competing solutions as the principal, globally institutionalized response to human basic needs and rising popular demands for ever greater material welfare. However challenged or maligned, it forms a formidable, autonomous power structure, with its own decision-making processes and actor incentives for decision and action. Actors associated with the market system, state and nonstate, have successfully frustrated alternative solutions for feeding, clothing, sheltering, and, more generally, for fulfilling human strivings for increasingly greater material well-being.

A global market system, as a solution to the Welfare imperative of governance, also poses formidable problems for the capacity of the interdependent peoples of the globe to address, coherently and cooperatively, their multiple and clashing demands for "more now" and for the continuing improvement of their material lots. Conventional wisdom—popular, partisan, and academic—may well stipulate that global markets represent the best available response to the imperative of Welfare.[2] The more relevant questions are whether the market system is good enough and, even if it is the best institutional solution available, whether it can elicit support of the world's populations to ensure its retention and replication. Relative to the challenges confronting the institution of global capitalist markets, pressured by a rising world population projected to reach nine to ten billion by 2050, Keynes's lament that "it doesn't deliver the goods" is no less true for our time than for his.

This chapter begins at the end of the story of the triumph of the market system. The long, arduous, and costly climb of the market system to ascendancy is covered in a voluminous literature well beyond the specific focus of this discussion.[3] What we want to determine, rather, are the flaws and failures of the market system today as a solution to global welfare. That diagnosis is the starting point for seeking workable remedies and reforms.

Since a fully satisfying and comprehensive evaluation of the effectiveness of global markets can scarcely be attempted here, the discussion will be limited to an examination of three major shortcomings: (1) the disposition of the system to implode, notably its financial component that supplies the capital, credit, and liquidity to keep the market engine running; (2) the market system's unequal and inequitable allocation of income and wealth to the world's populations as a consequence, recognized by Karl Marx almost two centuries ago, of the imbalances of political and economic bargaining power distributed by the market system among the members of the global society; and (3) the system's chronic inability to surmount poverty or achieve full global employment, however much it has helped to lift billions out of subsistence or sub-subsistence conditions.

These systemic flaws do not cover other significant and glaring market failures. Added to the three noted above, these include, among others, (4) the asymmetries of information available to economic actors at odds with the expectations of pure liberal economic theory, which expects a balance of information between suppliers and consumers or investors and credit agencies in their transactions; (5) the neglect of the market system to account for externalities or spillover costs in producing wealth, a shortcoming already visited in chapter 4; (6) the failings of the market system to provide sufficiently for collective goods indispensable for the survival of a global society; (7) the tendency at the opposite pole of implosion to move toward monopoly and the elimination of free market transactions; and (8) the moral paucity of the utilitarian normative value system underlying the market system that reduces all social exchanges, trivial and fundamental, to prices, profits, and material outcomes, thereby weakening and risking the evisceration of vital and strictly noneconomic social relations. Among the most important of these is social justice, indispensable for the effective and legitimate workings of human societies—*What Money Can't Buy*, in the words of Michael Sandel.[4]

Each of these weaknesses merits a volume, treatment of which is a life's work. It is also important to underline again that these eight shortcomings scarcely cover the full scope of market failures. Given the constraints of space, other, important market failings, like alternative ways to measure welfare than gross domestic product (GDP) and per capita income, will not be developed.[5] The object of this discussion is not the development of a definitive theory of the market system or its moral values or norms of behavior.[6] Rather, the aim here is narrower but important: to insist on the imperative of Welfare as a central determinant of global governance with its unique institutional rules, laws, protocols, processes of decision, supportive power resources, and multiple actors performing on a global stage.[7]

Chapters 5 and 6 submit that the market system is a necessary but insufficient solution to the global imperative of Welfare. This critique of three of its principal shortcomings—implosion, inequality and inequity, and poverty—is designed to serve as a surrogate for a more comprehensive analysis of the market system. It will also help to identify in broad outline the hard work that remains to perfect the market system as the provisional solution to the governmental imperative of Welfare. As Keynes suggests, there are no readily available substitutes for the market system. Absent alternatives, then the challenge confronting the states and peoples of the world society is to reform the system to address its flaws rather than simply hope that these are self-correcting. The dysfunctions of the market system belie this optimistic expectation.

Systemic Risk: The Perfect Storm of the Financial Meltdown of 2007–2008

It is difficult to exaggerate the significance of the financial breakdown of 2007–2008. The systemic risk it posed to the global financial system impacted ipso facto on the stability and sustainability of the more encompassing economic market system. In daily providing trillions of dollars of liquidity to the market system, the financial subsystem acts as the circulatory lifeblood of the market system.

In 2006 the GWP was approximately $47 trillion. The capitalization of the world stock markets surpassed this figure, topping $51 trillion. Domestic and international bonds exceeded these measures and stood at $68 trillion. The emergence of a host of new financial instruments by an expanding number of banks, investment and insurance firms, hedge funds, and private traders led to the creation of an ever greater mountain of unmanageable debt held by investors across the globe. Between 2002 and 2006, the indebtedness of the financial sector of the US economy rose from $10.1 trillion to $14.3 trillion. By 2007 the indebtedness of the financial sector reached $16 trillion.[8] Between 2001 and 2007, just before the financial meltdown, the total amount of US mortgage debt doubled from $5.3 trillion to $10.5 trillion.[9] Niall Ferguson captures the dimensions of this crisis in observing that at the beginning of the century, "Planet Finance" had eclipsed "Planet Earth."[10]

The global financial meltdown at the end of the first decade of this century exposed not only structural weaknesses of the global markets but also the failures of state actors responsible for ensuring market solvency to anticipate such a disastrous breakdown and, in its aftermath, to mitigate its damaging effects. The almost total dissolution of global financial markets and the resulting freezing of credit and capital flows produced the deepest recession of the postwar period, approaching the devastation of the Great Depression of the 1930s. If the sources of the collapse are, for analytic purposes, divided into state, market, and democratic political failures, it becomes readily apparent that these three power centers and the institutions they support were complicit, individually and collectively, in engendering the crisis.

The global meltdown of 2007–2008 is remarkable for at least three reasons. First, few who were engaged in the financial system from top to bottom foresaw its collapse. This "black swan" event was not anticipated even by those who expected the market system and its financial component to be subject to periodic and inescapable booms and busts.[11] This informed minority also subscribed to what had been heretofore a widely accepted expectation that business cycles and the ups and downs of capitalist markets were endemic to a free market system. Crisis market behavior was something deeper and more damaging, but no less intrinsic to market behavior if the conditions for breakdown arose and no countervailing governmental balance was invoked to preclude the collapse. In this sense, a global financial implosion could be viewed as a "white swan," as one keen analyst noted—namely, that crisis economics should be included as a probable, if unlikely, event as a part of the normal workings of markets. What is particularly striking about the 2007–2008 financial crisis is the failure of policy-makers, private market actors—notably financial institutions—to rely on economic models that incorporated "black swan" events into their thinking.

Second, the threat posed by the financial crisis to the global economy was graver than a typical downturn of the business cycle. The crisis raised the prospect of the collapse of the entire global financial system. Previous financial crises, like the Panic of 1908, never approached these extreme limits. The 2007–2008 meltdown raised fundamental questions about the comforting expectation that a downturn in the business cycle would always be followed by an upswing in the cycle and that an eventual, automatic rebalancing and recovery of global markets would result without governmental intervention.

Third, in contrast to the Great Depression, whose roots can be traced to the upheavals and economic dislocations of World War I—which destroyed the global interdependent economic system of the prewar period—the unfolding of the 2007–2008 threat to the world economy was due to the deliberate, if misguided, decisions of financial actors and to the perverse incentives at work within the system that disposed them to pursue their private and personal self-interests in ways to undermine the very market system on which their material interests depended. The incentive structures in place prompted almost all implicated actors—indeed, urged—them to make increasingly risky bets and assume mounting leveraged debt, gravely damaging their personal or corporate interests and ipso facto the global financial system.[12]

As long as what was increasingly becoming a global Ponzi game continued, few players could resist taking greater risks. Chuck Prince, the discredited CEO of Citigroup, captured the pressures on him from shareholders and competitors (not to say those which were self-imposed) in rationalizing the great losses incurred by his corporation when the financial bubble burst. Prince lamented that "when the music stops, in terms of liquidity, things will be complicated. But as long as the music is playing [liquidity in lending is available], you've got to get up and dance."[13]

Financial actors, principally large investment firms and hedge funds, have pressing incentives to keep making investments in the game to make gains or forfeit them to their competitors. If they did not "dance," others would reap these rewards. What is tricky is knowing when the music is about to abruptly stop and the game is over. Prince and a host of other speculators naively expected that, with the then seemingly inexhaustible availability of liquidity in global market transactions, the music would not stop anytime soon, if ever. Partially blinded by their pursuit of short-term profits, they were unable to foresee, some willfully, the warning signs of a coming collapse: the outcome of a precipitous cascade of defaults on housing loans, principally subprime mortgages; a steep fall in housing prices for the first time in the postwar period; a rapid increase in interest rates; and ever larger and accelerating demands of creditors for more collateral to guarantee shaky loans. The end game was the disastrous drying up of credit, when it was most needed, as banks and other financial institutions refused to lend to each other, much less to qualified, credit-borrowers. None could ascertain whether their loans would be repaid. Much like a run on an insolvent bank, the run now was on the global financial system as a whole.

As late as June 2007, Chuck Prince, like many of his counterparts in the financial community, justified the exposure of Citigroup to hypertrophied risk-taking in financial markets and the erosion of underwriting standards on the widely held assumption that global liquidity to support these excesses was sufficient to keep the music going: "The depth of the pools of liquidity is so much larger than it used to be that a disruptive event now needs to be much more disruptive than it used to be. At some point, the disruptive event will be so significant that instead of liquidity filling in, liquidity will go the other way. I don't think we're at that point."[14] The pools of liquidity that Prince was relying on to make good Citigroup's bets on lame assets were drying up as he spoke. As John Cassidy notes, "The logic of rational irrationality has rarely been spelled out more clearly."[15] If all actors try to offload their holdings at the same time, especially their toxic assets, which no one wants to buy, there is a run on the system itself. In that circumstance, as Keynes observed, "there is no such thing as liquidity of investment for the community as a whole."[16]

Within the global financial bubble, which the individual decisions of financial actors collectively created, all might well be viewed as acting rationally in pursuing their particular interests. Not to move with the herd was to risk being trampled by it. In retrospect, what was not apparent to anyone was that most financial players were all unwittingly cooperating in putting the market system at risk. In a perverse reversal of the expectations of Adam Smith's "hidden hand," financial actors—private and public—relentlessly pursued their own parochial interests in ways that served to undermine and threaten to destroy the system that ensured realization of their material well-being—or at least that of the corporations they were pledged to serve with due diligence.

The events of 2007–2008 revealed that, contra Adam Smith, the self-interested behavior of actors could, ironically, bring the system down.[17] Falsified was the conventional wisdom of most financial experts that bad bets would always be penalized or punished by the system, short of the collapse of the system itself, and that markets were always self-correcting with no need for state or outside help.[18]

State Actors: Failures of Commission and Omission

The unwitting coconspirators of the financial collapse were (a) clutches of actors associated with multiple and overlapping (and uncoordinated) state regulatory and financial agencies; (b) a vast array of private actors heavily engaged in financial markets, notably large investment firms, hedge funds, and an expanding universe of private traders and brokers—that emerged as an enlarging network of shadow banks; and, finally, (c) millions of improvident home buyers and consumers eager to live beyond their means by assuming subprime mortgages and by incurring credit card and other forms of debt for which they lacked the means—or felt the obligation—to repay, many using their home equity as an ATM machine.

The actors and factors leading to the collapse of the financial market system, described below, are not ordered in any priority of causal impact on global financial markets. There is not sufficient data, much less consensus among professional observers and analysts, to definitively accord responsibility for the collapse.[19] Some charge that the source of the meltdown was the federal government through one or more of its sprawling and decentralized regulatory agencies.[20] Others criticize Congress and presidents Bill Clinton and George W. Bush for pressing governmental agencies to make easy credit available to poor-risk borrowers.[21] Others are convinced that fault lies primarily with the private sector and greedy, overreaching banks, investment houses, credit rating agencies, and a vast array of smaller financial brokers and traders.[22] This discussion advances a balanced approach, citing these sets of actors as culpable, though blame is allocated to members in different shades of gray.[23]

What the record so far discloses is that these three sets of interdependent actors were (and are) in one way or another deeply implicated in the assault on the global market system. However responsibility is allocated across these actors, there is little doubt that unregulated, unfettered free global financial markets are highly vulnerable to systemic risk and implosion as a consequence of the uncoordinated but converging initiatives of a wide spectrum of actors, most of whom had never had any direct connection with each other. Like Agatha Christie's vengeful passengers on *Murder on the Orient Express*, all were culpable, but no one is willing to accept personal responsibility. That inherent exposure to systemic collapse goes beyond the ups and downs of the business cycle. In a complex, interdependent global society of seven billion principals and their multiple agents, uncertainty about the future prospects, even survival, of the market system is endemic to the unpredictable dynamism of actor economic and financial transactions.

What occurred was a "perfect storm." Unlike passing weather fronts, this crisis was in the making for a long time. The financial bubble and the volatile forces working within its fragile membrane were gathering strength over several decades before they exploded in a self-sustaining chain reaction over 2007–2008. Decades were required for the contributions from these varied sources to eventually converge to produce the global meltdown. The inputs of the bewildering cluster of alphabet financial agencies of the US federal government, notably the Treasury, the Federal Reserve, and government-sponsored enterprises (GSEs Fannie Mae and Freddie Mac), to the gathering storm are key starting points to understand the role of state policies and institutions in the catastrophe.

State actors contributed to market system risk through a mutually contradictory combination of intervening too much in financial markets, to their detriment particularly in pressing for greater home ownership, or too little. The latter omission was particularly disruptive. Over a decade or more financial markets were gradually deregulated and, in tandem, governmental regulatory bodies either were precluded from exercising oversight over an exploding securities market in derivatives, credit default obligations, and other dubious financial vehicles by Congress, or were dysfunctional or co-opted by the actors that they were supposed to regulate, to preclude a systemic financial crisis. The disquieting results of these multiple lapses were inadequate and self-defeating ad hoc responses, monetized in trillions of dollars in taxpayer obligations, no small amount of which was wasted, fraudulently pilfered, or ineffective in stabilizing a profoundly shaken global financial system.[24]

The roots of the financial crisis can also be partially traced to the interest of both political parties and the Congress to encourage and facilitate home ownership, which became referred to, ironically, as "the American Dream." Congress created Fannie Mae and Freddie Mac to buy both governmental and conventional private mortgages and to issue securities for those mortgages that it guaranteed. The purchase of these mortgages freed up bank credit that could be used to issue additional mortgages in pursuit of the goal of increasing home ownership.

GSEs are a special private-public corporate entity. As private entities they could issue stock and assume much of the properties and market power of a corporation. As government-sponsored entities, they could implicitly draw on the full faith and credit of the US government to borrow at interest rates below those of private corporations, even triple-A rated corporations like General Electric. Their securities were particularly attractive to investors, who viewed them as tantamount to US treasury notes. The federal government was expected to back defaults on mortgage payments, though this guarantee was nowhere spelled out in legislation. The initially prudent policies of Fannie Mae and Freddie Mac bolstered their reputations and credit ratings. They strengthened investor confidence in dealing primarily, at the start, in quality mortgages. These were issued to borrowers who were employed, who had good credit scores, and who could meet tough equity requirements for loans.

These stringent policies were progressively weakened within the GSEs as leadership changes in the 1990s brought to these corporate helms CEOs who gradually shifted GSE priorities: to increase market shares of mortgage holdings of decreasing credit worthiness so as to keep pace with Wall Street and private mortgage underwriters; to enhance salaries for GSE CEOs as compensation for greater entrepreneurial success; and to increase profits for the GSEs in responding to shareholder expectations for higher yielding dividends and capital gains. Downgraded was the original and privileged mission of the GSEs—namely, to expand home ownership and to develop that mission by placing housing on a solid financial foundation.[25]

Congressional legislation fostered these changes in priorities. In the 1990s, Congress stipulated that 30 percent of the mortgages purchased by GSEs were to support homeownership to low- and middle-income families, so-called underserved borrowers. To meet the requirement that banks underwrite increased loans to low- and middle-income families, standards of eligibility were progressively relaxed. By 1997, according to one estimate, Fannie Mae was purchasing 97 percent of these mortgages with as little as a 3 percent down payment. By 2001 GSEs were guaranteeing and buying mortgages that lacked adequate credit checks and with no money down.[26]

The GSEs and the private financial sector were locked in self-destructive competition to capture an increasingly larger share of the mortgage market, largely through the issuance of subprime mortgages to homebuyers with weak credit ratings and little prospect of employment capable of meeting their loan obligations. The securitization of these toxic assets and their dissemination around the globe fueled the creation of a financial bubble in subprime mortgages of unprecedented scope. The continued speculative rise in housing prices and the incentive that this rise afforded home owners to increase home equity loans spurred further the frenzy in making risky loans of all kinds—mortgages, credit card debt, car and student loans, and so forth. This dysfunctional incentive structure drove lenders and borrowers to assume ever-larger debt and risk-taking or be left out of the financial gains to be realized as long as the bubble did not burst.

The GSEs, which were late in the game of speculation in subprime mortgages,[27] were forced, ironically, to return to their primary mission, to provide increased liquidity to prop up a volatile and failing housing market. By 2008, when the financial bubble eventually burst, sparked by the collapse of the subprime mortgage market, the GSEs owned or guaranteed $5.3 trillion in mortgages, a large portion of which was in rapidly depreciating housing assets. Against this indebtedness the GSEs held only $84 billion in reserve, or less than 2 percent. They added to their insolvency by also keeping subprime mortgages on their books in a futile quest to yield greater corporate profits and dividends to their stockholders and to ensure GSE CEOs and top employees increased compensation.

Facing bankruptcy, the US Treasury induced Congress to pass emergency legislation to place the GSEs into conservatorships. As two analysts concluded, "For decades, Fannie and Freddie had worked to maximize profits at the expense of its government mission. Now that mission was paramount."[28] Illusory was the expectation that this mission could be achieved through the unfettered workings of the market system in response to the incentives for profit that it generated.

What was not anticipated was the fact that GSE defection from its primary mission would cast taxpayers in the unsought role of guarantor of last resort of the toxic assets on the GSE books. The magnitude of the federal government's action in essentially nationalizing Fannie Mae and Freddie Mac is suggested by the debt and other obligations assumed by the US government. These amounted to over $5 trillion, which in 2007 were greater than the public debt then owed by the federal government.[29] The US Treasury was obliged to pledge $200 billion in taxpayer funds to guarantee that the two mortgage giants would pay their debts,[30] while preferred stockholders in Fannie and Freddie were largely wiped out.

The roles of the Federal Reserve and the US Treasury are also important to understand the causes of the financial breakdown. The acts of omission and commission of these two principal institutions to oversee and regulate financial markets are more complex than can be fully detailed here. Federal Reserve and Treasury leadership failed on several counts: initially failing to predict or anticipate the financial meltdown, abetting the crisis by fueling liquidity, moving slowly to contain the crisis, and finally pursuing weak and feckless policies to mitigate the disruptive and damaging effects of the financial breakdown. The important point to be drawn from their acts of omission and commission that contributed to the financial crisis is that the regulatory system of banks and financial institutions, over which the Federal Reserve and Treasury preside but do not fully control, was totally unprepared to address the systemic risk to the entire global financial system whose workings revolve around the American component.

Largely through ad hoc responses to each unfolding phase of the financial crisis, these institutions barely saved the financial system from complete collapse. Some initiatives were remedial and partially worked, though in every instance at substantial cost to taxpayers. The bailout of AIG, described below, which is the largest insurance corporation in the world, illustrates a costly public lifesaving intervention. Other responses were poorly conceived and disastrous. The bankruptcy of Lehman Brothers is a case in point wherein the failure of the federal government to act to forestall its collapse had disastrous consequences for the global financial system. Neither the Federal Reserve nor the US Treasury grasped how deeply embedded and indebted Lehman Brothers was in the tightly woven fabric of the global financial system. In failing to save Lehman, the American government's inaction allowed the firm to unravel overnight. With its rapid dissolution, the entire global financial system froze.

Federal Reserve Chairman Ben Bernanke and Treasury Secretary Henry Paulson insist that they were acutely aware of the systemic, worldwide impact of the Lehman bankruptcy. Bernanke characterized it as an "epic disaster."[31] Citing Tim Geithner, New York Federal Reserve chairman, Bernanke's case for governmental inaction pivoted on the claim that "Without a buyer, and with no authority to inject fresh capital or guarantee Lehman's assets, we had no means of saving the firm."[32] The weakness of this defense is that neither Paulson nor Bernanke (much less Alan Greenspan) had ever proposed to Congress well before the crisis erupted that Congress provide the needed authority for the government to act to preclude a systemic collapse of the global financial system. There is little likelihood that Congress would have provided this authority in light of the ruling coalition's commitment to the principle of a self-regulating market system. But the Federal Reserve and the Treasury would have at least been on record as acting with due diligence to prevent a systemic breakdown of the global financial system. Clearly lacking were national and international political controls to save the market system from itself. Nor are they readily available today.

Congress has scarcely addressed these governmental failings although more than a half-decade has passed since the crash. Much less has transnational banking cooperation been strengthened, principally between the United States and the European Union, the European Central Bank, and the respective national banks of the EU. The Dodd-Frank bill to reform and strengthen governmental financial regulation remains untested. As Alan S. Blinder, a former vice chairman of the Federal Reserve, concluded in his explanation of the financial collapse, "The battle for financial reform still rages. Rules remain to be written, interpreted, and rewritten—not to mention implemented. . . . We won't know how the new authority for liquidating financial giants will work until we actually use it. And I have not even mentioned the difficulties of homogenizing U.S. rules with foreign rules, which are generally different and lag behind ours."[33]

JP Morgan's large losses in the spring of 2012 as the result of risky market speculations, reminiscent of the 2007–2008 meltdown, dramatize the systemic weaknesses of the prevailing financial regime. Market losses totaled approximately $6 billion. Added fees and charges to settle its case with governmental regulators brought its total losses to $10 billion. The bank put depositor funds, guaranteed by the federal government, at risk because there were no effective regulatory mechanisms in place to have precluded the wagering of these bad bets.[34]

Bernanke's predecessor, Alan Greenspan, was among the most prominent contributors to the slow and then accelerating meltdown. His ideological certainty about the efficiency and effectiveness of free, unfettered markets shaped his responses to the financial crisis.[35] He was convinced that there was little need and much mischief in exercising the regulatory powers of the Federal Reserve to stanch predatory mortgage lending and the weakening of lending standards. The latter included falsifying the credit worthiness of borrowers or requiring little or no down payments for mortgages. Greenspan resisted using Federal Reserve powers to monitor subprime lenders, arguing that "for us to go in and audit how they act on their mortgage applications would have been a huge effort, and it's not clear to me we would have found anything that would have been worthwhile without undermining the desired availability of subprime credits."[36]

Greenspan expressed the same optimistic view in refusing to exercise the regulatory power of the Federal Reserve over credit default swaps and other forms of derivatives: "Risks in credit financial markets, including derivatives markets, are being regulated by private parties. There is nothing involved in federal regulation per se which makes it superior to market regulations."[37] For Greenspan the best regulation was little or no regulation. The market was self-correcting. Those who made risky choices lost; those who were prudent and prescient won.

Rather than contain the toxic spread of subprime mortgages, the immediate trigger for the global financial collapse of 2007–2008, the Federal Reserve under Greenspan threw fuel on the fire in lauding their utility in increasing home ownership. On that score his thinking and that of prevailing congressional sentiment converged. Greenspan was no less oblivious to the negative implications of using subprime mortgages to underwrite a mountain of public and private debt, spurred by the spread of new and volatile financial instruments. Flooding the global financial markets were collateralized debt obligations (CDOs), credit default swaps (CDSs), and structured investment vehicles (SIVs)—monetized in hundreds of billions of dollars.

What is noteworthy about Federal Reserve myopia in this period, in failing to pursue its obligation to stabilize financial markets through its monetary authority—principally its influence over interest rates—and its regulatory authority over banks and financial institutions, are the causal links between these powers and the explosion in real and notional value of these dubious financial instruments. Instead, the Fed's rapid lowering of interest rates to address the dot-com bubble at the turn of the century helped usher in the subprime mortgage bubble a half-decade later. Critics note that when the Federal Reserve acted quickly to lower interest rates, it then kept these low rates in place for too long a time. The effect was to pump vast sums of easy credit into the financial system to stem the damage of the collapse of the technology bubble only to inflate "an entirely new one."[38] By keeping the Federal Reserve fund rate at 2.5 percent between 2001 and 2005, interest rates more generally were also kept low. The incentive to borrow and risk huge funds spread from home owners and consumers to businesses and speculators. Between 2002 and 2006, total US debt from all sources jumped from $31.84 trillion to $45.32 trillion, an increase of 42.3 percent. By 2006, total indebtedness of the country rose to 350 percent of GDP, with the financial sector accounting for the largest share of this total.[39]

As one significant element of the developing perfect financial storm, the Federal Reserve was unwittingly providing massive amounts of easy credit at the very time that the private sector was creating new, risky financial instruments, spurred by access to easy money. The unregulated expansion of markets in these instruments, resting increasingly on paper transactions and not real, tangible material assets, threatened the global system itself. In an appearance before a congressional committee at the height of the crisis, Greenspan explained that "the boom in subprime lending occurred because of the huge demand for investment opportunities in a global economy."[40] He blamed the crash on a failure by investors to properly assess the risks from such mortgages, which went to borrowers with weak credit. Of the billions of dollars of losses suffered by financial institutions because of their investments in subprime mortgages, Greenspan said he had been shocked by the failure of banking officials to protect their shareholders from bad decisions. A critical pillar to market competition and free markets broke down. Greenspan had no explanation: "*I still do not understand why it happened.*"[41] So much for the reliability of self-regulating private financial actors to effectively pursue their personal interests, much less to ensure the stability and survival of the global financial system.

Greenspan's successor, Ben Bernanke, was no less caught up initially in the thrall of the optimistic assumptions of the self-correcting capacities of financial markets and no less initially enamored about the alleged positive advantages of the multiplying financial instruments issuing from Wall Street and other sources. Economists at the Federal Reserve shared Greenspan's assessment of unregulated financial markets. In 2005 three Federal Reserve economists lauded what they believed were the positive benefits to the market of financial innovations, implicitly unchecked by the Federal Reserve:

"Improved assessment and pricing of risk, expanded lending to households without strong collateral, more widespread securitization of loans, and the development of markets for riskier corporate debt have enhanced the ability of households and businesses to borrow funds."[42] It was precisely these activities that were the undoing of the financial system.

It would be misleading and grossly unfair to attribute the principal cause of the crisis to any one individual. Greenspan's untutored understanding of the workings of financial markets was not singular or peculiarly aberrant. An array of leading economists, analysts, and political elites shared the untested assumptions about the market's self-correcting capacity. What became evident in the wake of the financial crash was that the economic models they relied upon were fundamentally flawed. Financial operatives were able to create and trade trillions of dollars in assets whose value few, if any, understood. Nor were financial markets able to accurately price these paper instruments.

Uncertainty and the resulting paralysis of the financial system, public and private, was the inevitable, if unforeseen, result. In freezing financial and credit markets, the global economy itself was placed in peril. Under these conditions, global markets could not be reassured. The multiple actors who implicitly conspired to cause the crisis lacked the vision and means to correct their failures absent collective governmental action on a scale equal to the crisis. Effective intervention tools were nowhere readily available. The expectation that banks and traders were sufficiently informed to protect themselves against the risks they ran simply proved wrong and wrongheaded. The models were broken because systemic failure had not been included in their estimates or expectations.[43] The existence of "black swans" was ruled out by assumption.

The ruling majorities in the House of Representatives and the Senate, with bipartisan support of Republicans and Democrats and that of the White House of President Bill Clinton, were no less caught up in the financial frenzy. The legislative and executive branches were as one in supporting the extension of easy loans to low income groups. The Congress, as noted earlier, also pressured Fannie Mae and Freddie Mac to follow suit. These well-intentioned policies contributed to the unwitting extension of credit to otherwise suspect creditworthy borrowers, whether to buy a home, to exploit their home equity, or to seek loans for purposes of excessive consumption beyond their means to repay.

In repealing the Glass-Steagall Act of 1933, Congress extended additional support for the boom in subprime mortgages and asset innovation. Glass-Steagall prevented commercial banks from using depositor funds to invest in selling stocks and bonds, issuing and underwriting financial securities, and the like. The wall between commercial and investment banking acted as a barrier to large-scale speculation in investments and as a brake on the development of new, tradable financial instruments. The passage of the Gramm-Leach-Bliley Act in 1999, which effectively repealed Glass-Steagall, made available a vastly increased pool of liquid funds to bankers, who no longer had to be constrained by New Deal legislation. The wall between commercial banking and investments came tumbling down.

In a fundamental sense, the emergence of an expanding universe of "shadow banks" had already superseded the formal repeal of Glass-Steagall. The commercial banking system during the Glass-Steagall era of over sixty years fell under the regulatory sway of the Federal Reserve and Federal Deposit Insurance Corporation (FDIC). Banks were obliged to submit themselves to regulation and to meet federally mandated reserve requirements in exchange for access to the Federal Reserve as the lender-of-last-resort. The significance of this regulatory regime was to limit the profits of banks, since they had to adhere to constraints covering liquidity, leveraging, and capital.

To get around these limits, a large array of new financial institutions, including branches of regulated banks, sprung up. These new actors formed what became a global shadow banking system. This sprawling network of "banks" rivaled commercial banks, which were under Federal Reserve and FDIC regulation, in size, capitalization, and lending power. Shadow banks consisted of traditional big investment firms, like Goldman Sachs, Bear Stearns, Lehman Brothers, and Morgan Stanley, as well as large hedge funds and multinational corporations (e.g., General Electric or General Motors). Also included were global insurance firms, like AIG, as well as thousands of mortgage brokers and small traders. These new financial players, commanding hundreds of billions of dollars in assets, acted in every way like banks, with one critical exception: they were not regulated. And they successfully lobbied, fueled by their ill-gotten gains, to preclude or weaken legislative oversight of their activities.

Shadow banks largely effaced the line between commercial banking and investment banking firms. The passing of Glass-Steagall implicitly recognized its increasing irrelevance as the ocean of available funds and credit from shadow banks vastly increased the speculative opportunities of the finance industry. Traditional commercial banks could not use the deposits of their clients to sell and trade stocks and bonds, invest in real estate, and securitize all kinds of loans for sale and profit on the open market. By the turn of the century all major traditional banks, like JP Morgan, had already created subsidiaries to trade and invest in dubiously backed securities.

In 1998, the collapse of Long Term Capital Management (LTCM), a giant hedge fund and prominent member of the shadow banking industry, foreshadowed the 2007–2008 crisis. Dealing heavily in derivatives, LTCM relied on sophisticated mathematical models to predict market movements in placing investor deposits at risk to increase LTCM's profits and to ensure large fees and outsized compensation for its managers. When LTCM's bets went sour and the firm faced imminent bankruptcy, the Federal Reserve of New York hastily arranged for fourteen banks and investment firms to provide sufficient equity to prevent LTCM's collapse. So much for the self-correcting mechanisms of the market, which were expected to inflict penalties on losers. LTCM was too big and its portfolios too interwoven with the assets of other financial actors to be permitted to fail.

What is extraordinary about this ad hoc solution is that no lessons were drawn from LTCM's collapse. The derivative market, inflated by leveraged debt monetized in trillions of dollars, threatened the entire financial system no less than the speculation in subprime mortgages would less than a decade later. Auditors discovered that LTCM had a leveraged ratio of 250 to 1—that is, only one dollar of LTCMs funds covered every $250 in debt on its books. The notional value of its derivatives was estimated in excess of $1.25 trillion.[44]

LTCM's excesses were deliberately pursued to the brink of bankruptcy, although two Nobel Prize laureates in economics, celebrated for their contributions to quantitative theory, were on its board of directors. Not without irony they were cited for their innovative work in the quantitative analysis of global market behavior. The best and brightest were no less subject to financial hubris than their less-celebrated counterparts. As Robert J. Shiller and George A. Akerlof remind us, free markets generate incentives for "animal spirits" and "irrational exuberance" to manifest themselves in the behavior of market actors, impelling them to their own, self-designed destruction—and that of the market system itself.[45]

Private Sector Contributions to the Meltdown

The continuing flood of conflicting accounts of the financial meltdown in books, journal articles, public documents, congressional hearings, and ceaseless media analyses currently precludes any definitive assessment of the private sector contributions to the crisis.[46] The aim here is rather to underline the structural flaws in the workings of free markets absent public regulation. Seriously undermined is the expectation of maximum payoff to all participants as well as maximum social benefit if the market is allowed to work unfettered and free from governmental intervention.

Markets, most notably in contemporary financial transactions, are disposed to implode if left unregulated by the state or by some other governing body with clout and authority to preclude implosion. Conversely, too much state intervention and control, with a centralized state economic system as the pertinent referential experience, impedes innovation, efficient and effective allocation of scarce investment sources, and sustained economic growth. Striking this balance is easier said than done. It was impossible during the wild speculative fever of the first decade of the twenty-first century, given the incentives driving public and private actors to work against their own self-interests.

A key starting point to understand the financial meltdown begins with the progressively significant impact of expanding financial transactions on national economies and on the global economy as a whole. This relentless expansion over a generation, with roots going back to the immediate postwar period, provided the material conditions for the almost worldwide financial collapse of 2007–2008. Between 1945 and 2010, the value added of the finance and insurance sectors in the United States as a percentage of GDP grew from approximately 2.5 percent to approximately 8.5 percent.[47] In the United Kingdom the percentage increase from the 1970s grew from 5 percent to 9 percent—more than tripling in the United States and doubling in the United Kingdom.[48]

This growth is further dramatized by the dollar value of trading in the US financial markets compared to GDP. In 1956, GDP represented almost 80 percent of the financial turnover of financial transactions. The GDP percentage dropped each year to reach approximately 18 percent in 1980 and less than 2 percent in 2000. Estimated financial turnover for 1956 was $534 billion, ballooning to approximately $227 trillion in 1990 and doubling to $508 trillion a decade later, excluding trillions more in derivative transactions that are not registered on open market trading exchanges.[49]

The collapse of a host of banks, the loss of employment of thousands of traders and brokers, and the near and actual bankruptcy of most large investment banking firms had a globally damaging impact on the world economy of a scope and depth to equal the depression of the 1930s. An April 2009 International Monetary Fund (IMF) study of the financial crisis estimated that bank losses would exceed $4 trillion. The write-down for 2009 was estimated at $2.8 trillion. Compared to a global GWP of $58 trillion, this loss represented almost 5 percent of global income. During 2007–2009, 168 US banks failed with deposits of just over 3 percent of GDP. If three large banks saved by federal intervention from bankruptcy are added, the percentage loss increases to 16 percent in 2008. The FDIC listed over 829 banks in the second quarter of 2010 as stressed and in serious trouble.[50] The 2009 IMF report also estimated that over $10 trillion would have to be expended by governments, notably in the United States and Europe, to prevent the collapse of the global financial system.[51]

The negative impact on the world economy was dramatic. In the United States, investment in 2009 fell at an annual rate of 49 percent. Exports dropped by 31 percent. The US GDP, on an annualized rate, fell 2.8 percent.[52] The steep decline in demand for goods and services forced mass layoffs. At the height of the financial crisis with the bankruptcy of Lehman Brothers and the near collapse of AIG, the world's largest insurance corporation, more than five million jobs were lost. Unemployment rose from 6.2 percent to 9.5 percent in the United States and remained at above 8 percent for the next four years. In Europe the downturn and economic dislocation of the recession brought on by the financial meltdown was much worse. Icelandic banks essentially went bankrupt. The invidiously labeled PIGS (Portugal, Ireland, Greece, and Spain), as well as Italy, confronted large and mounting public debts, threats of sovereign bankruptcy, and large-scale unemployment exceeding that of the United States. Between April 2008 and March 2009, world industrial production fell by almost 15 percent,[53] *The Wall Street Journal* reported owners of stock lost $8 trillion between January and October 2008 or a drop of approximately 40 percent. The same percentage loss also impacted on foreign investors abroad.[54]

The trigger for the collapse was the bursting of the housing bubble in the United States in 2007–2008, driven by the disintegration of the subprime mortgage market. Prime mortgages are accorded to clients with strong credit ratings. Creditworthiness is measured typically by a FICO score of 725. Below this number are subprime loans. The name FICO is derived from the Minneapolis firm, Fair Isaac Corporation, that developed the original model over fifty years ago. The score starts at 350 to an end point of 850. A FICO score below 600 is rated to post a risk of failure of 51 percent, a score between 600 and 649 of 31 percent.[55]

Until the late twentieth century, the GSEs, which were the principal guarantor of residential mortgages, largely underwrote prime mortgages. Due to legislative and public pressures, less creditworthy borrowers, with falling FICO scores, were extended loans by brokers and large mortgage companies like Countrywide and Ameriquest. Dubious loans were increasingly taken on GSE balance sheets. The higher returns to be made from subprime loans attracted private investors. Washington Mutual, a major subprime mortgage lender acquired by JP Morgan to escape bankruptcy, reported that subprime loans were roughly seven times more profitable than prime mortgages.[56]

The expanding issuance of subprime loans grew apace between 2000 and 2006, the last year marking the height of the subprime rise. By March 2007, US subprime mortgages were estimated to be monetized (as distinguished from real market value) at $1.3 trillion with over seven million first-lien mortgages. A general, systemic relaxation of credit standards spurred the rapid growth of these instruments. Subprime mortgages assumed many forms: no documentation Alt-As (a FICO just below prime); high-LTV (loan to value);

adjustable rate mortgages (ARMs); NINJAs (no income, no job, no assets); or interest-only loans, whose premiums often ballooned in a short period of time. Loans were made with little or no collateral. Very large loans, which GSEs could not handle, were still awarded to questionable borrowers.[57] At the time of the collapse of housing market in 2007, approximately 20 percent of original mortgages were subprime.

A sizeable proportion of subprime mortgages were extended through "teaser" loans in which the first two years would be offered at a lower rate, with a balloon rise in succeeding years—so-called 2/28 loans. The sizable and rapid increase in nonbank independent mortgage originators aided this process. Countrywide, which became among the largest underwriters of subprime mortgages, expanded this branch of its services by using independent brokers rather than relying on its own staff. Management leadership took this step to increase profits but at the expense of a loss of control of these feeders or over the quality of the mortgages that they were originating. Once the mortgage was transferred to Countrywide or to other larger mortgage firms, the broker who was paid a fee for service no longer assumed any obligation for the repayment of the loan.[58] This incentive system placed a premium on creating and churning mortgages. This system partially explains why two-thirds of all US mortgages leading to the bubble burst in 2007 were granted through a broker who had no physical contact with the borrower.[59] Of more significance is the dubious practice wherein the funder of a loan is not the one who originates it.

What transformed these subprime mortgages into a system-threatening process was the securitization of these loans and the extension of this flexible, if volatile, financial instrument to all other forms of debt, including credit card, car and student loans (a market monetized at over $1 trillion), and a vast array of other financial vehicles.

Securitization involves the bundling of varied forms of contractual debt into bonds. Once "sliced and diced" into securitized assets, they were sold to investors. Wall Street further refined the securitization process by creating from these pools of securitized assets different levels of assigned risk to tranches to meet the demand, stimulated by Wall Street, of investors who wished to define different levels of risk that they preferred to assume. Investors included foreign and domestic municipalities, pension funds, German savings banks, Icelandic and Chinese commercial banks, hedge funds, and armies of investment advisers and financial managers—like UBS, which induced trusting, uninformed clients to buy these toxic assets. Some, like Goldman Sachs, actually bet against their clients in marketing these risky products, such as its Tricia fund.[60] These securitized instruments were particularly attractive to Wall Street firms. They made billions trading in these securities;

they could lend warehouse lines of credit to mortgage firms to make these loans and then bundle them for additional sales; and they could make more gains by organizing the sale of stock of moneylenders, like Associates Household and the Money Store.[61]

The ironic rationale for securitization was the advantage this instrument purportedly offered in distributing risk. No less than the chairman of the Federal Reserve, Alan Greenspan, was an enthusiastic proponent of securitization as an innovative financial instrument that ostensibly made global financial markets more flexible, economically productive, and profitable for all parties. Banks, too, could sell their mortgages to Wall Street. In getting these obligations off their balance sheet, they could make more loans, since reserve requirements would have been met. International standards determining bank capital adequacy under Basel I rules considered mortgage loans prime assets and accorded them privileged rankings in determining the reserves banks had to retain.[62] Securitization had the opposite result of its intended aim. Rather than share and lower risk to investors, securitization concentrated risk in the financial sector.[63]

The three major rating agencies—Standard and Poor's, Moody's Investors Service, and Fitch Ratings—helped to stampede the frenetic purchase of subprime loans and their securitization by Wall Street. Since the 1970s these three firms essentially assumed the position of oligopolists. Legislation assigned them a privileged status in the industry of evaluating assets. Entry requirements for competitors were difficult to meet. The Securities and Exchange Commission required that for an applicant to gain status as a nationally recognized statistical rating organization (NRSRO), it must have been in business several years and had major clients. These were catch-22 conditions, since the major clients were already tied up by the big three. Moreover, many large funds, notably pension fund managers, were obliged to invest only in high-grade assets rated by these firms.[64]

At the start, investors paid these rating agencies for their services. That model was abandoned in the decades before the turn of the century in favor of fees being paid by the issuers of bonds and other investment vehicles. Immediately a basic conflict of interest arose between the economic and financial incentives of rating firms and investor reliance on the evaluations of these rating firms, since the fees of these rating agencies depended on being chosen by investment issuers. The competition for contracts and resulting fees disposed these rating agencies to look favorably on new issues. "Rate shopping" these agencies by firms issuing investment products was a common practice. Bethany McLean and Joe Nocera recount the story of UBS banker Robert Morelli's threat to Standard and Poor's on hearing that a UBS product was about to be downgraded. "Heard your ratings could be 5 notches back of moddys [*sic*] equivalent," noted Morelli. "Gonna kill your resi biz. May force us to do moodyfitch only."[65]

These structural flaws in the relation between issuers and rating agencies versus investors deepened and became increasingly more questionable, if not fundamentally corrupt, when the big three also began advising issuers of bonds on how to package these assets to gain top ratings. The vicious circle was complete: to increase their fees, rating agencies advised issuers how to sell investment bonds, which they then turned around and assigned a high rating to. It is in this context that these rating firms assigned Triple-A ratings to a package that included subprime, securitized mortgages, although they were later to admit that they did not fully understand the composition of these securitized assets and their toxicity.

If the rating agencies allowed themselves to be misled, it was no wonder that gullible investors were not only induced by their interest-conflicted investment advisors to believe that these were sound assets but also persuaded that they were buying risk-insulated securities, certified by these misbegotten rating agencies. Seven years after the financial crash of 2007–2008, nineteen state attorneys general and the federal government finally succeeded in extracting $1.5 billion from Standard and Poor's for its role in falsifying the creditworthiness of near-worthless assets. The penalty may deter rating agencies from issuing false credit evaluations. That expectation will depend on the cost-benefit relation between the gains in fees and market share won through prevarication versus the possibility that governmental penalties might have to be incurred as the price of doing business. The conflicts of interest that led to this damaging financial behavior were not addressed by the settlement, and Standard and Poor's admitted to no legal wrongdoing.

These multiple forms of bundled securitized bonds assumed a life of their own. Wall Street firms—Goldman Sachs, Morgan Stanley, Merrill Lynch, and others—transformed these securities into collateralized debt obligations (CDOs) and other forms of paper-tradable products. The complexity of CDOs exceeded the ability of either sellers or buyers (or insurers) to understand the products they were trading or the capacity of the market to accurately price them. Maximum uncertainty under conditions of irrational seller-buyer confidence is captured in this description offered by two perceptive critics of the meltdown:

> Start with a thousand different individual loans. . . . Package them together into an asset-backed security (ABS). Take that ABS and combine it with ninety-nine other ABSs. . . . That's your CDO. Now take that CDO and combine it with another ninety-different CDOs, each of which has its own unique mix of ABSs. . . . In theory, the purchaser of this CDO is supposed to somehow get a handle

on the health of ten million underlying loans. Is that going to happen? Of course not.[66]

The same mind-boggling transformation of financial instruments into worthless paper also affected CDSs. These instruments have been around for a long time. They are, when used prudently, useful hedges, for example, against unforeseen changes in the price of gasoline for airlines, spikes in interest rates, price fluctuations of farm products or traded commodities. In its traditional form, a CDS represented an insurance contract between a buyer seeking protection against the possibility of a default on specific bonds for which he pays a seller a yearly premium. The latter is obliged to cover the loss on the face amount of the reference bond or loan in case of default.

In the frantic subprime mortgage era, CDSs assumed a new life. They morphed, from standard vanilla insurance policies to protect against defaults on ABSs and other securitized mortgaged bonds, into vehicles for highly speculative bets among thousands of active players around the globe—a giant, sprawling global computerized casino. Purchasers of CDSs did not actually have to own either whole or part of the asset that was the object of the bet. Perversely, those betting in CDSs, like Goldman Sachs, had an incentive to have the pledged assets for which the CDS was the guarantee to default.

Transactions in CDOs and CDSs were principally between two parties. They were not recorded on any exchange. These transactions were also insulated from securities laws and regulation. Congress passed legislation in 1999 specifically forbidding the Commodity Futures Trading Commission (CFTC) from regulating derivatives. CFTC director Brooksley Born had proposed their regulation as a form of futures trading. Congress, the Treasury under Robert Rubin, and White House economic advisors in the Clinton administration supported the prohibition to regulate derivatives, while insulating Born from the administration's financial policy decisional process.

The result of weak or nonexistent regulation was the unimpeded enlargement of the nontransparent derivatives market. The notional value of the CDS market as a central component of the derivatives market was estimated to be over $60 trillion at its height just before the subprime housing collapse in 2007–2008.[67] With all forms of derivatives, more generally, debt was used by speculators—banks, investment firms, hedge funds traders, and others—to purchase more debt. Managers of CDOs were paid a percentage of the fund in the CDO. This fee created an incentive to create and churn CDOs. The cash flow generated by the assets in CDOs yielded fees for all those engaged in these transactions up and down the line of these exchanges—Wall Street firms, bankers, CDO managers, rating agencies, and a cast of anonymous enabling and supporting actors.[68]

As early as 2002, Warren Buffett predicted the collapse of this mounting financial edifice in securitized mortgages, CDOs, and CDSs. "I view derivatives as time bombs, both for the parties that deal in them and the economic system," wrote Buffett in his 2002 Berkshire Hathaway annual report. "The derivatives genie is now well out of the bottle and these instruments will almost certainly multiply in variety and number until some event makes their toxicity clear. Central Banks and governments have so far found no effective way to control, or even monitor, the risks posed by these contracts. In my view, derivatives are financial weapons of mass destruction, carrying dangers that, while now latent, are potentially lethal."[69]

The event that made the "toxicity clear" about derivatives was the collapse of the housing market in 2007–2008, triggered by the rapid increase in subprime defaults. In 2006 the share of delinquent subprime loans rose to the predicted rate of FICO projections of 51 percent and continued to rise in the following years.[70] Subprime borrowers matched the greed of financial firms and traders in manipulating them to overextend themselves and in conspiring in the vast duplicity of mortgage originators in falsifying the creditworthiness of borrowers. Like Citicorp's Chuck Prince, who was more candid than most in participating in these deceptions, investors believed (hoped, really) that liquidity would always be readily available to cover these risky loans and that housing prices, which had never declined since the Great Depression, would continue to rise to facilitate the refinancing of these shaky deals which now blanketed the country. A collapse would not be, as typically before, localized to a specific town or state but would infect the real estate and financial markets of the nation and the globe—extending as far away as a small Norwegian municipality that improvidently invested in this flawed asset, with the result that the city was saddled with tens of millions of dollars in debt.

Much of the source of the toxicity was embedded in the contracts for subprime mortgages. An extraordinary two-thirds of all subprime mortgages at the height of the housing bubble were in the form of 2/28 hybrid adjustable rate mortgages (ARMs).[71] A 2/28 mortgage might begin at 3–4 percent, but be reset in the turbulent credit stresses of 2007 at 13 percent in following the LIBOR rate plus margin.[72] Subprime homeowners were in no position to meet these increases, nor were they eligible, as bad credit risks, to refinance their loans. That they were culpable in this mutually contrived Ponzi game is suggested by the fact that 82 percent of these ARMs were for the refinancing of a home rather than first mortgages. An estimated 60 percent of these mortgages were being used to take funds out of what equity existed in their homes for the purpose of spending beyond the means and economic prospects of the borrowers.

It comes, then, as no surprise that millions of homes would be foreclosed and large numbers of homeowners would simply walk away from their mortgage obligations. Millions of homes were now underwater—that is, the market price of the home was below the principal owed on the mortgage. In 2008, a total of 3.2 million homeowners were ensnared at some stage in the foreclosure process. This number rose to 3.9 million a year later. Over one million houses were sold at auction in 2009 at prices that one analyst estimated were 25–30 percent below market value. According to the Mortgage Bankers Association, foreclosures and distressed sales increased from 0.4 percent of all outstanding mortgages to over ten times that rate or 4.58 at the end of 2009.[73]

Since the mountain of CDOs, CDSs, SIVs, and other exotic financial instruments were so entwined in the subprime mortgage market, it was no wonder (though still a surprise for most of the actors involved in derivatives and subprime mortgages, including the Federal Reserve) that "as homeowners defaulted on their mortgages, the value of the securities derived from those loans collapsed and the bust began."[74]

What was unfolding was not only a run on those firms and the loss of hundreds of billions of dollars to investors holding these highly leveraged securities but also a run on the financial system itself. Where the bubble began to deflate can be subject to debate. The collapse of Bear Stearns is one starting point that reveals the unsustainable debt exposure of the firm, resulting in its fire sale to JP Morgan in March 2008, a premature birth midwifed by the New York Federal Reserve. The story starts almost a year earlier in July 2007 with the collapse of two Bear Stearns hedge funds, which were hostage to the vagaries and unpredictability of the derivatives market. Their collapse foreshadowed the dissolution of Bear Stearns in March 2008. The two funds included the Bear Stearns High-Grade Structured Credit Fund and its High-Grade Structured Credit Enhanced Leveraged Fund. Tracing the sequence of flawed decisions leading to their demise is an object lesson of how other Wall Street firms were impacted by the implosion or the subprime mortgage market. The strategy pursued by both funds can be characterized as leveraged credit investment. At its base, both funds invested heavily in CDOs. These were largely composed of triple-A rated securities or subprime, mortgage-backed securities. The higher interest rate over the cost of borrowing to acquire these CDOs prompted their acquisition through highly leveraged borrowing reaching ratios of thirty-to-one in capital backing of these securities.

The next step in the process of self-destruction involved the purchase of CDSs to hedge against the risks posed by hypertrophied holdings of CDOs. As long as markets remained stable (everyone continues to "dance"), profits were guaranteed. These were sufficient to cover the costs of borrowing and the inflated expenses of hedge fund managers and investment brokers. In the

Bear Stearns case these amounted to 1–2 percent of the fund's assets of over a billion dollars for the two funds combined and a 20 percent incentive fee of all profits. In taking enormous risks in borrowing short and investing long in illiquid assets, fund managers at Bear Stearns and other large investment houses were acting rationally, as economic models would have predicted, but at the risk of bringing down the financial system on which their institutions depended for making money. It made economic sense for managers to bet against both their institutions and the system and, as the record of who gained and lost in these ventures revealed, to walk away from the debacle with personal fortunes.

With the rapid rise in subprime defaults in 2006 onward, the CDOs and CDSs, which used these securities as collateral for the debt binges of financial entrepreneurs and managers, also began to drop precipitously in value in a predictable pattern. Lenders to these hedge funds began to insist on more cash and collateral to back their loans. Defaulting subprimes could not provide that confidence. Funds had to draw on their own capital, vastly overstretched as a function of leveraged credit borrowing. "Simply put," as one informed and sententious description of the fall of these hedge funds noted, "as prices on bonds fell, the fund experienced losses, which caused it to sell more bonds, which lowered the prices of the bonds, which caused them to sell more bonds—it did not take long before the funds had experienced a complete loss of capital."[75] In July 2007, both hedge funds declared Chapter 15 bankruptcy. All investor deposits were wiped out. The fund managers who were accused of fraud were later found not guilty by a jury in November 2009.[76]

The collapse of the Bear Stearns hedge funds was the beginning of the end for the firm. In March 2008, facing the same pressures from creditors as its subsidiaries before, the firm was on the brink of declaring bankruptcy. The Federal Reserve initially contemplated this disaster as the cost of market imposition of penalties for the bad bets a firm had made. Reserve auditors discovered, however, that Bear Stearns was not only too big to fail but also too "interconnected" to fail. The firm at the cusp of bankruptcy was involved in some one hundred fifty million trades on its books with more than five thousand different traders and firms or counterparties to these trades. Its potential collapse, like the actual bankruptcy of Lehman Brothers shortly thereafter, would create a negative domino effect, threatening the entire global financial system.

Exercising emergency legislative authority, which it had not invoked since the Great Depression, the New York Federal Reserve arranged for JP Morgan to purchase Bear Stearns at $10 a share. The price of its shares a year earlier was in the range of $170. Since funds were extended to a bank—funds not available then to investment firms like Bear Stearns—the move was viewed as legal in exercising the Reserve's authority to pump liquidity into the banking system, specifically making billions available to JP Morgan to consummate the fire sale, in "unusual and exigent circumstances." Timothy Geithner, the head of the New York Federal Reserve, justified this extraordinary action in systemic terms: "It became clear that Bear's involvement in the complex and intricate web of relationships that characterize our financial system, at a point in time when markets were especially vulnerable, was such that a sudden failure would likely lead to a chaotic unwinding of positions in already damaged markets."[77]

The subsequent rapid unraveling of Lehman Brothers in September, larger than Bear Stearns, more indebted for much the same reasons, and even more globally interconnected and interdependent, was permitted to roil world financial markets without outside private or public assistance to prevent bankruptcy. One analyst calculated that, given the leverage ratios of debt to capital of thirty to one, a decline in the firm's assets—a vulnerability impacting both Bear Stearns and Lehman Brothers—would wipe out their capital—which is precisely what occurred.[78] The rationale offered by the Federal Reserve to allow this disaster to occur turned on its claimed lack of legislative authority to prevent Lehman's bankruptcy. Unlike the JP Morgan bank takeover of Bear Stearns, there were no private banks willing to underwrite Lehman Brothers. The United Kingdom's Barclays Bank rejected an eleventh-hour Federal Reserve overture to assume Lehman's assets as too costly and risky. Lehman Brothers, which had been in business for over a century, declared insolvency, engendering a worldwide run on the entire financial system.[79]

In this volatile period between the spring and fall of 2008 several other mergers were hastily and haphazardly orchestrated. The Federal Reserve induced Bank of America to become the largest shareholder of Countrywide Financial in July 2008 and to absorb the larger and more prestigious Merrill Lynch for $50 billion on September 15, 2008, just as Lehman Brothers was being dissolved. Wells Fargo bought Wachovia with over $300 million in assets in October 2008. To prevent the disintegration of AIG, which was the largest insurer of CDSs to derivative speculators, the Federal Reserve, fearing an even deeper and more profound negative impact on the global financial system than the collapse of Lehman Brothers, injected a $182 billion loan to save AIG. The government assumed majority control of the firm, essentially nationalizing it.

The run on the shadow banking system and its bewilderingly rapid disintegration also had a massive negative impact on the trillion-dollar money market and repurchase-agreement or "repo" markets. To finance demand for funding subprime mortgages and other securities, banks developed short-term financial vehicles to warehouse these loans. By the spring of 2007, this market swelled to $1.7 trillion. Money market purchases of this commercial paper appeared attractive, and traders in this market became increasingly tied to the commercial paper market. As doubts and fears arose about the creditworthiness of commercial paper, confidence in money markets was also negatively affected. Lehman's demise, along with its money market fund, Reserve Primary Fund, prompted a global run on the $4 trillion money market system. For the first time in its development, a dollar invested in money market funds was less than one dollar in value. The money market panic was also of a piece with the repo market. To prevent the collapse of money market funds, central to the banking and investment system, the federal government had to take the extraordinary step of guaranteeing all existing money market funds.[80]

Summing Up

What explains this incipiently total collapse of the financial system? The discussion so far has shown that public and private financial actors were complicit in bringing about the debacle, each with its own particular interests at stake. If one steps back a moment to survey this disparate and sprawling field of loosely coordinated but deeply interconnected and interdependent actors, ensnared in a progressively corrosive system marked by unrelieved excessive risk taking,[81] it is not unreasonable to conclude that the global financial system and the perverse incentives that it generated "caused" or comprised a principal explanatory cause of the unraveling. The global expanse of shadow banks overwhelmed the already weak and divided and sometimes warring regulatory bodies, which were charged to oversee the financial system. This balkanized network of banking agencies included Wall Street's large investment firms, the GSEs, GE and GM investment branches, as well as those of other large international corporations with financial branches, and flocks of traders and brokers. These units, if regulated at all, fell under the regulation of different and competing governmental agencies, or, as in the case of dealers in derivatives, they escaped regulation completely.

Johan Lybeck lists at least nine such agencies. These include, among others, the Federal Reserve, the Office of the Comptroller of the Currency, the Federal Deposit Insurance Corporation, the Office of Thrift Supervision, the Securities and Exchange Commission, and the Commodity Futures Trading Commission.[82] Neil Barofsky adds to this list of overlapping regulators. Included is the Department of Justice, responsible for the civil or criminal prosecution of fraud, and a sprawling and friction-generating system of inspectors general within each of the departments of government as well as agencies of Congress, including the General Accounting Office and dedicated inspector general units, like the Troubled Asset Relief Program (TARP), discussed below.

In light of the exaggerated confidence in self-regulation of financial markets by successive Federal Reserve authorities, what fragmented regulatory authority was available to these agencies was not exercised until it was too late to stem the tide of collapse. As critics of governmental policies and accountability underscore, the responses of the federal government under both the Bush and the Obama administrations were marked by wholesale failures to hold banks accountable once hundreds of billions of taxpayer funds were distributed to the banks and financial institutions to restart the American and global economy.[83] If the patchwork of US regulators was AWOL, there certainly existed no global mechanism of regulation to fill this void. The nation-state system, as chapter 4 detailed, is structurally unable to address global issues or to provide the supportive collective goods to fully ensure the safety and integrity of the global market system.[84]

These governmental and agency institutional deficiencies, public and private, go a long way to explain the crisis, but not far enough. Their contributions to the systemic meltdown have to be supplemented by an understanding of the personal incentives and motivations of the major players working within this actor-created system to favor personal over corporate and systemic interests. Compensation for CEOs and financial traders was based on bonuses, and not, for example, on stock options that (if not subject to manipulation and fraud) can in theory provide a better measure of the value of the contribution of a CEO to his corporation's bottom line. Instead, compensation in financial markets was distributed as a function of the performance of mortgage originators' capacity to generate loans, or to resourcefully imaginative investment traders who could invent new, flawed products to sell to gullible investors.

On this basis, the major Wall Street investment banking firms—Goldman Sachs, Morgan Stanley, Merrill Lynch, Lehman Brothers, and Bear Stearns—paid $25 billion in bonuses in 2005 and $36 billion a year later; they continued to pay large bonuses in the wake of the financial collapse, in some instances using governmental bailout funds to continue the practice, now euphemistically transformed from "performance" to "retention" bonuses. The public outrage over these practices reached a heightened pitch when AIG, recipient of $182 billion in bailout funds, announced in March 2009 that it was going to pay $165 million in bonuses to its traders and executives.[85] Recipients of governmental and taxpayer largesse also used part of these assets to lobby Congress to resist putting caps on executive compensation and to weaken regulations of the financial sector, most notably derivatives.[86]

What this pay system created was an incentive to make mortgage sales with little or no credit foundation or to make increasingly large and risky bets with the capital of a firm or its depositors. The Bear Stearns hedge fund collapse is illustrative. Similarly, the Financial Services branch of AIG in London put the home company, which was solvent, at risk. The fees collected in issuing CDSs appeared to be "free," riskless money, because it appeared to all of the principals that a meltdown of crisis proportions was inconceivable. In any event, that contingency never appeared in the models or stress tests conducted by banks and investment firms. No "black swans" appeared on the screen in running these defective models. This same reckless behavior among employees and CEOs was no less manifested in all of the institutions recounted above, including most especially Countrywide, Ameriquest, Merrill Lynch, and, of course, Lehman Brothers.

More to the point, there appeared to be few or no personal risks in risking a firm's resources or those of depositors. Not only did underlings profit greatly, but CEOs did even better. In 2006, James E. Cayne of Bear Stearns was paid $33.85 million; Richard S. Fuld Jr., of Lehman Brothers, $40.5 million; Lloyd C. Blankfein of Goldman Sachs, $54.7 million; John J. Mack of Morgan Stanley, $41 million; Stanley O. Neill of Merrill Lynch $48 million; Charles Prince of Citicorp, $26 million; and Kenneth Lewis of Bank of America, $28 million.[87] As Lehman Brothers' positions became more tenuous in 2007, Fuld still received $73 million in bonuses.[88] O'Neill decamped from Merrill Lynch when incorporated into the Bank of America with a platinum parachute of $162 million in compensation.[89]

Additional incentives to feather one's own financial nest arose from infirmities of the governance of investment firms and banks. This principal-agent problem stems from the asymmetrical information available to CEOs versus their governing boards. The management advantage was further bolstered by the incestuous relationship that developed between CEOs and their governing boards to mutual material advantage. Such a corrupting relationship undermined their obligation of due diligence in pursuing the interests of the corporation and stockholders. This evasion of faithfully fulfilling the principal-agent obligation at the CEO level percolated throughout these firms from top to bottom. Employees were both principals and agents, often with little or no sense of responsibility upward or downward other than advancing, first and foremost, their own fiduciary interests.

Stockholders who may have been expected to hold their multiple agents responsible were no less conflicted. If the firm was posting profits and distributing dividends, there was little incentive to question management practices or strategies. Depositors might also have been expected to ride herd on banks.

That their deposits were guaranteed up to $250,000 by the FDIC discouraged criticism or critical evaluation of banking balance sheets.[90]

This tour of the horizon of the financial crisis finally brings us to the most ambitious effort of governmental officials to staunch the bleeding of the financial system: TARP, the Troubled Asset Relief Program. The original justification for a Treasury request to Congress for $700 billion in loan authorizations was to purchase the toxic assets languishing on the books of banks. This would have provided needed liquidity, which was supposed to inject confidence among bankers and financial firms to resume loaning to each other, investors, and the public. Despite the failure of the market to accurately price these assets, governmental acquisition of these assets through negotiation with the banks and financial institutions at prices roughly reflecting their diminished value would have provided the government with the leverage needed to modify loans or the principal on underwater mortgages—in which the mortgage owned was greater than the market value of the property. Instead, that option was consigned to the mortgage holders, which had little or no incentive to keep homeowners in their homes.[91]

Contravening the justification advanced by the Bush administration for TARP—to help homeowners—the program's focus shifted rapidly to the recapitalizing of shaky banks. Treasury Secretary Hank Paulson foisted most of the initial half of TARP funds in governmental loans on the eight largest banks of the nation, whether they wished to have loans or not. The aim was to assure investors and depositors of the adequacy of liquidity in the system and confidence in the banking system. Bank of America also booked $118 billion in guarantees to sweeten its government-pressured purchase of Merrill Lynch. Other banks, including 356 smaller institutions,[92] received lesser amounts.

Criticisms of TARP have not subsided since its inception and gradual downsizing. Homeowners who were supposed to receive aid to keep their homes received scarcely any assistance. TARP money was not used in an appreciable degree to increase lending to housing or modify existing loans. Although $50 billion was available for these purposes, only 2 percent, or $1 billion, was allocated for this purpose. In fact, studies show that large TARP banks issued more risky loans after receiving federal aid.[93]

Big banks were privileged over small banks. Since no conditions were attached to banks in using their TARP funds, the Treasury could not or would not determine whether banks were using these loans for the purposes for which TARP was designed rather than helping them build up reserves for future credit losses, pay back other more expensive loans than TARP, advance aggressive bids for other banks, or increase the compensation of corporate heads.[94] Transparency of the Treasury-bank contracts was among the first casualties of the implementation of TARP. What mattered most was getting the funds out the door as quickly as possible.[95] Meanwhile TARP was used to save General Motors and Chrysler from bankruptcy, estimable but never envisioned as objectives within TARP's original mandate.

So what can we conclude about the status of the financial system today? No single government has control of the global financial system or the resources and authority to achieve this objective. There are few mechanisms in place to facilitate, much less compel, cooperation among banks and investment banking firms—certainly not the entire system of shadow banks. The US financial crisis operates seemingly independently of the European sovereign debt crisis, although it is obvious that the economies and financial institutions of the Western states are interdependent. It was once commonplace to say that when the US economy coughed, Europe caught a cold. Now both are vulnerable to mutual infection of incipiently fatal pneumonia-like proportions.

What is clear, too, is that TARP did not kick-start the credit system. As the LIBOR scandal in 2012 unfolded, involving Barclays and other top London banks for manipulating the setting of daily interest rates for their own advantage, banks also revealed that they resisted lending to each other. They remained skeptical of each other's credit standing and solvency.[96] The derivatives market remains no less opaque than it ever was.

The problem of "too big to fail," or, more precisely, "too interconnected to fail" (or jail), has grown more problematic and destabilizing. Governmental intervention and bailouts have consolidated the banking sector. Hitherto shadow banks, like Goldman Sachs and Morgan Stanley, are now major actors in the banking system. As Neil Barofsky summarizes, "The top banks are 23 percent larger than they were before the crisis. They now hold more than $8.5 trillion in assets, the equivalent of 56 percent of our country's annual output, up from 43 percent just five years ago. The risk in our banking system is remarkably concentrated in these banks, which control 52 percent of all industry assets, up from 17 percent four decades ago."[97]

These institutions are mutually dependent on each other and all are entwined with the government. If central banks and governments were always assumed to be lenders of last resort, they have now become investors of last resort. The result is the institutionalization of moral hazard into the global financial and economic system—but with no clear guidelines, reliable strategies, or broad-based public support to navigate the shoals of these hazards and to strike a working and productive, mutually equitable balance response to the claims of all actors, most notably taxpayers who are the foundation and ultimate guarantors of the system.

The stupendous costs and the scope of the global destabilization of financial markets have yet to be fully assessed. The likelihood of a definitive reckoning sometime soon is problematic. The implicated governmental and private sector actors have their own self-interested narratives to explain the collapse and advance conflicting solutions to prevent another meltdown, as the numerous citations running along this discussion evidence. What is known is that approximately nine million jobs were lost in the aftermath of the meltdown. Between January 2007 and December 2011, there were 8.2 million foreclosure starts and 4 million completed foreclosures. In the fourth quarter of 2011, there were still 11.1 million residential properties, 28 percent of the US total, that were underwater.[98] Aside from trillions of dollars in losses in retirement accounts, Americans also suffered losses of $6.5 trillion in housing valuations.[99] What might be viewed as a housing bubble was actually a threat to the global economy and took a vast human toll on millions of investors, pension funds, homeowners, workers, and taxpayers in the United States and abroad.[100]

The Treasury and Federal Reserve handling of AIG's insolvency captures the overall failure of governmental units to hold bailed-out banks and financial institutions, like AIG, accountable for how they used TARP funds. Thanks to congressional intervention, which precluded regulation of the derivatives markets, there was a complete lack of governmental regulation of the CDS market. AIG dug a bankruptcy hole for itself in allowing its London Financial Products division to underwrite billions of dollars in CDSs. The billions in dollars in fees collected on these counterparty contracts were viewed as "free money," since it appeared inconceivable that AIG would have to meet its insurance obligations if debtors and mortgage holders failed to meet their assigned payments. In August 2007, as the financial system was beginning to rapidly unwind, the director of the London office asserted that "it is hard for us, without being flippant, to even see a scenario within any kind of realm of reason that would see us losing one dollar in any of those [CDS] transactions."[101]

Neither the Treasury nor the Federal Reserve held AIG (or other TARP recipients) accountable for how they used TARP funds. AIG received taxpayer guarantees of $182 billion to meet its counterparty obligations. The latter were not induced to accept a "haircut" (that is, a percentage loss on these contracts), because Treasury officials believed that the failure to provide full faith and credit on these contracts would further depress a weak and faltering financial system. Yet Treasury subsequently acquiesced in AIG's use of its resources, now mixed with TARP funding, to award $168 million in bonuses to almost all of its employees, with its top leadership receiving up to $2 million. The rationale for Treasury's acquiescence was that these officials, who were responsible for AIG's insolvency, had to be retained to dig AIG out of bankruptcy. The institutionalization of moral hazard at the corporate level was further reinforced at the level of corporate leadership and management.

It seems fair to say that the housing and financial bubble, driven and bloated by CDSs and CDOs, was largely caused by the relatively free and untrammeled workings of the free market. Few governmental regulatory controls were in operation to prevent the breakdown or ameliorate its burdensome impacts on millions of people. Indeed, governmental policies, like those fostering homeownership, spurred not only GSEs but also Wall Street to expand the bubble.

Much in evidence is Adam Smith undone. The "irrational exuberance" of private (and public) actor behavior,[102] each actor pursuing rationally his self-interest, had the paradoxical result of undermining the free market system itself. Somewhat akin to Joseph Conrad's "Secret Sharer," there lurks the potential fatal flaw of free markets and unregulated actor behavior destroying the institution on which rational economic behavior can be understood and predicted at the margin—but not at the level of the global system.[103] To put the problem in economic terms, there is a misalignment between private incentives for gain and their alleged contribution to public good. Adam Smith's expectation of convergence of private and public interest is nowhere apparent in the financial meltdown of the first decade of the twenty-first century. Smith's expectation was frustrated when private incentives were not aligned with socially beneficial results, much to the disadvantage and disrepair of society as a whole. Super-rich actors within the market system have a particularly significant impact on market meltdowns and on the prospect and possibility of an implosion of the market system becoming a reality.[104]

Notes

1. Technically, the present market system is more a semifree system, given tariffs and other barriers to trade, subsidies, etc., as well as state regulations, which impede the operation of a perfect free exchange system. See for example, *The Economist*, a staunch partisan of the market system, which observes that the market system has increasingly been modified by what *The Economist* terms "state capitalism" (e.g., January 21, 2012, issue).

2. Defense of the market system is found in the writings of Milton Friedman and his colleagues, who formed what has become known as the Chicago school. These theorists dominated the award of Nobel prizes in economics at the end of the twentieth century. Also important, more from a philosophical than an economic perspective, is the thinking of Friedrich von Hayek and the Austrian school of economics. See Friedman (1962); Friedman & Friedman (1980); Friedman & Schwartz (1963); Hayek (1967).

3. The history of human economic exchange provides the context for this development of a theory of governance. Some places to begin to get hold of this history include, *inter alia*, Beaud (2000); Cameron (1993); Findlay & O'Rourke (2007); Frieden

(2006); Jones (1987); Kindleberger (1983); Landes (1969, 1998); Schumpeter, 1954). Useful, too, is to view the evolution of economic systems from the perspective of sociology. See Smelser & Swedberg (1994).

4. Sandel (2012); Sandel's critique is preceded by the philippic of Karl Polanyi (1944).

5. See, for example, Kahneman et al. (2004, 2006).

6. Kahneman & Kreuger (2006); Kahneman et al. (2004, 2006); Kreuger & Schkade (2008).

7. Lindblom (2001) suggests the insight that all economic activities are performances.

8. Cassidy (2009, pp. 224–25).

9. Barofsky (2012, p. 87).

10. Ferguson (2008, p. 5).

11. Roubini & Mihm (2010). Roubini draws heavily on the work of Hyman Minsky. Cassidy (2009) also relies on Minsky's work in criticizing prevailing optimistic academic and business models of financial and economic behavior. The reference to a "black swan" event is attributed to Nassim Nicholas Taleb, who popularized the notion of improbable occurrences with large but unanticipated consequences—an insight that is particularly relevant to the 2007–2008 crisis. See Taleb (2007).

12. JP Morgan is one notable exception, but it, too, lost several billions of dollars in risky hedging transactions that turned sour. See the testimony of CEO Chairman Jamie Dimon before Congress, *New York Times*, June 13, 2012.

13. Quoted in Wessel (2009, p. 105). Prince's rationale for his irrational behavior illustrates precisely the disposition of the market system to generate self-destructive incentives under the guise of rational behavior. See Akerlof & Shiller (2015, especially pp. 23–43), which supports the proposition of this chapter that the market system is susceptible to breakdown and implosion unless governmentally regulated to preclude its self-destructive tendencies.

14. Quoted in Cassidy (2009, p. 297).

15. Ibid. Robert Shiller discusses this same herd mentality with respect to the stock market bubbles of the turn of the century. See Shiller (2005). Two other relevant works of the impact of psychology on economic behavior leading to undermining the expectations of rational actors seeking to maximize their material wealth and self-interests are Akerlof & Shiller (2009); Frank (2011). Blinder (2013) provides an overview of the crisis.

16. Ibid., p. 299.

17. Cassidy (2009) develops this point at great length. See also Robert H. Frank (2011), who dwells on the paradoxes of Adam Smith's "Hidden Hand" as insufficient to provide for public goods or the common good.

18. Greenspan (2007).

19. The split report of the Financial Crisis Inquiry Commission, created by Congress, mirrors the division of opinion across the vast and growing literature and commentary to explain the causes of the financial crisis. Besides the report of the Financial Crisis Inquiry Commission (*The Financial Crisis Inquiry Report: Final Report of the National Commission on the Causes of the Financial and Economic Crisis in the United*

States [Washington, DC: Government Printing Office, 2011]), see Cassidy (2009); Friedman (2011); Lybeck (2011); McLean & Nocera (2010); Posner (2010); Rajan (2010); Stiglitz (2010); Posner (2009).

20. Friedman (2011); Wallison (2011).

21. Rajan (2010).

22. Posner (2010, 2009); Stiglitz (2010).

23. Compare Lybeck (2011); Roubini & Mihm (2010). See also the report of the majority of the Financial Crisis Inquiry Commission, n. 24 (cited in note 19 above). Wessel (2009, pp. 54–55) neatly summarizes the actors who warrant blame.

24. Barofsky (2012).

25. Morgenson (2011) describes the contribution of both parties in Congress, and the GSEs in creating the financial bubble. See also McLean & Nocera (2010, passim) for a briefer, more sympathetic account.

26. Wallison (2011).

27. This is the view of McLean & Nocera (2010); Roubini & Mihm (2010). With the exception of its Republican members, this is largely the view of the Financial Crisis Inquiry Commission (2011, n. 24).

28. Financial Crisis Inquiry Commission (2011, p. 354). See also pp. 351ff. For a critique of GSE and federal governmental policies keyed to increasing home ownership, see Wallison (2011).

29. Wessel (2009, p. 180).

30. Ibid., p. 186.

31. Bernanke (2015, p. 268).

32. Ibid. See also Paulson (2010).

33. Blinder (2013, p. 318).

34. *New York Times*, June 27, 2012, Business Section, pp. 1–2.

35. Greenspan (2007).

36. Quoted in Roubini & Mihm (2010, pp. 73–74).

37. Cassidy (2009, p. 231).

38. Ibid., p. 73. Wessel (2009) covers these points at length. See also Roubini & Mihm (2010, p. 73).

39. Cassidy (2009, pp. 223–24).

40. Quote in a review of Greenspan's congressional testimony, http://ruleofreason .blogspot.com/2008/10/greenspan-recants.htm.

41. Ibid.

42. Quoted by Floyd Norris in the *New York Times*, July 18, 2013.

43. Cassidy (2009 [italics added]) develops this point at length. See also Collander et al. (2010); Roubini & Mihm (2010); Stiglitz (2010, pp. 238–74).

44. McLean & Nocera (2010, pp. 96–97, 106–7).

45. Akerlof & Shiller (2009); Shiller (2008).

46. For a sampling, consult the numerous notes to this chapter.

47. *Economist's View*, October 27, 2011, p. 1.

48. Ibid.

49. Wikipedia lists seven governmental and private sources for these figures. See http://en.wikipedia.org/wiki/Financialization.

50. The figures are taken from Lybeck (2011, pp. xi–xiii). The banks included Citigroup, Bank of America, and Wachovia Bank.

51. IMF (2009); also Cassidy (2009).

52. http://data.worldbank.org/indicator/NY.GDP.MKTP.KD.ZG.

53. Ibid.

54. *Wall Street Journal*, October 11, 2008, p. 1.

55. Lybeck (2011, pp. 127–29).

56. McLean & Nocera (2010, p. 134).

57. Friedman (2011, pp. 16–17).

58. Ibid., p. 34.

59. Lybeck (2011, p. 114).

60. McLean & Nocera (2010, pp. 270–73, 278–80); also Morgenson & Story (2009).

61. Morgenson & Story, p. 34. Lybeck (2011, pp. 163ff.) discusses the complex process of securitization. See also Ashcraft & Schuermann (2008).

62. Jablecki & Machai (2011).

63. Acharya & Richardson (2011).

64. Roubini & Mihm (2010, pp. 196–99).

65. McLean & Nocera (2010, p. 118 [spellings in the original]).

66. Roubini & Mihm (2010, p. 194). Barofsky (2012, pp. 86ff.) makes the same point.

67. Shah Gilani, *Money Morning*, September 18, 2008.

68. McLean & Nocera (2010, p. 121).

69. http://www.fintools.com/docs/Warren%20Buffet%20on%20Derivatives.pdf.

70. Lybeck (2011).

71. Cassidy (2009, pp. 258–59). Cassidy describes egregious forms of predatory lending.

72. Fourteen London banks meet each day to set what is termed the London Interbank Offered Rate (LIBOR). It is the rate that banks charge each other for short-term loans. This segment of the banking industry also proved corrupt as LIBOR banks set interest rates to increase their profits at the expense of other investors. See "Banks Go Wild," *New Yorker*, July 30, 2012, p. 25.

73. Lybeck (2011, p. 131).

74. Roubini & Mihm (2010, p. 19).

75. http://www.investopedia.com/articles/07/bear-stearns-collapse.asp#axzz21fuBri39.

76. *New York Times*, November 10, 2009.

77. Quoted in Cassidy (2009, p. 319).

78. Cassidy (2009, p. 313).

79. See McDonald (2009) for a narrative account of the Lehman collapse.

80. Roubini & Mihm (2010).

81. Knight (1921) is the foundational study of the effects of uncertainty on economic behavior.

82. Lybeck (2011, pp. 358–59).

83. See Barofsky (2012).

84. Blinder (2013); Rajan (2010). Blinder and Rajan discuss the absence of adequate international institutions to regulate financial markets in their evaluation of the financial crisis. Beck (2007) provides a sociological interpretation of a world at risk that complements their analyses.

85. McLean & Nocera (2010, p. 362).

86. Roubini & Mihm (2010, p. 222).

87. Cassidy (2009, p. 289).

88. Lybeck (2011, p. 171).

89. McLean & Nocera (2010, p. 321).

90. Bhide (2011, especially pp. 92ff.).

91. Barofsky (2012) details the failure of Congress and two administrations either to help Main Street or to impose costs (not to say initiate civil and criminal action) on those in the banking industry who did not exercise due diligence in meeting their fiduciary responsibilities. Buttressing Barofsky is Bair (2012); Sheila Bair is the former director of the FDIC.

92. Bair (2012, p. 99).

93. http://www.federalreserve.gov/pubs/ifdp/2012/1043/ifdp1043.pdf.

94. Lybeck (2011, p. 224).

95. Barofsky (2012, especially pp. 79ff.).

96. See the BBC's explanation of LIBOR as well as the scandal involving major English banks that daily published, not always without self-interested manipulating, the short-term lending rate. One LIBOR executive, Tom Hayes, has been convicted of fraud. See http://www.bbc.co.uk/news/business-19199683. As of this writing six others are under indictment. *New York Times*, October 7, 2015, p. B6.

97. Barofsky (2012, p. 229).

98. Stiglitz (2012, pp. 293–94).

99. Ibid., p. 13.

100. The citations for these statistics are drawn from Barofsky (2012, p. 254), who cites reports of the Federal Reserve for 2011, the National Foreclosure Report for March 2012, and the Federal Housing Agency.

101. Ibid., quoted on p. 141.

102. Shiller (2005).

103. This discussion focused on the breakdown of the global financial system is limited to identifying the underlying proclivity of the market system to generate self-damaging incentives for actor behavior, leading to its systemic undoing. It makes no pretense to explain all of the underlying motivations, which may have prompted individual, corporate, or governmental actors to blindly cooperate in unintended ways to risk the collapse of the market system. Relevant is Robert Frank's thesis that Darwin's theory of human evolution warrants examination as an amendment to address weaknesses in prevailing market theory. See Frank (2011).

104. This is the message of two recent volumes about the disposition of the super-rich to undermine their own interests and wealth in the unchecked pursuit of ever-greater economic wealth and power. See Freeland (2012). This is also the implicit argument posed by Joseph Stiglitz (2012).

6

The Market System II

The Challenges of Inequality and Poverty

Capitalism is failing to produce what was promised, but is delivering on what was not promised—inequality, pollution, unemployment, and, most important of all, the degradation of values to the point where everything is acceptable and no one is accountable.[1]

—Joseph E. Stiglitz, *The Price of Inequality:
How Today's Divided Society Endangers Our Future*

The outstanding faults of the economic society in which we live are its failure to provide for full employment and its arbitrary and inequitable distribution of wealth and incomes.

—John Maynard Keynes, *The General
Theory of Employment, Interest and Money*

BESIDES THE TENDENCY OF SYSTEMIC breakdown, outlined in chapter 5, the market system also confronts two other formidable challenges: the growing, unequal, and inequitable distribution of income and wealth across the populations of the world society; and chronic and seemingly irremediable poverty, affecting billions of people and households around the world. These vulnerabilities, as the Nobel laureate Amartya Sen and others have stressed,[2] are not given sufficient weight. Typically, they are treated as market imperfections or failures, which the market system can resolve through its own self-correcting mechanisms. This understanding of the market system simplifies the conditions and constraints under which markets actually operate. Too often assumed is a potentially frictionless system of economic exchanges, driven by rational, self-interested actors. Deviations from expected pure market behavior are viewed as breakdowns, which the market system over time can purportedly rectify on its own account.

This chapter challenges this optimistic assumption. Absent the intervention of the state's coercive and regulatory power, supported by populations demanding greater equality and equity in the distribution of incomes and wealth as well as ways to escape poverty, the structural flaws of the market system cannot be easily relaxed or surmounted through its own devices. The aim of reform is not to weaken the market system but to set the conditions for its support by the state system and by the expectations of the world's populations in such a way that promises to make global markets work more effectively and efficiently than they do now to serve the greatest number for the greatest material good.

The Market System and the Unequal Distribution of Income and Wealth

To what extent can the market system account for the increasing inequality (and inequity) in the distribution of income and wealth within and between states and over the whole of the world's population? This question, superficially, is somewhat anomalous. Markets are supposed to distribute income and wealth unequally. This comes as no surprise. After all, the market system is a quid pro quo system.[3] Former British prime minister Margaret Thatcher states the case for inequality, paradoxically, as a principle of social justice: "It is our job to glory in inequality and see that talents and abilities are given vent and expression for the benefit of us all."[4]

As Joseph Stiglitz reminds us, "Competitive markets, working through the laws of supply and demand, determine the value of each individual's contributions."[5] Under the assumptions of a pure market system, economic actors, theoretically, receive rewards equal to their marginal productivity or contributions.[6] Following Adam Smith, personal gain and social good converge through the market's hidden hand. Self-interest and public goods are mutually fostered without the need for appeals to altruistic purpose, much less for the coercive intervention of the state.[7] The latter move, predicable of economic systems before the installation of the market system, chronically proved suboptimal in facilitating and in maximizing economic growth, technological progress, or equitably distributing the wealth that was created.

Until the development of industrialization and its globalization through the market system, human capacity for creating wealth was at a low and static level. The world's populations were in the thrall of Thomas Malthus's dismal prediction that human population growth would always exceed food supplies.[8] The resulting equilibrium would neither produce more wealth nor enhance the health and well-being of a larger population. A market system driving global industrialization, including that of scientific agriculture, and its successor, informational counterpart, surmounted the seemingly permanent Malthusian limits of scarcity. Since the 1800s, the world's populations have enjoyed continuing growth in global world product (GWP), topping $70 trillion in 2011, in supporting the largest population in human history. Under a threshold of 1985 dollars in purchasing power parity (PPP), world per capita income rose from $659 to $4,912 between 1820 and 1992.[9]

If markets distribute income and wealth unequally and, presumptively, equitably as a function of the generally acknowledged and accepted quid pro quo normative properties of a market system, why does this condition pose a problem and potentially a fatal flaw of the system? Even prominent economists like Paul Krugman and Joseph Stiglitz, severe critics of market workings, defend the system while arguing for reforms, specifically, to address inequality and poverty.[10] The market's unequal distribution of wealth would not pose a problem if, indeed, private gain and public social welfare converged. That is not how the market system is working today. Nor can it be expected to harmonize these two contesting aims anytime soon without public and governmental assistance.

There is a growing, dysfunctional, and destabilizing gap—economic, political, and moral—between those at the top of the income scale and those in the middle and at the bottom within and across developed and developing states. The source of concern is not, in principle, the incentive structure of the market to reward unequally in response to quid pro quo norms. Rather, the market system is susceptible to economic and political manipulation by actors who are rewarded in excess of their marginal productivity and actual contributions to public good. For example, the top twenty-five hedge fund managers in 2014 earned $11.62 billion.[11] Income that might normally be taxed at a progressive rate is taxed at a lower dividend rate for hedge fund managers thanks to protective legislation that accords them gains well beyond the economic contribution that they make to their investors and, even more so, to the general public good.

Under ideal assumptions of perfect competition and complete efficient and effective market operations, the returns to a worker or an investor "are in fact equal to the benefits to society that his actions contribute."[12] What has happened since the 1970s is a misalignment between private gain and public benefit to the enlarging advantage of the former at the expense of the latter. Created is a broad spectrum of inefficient economic outcomes. These market failures are partially, but significantly, a consequence of the unequal allocation of income and wealth as well as of disproportionate imbalances in the distribution of political power across populations, favoring those with wealth to the disadvantage of the less fortunate. One particularly damaging consequence, discussed below, is the loss of opportunities for economic and social advancement of untold members of an affected community.[13]

Rents and *rent-seeking* are particularly important to understanding why inequality is a serious market flaw. They refer to payments to economic actors, corporations, or individuals, that exceed the value of their contributions to a product or service and to the value of the social good that is created. The previous chapters provided multiple examples of a dysfunctional financial market system, which distributed huge profits to actors well beyond the marginal personal and social value of their contribution to the quid pro quo system. Rents are the difference, so to speak, between the inequitable income received by an actor and the lower amount he or she should have expected if the market were operating according to the theory of a pure market system.

Included, too, in rent-taking are corporate welfare (e.g., tax breaks for oil producers and hedge fund managers), subsidies to manufacturers or farmers (e.g., globally noncompetitive cotton and sugar producers), price fixing, lax enforcement of business and financial practices, rigged fire sales of public lands and property to privileged buyers (e.g., Russian oligarchs), tariff protection for uncompetitive industries, and so forth. In greater or lesser measure, rents and rent-seeking have now become deeply embedded in the political processes and economic practices of developed and developing states. As suggested earlier, it is particularly pronounced in the United States, which supports a political process that has elevated special legislation to promote rent-taking to the level of big business.[14]

What Are the Facts about Inequality?

Reliable sources, however much they post different results, conclude that, since approximately the 1970s and 1980s (and even before, depending on the data being used), most developed states evidence a growing disparity in the distribution of income to individuals as well as increasing gaps in household income between those at the top and bottom 10 percent of households.[15] While economists differ in their methods and findings in measuring inequality in income and household distributions across developed and developing states as well as in their evaluations of the economic, social, and political consequences of these trends, there is general agreement that there is a growing and chronic gap in income distribution between the top 10 percent of the populations of the states covered in these surveys and the rest of the population. This is especially the case between the top 1 percent and the remainder of each state's population.

Since the 1980s, the democratic OECD (Organisation for Economic Co-operation and Development) countries experienced a 1.7 percent annual average increase in real disposable household incomes. In a majority of cases the richest 10 percent grew faster than those of the poorest 10 percent. In this period the average income of the richest 10 percent is approximately a ratio of 9 to 1 relative to the poorest 10 percent. The ratio increases to 14 to 1 for the United States, topped by Mexico and Chile at 27 to 1.

The same imbalance can be viewed from the perspective of the Gini coefficient measure. It is a standard measure of income inequality that ranges from zero (when all receive identical incomes) to one (when all income goes to only one person). In the mid-1980s, the Gini coefficient for OECD countries was at .29. Twenty years later it increased to .316. The coefficient rose in seventeen of twenty-two countries. It climbed by more than four basis points in Finland, Germany, Israel, Luxembourg, New Zealand, Sweden, and the United States.[16]

By 2010, the top 1 percent of US households captured 20 percent of total national income. The top 0.1 percent received 8 percent. These levels were last recorded in the 1920s just before the Great Depression.[17] Even within the 1 percent the gap between the lowest percentile (99th to 99.5th percentile) and the top .01 percent is dramatic. Of the income captured by this 1 percent of the population the bottom percentile increased 4.6 percent ($418,000), while the top one hundredth of 1 percent rose by 21.5 percent ($23.8 million). While the 1 percent suffered great losses in the great recession of 2008, it also rebounded more quickly than the rest of the population, receiving 93 percent of the income growth in the first full year of the recovery in 2010. As the Piketty and Saez data reveal, the average income of the top 1 percent "increased nearly 12 percent ($105,000) in the first year of the recovery while the average income of households in the bottom 90 percent of the distribution remained at its lowest level in nearly 30 years."[18] Since 1979, the top 1 percent change in after-tax income grew almost 300 percent; the next 19 percent, 65 percent; the middle 60 percent, 28 percent; and the bottom 20 percent, 18 percent.[19]

Joseph Stiglitz humanizes the implications of these cold percentages of growing income disparities on households: "The top 1 percent get in one week 40 percent more than the bottom fifth receive in a year; the top 0.1 percent received in a day and a half about what the bottom 90 percent received in a year; and the richest 20 percent of income earners earn in total after tax more than the bottom 80 percent combined."[20] Between 1982 and 2012 the share of national income going to the richest 1 percent of Americans doubled, rising from 10 to 20 percent.[21] The share going to the top .01 percent quadrupled in this period from 1 to 5 percent, covering a small set of sixteen thousand families with an average income of $24 million. That is larger than the same group received a century ago in the heyday of Fords, Carnegies, Rockefellers, and the robber barons.[22] The sustained unequal distribution of income also has a significant impact on wealth ownership and creation. The top fifth of the US population possesses approximately 85 percent of the nation's wealth.[23]

These income disparities across developed states are mirrored and accented in the income distributions within the states of emerging economies.[24] These states report significantly higher levels of inequality than OECD countries. South Africa, Brazil, Argentina, Russia, China, India, and Indonesia, which have more than half of the world's population, reveal increasing inequality in emerging economies. The Gini coefficients of these states are significantly greater than the OECD average. Except for Brazil, Argentina, and Indonesia, the others actually experienced increased inequality between the early 1990s and the late 2000s.[25] In this period, South Africa registered a Gini coefficient of 0.7. It was followed by Brazil (0.55), Argentina (0.45), Russia (0.43), China (0.42), India (0.37), and Indonesia (0.32).

Measuring inequality becomes more complex if the focus shifts from inequality within states to between states and then to global inequality. François Bourguignon and Christian Morrison developed intrastate, interstate, and global measures of inequality from 1820 to 1992. They found that inequality rose continually from the Industrial Revolution to World War I. The Gini index climbed from 0.50 to 0.61. The Gini index between states rose from 0.05 in 1820 to 0.50 in 1992. In the same time period, the Gini index for global inequality rose from .45 to .83.[26]

Since the beginning of the Industrial Revolution, the income inequality of what Bourguignon and Morrison cite as "world citizens" has largely followed a trend line of increasing inequality. The principal, if temporary, exception to this trend was the period immediately following World War II until approximately the 1970s and 1980s.[27] Over the period studied by Bourguignon and Morrison, the share of world income going to the bottom 20 percent fell from 4.3 to 2.2 percent. During the same period, the share going to the top 10 percent rose from 34 to 53 percent. Branko Milanovic of the World Bank buttresses this conclusion, attributing widening inequality over this long period to European colonial practices, favoring the interests of the metropole over subjugated populations and retarding their industrialization and economic growth.[28]

The data for global inequality since 1950 become even more complex and difficult to assess if China and India are included in or excluded from the mix. With these two states included, the World Bank shows global inequality decreasing in the second half of the twentieth century, a trend confirmed by the Bourguignon and Morrison study.[29] Conversely, as Robert Hunter Wade suggests, "One combination of inequality measures does yield the conclusion that income inequality has been falling—PPP-income per capita weighted by population, measured by an averaging coefficient such as the Gini. But take out China and even this measure shows widening inequality."[30] If inequality besets the Chinese population, the rapid industrialization and double-digit economic growth of China since the 1980s has had the effect of dampening global inequality. If China is excluded, the trend line of inequality between states continues its steep upward trajectory.[31] While the growth rate and increases in the per capita income of the Chinese population (and to a lesser extent in India) have had the effect of decreasing inequality across the world's populations, inequality within China (and India) has actually increased in the face of impressive economic growth.[32]

Figure 6.1 depicts these seemingly paradoxical counterflows of global inequality. If China is included in the estimates of global income distribution, inequality between 1950 and 1998 shows a marked decline. If China is excluded, the trend toward global inequality shows a marked increase over this period. As Raphael Kaplinsky notes, in citing Branko Milanovic's findings, "China accounts for almost 20 percent of the global population. So it is almost an arithmetic certainty that this will show up as an improvement in global income distribution, despite the paradoxical fact that, at the same time, China's internal income distribution became considerably more unequal; in 2003 there was an increase in the numbers living in absolute poverty."[33]

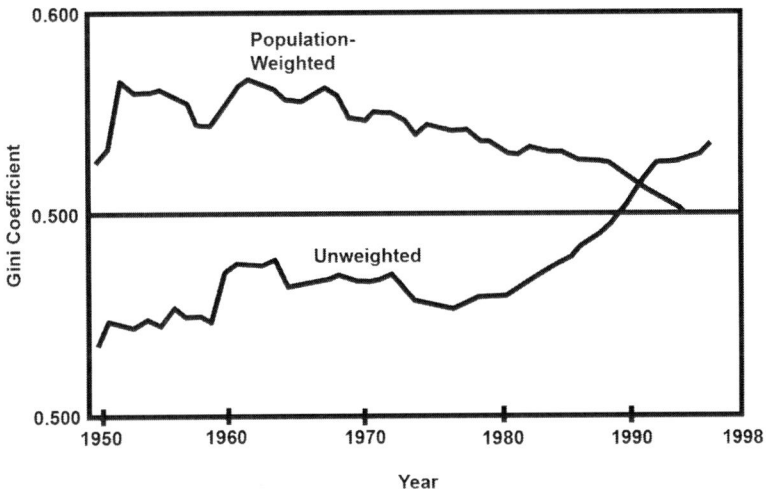

FIGURE 6.1
Weighted and Unweighted Income Distribution (Gini Coefficients), 1950–1999
Source: Raphael Kaplinsky, *Globalization, Poverty, and Inequality: Between a Rock and a Hard Place* (Cambridge: Polity Press, 2005), 46.

Explaining Inequality

If economists and policy-makers agree that there is an increasing disparity of incomes to individuals and households since the 1970s and 1980s, and that, with few exceptions, these trends are becoming more acute, there is widespread disagreement in explaining why these gaps are occurring. Three lines of explanation are generally advanced. The first focuses on globalization—that is, the increasing integration of trade, finance, and labor flows, which blurs state boundaries and control. The second stresses technological innovation and its global spread as the force behind inequality. These two seemingly contrasting explanations would appear to be different sides of the same coin. As the *Economist* survey of global inequality observed, "Technology accelerates globalization, and globalization accelerates technological progress."[34] Viewed another way, an informational and knowledge-based global economy privileges skilled over unskilled labor as well as creative innovators and issuers of new financial instruments over the contributions of those associated with traditional industries and services.

A third perspective moves from economic explanations to imbalances in political power between top earners and those below, especially the top 1 percent in what appear to some observers as the global spread of a winner-take-all society.[35] Thomas Piketty's *Capital in the Twenty-First Century* identifies the holders of capital as the principal source of income inequality. His exhaustive empirical analysis shows that in the modern period, notably since the 1970s, the rate of capital accumulation greatly exceeds the rate of economic growth. This inequitable trend line portends the continuing accumulation of wealth in the hands of an increasingly small number of individuals and families, heralding another "Belle Époque" and the institutionalization of inequality in democratic societies.

Fully explaining how structural inequality as a function of political influence and power exercised under conditions of increasing economic inequality has developed in contemporary democratic societies goes beyond the scope of this discussion. What this discussion stresses is the rent-seeking behavior of actors to manipulate the outcomes of market transactions to receive returns in excess of their actual contributions to the production of wealth and their capacity and incentive to use those excessive gains to ensure and grow those gains further, whether through monopolistic practices or influencing state policies and regulatory agencies to favor their interests. Created is a crisis not only for the market system but also for the political system fostering inequality.

Each explanation provides a plausible but, alone, not a fully convincing case to explain inequality.[36] Together, these three lines of analysis furnish a more comprehensive, if still incomplete, point of departure to explain income inequality. What emerges from these interdependent explanations is a circularity across these three domains wherein an initial driver of inequality produces an effect that is then transformed into a cause of inequality, each feeding and transforming cause and effect in a feedback loop.

The globalization of markets contributes significantly, if not conclusively, to an explanation for income inequality, notably within countries.[37] The vast expansion of the global labor market with the entry of workers from emerging economies, particularly from China and India, has put great competitive pressures on all workers, particularly low-skilled labor. Since the 1980s, these same downward pressures on income are also increasingly affecting even high-wage earners in the developed states.

Worker power to bargain for higher wages and favorable working conditions and benefits in the developed states of the OECD has appreciably declined relative to capital, investors, and management. Outsourcing jobs to the emerging economies produces increased unemployment, shorter working hours, higher worker turnover, and decreased wages in developed states, a condition that promises to be permanent in a globalizing world. Investors can also threaten to move their capital elsewhere unless workers agree to concessions, such as cuts in health and pension guarantees or the imposition of two-tiered wage systems for older and younger workers to accommodate corporate and investor demands for greater profits. These same dynamics work with increased effectiveness in developing states where unionization is largely unavailable to indigenous labor.

The decline of union membership and bargaining power, which has accompanied these trends, is a significant factor to explaining growing inequality within the global society. The OECD report on inequality reports a steep decline in union membership. With 1980 as 100 percent for the index of union density, the number of union members, as a proportion of all employees eligible to be members, has fallen to 60 percent, with the trend line continuing to slope downward.[38] A parallel drop in employment protection can also be noted, falling from 100 percent in 1980 to approximately 75 percent in 2006. This decrease in worker protections and the unraveling of social safety nets characterize both developed and developing states. Added to these blows to income returns for labor has been the progressive trend across states in the market system to reduce the regulation of goods, services, and financial transactions and to make labor markets more open and adaptable to market competition. Here the index for regulation in this time period drops precipitously from 100 percent to below 30 percent.[39]

Rapid technological progress and the dissemination of best practices around the globe also explain progressively more income inequality. Unskilled workers are especially hard hit. The greater skill required to keep pace with technological change and the increased sophistication of equipment command greater wages for those with these capabilities. This finding is consistent with traditional international trade theory. Increased trade integration is associated with higher wages going to skilled workers in richer countries, producing greater inequality in those countries.[40] What is also interesting to note is that the returns on greater productivity have gone more to management and investors than to labor. Those who profit from these changes in laws and regulation are again the top wage earners. Most of these gains are estimated to go to the top 20 percent.[41]

Outsized market inequalities result in increased political and economic bargaining power for top income earners, particularly the 1 percent within a progressively winner-take-all global economy, as well as corporate leadership, and holders of capital. This income elite uses its enhanced political power to reinforce and solidify a market system rigged to inequality.[42] As Joseph Stiglitz concludes in his study of inequality and its costs, "while market forces play some role in the creation of our current level of inequality, market forces are ultimately shaped by politics."[43] This is also the conclusion of an exhaustive OECD study of inequality.[44] How does political power in the hands of the top wage earners result in laws and institutions favoring their interests?

The obvious answer is money. Individuals and corporations invest their economically enhanced wealth to increase their power to write laws, co-opt or capture regulatory bodies, and influence local, state, and national elections and policies to favor their interests. The unraveling of regulations over product, service, and financial markets favors top earners. The weakening of unions and the relaxation of environmental protections did not result simply from superior economic analysis and the compelling virtues of free markets. These major changes in laws, regulations, and control over the membership of regulatory bodies were largely the product of the exercise of political power by those with the economic resources to advance their interests.

This is the conclusion of a major study of the politics of inequality in the United States by Larry Bartels, with specific reference to party competition, presidential terms, and Senate votes on public policy issues. Bartels responds to the question posed by Robert Dahl: "In a political system where nearly every adult may vote but where knowledge, wealth, social position, access to officials and other resources are unequally distributed, who actually governs?"[45] With respect to Senate voting, Bartels's study shows a strong correlation between Senate votes and the preferences and interests of rich constituents versus those of lesser means.[46] Bartels concludes "that affluent people have considerable clout, while the preferences of people in the bottom third of the income distribution have *no* apparent impact on the business of the Senate in three successive Congresses or specific salient roll call votes on governmental spending, the minimum wage, civil rights, and abortion. The statistical results are remarkably consistent in suggesting an utter lack of responsiveness to the views of millions of people whose only distinguishing characteristic is their low incomes."[47]

What Robert Michels might have termed an "iron law of oligarchy" is embedded in the market system, unless counterbalanced by the political power of those in lower wage groups.[48] The market system cannot be portrayed accurately as a model of perfect competition. Pure models have utility for analytic purposes to provide a base point to identify market imperfections. As a depiction of how markets work, suspended between the institutions of power of the state and the politics of inequality, these models are wanting and misleading. The global market system is a hybrid of economic and political constraints and opportunities, biased in favor of those with greater economic and political power to define the rules of economic transactions and income distribution.

Specifically, the "marginal productivity theory" of economic textbooks does not work in practice to explain the outcomes of the prevailing workings of the market system. The proposition that private rewards and social contributions are equal, in fact, offers increasingly less explanatory power for who gets what, how, and why from the operations of the market system—that is, who makes rules, governs, and privileges certain preferences over others. There is deep and growing disconnect between the skewed tendencies toward inequality of the market system and the predictive power of "marginal productivity theory."

The transformation of the market system from pure market operations to a hybrid economic-political power machine took much doing. Chapter 5 has already sketched the rise of state capitalism.[49] Short of state takeover of the economy, there is also a growing and more prominent trend for state policies, as Bartels suggests, to privilege the preferences and interests of the rich. In the United States and elsewhere throughout the market system, notably in the developed states, armies of lobbyists work tirelessly at all levels of government to foster the economic interests of their clients. The Center for Responsive Politics (CRP) posts a comprehensive listing of these lobbying services for the United States. While all lobbying activities are not related exclusively to seeking legislative perquisites, subsidies, tax breaks, tariff protections, relaxed regulations, and rents, the overwhelming amount of publicly reported spending on lobbying (data on corruption being not readily available) is for these and related economic benefits to individuals and corporations. The CRP notes that spending for lobbying doubled between 1998 and 2011 from $1.44 to $3.33 billion.[50] Top spenders between 1993 and 2011 included the US Chamber of Commerce ($886 million), General Electric ($272 million), the American Medical Association ($274 million), and the American Hospital Association ($274 million).[51]

The number of lobbyists working in Washington is impressive. Lobbyists from a wide spectrum of businesses numbered approximately 5,000 in 2012: health, 2,758; finance, insurance, and real estate, nearly 2,200. The number of industries and lobbyists serving them are too numerous to recount here; reference to the website of the Center for Responsive Politics[52] is suggested. What is particularly interesting is the recruitment of former legislators and legislative professionals by lobbyist organizations. For these three industries, the percentage of so-called revolvers for business is 54.3 percent; health, 46.8 percent; and finance, insurance, and real estate, 55.3 percent. Lobbying firms are also big business. The top three recorded over $1 billion in revenues between 1998 and 2012.[53]

Spending on elections to choose candidates and influence policies is especially significant in the United States. Elections, combined with intensive lobbying, have produced policy results that have resulted in legislation and administrative rulings favoring the unequal distribution of income. This spread between the rich, middle class, and poor has widened despite countervailing social safety nets like Social Security, Medicare, Medicaid, food stamps, and negative tax schemes to provide income to subsistence families. Electoral expenditures reached all-time highs in 2012 in no small part due to the decision of the Supreme Court in *Citizens United v. the Federal Election Commission*. In equating money with freedom of speech, the Court held as unconstitutional prohibitions on the amount of money that could be spent on election campaigns by corporations, labor unions, and other bodies, if spending was directed at advocacy and not expressly for a candidate.

The Court's ruling led to the creation of so-called Super PACs. They could attract unlimited funds and spend as much as they wished for advocacy purposes. The Center for Responsive Politics estimates that over $6 billion was spent on the presidential and congressional primaries and elections in 2012. The two US presidential candidates each spent roughly $1 billion. Another approximately $1.7 billion was spent in House and Senate races. The remainder was expended by party organizations and some 1,063 Political Action Committees (PACs). Early reports on spending by candidates for the office of president in 2015 strongly suggest that spending on election campaigns will exceed the 2012 totals.

While it is not clear what impact increased spending will have on election outcomes, there is little doubt that large donors are intent on preserving their economic and political positions by supporting candidates who foster their interests and ideological orientations. The decline in taxes paid by the super-rich over the past decade swells the political power of this group. Incentives are created for the rich to make direct payments to the campaigns of legislators who support them or to mount PAC-directed electoral campaigns to garner public support. There is little difference from an economic point of view between investing in legislative or presidential campaigns to gain rents or to influence regulatory bodies and in promoting a new product or service to reap profits and capital gains. The complexity of American tax laws and the multiple avenues available to decrease individual and corporate taxes provide substantial resources to shape the tax laws or subsidies going to corporations to advantage the rich and super-rich.

There are two additional factors that should be taken into account to explain chronic income inequality: prevailing economic theory and changing public norms about appropriate levels of income. Economic theory has not kept pace with market failures arising from imperfections in economic transactions and from distortions in state policies favoring the economic and political power of those on top. Nouriel Roubini has been particularly pointed in his criticism of economic theory as a contributor to the governmental policies that were significantly instrumental in leading to the financial meltdown of 2007–2008. Along with a rising chorus of others,[54] he has underlined the outsized incomes of hedge fund managers and CEOs, monetized in the billions of dollars—some of whom received these high incomes, although their funds or firms were driven to ruin and some to bankruptcy.[55]

Not without irony, the Federal Reserve, which is responsible for bank regulation, was largely dominated by directors who viewed outsized CEO and hedge fund compensation as expected market outcomes. This was clearly the position of Alan Greenspan, the long-time director of the Federal Reserve. It may well be the case, from a counterfactual point of view, that markets will eventually reach an equilibrium that restores in practice the theory of marginal productivity as well as full employment, but as John Maynard Keynes observed, we're all dead in the long run.

Related to the problematic explanation of market operations of key elements of prevailing economic theory is the gradual change in public norms in the postwar era about income inequality, particularly among the class that has most benefited from these disparities. At the corporate level, with the financial sector in the lead, there has been a marked shift toward a winner-take-all disposition at the expense of labor and even investors. Lloyd Blankfein, CEO of Goldman Sachs, a significant contributor to the financial meltdown of 2007–2008, remarked that Goldman Sachs's profits and, implicitly, his outsized salary were justified. As he asserted to reporters, he and his financial brothers and sisters were "doing God's work,"[56] the excessive risks taken by them to the contrary notwithstanding. Only the surface of this complex issue of corporate executive compensation can be covered here. Suffice it to say that the problem globally is real and acute, particularly in the United States, and that this defect in the governance of the global society is linked deeply to globalization, technological innovation, laws and institutions discriminating against the less economically fortunate, and flawed socioeconomic and normative thinking in support of this broken system.

The Implications of Inequality of Income and Opportunity

The disagreement over the scope of income inequality and its causes among economists, policy analysts, and decision-makers is further accented and deepened in the discord over the implications of this trend. Expert opinion varies widely and is internally contradictory. At one pole of opinion there are those, like Greenspan, who see no fundamental problem. Free markets are expected in the long run to eventually resolve what is viewed as a temporary anomaly in the workings of the market system. Robert Lucas, a Nobel Prize winner in economics, argues that "of the tendencies that are harmful to sound economics, the most seductive and . . . poisonous is to focus on questions of distribution."[57]

At the opposite pole are those who see imminent threats not only to the market system but also to the survival of open societies.[58] In between is a host of other viewpoints, reservations, and qualifications about the socioeconomic, political, and normative implications of income inequality and about what reforms are relevant to ameliorate the adverse effects of inequality. Despite these uncertainties and clashing expert opinions, several adverse systemic effects of income inequality and their interdependent and synergistic impacts on each other can be identified.

First, great discrepancies in income dispersion generate increased rent-seeking behavior by top earners and powerful corporations and their leadership. Second, since by definition rent-taking marks gross inefficiencies in the operations of the market system, it also has the effect of constraining or limiting social investments in education, health, infrastructure development, and public availability of parks and leisure. These are the preconditions for continued economic growth and expanded social welfare. Decreases in public goods also foster unemployment not only in the provision of these and other public goods but also in reducing the income of workers whose marginal propensity to consume is higher than wealthy wage earners. Less income in the hands of consumers—that is, those in the lower 80 percent of the population—results in lower demand for products and services.

Third, there is accumulating evidence that skewed distribution of incomes, favoring top earners, inhibits economic growth. International Monetary Fund (IMF) economists find that inequality and unsustainable growth are two sides of the same coin.[59] Their research challenges the notion that increasing income inequality can be rationalized as an efficient market outcome. Income distribution survives in their research "as one of the most robust and important factors associated with growth duration."[60] Their cross-national data evidence that a 10 percent decrease in inequality has the effect of increasing the economic growth of a country by 50 percent. As the authors conclude, "Remarkably, inequality retains a similar statistical and economic significance . . . despite the inclusion of many more possible determinants. This suggests that inequality seems to matter in itself and is not just a proxy for other factors. Inequality also preserves its significance more systematically across different samples and definitions of growth spells than the other variables. Inequality is thus a more robust predictor of growth duration than many variables widely understood to be central to growth."[61] Other research buttresses this finding.[62]

Of course the factors explaining economic growth or its absence are more complex than attributing changes in patterns of growth solely to rents and rent-seeking. Added, too, among the most important factors are the quality of a state's economic and political institutions, a commitment to open market operations and competition, national macroeconomic policies fostering stability, and the promotion and provision of human capital and know-how. Research is showing more equitable and economically balanced income equality, consistent with measures of differential factor contributions to national (gross) and global world product (both GWP), is increasingly understood as a driver of growth, while, conversely, greater inequality is a brake on growth within, between, and across states.[63]

Fourth, if it is assumed that income inequality decreases economic growth, then it follows that the GWP pie is smaller and income wedges, especially for labor, are thinner. In human terms, inequitable income distributions adversely affect billions of individuals and households. If the focus moves from an abstract macro level of analysis to a micro look at the effects of income inequality on those at the lower-than-80-percent levels (and most particularly at the lowest quintile), significant negative changes in the material prospects of these groups appear to be developing.

To the issue of the negative effects of increased inequality of income within states must be added the complementary challenge of the rise in inequality of opportunity for the disadvantaged members of each state. The unemployed or lower paid unskilled workers have increasingly fewer opportunities to acquire the education and skills they or their children need to compete in a globalized economic market system. Decreased access to basic health services, adequate diet and clean water, and supportive environments have the same restraining impact on opportunities to increase income and to facilitate social mobility. The loss of opportunities for economic and social advancement in the United States is highlighted in a recent study by Robert Putnam.[64]

Many scholars and policy analysts have increasingly challenged the focus on income inequality as an adequate measure of income and wealth disparities within and between states and globally. The OECD comprehensive study, *Divided We Stand*, identified three principal causes of income inequality: globalization, technology, and state and international institutional constraints. Going further and deeper, critics raised the issue of social justice and the multiple socioeconomic, political, and environmental determinants of an individual's or group's capacity to earn income. It is not enough to assess the equity of the distribution of outcomes—that is, income. More important, the issue of equity revolves around the fairness or equity of the broadly social allocation of resources and capabilities available to those engaged in market exchange or their incapacity to enter into this quid pro quo system absent their capacity to surmount the barriers to equality of opportunities.[65]

John Roemer and other economists distinguish between the capacity of an individual to earn income as a function of his or her endowments, talents, discipline, hard work, and luck, and the social factors that either facilitate or frustrate that pursuit. These multiple social factors (too numerous to recount here) are stipulated to be beyond the capacity of the individual to change in any fundamental way. For example, a study of inequality of opportunity in Brazil that persisted over generations identified four main, pre-market factors inhibiting income acquisition: parental schooling, father's occupation, race, and religion.[66] This study found that family background was the most significant.

World Bank economists have added to this study by creating two measures to assess the relative inequality between states with respect to opportunities for income growth. They have developed a coefficient of "inter-generational elasticity of income."[67] It provides a rough measure of the degree to which parental position influences children's relative income or education. The higher the coefficient, the less socioeconomic mobility results. Scandinavian countries have low coefficients, passing along only about 20 percent of the parents' wealth. China registers at 60 percent. The United States is also high wherein half of the parents' wealth is passed to their children. Mobility in China and the United States is lower than most European states.[68]

A second measure relates the inequality of opportunity to a percentage of total inequality within a state. Again the Scandinavian countries provide more opportunities for income growth for their populations than Brazil or the United States. That is, limits to efforts of individuals to improve their lot over which they have no control are lower than those experienced in other OECD countries in contrast to the United States. While it is widely held in elite and popular circles that the United States is a mobile society in which equality of opportunity is amply afforded its citizens, evidence points in the opposite direction. Overlooked is the significant influence of income in-equality on narrowing the range of opportunities available to individuals to improve their particular material lots, social status, affordable education, and, more generally, a more fulfilling quality of life.

Of particular interest is the development by World Bank researchers of a "Human Opportunity Index."[69] This index comprises measures of human access to key pre-market conditions for economic success. Among the most important are education (considered the most significant determinant of future economic income growth for individuals), health, immunization to disease (particularly children), and nutrition. The World Bank's 2006 report on development stresses the particular vulnerability of women who are dis-advantaged on all of these measures.[70] These same drawbacks adversely affect groups discriminated against because of ethnic or tribal identities or cultural or religious orientations.

Associated with these personal elements are critical public goods, such as the quality of government, the absence of corruption, good roads, and trans-portation systems to bring produce and goods to market, adequate credit facilities, the observance of the rule of law, and personal and group security, free from local and regional conflicts. While some of these impediments to the equalization of opportunities for income growth are found in developed states, most of the global impact on inequality of opportunities falls on the populations of the developing world. Among these, the most adversely af-fected are the populations of sub-Saharan Africa.

Income disparity, occasioned both by the inequality of income and op-portunity within (and especially between) states and at a global level, creates a sense of unfairness among large segments of the world's populations. These inequities are daily communicated to the world's underprivileged through the media and online social networks. As worker income declines and perceptions of increasing inequality of opportunity persist, the support of economically disenfranchised populations for the market system is gradually withdrawn. Increased pressures are exerted on populations to explore radical alterna-tives to what are viewed as the failures of the market system to improve their material welfare. The threat is raised that the market system, which has been instrumental, whatever its flaws, in moving billions out of abject poverty, may unravel and place global governance, inherently fragile and unstable, at seri-ous risk of breakdown. The economic upheaval between World Wars I and II and the overthrow of democratic governments in Europe, notably Germany, illustrate the reality of this potential breakdown of the market system and misguided popular support for authoritarian alternatives.

Under the impact of rising inequality of incomes and of opportunities, open societies are placed under increased stress and exposed to rising internal conflict. As several analysts warn, democratic government, too, is put at risk.[71] As those at the top strive to protect their privileged interests and to extend their power, they not only expose the market system to implosion but also, ironically, place their own positions in jeopardy. The widening domestic political conflict affecting the debtor states of the European Union, dramatized by the economic reversals of Greece, highlights the vulnerabilities of open societies to the destabilizing effects of income inequality.

Popular revolts against chronic poverty and inequality, evidenced by the Arab Spring, fueled by demands of populations for greater economic welfare and for an increased say over their political lives, are not isolated events. These movements evidence deep fissures, not to say inequity, in the stability of the market system as it works—or fails to work—today. An appreciation of rising inequality of income and of opportunity within and between states as well as at a global level also underscores the crisis of global governance. One need not accept the millennial Marxist predictions of the inevitable demise of market capitalism to acknowledge that chronic and growing economic inequality prompts upheaval, social tumult, demands for radical regime change, and appeals to force by disadvantaged groups and terrorists to rectify real and perceived inequities. Even short of violence, democratic rule and the equal application of the rule of law are also eroded by the spread of rampant inequality across the world's populations. Recent research that projects the global distribution of income in 2050 concludes that "unless the OECD countries start growing more slowly than is now commonly assumed or broad swaths of the developing world substantially improve their economic performance beyond that experienced in the last 25 years, the global income distribution will soon start to worsen again."[72]

Poverty and the Market System

What, then, can be said with some assurance to be the impact of the market system on poverty? More generally, drawing from the evidence explaining inequality, what can be said of the impact of the contemporary world order, within which the market works, on poverty? It is difficult to isolate the impact of the market system, the distribution of power of actors working within it, and their differential responses to the incentives that the power structure of the market system generates. The problem of a reliable assessment is further complicated beyond the possibility of definitive resolution. Concerned elites—social scientists, policy analysts, and decision-makers—hold, objectively, multiple and conflicting notions of what poverty is. They and the diverse populations of the world also attach radically contrasting subjective values to its significance and persistence as an issue amid a global sea of unprecedented wealth.

The notion of absolute poverty would seem to be an empirically uncontested point of departure in defining poverty. Every human requires adequate food, clothing, shelter, and a supportive physical environment simply to survive. Poverty and inequality are, in principle, distinguishable. "As these terms are normally defined," World Bank economist Martin Ravallion explains, "poverty is about absolute levels of living—how many people cannot attain certain predetermined consumption needs. Inequality is about the disparities in levels of living—for example how much more is held by rich people than poor people."[73] Even this definition of absolute poverty is not easily translated into universally applicable bundles of basic physical needs. Human populations are heterogeneous as a function of where they live—their hot or cold climates, seasonal changes, availability of a wide spectrum of different foods, and population pressures on resource scarcity. Standardizing poverty across seven billion humans and their households does not admit to a simple solution. What can be said with some confidence is that to properly understand absolute poverty, it must also be situated, paradoxically, in a relative context.[74]

This move also raises problems. In shifting attention from absolute to relative poverty, a more intractable set of notions of poverty arises. What is a necessity for the disadvantaged in rich states, like the United States or France, is hardly the same for those living in the least developed states of the globe. The World Bank standard of one-dollar purchasing power parity (PPP), as the standard of poverty, defined by the poor in the fifteen least developed states, is scarcely applicable to Americans or Europeans, among whom the standard is more than thirteen times that level.[75] Accordingly, middle-income countries will also have a higher poverty line than low-income countries. The notion of poverty is implicitly defined by the relevant population under examination. A material standard blurs into a subjective determination of what constitutes absolute poverty.

Over two centuries earlier, Adam Smith recognized this complexity in attempts to fix the definition of absolute poverty for all time in noting that what are the necessities for survival and thriving in a society differ across communities: "By necessities I understand not only the commodities which are indispensably necessary for the support of life, but whatever the custom of the country renders it indecent for creditable people, even of the lowest order, to be without."[76] Absolute poverty, even when reference is made to a particular community, is not a static notion. It is rooted in changing community mores. What is considered to be the proper line between those living above and below a poverty line, defined by the bundle of needs that have to be fulfilled by a particular human community, changes over time as human values respond to shifts in consumption levels and patterns as well as community values. When television sets were first introduced into the market, they were considered a luxury for many households. Now they are an expected element of the material possessions of the poor in many countries. The same can increasingly be said of smartphones and Kindles, but not Apple watches and luxury cars.

Adam Smith's broader understanding of poverty prompts thinking to go beyond a simple representation of poverty as sufficient income to survive to probe the conditions that produce poverty. To eliminate poverty, the challenge is not only to provide humans sufficient means to live above some abstract line defining poverty but also, and more important, to eliminate the causes of poverty itself. This challenge explains the increasing interest of analysts and international organizations, notably the World Bank, whose mission is to lower the incidence of poverty, in shifting from a focus on economic development and growth to an evaluation of the multiple conditions that sustain the chronic poverty of billions.

The evolution of thinking toward this larger conception of poverty has been building over several decades among economists and social scientists. Among the first was Peter Townsend, whose magisterial survey of *Poverty in the United Kingdom* set a high standard for evaluating absolute and relative poverty.[77] Townsend's encompassing understanding of poverty was given global voice by Amartya Sen, a Nobel Prize recipient in economics.[78] Sen argues that poverty should not be depicted or understood solely as inadequate income. It requires both a notion of human access to capabilities to rise from poverty and measurement of these deprivations to determine the challenges facing states and populations.

There has now developed an accumulation of data and measures about these capabilities, which are stipulated to contribute to poverty and, conversely, whose elimination or remission are requirements to escape poverty.[79] An inventory of the annual World Bank *World Development Report*,[80] the UN *Human Development Reports*,[81] and the voluminous literature[82] that has accumulated over the past generation stresses one factor or another or multiples as essential to an explanation of poverty and ipso facto what factors have to be addressed to surmount this condition. Included, among others, are access to education, nutrition, health, sanitation, disease control, and literacy. To these are added more equal distribution of income, empowerment and voting rights for the poor, access to credit, land reform, diminution of ethnic and religious conflicts, greater transparency of and control over extractive elites and corruption, the rule of law, and expanded foreign aid and public works projects. The list goes on.

So large and complex a set of factors and indexes to explain poverty and its elimination indicate the lack of consensus among expert observers over how to conceptualize poverty or how to marshal the economic resources and political will to cope with this problem on a global scale. In reviewing the debate over whether globalization and growth reduce poverty, Angus Deaton, a leading scholar of poverty, advances the limited and cautious generalization that there is not much common ground among informed observers about how to measure, evaluate, or reduce global poverty: "When economic growth benefits everyone in equal proportion, the incomes of the poor grow at the same rate as does mean income. . . . If economic growth is unequally distributed, the effects of growth on poverty reduction will be less (or more) depending on whether the incomes of the poor grow by less (more) than average. So much, but perhaps not much more, is common ground."[83] That is neither an arresting insight nor an encouraging conclusion about what is shared, common knowledge about poverty.

What can perhaps be said more confidently than in the recent past is that the once-dominant explanation and solution to poverty, conventionally referred to as the Washington Consensus,[84] has lost ground under withering criticism and poor results in implementing its stiff recommendations, popularly summarized by Thomas Friedman as the "golden straitjacket."[85] This approach to economic development and the reduction of poverty was supported by the second Bush administration, the World Bank, the International Monetary Fund, the Inter-American Development Bank, and the US Treasury. The rigorous policy of the "golden straitjacket" insisted that developing states integrate into the global market system as quickly as possible. A typical passel of proposals advanced by these agencies (and their economist partisans) demanded "opening countries to foreign trade and investment flows, privatizing state-owned enterprises, deregulating businesses and industries, and implementing restrictive fiscal and monetary policies."[86] Until recently, signaled by the World Bank's shift from development to poverty reduction, this unfettered, free market approach and the tough demands that it made on developing states to adapt to market competition ignored or marginalized issues of equity in the distribution of income within states, poverty reduction, and the creation of better conditions, especially for education and skill development, to increase opportunities for the poor.[87]

Measuring Poverty

Given the conceptual confusion and dispute over what poverty *is*, the deep splits over how to evaluate poverty as a human condition, and controversy over how to eradicate it, there should be no surprise to discover that these divisions of opinion would also affect the measurement of poverty. Measures and methods of assessing poverty, within and between states, present

equally perplexing challenges as those posed by efforts to understand absolute poverty. These measurement issues cannot be sidestepped. Absent some
yardsticks for poverty, it is next to impossible to devise effective policy responses to cope with the problem. Briefly sketched below is the spectrum of
prevailing opinion and findings advanced by policy analysts and experts on
global poverty about how to measure poverty. This discussion sets the stage
to address the question, posed earlier, of whether globalization, defined as the
integration of states into a global market system, has helped or hindered, even
retarded, global economic growth and the equitable distribution of income
and wealth across the world's populations.

The estimates of global poverty developed over several decades by the
professionals of the World Bank in cooperation with leading economists and
social scientists are currently widely accepted, disputes and criticisms over
World Bank data and methods notwithstanding. [88] The World Bank stan-
dardizes its measure of poverty by adopting the method of translating local
currencies into purchasing power parity measured in terms of US dollars
(PPP$). Currently, 2005 is used as the benchmark year, replacing a previous
1993 PPP$ calculation. Prices are converted to those at the time of the rel-
evant household survey using the local consumer price index (CPI). The poverty rate is then calculated from each particular country survey. The mean or
average poverty line for the poorest 15 countries is stipulated as the basis for
the poverty lines described in table 6.1. The most recent World Bank survey
covers 115 countries and samples 1.23 million households for the 2005 data
set, covering 90 percent of the populations of the developing world within
two years of 2005.[89]

Poverty lines for each country are defined as those alleged to be socially
relevant to each country. As a basic measure of absolute poverty, reference is
made to a bundle of goods reflecting minimal subsistence food-energy needs
and varying nutritional intake of calories available to different populations.
For example, for India "a daily food bundle comprises 400g of coarse rice and
wheat and 200g of vegetables, pulses, and fruit, plus modest amounts of milk,
eggs, edible oil, spices and tea."[90]

Two complementary measures are used by economists Shaohua Chen
and Martin Ravallion: "Poverty is assessed using household expenditure on
consumption per capita or household income per capita as measured from
the national sample surveys."[91] Aggregate global poverty lines are listed in
PPP$ for $1, $1.25, $1.45, $2.00, and $2.50 for consumption below each poverty line. These are displayed in three-year intervals between 1981 and 2005.
Noteworthy is the decline at each PPP$ level in this period. For example, at
the $1.25 level, the percentage of those living below this line in the developing
world fell from 51.8 percent in 1981 to 25.2 percent in 2005 (the latter figure

TABLE 6.1
Regional Breakdown of the 2005 Poverty Rate and Number of Poor

Region	Poverty Line in 2005 prices			
	$1.00	$1.25	$2.00	$2.50
(a) Poverty rate (percent living below poverty line)				
East Asia and Pacific	9.3	16.8	38.7	50.7
Of which China	8.1	15.9	36.3	49.5
Eastern Europe and Central Asia	2.2	3.7	8.9	12.9
Latin America and Caribbean	5.6	8.4	16.6	22.1
Middle East and North Africa	1.6	3.6	16.9	28.4
South Asia	23.7	40.3	73.9	84.4
Of which India	24.3	41.6	75.6	85.7
Sub-Saharan Africa	39.9	51.2	73.0	80.5
Total	16.1	25.2	47.0	56.6
(b) Number of poor (millions)				
East Asia and Pacific	175.6	316.2	728.7	955.2
Of which China	106.1	207.7	473.7	645.6
Eastern Europe and Central Asia	10.2	17.3	41.9	61.0
Latin America and Caribbean	30.7	46.1	91.3	121.8
Middle East and North Africa	4.7	11.0	51.5	86.7
South Asia	350.5	595.6	1,091.5	1,246.2
Of which India	266.5	455.8	827.7	938.0
Sub-Saharan Africa	304.2	390.6	556.7	613.7
Total	875.9	1,376.8	2,561.6	3,084.6

Source: Shaohua Chen and Martin Ravallion, "The Developing World Is Poorer Than We Thought, But No Less Successful in the Fight Against Poverty." © World Bank, 2008, https://openknowledge.worldbank.org/handle/10986/6322.

License: Creative Commons Attribution CC BY 3.0.

is shown in table 6.1). If China is excluded, the decline in poverty at the $1.25 line is less, falling from 39.8 percent to 28.2 percent.[92]

Interestingly enough, if China is excluded, the number of global poor actually increases in this period from 1,061.1 to 1,169.0 million. At the $2.50 line, the increase in number of the world's poor is even more dramatic when China is excluded, ranging from 1,759.5 million in 1981 to 2,611.0 million in 2001, affecting approximately 40 percent of the world's population.[93] If China is included, the UN Millennium Development Goal (MDG) of halving the 1990 poverty rate by 2015 is on track. Absent the dramatic decrease in the poverty levels in China, the developing world will not be able to achieve the MDG, according to World Bank estimates.[94] A global recession in the wake of the 2007–2008 meltdown and decreasing aid from the developed to the developing world (the United States commits less than two-tenths of 1 percent of GDP to foreign assistance) reinforces this bleak conclusion.

The pattern of poverty reduction between 1981 and 2005 is more complex than global totals reveal. As Shaohua Chen and Martin Ravallion's data show,[95] only East Asia and the Pacific and, specifically, China, enjoyed a dramatic decrease in poverty, measured at the $1.25 PPP. In this period the East Asia and Pacific poverty rate fell from 77.7 percent of the population living below this line (84.0 China) to 16.8 percent (15.9 China). In terms of population, the number moving above the $1.25 line in East Asia and the Pacific is nothing less than phenomenal. In 1981, 922 million in this region (730 China) were living below the international poverty line of $1.25 PPP. In 2005, these numbers fell to 176 million (106 China), as shown in table 6.1.

Between 1981 and 2005 poverty in East Europe actually increased from 1.7 percent of the population to 3.7 percent, as a consequence of the implosion of the Soviet Union and the loss of its East European satellites. While Latin America and the Caribbean, South Asia (with India), and sub-Saharan Africa registered decreases in the percentage of the population below the $1.25 line, each of these regions actually had more poor in numbers at the $1.25 than before, as a consequence of population growth. These increases in millions are as follows: Latin America (42 to 46.10); South Asia (548.3 to 595.6) and with India (420.5 to 455.8). Sub-Saharan Africa showed little decrease in the percentage of the poor at the $1.25 line (53.7 to 50.9), while the number of estimated poor rose from 213.7 to 390.6 million.[96]

Given the heterogeneity of the world's populations, developing consensus among experts on how to compare and represent poverty poses formidable measurement challenges. The World Bank's measures, outlined in table 6.1, will be relied upon for purposes of this discussion.[97] It should be noted that there is widespread disagreement on how to measure and value poverty as a global problem. World Bank economists also provide competing measures of poverty depending on the year under examination. World Bank economists Chen and Ravallion alternatively presented 1993 and 2005 as the benchmark years to calculate PPP$ rates.[98] Re-estimating the data from earlier surveys and updating those to 2005, they concluded that the world's populations were poorer than they originally believed. The estimates for 2000 and 2005 differ sizably, depending on what benchmark is used. In 2000, for example, the difference in the number of those in poverty, using 1993 and 2005 benchmarks, was a nontrivial 587 million. This difference, while less, appeared again in the re-estimations for 2005, totaling 408 million.

How are major discrepancies in expert calculations to be explained? The surface explanation turns on the conflicting poverty lines preferred by each analyst, the different uses of PPP exchange rates to convert incomes from local to international currencies, the different methods employed, and the varying calculations of mean incomes and consumption patterns within the selected and differing sets of states covered in these surveys over different periods. These confusing and contrasting estimates of poverty make comparisons problematic. They only partly explain the roots of discord among expert observers. The more fundamental reason for discord over the facts and value of poverty is rooted in the heterogeneity of the world's populations. This has led some analysts to throw up their hands and assert that "comparability and global representation are therefore impossible to achieve."[99] Certainly, as Ravallion concedes, "A conventional poverty measure can hardly be considered a sufficient statistic for judging the quality of people's lives."[100]

The significance of these poverty statistics, however much they differ from analyst to analyst, is that they underline the chronic existence of large-scale poverty around the world. Even those who prefer lower numbers of poor concede that hundreds of millions are mired in these wretched conditions. If the poverty line is set at $2.50 PPP, the number in poverty goes up sharply. If the World Bank estimates in table 6.1 are taken at their face value, 57 percent of the world's populations live below this poverty line, representing 3085 million people or approximately 40 percent of the world's population in 2005. This excludes hundreds of millions more, including those in the developed states, who are just above the $2.50 poverty line. Can the market system address this challenge?

Assessing Market System Responses to Poverty

Almost all economists agree that economic growth does reduce absolute poverty, an empirical generalization that is hard to deny.[101] That convergence begs the question of whether the market system has been a key contributor to economic growth for the world's populations. The factors that explain economic growth are by no means universally acknowledged. There is no theory of economic growth subscribed to by all—economists, social scientists, policy analysts, or, and much less so, political actors and the interested and informed public. When the empirical question of economic growth merges with the question of the equity of the distribution of income and wealth, controversy over rival views about poverty becomes more intense and inconclusive.

Note that some people, insulated from global markets, were remarkably successful in achieving high levels of economic growth. As Eric Jones shows, the Japanese people reached a very high level of sustained economic growth, although the society was essentially closed to foreign trade and economic exchange with the outside world between the beginning of the seventeenth century and Japan's forced opening to world trade by the United States in 1854.[102] Similarly, the European peoples grew economically although their economic relations were largely confined to one region of the world.[103] Their

upward economic climb took centuries of punctuated economic development. Growth began to rise with colonial expansion, beginning in the fifteenth century. It was then accelerated by the Industrial Revolution and the
emergence of a global market system.

Figures 6.2 and 6.3 chart the steep increase in the world's population since
1800 and the parallel growth in per capita income from this period until
now. While growth cannot be attributed solely to the creation of a market
system, absent the erection of a free exchange system, as envisioned by Adam
Smith,[104] it is difficult to argue that the market system did not play a crucial
role in driving economic growth and increasing per capita income. This is
not a wholesale and unconditional endorsement of the market system as
the explanation for economic growth. That is too simple a response to this
conundrum, whose solution remains elusive. That said, the plausible and
empirically grounded response to the question of whether globalization, or,
more precisely, the market system, helps or hinders the reduction and elimination of poverty is this: The market system has been decidedly helpful.

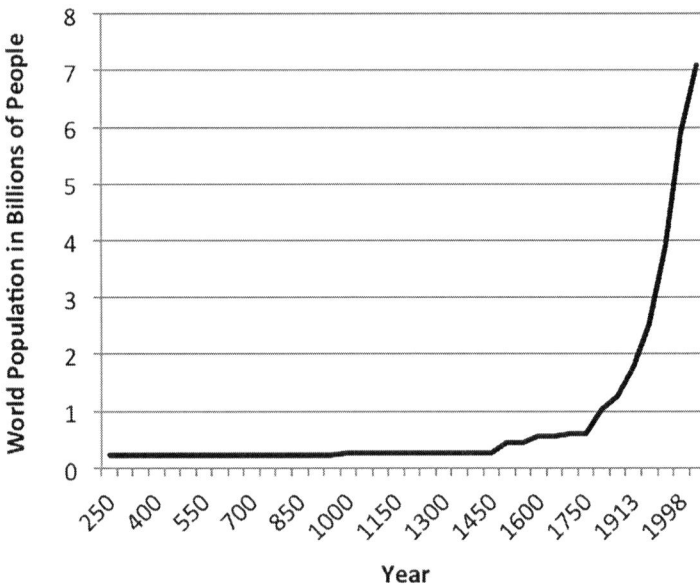

FIGURE 6.2
World Population Increase (250–1998 AD)
Source: Based on data from Angus Maddison, *The World Economy*, vol. 1, *A Millennial
Perspective*, and vol. 2, *Historical Statistics*. Development Centre Studies (Paris: OECD,
2001), 241, doi:10.1787/9789264022621-en.

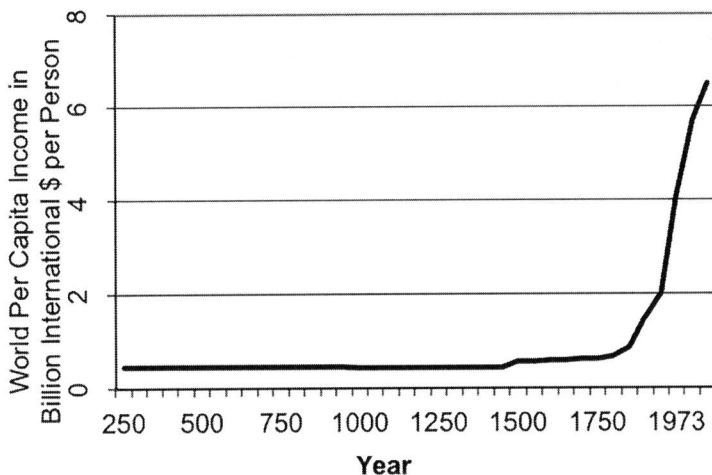

FIGURE 6.3
World Per Capita Income Increase (250–1973 AD)
Source: Based on data from Angus Maddison, *The World Economy*, vol. 1, *A Millennial Perspective*, and vol. 2, *Historical Statistics*. Development Centre Studies (Paris: OECD, 2006), 642, doi: http://dx.doi.org/10.1787/9789264022621-en.

Conversely, with billions of humans living in absolute or near-absolute poverty around the world, including many in developed states of the OECD, it would appear that Lord Keynes's observation at the head of this chapter has weight—namely, that the global capitalist integration of markets is not delivering on its promises of the greatest good for the greatest number. On this score more than a few economists of poverty would argue that the existence of widespread poverty in a world of abundant and growing wealth is evidence of a market failure.[105] The latter refers particularly to "credit, insurance, land, and human capital."[106] As the World Bank's 2006 *World Development Report: Equity and Development* concludes, "Institutions and policies that promote a level playing field—where all members of society have similar chances to become socially active, politically influential, and economically productive—contribute to sustainable growth and development. Greater equity is thus doubly good for poverty reduction: through potential beneficial effects on aggregate long-run development and through greater opportunities for poorer groups within any society."[107]

The World Bank's prescription for reducing market system outcomes of inequality and poverty is largely through nonmarket power—that is, empowering the disadvantaged: "Government policies are what they are—from Mali to Chile—because someone is making them. No group is power*less*, unless some other group is power*ful*. If an inequitable distribution of opportunities means that the investment climate for large groups is poor, this is intimately linked to the lack of power in those groups to affect the decision-making processes that could lead to changes in the distribution over time. And if power is imbalanced, it is because wealth and economic opportunities are uneven. Inequality traps are vicious circles, with economic and political inequalities mutually reinforcing one another."[108] The empowerment of the poor must also extend logically to international institutions and their policy-making rules as well as the economic policies of developed states—for example, the elimination of subsidies to inefficient cotton and sugar producers in the United States—that undermine the competitiveness of farmers in the developing world.

Absent an orchestrated global state strategy to empower the poor, the World Bank solution, however estimable in principle, remains a counsel of virtue. In light of the discussion earlier on the causal relation between the unequal distribution of income and wealth to the top 10–20 percent of the world's populations and the political power wielded by these actors and their ability to frame the poverty issue to their liking, the prospect of substantially decreasing poverty by inducing developed states to help the grossly disadvantaged and poor is highly unlikely. More is needed than achieving the United Nations' MDG, which sought "to halve, by the year 2015, the proportion of the world's population of the world's people whose income is less than one dollar a day."[109] That would have resulted in moving millions above the one-dollar-a-day line but would not necessarily have raised them from what would still be a wretched condition. As Ravallion reminds us, "Redressing the antecedent inequalities of *opportunity* within developing countries as they open up to external trade is crucial to realizing the poverty-reducing potential of globalization. That is the real challenge facing policy-makers striving for pro-poor growth."[110]

There is evidence that, where such state-led prerequisites for gainful market system exchange have been implemented, integration into the market system has reduced poverty, even if large-scale inequalities persist, as in China.[111] A prudent strategy is not to precipitously expose developing states and unskilled and noncompetitive populations to the rigors of the market, some rules of which are clearly discriminatory, but to determine *how* to expose these populations to the market system. There will always be winners and losers in competitive markets. What needs to be done is to shape state and global institutional policies to fit the particular needs and circumstances of each population. The attraction of the Washington Consensus solution of immediate exposure to the market system has increasingly lost ground, since one suit scarcely fits all.[112] Access to education, health, nutrition, clean water, and so forth first must be in place to position populations to compete successfully in the market system. Even that formula has to be qualified since a sector of a country's economy may well expose itself to foreign competition and still be unable to complete successfully. Numerous examples can be cited, including Mexican farmers exposed to American agricultural producers or furniture manufacturers in South Africa, who went bankrupt when their products could no longer survive in global competition with other developing states.[113]

A Summing Up: The Promiscuity of the Market System

Chapters 5 and 6 have evaluated key components of the market system's record as a solution to the imperative of Welfare, one of the three indispensable and mutually dependent elements of the governance of all human societies. The challenge of presenting a convincing assessment of the workings of the market system is compounded by the deep discord among economists in addressing this issue. Reconciling the rival theories of monetarists and Keynesians (much more those of Marxists) exemplifies the unlikely harmonization between these competing schools of thought over facts and values anytime soon. The approach assumed here is to abandon the notion that there currently exists a pure market system or that such a system can ever fully be instituted globally. The market system we experience is a hybrid based only partially (but significantly) on the principle of open, free economic transactions. Economic actors—individuals, groups, corporations—are also bounded by the power and claims of those actors associated with the governing institutions of order (coercion) and legitimacy (the right to rule).

Recall that the imperatives of governance—the socially constructed institutions of Order, Welfare, and Legitimacy—are also structures of power. Left alone to their unfettered processes of decision and action, they are "promiscuous." As Michael Mann reminds us,[114] those controlling each of these power structures have incentives to subordinate the other imperatives of governance to their focused concerns and interests. Their monopolistic success can only be at the expense of effective and just governance. Partisans of the market system, not less than their counterparts working in the power structures of order and legitimacy, are perpetually at sixes and sevens in governing the world society.

Given space limitations, I have chosen to focus on three weaknesses of the market system as central to an evaluation: the tendency of the system to implode if left unregulated; the excessive, unequal, and inequitable distribution of income that it perpetuates on billions of the world's populations; and the chronic existence of pervasive absolute and relative poverty in a sea of untold wealth, swelling ever more beyond what has already been accumulated.[115] The norm of self-interest as a driving force for personal and collective economic gain is a powerful instrument for economic growth and for increasing per capita income of the world's populations. Only individuals can legitimately define their economic and material interests and values. The market system allows them that opportunity to a greater degree than alternative ways of organizing the Welfare imperative.

The aim of this partial diagnosis of market system failures is to underline two paradoxical conclusions. The first is that there exists no alternative to the market system as, provisionally, the optimal way—or, negatively stated, the least bad institutional option—to address the Welfare imperative. The second point is that, unless its failures are addressed, including those going beyond those covered in these chapters, support for the market system and its legitimacy, the imperative of governance developed in the next chapter, there is the likely prospect that it may be rejected by the world's populations or impaired in its best workings by misguided and uninformed public sentiment with no ready alternative to replace it. John Maynard Keynes foresaw this dismal outcome almost a century ago, as the quotation in chapter 5 recounts.

We now turn to the third leg of OWL governance—Legitimacy. The crisis over Legitimacy, endemic to the currently insurmountable divisions among the contesting populations of the global society, will certainly continue long into the future. There is every prospect that this crisis will grow and become increasingly intractable. This parlous state arises from two interdependent sources. The first is the wide range of conflicting solutions to the Legitimacy imperative, covered in previous chapters, which command widespread support, both elite and popular. The second arises from the failure of the democratic global states and peoples to live up to the ideals of popular government. The gap between democratic promise and realization is addressed in chapter 7.

Notes

1. Stiglitz (2012, p. xviii).
2. See Sen (1992, 2000 ["Social Justice"]). For inequality, the essential work is Thomas Piketty's magisterial *Capital in the Twenty-First Century*, which traces inequality across all of the major world economies over almost two centuries. Of particular interest to this discussion is the period from roughly 1913 to the present; see Piketty (2014). For the United States in the current period, see Stiglitz (2012, 2015). More generally for the United States and Europe, consult Atkinson (2015).
3. Lindblom (2001).
4. Quoted in Wade (2004, p. 582).
5. Stiglitz (2012, p. 30).

6. Ibid.

7. Coase (1988).

8. Malthus (1836/1964).

9. Bourguignon & Morrison (2002).

10. See the views of two Nobel laureates in economics: Krugman (2009); Stiglitz (1989, 2002, 2006, 2010, 2012). Relevant, too, among distinguished economists are the views of Dani Rodrik (1998, 2012) and Nouriel Roubini (Roubini & Mihm [2010]). Finis Welch (1999) provides a defense of inequality, more as a positive attribute of the market system than as a failure.

11. *New York Times*, May 5, 2014, Business section, p. 1.

12. Stiglitz (2012, p. 34).

13. See Putnam (2015).

14. This is a central theme of the Stiglitz volume on inequality; see Stiglitz (2012).

15. Several sources were relied upon to supply data. Particularly helpful were OECD (2011); Salverda, Nolan, & Smeeding (2009). The latter citation, *The Oxford Handbook of Economic Inequality*, provides a comprehensive survey of the problem. Especially relevant of its twenty-seven chapters are those on the measurement of inequality (pp. 40–70), the functional distribution of inequality based on households (pp. 71–100), and the accumulation of wealth through sustained unequal dispersions of income (pp. 101–26). A summary of the longer OECD study is found at http:// www.oecd.org/els/socialpoliciesanddata/49499779.pdf. See Stiglitz (2012, p. 310) for citations to UN and EU data. These affirm the trend toward increasing inequality, though the calculations of these sources differ from the OECD study.

For long-term trends in income inequality among Western democracies, the principal source is Piketty (2014). For briefer treatments, consult Piketty & Saez (2003). Updates are found in Alvaredo et al. (2013); Atkinson & Piketty (2007); Atkinson, Piketty, & Saez (2009). The Center on Budget and Policy Priorities, relying on Saez data, delineates the increasing gap between the top 1 percent in the United States and the remainder of the population since the recovery from the great recession of 2008: http://www.cbpp.org/cms/index.cfm?fa=view&id=3697. Congressional Budget Office data are also referenced in this summary of Saez findings.

Complementing these data sets is that of the World Income Inequality Database (WIID), provided by the World Institute for Development Economic Research (WIDER) at the UN University, http://www.wider.unu.edu/research/Database/ en_GB/database/. For a brief overview of US trends in income inequality, consult US Congress (2011).

16. OECD (2011, pp. 22–25).

17. Raghuram Rajan (2010) extensively develops a series of fault lines in the market system that goes well beyond what can be developed here. His informed analysis bolsters the more circumscribed discussion of market failures of this volume in which the market is both the solution and the problem of achieving global welfare.

18. http://www.cbpp.org/cms/index.cfm?fa=view&id=3697. For the Piketty and Saez update to January 23, 2013, see http://elsa.berkeley.edu/~saez/saez-UStopin-comes-2010.pdf.

19. Ibid.

20. Stiglitz (2012, p. 4).

21. *Economist*, October 13, 2012, p. 2.

22. Boardman (1979).

23. Ibid., p. 147. See also Davies (2009).

24. OECD (2011, pp. 47ff.). See also *Economist*, October 13, 2012, pp. 2ff.

25. Ibid., pp. 49–51.

26. Bourguignon & Morrison (2002); see also Milanovic (2011).

27. Bourguignon & Morrison (2002).

28. Milanovic (2003).

29. Ibid.

30. Wade (2004).

31. Kaplinsky (2005, especially chapter 2, pp. 26–52).

32. Ibid., pp. 37–38.

33. Ibid., p. 45.

34. *Economist*, October 13, 2012, p. 10.

35. Frank & Cook (1995).

36. This cautionary point is underscored by Timothy M. Smeeding (2002), a leading expert on cross-state trends in income inequality.

37. Two works that focus on globalization as a driver for inequality are Andrain (2014) and Hytek & Zentgraf (2008).

38. OECD (2011, p. 30).

39. Ibid.

40. Kremer & Masking (2006).

41. Stiglitz (2012, p. 65).

42. Freeland (2012); Noah (2012); Roubini & Mihm (2010); Stiglitz (2012).

43. Stiglitz (2012, p. 287). See also Stiglitz (2015), which develops the political thesis for income inequality.

44. OECD (2011). For a summary of OECD findings, see pp. 40–42 of the summary of this longer document: http://www.oecd-ilibrary.org/social-issues-migration-health/the-causes-of-growing-inequalities-in-oecd-countries_9789264119536-en.

45. Dahl (1961, p. 1).

46. Bartels (2008).

47. Bartels (2008, p. 285). I have used Bartels's careful study as a proxy for a growing scholarly literature that supports his general conclusion that American democracy has gradually morphed from a popularly representative democracy (qualified by Robert Dahl's notion of polyarchy) to an oligarchy and even a plutocracy in some policy areas in which rent-seekers control policy outcomes (e.g., hedge fund managers). For scholarly works supporting Bartels's research on rent-seeking behavior and political privilege, see Alvarado et al. (2013); Andrain (2014); Atkinson (2008, 2015); Atkinson & Piketty (2007); Gilens (2012); Jacobs & King (2008).

48. Michels (1966).

49. See Wade (1990) for an overall appreciation of the role of government in fostering economic growth. See also Hirst, Thompson, & Bromley (2009); Kaplinsky (2005), who depict globalization more in terms of state intervention in the economy than a borderless global economic system. See also chapter 4 and citations there covering the same point.

50. http://www.opensecrets.org/lobby/index.php.

51. Ibid.

52. http://www.opensecrets.org/about/.

53. Ibid.

54. See note 17 and references to Krugman, Stiglitz, Roubini, and Rodrik, among others.

55. For a contrary, minority view on CEO compensation, see Kaplan (2008).

56. Remark of November 9, 2009, cited in the HuffPost Business, http://www.huffingtonpost.com/2009/11/07/goldman-sachs-ceo-lloyd-b_0_n_349620.html.

57. Quoted in *Economist*, October 13, 2012, p. 4. Friedrich von Hayek (1944, 1948, 1960) makes the case for personal liberty as a function of free and unfettered markets.

58. Contrast Welch (1999) and Stiglitz (2012) respectively, at the extremes of these two poles.

59. Berg & Ostry (2011, *Inequality*); see also Berg & Ostry (2011, "Equality and Efficiency").

60. IMF (2007, p. 13 and note 22).

61. IMF (2007).

62. Easterly (2007); Ferreira & Ravallion (2009). Space constraints preclude a comprehensive review of the economic literature measuring the impact of inequality on growth. I have chosen to side with the recent findings of studies conducted by the OECD and the IMF: IMF (2007); OECD (2008, 2011). For a nuanced review of these conflicting findings, see Voitchovsky (2009).

63. This is the conclusion of the OECD study on inequality (2011).

64. See Putnam (2015).

65. For example, see Arneson (1989); Bourguignon, Ferreira, & Menendez (2007); Cohen (1986, 1990); Dworkin (1981 ["What Is Equality? Part 1"; "What Is Equality? Part 2"]); Rawls (1971); Roemer (1998); Sen (1980, 1985 [*Commodities*]). Key to this debate is the World Bank's *World Development Report for 2006: Equity and Development* (2006).

66. Bourguignon, Ferreira, & Menendez (2007).

67. World Bank (2006, pp. 29–30).

68. *Economist*, October 13, 2012, p. 15.

69. Ibid., p. 10.

70. World Bank (2006).

71. See especially Rodrik (1998, 2012). Also relevant is Fukuyama, Diamond, & Plattner (2012).

72. Hillebrand (2008, pp. 1ff.).

73. Ravallion (2010, p. 26).

74. Ibid., p. 27.

75. See the World Bank brief outline of how it measures poverty: http://econ.worldbank.org/WBSITE/EXTERNAL/EXTDEC/EXTRESEARCH/0,,contentMDK:22452035~pagePK:64165401~piPK:64165026~theSitePK:469382~isCURL:Y,00.html. Also see Chen & Ravallion (2010), which estimates that the poverty line for the United States is thirteen dollars per person per day.

76. Quoted in Kaplinsky (2005, p. 28). The quote is drawn from Peter Townsend. He humorously notes that, while Smith included linen shirts and leather shoes in his list of necessities, he excluded beer, ale, and wine because, he believed, "'custom nowhere renders it indecent for people to live without them.'" See Townsend (1979, pp. 32–33).

77. Ibid.

78. See, among others, Sen (1980, 1985 [*Commodities*, "Goals"], 1992, 2000 ["Decade," "Social Justice"]). For a general overview of Sen's work, with particular focus on gender inequality and opportunities, see Agarwal, Humphries, & Robeyns (2005).

79. Sachs (2005).

80. See http://econ.worldbank.org/WBSITE/EXTERNAL/EXTDEC/EXTRESEA RCH/EXTWDRS/0,,contentMDK:20227703~pagePK:478093~piPK:477627~theSit ePK:477624,00.html.

81. http://hdr.undp.org/en/reports/global/hdr2011/.

82. Aside from the references already noted and those below, a sampling of relevant studies includes Adams (2004); World Bank (2011); Danzinger & Haveman (2001); Dehesa (2007); Godinot (2012); Hughes et al. (2009); Hulme & Toye (2007); Kohl (2003); Logan (2002); Santarelli & Figini (2004); Sinha (2003); Tausch & Heshmati (2012).

83. Deaton (2010, p. 187).

84. The term "Washington Consensus" was coined by World Bank economist John Williamson; see Banerjee, Benabou, & Mookherjee (2006).

85. Friedman (2000, 2006).

86. Banerjee, Benabou, & Mookherjee (2006, p. xxv).

87. Note that the 2006 World Bank *World Development Report* was devoted specifically to "Equity and Development"; see World Bank (2006).

88. The description of World Bank data acquisition of poverty and methods are drawn from the publications of Shaohua Chen and Martin Ravallion, the World Bank's top statisticians and research directors, and the summary presentation of their measurement of global poverty in a World Bank research note, "Knowledge in Development Note: Measuring Global Poverty." See: http://econ.worldbank.org/WBSITE/ EXTERNAL/EXTDEC/EXTRESEARCH/0,,contentMDK:22452035~pagePK:641654 01~piPK:64165026~theSitePK:469382~isCURL:Y,00.html.

89. Chen & Ravallion (2010, p. 1590).

90. Ibid., p. 1585.

91. Ibid., p. 1590. Note that there are hosts of problems in using these or other measures and methods to produce comparable poverty estimates. These are discussed at length in Chen & Ravallion (2010); neither these survey and data issues nor the respective merits of using a "survey-based method," based on aggregating surveys across states or a "rescaling method," employing national income accounts, are reviewed here. The object of this discussion is to underline the shortcomings of the market system to solve the problem of chronic poverty. It is sufficient for this discussion to clearly establish that hundreds of millions around the globe, principally in the developing world, and most especially in sub-Saharan Africa, live in dire circumstances, whether the World Bank data and methods or those of its critics are used.

Of course, important policy issues are raised, depending on whose data and methods are used, but those conflicts largely fall outside the scope of this analysis. For a fuller review of the data and methodological issues associated with measuring poverty, see also two indispensable volumes, which present comprehensive discussions of these issues and the conflicting positions of experts in the field: Anand, Segal, & Stiglitz (2010); Banerjee, Benabou, & Mookherjee (2006).

92. Chen & Ravallion (2010, p. 1598).

93. Ibid., p. 1599.

94. Ibid., p. 1600.

95. Chen & Ravallion (2010). See especially the tables and figures comparing changes in the percentages and absolute numbers of the poor at different poverty lines for six regions of the world (pp. 1598–1611).

96. Ibid., pp. 1603–6 for all five levels of poverty from 1981 to 2005.

97. For critiques of World Bank estimates of poverty, consult Bhalla (2002, 2003, 2010); Sala-i-Martin (2006).

98. See Chen & Ravallion (2010, note 97). At this writing, Ravallion is a professor of economics at Georgetown University.

99. Anand, Segal, & Stiglitz (2010, p. 150).

100. Ravallion (2010, p. 32).

101. Ibid., p. 37.

102. Jones (1988).

103. Jones (1987).

104. Consult chapter 3.

105. With few exceptions, notably Surjit S. Bhalla, many economists concur that the market system has failed to satisfactorily address poverty. There also appears growing consensus among developmental economists within the IMF, World Bank, and United Nations, registered in their annual reports, that the market system, particularly the extension of credit, could do more to alleviate poverty. See recent annual reports of the IMF and World Bank and the UN *Development Report*.

106. World Bank (2006, p. 2).

107. Ibid.

108. Ibid., p. 228.

109. Quoted in Pogge (2010, p. 102). Pogge notes that the MDG definition of poverty reduction is "calculated not as a percentage of world population, but of the faster-growing population of the less developed countries" (ibid.). This results in millions being left out of the calculation of the world's poor.

110. Ravallion (2010, p. 37).

111. Winters, McCulloch, & McKay (2004).

112. Consult Sachs (2005); Stiglitz (2002, 2006, 2012).

113. This point is made repeatedly with numerous examples by Kaplinsky (2005).

114. Mann (1986, 1993). Since the incentives for actor behavior and responses generated by OWL institutions and power structures can in theory never be reconciled, the conclusion is hard to resist that the governance of all human societies is fundamentally problematic and uncertain. The perpetual change in governing regimes over

the evolution of the species underscores this unsettling proposition. See Finer (1999) for references to governmental change over centuries.

115. For a discussion of market system failures that expands on my more limited critique, focused on global governance, consult the writings of Joseph Stiglitz, cited in this volume, and a recent work by Raghuram Rajan (2010).

7

Democratic Legitimacy Besieged

The price of preserving legitimacy is my life. Legitimacy is the only guarantee to preserve the country. The Egyptians declared to the whole world
that they have elected a president in a free manner.

> —Deposed Egyptian president Mohamed Morsi,
> quoted by Matt Brown, *ABC News*, July 5, 2013[1]

Legitimacy is best conceived as a source of power, not a veil to power, as
it is commonly described.

> —Christian Reus-Smit, *International Politics*[2]

PREVIOUS CHAPTERS EVALUATED the state and market systems. These
have become the prevailing, if still flawed, solutions to the imperatives of
Order and Welfare. Despite the continuing rivalry of states and competition
within the market system, the actors engaged in these solutions, respectively,
to Order and Welfare imperatives, largely accept the governing arrangements
associated with these imperatives. This chapter departs from that starting
point of actor willingness to work within the state and market systems and
their autonomous power structures in pursuing their interests.

There is no universal starting point in evaluating the imperative of Legitimacy. The imperative of Legitimacy is more daunting and intractable
than problematic accord on Order and Welfare imperatives. Humans have
resisted settling upon a core of universal values to legitimate the governance
of their societal relations and interdependencies. Absent progress in bridging
the clashing value systems of the world's populations, the likelihood of an

effective and just governance of the peoples of the globe will continue to be seriously arrested. Imperiled will be the state and market systems, too.

The challenge of Legitimacy is the principal weakness of global governance and the most resistant of the imperatives to resolve. There is a global society, as defined by this volume, but no world community susceptible to global rule by a universal state, providing a coherent and cohesive governing regime accepted as legitimate by the world's peoples and authorized to act directly on them with their consent. Nor is there any prospect of such a global state and regime emerging any time soon.[3] Given the deeply torn social composition of the world's populations, efforts to pursue such an objective are scarcely desirable. Such efforts would provoke globally scaled conflict and incur human and material costs likely to exceed those expended in creating the currently provisional solutions to Order and Welfare imperatives.

The struggle to define legitimate rule of the world's populations is dispersed within and across the state system. In these multiple settings, the conflict over competing representations of legitimacy, as the struggle over legitimate rule in Egypt lethally exemplifies, assumes a bewildering array of contradictory forms. What is true for Egypt can also be predicated for all of the peoples enveloped by the uprisings of the Arab Spring in 2010. Conflict over legitimacy extends no less to a host of other states and peoples around the globe. Witness the challenge of the Taliban in Afghanistan; the incipiently failed Pakistani state; communal strife in India; the multiple tribal and ethnic struggles in the Republic of the Congo, Mali, the Central African Republic, and South Sudan; or continuing turmoil in Ukraine with contesting factions seeking alignment with either Russia or the European Union.

Even in seemingly stable democracies, like the United States or France, there is much talk of illicit or illegitimate rule. Deep disputes arose over whether George W. Bush was legitimately elected in 2000 as president of the United States. He received fewer votes than his opponent but garnered a majority of electoral votes. A five-to-four vote of the US Supreme Court confirmed his election by halting further vote-counting in the contested state of Florida. The split vote of the Supreme Court ratified his election to be president of 300 million Americans, but at the expense of the principle of majority rule, the touchstone of legitimate democratic rule.

The issue of legitimate rule has been a continuing issue in French history since the French Revolution between opponents favoring a strong executive and those who viewed the legislature as the embodiment of the general will. More recently, opponents of the French Fifth Republic disputed the legitimacy of this regime for a generation after its adoption through a referendum in 1958. It created the office of president and provisionally legitimated the assumption to power of Charles de Gaulle in the wake of what was a coup d'état by the French military over the issue of Algerian independence.[4] Only with the election of a socialist president, François Mitterrand, a generation later was the legitimacy of the Fifth Republic Constitution confirmed and reconciliation between two opposed conceptions of legitimacy achieved after almost two centuries of discord over where to place the locus of legitimate rule.

For the reasons delineated below, the discussion of the Legitimacy imperative will be limited to the model of legitimate rule adopted in a variety of forms by the coalition of free, open democratic states and peoples. As the currently dominant, if partial and flawed, solution to the imperative of Legitimacy of global governance, this model is a feasible start on which to build toward a more comprehensive and inclusive understanding of legitimacy as a central component of human governance and a source of political and moral power.

However they may differ in their institutions or their political practices, there is sufficient accord among open, free societies on basic democratic norms.[5] These converging social compacts of an increasing number of states and peoples have two important implications for the legitimacy of global governance. First, in greater or lesser measure, each meets, however imperfectly, the demanding tests of a democratic regime. While convergence of the world's populations on liberal democratic norms cannot be expected anytime soon, probably never,[6] the expansion of democratic regimes does move in that direction to partially relax the conflicts posed by the currently competing and incommensurable solutions to the imperative of Legitimacy from state and nonstate sources. Second, given the trend toward adoption of the democratic model over the last two centuries, democratic regimes can also be viewed collectively as a unit of analysis for legitimate governance of the globe.

Gaining universal consent of the world's populations to a shared conception of legitimacy arises from the deeply contesting value systems held by the divided populations of the global society. As Albert Camus's *L'Etranger* makes abundantly clear, to be human is to have values and to make choices as a consequence of those values. The distinguishing property of a global society is the clash of values (not just civilizations), which define and determine legitimate rule. What is clear is that the democratic experiment is uneasily and precariously suspended within the larger and resistant webs of the global society populated by billions of actors who reject democratic OWL solutions, notably those associated with the imperative of Legitimacy. They work assiduously—employing force where effective—to defeat the democracies and install their alternative preferences for global governance.

Preserving and extending democratic rule in this conflict-ridden global domain is then a collective enterprise. If free government is not to perish from the earth, its collective survival will hinge on cooperative responses to the imperatives of governance—most notably in continually striving to establish democratic rule, civil liberties, and human rights worldwide as the basis for the legitimacy of global governance. There is a lot of work yet to be done to achieve this level of cooperation among democratic states and peoples. Preceding chapters have shown that democratic regimes and their supportive populations have failed to coordinate their policies and power to fully address the shortcomings of their responses to Order and Welfare imperatives. In varying degrees they also fail to live up to demands of democratic norms and practices.

This chapter reaffirms the proposition, articulated by Robert Dahl, that "the boundaries of a country, even a country as large as the United States, are now much smaller than the boundaries of the decisions that significantly affect the fundamental interests of its citizens. A country's economic life, physical environment, national security, and survival are highly, and probably increasingly dependent on actors and actions that are outside the country's boundaries and not directly subject to its government."[7] Under the pressures of globalization, extending democratic government to all of the world's peoples is among the most important challenges confronting free peoples today, a goal mightily resisted by nondemocratic regimes and no less so by billions untutored in democratic practices and virtues. Theoretically, if democratic government were extended to all peoples, the tension between the interdependencies of the world's populations and their ability to have a say in the governance of these entanglements would be eased, if obviously not fully resolved.

This chapter is divided into four sections. The first argues that a reasonable starting point in advancing toward a solution for legitimate global rule is to evaluate the solution devised by the democratic states rather than attempt to address the governmental preferences of their rivals.

The second section summarizes the case for popular government as superior to competing regime solutions to the imperative of Legitimacy.[8] It is important to go over this well-travelled ground in order to set the stage for the third section, which focuses on the unsolved problems raised by democratic rule as a solution to legitimacy. The shortcomings of this solution complement and extend those already developed for the state and market systems. The conjunction of these flawed solutions to OWL imperatives summarizes the current perils confronting the democratic experiment as a viable, if flawed, solution to global governance.

The final section moves from the nation-state to a global level to show that there exists a permanent "democratic deficit" in governing the interdependencies of the world's diverse peoples. Two key factors are singled out for special attention. First, there is the continuing imbalance of power within the principal international organizations created largely by the democratic global states to address the shared problems of the world's peoples. These refer principally to the United Nations, the World Bank, the International Monetary Fund, and the World Trade Organization. Power is divided unequally in these organizations. As a consequence, the capacity of many states to have a say over the decisions and policies of these organizations that affect their vital interests is marginalized or precluded. This puts the democracies in conflict with these affected states and peoples. Second, and more important, the democracies have failed to provide, sufficient and effectively, needed public goods for their own populations, much less for the world's populations. These shortfalls weaken the power and dilute the authority of democratic regimes to be the foundation for legitimate global rule.

Why Democratic Rule as a Solution to Global Legitimacy?

As chapter 3 argues, Legitimacy is an imperative of governance predicable of all human societies. It is a necessary and unavoidable component of just and effective rule. Recall that legitimacy, as an autonomous source of power, is the right of authorities to issue rules to govern subject populations and their reciprocal obligation to obey those directives. Ideally, legitimacy rests on free and unconditional consent to obey those officials and institutions invested with authority to govern the exchanges and transactions of the populations under their direction. Rules based solely on force, coercive threats, extortion, and intimidation—as Rousseau well stipulated centuries ago—is inimical to right rule, based on the principles of the freedom and equality of all human beings. Human societies ruled largely by force have obviously persisted and replicated themselves. Whatever the duration of survivability of these regimes may have been, populations in the modern era—dramatized initially by the American and French revolutions and, subsequently, by uprisings across the globe—have increasingly opted for freely elected, popular, representative democratic rule as the gold standard of legitimate governance, a trend that persists despite its irregular and unpredictable movement, with fits and starts and setbacks along the way.

Over the long course of human social evolution, few, if any, regimes offer themselves as illegitimate. No government or its leaders admit that their regime is bereft of authority to rule their subjects or that their subjects are not obliged to obey their commands, however perverse their notion of legitimacy may be. The regimes of Adolf Hitler's Germany, Joseph Stalin's Soviet Union, Mao Zedong's China, and Fidel Castro's Cuba are contemporary examples of flawed assertions of legitimate rule, resting on coercion and intimidation, not consent. Countless other examples can be multiplied to reinforce the centrality of legitimacy to governance even for those who corrupt any reasonable understanding of legitimacy resting on free and unfettered popular consent. The claim or mantel of legitimacy is a telling instrument of power and indispensable to effective governance.

This broad declamation of the fusion of legitimacy with governance begs the question of the substantive warrant of each regime's claim to authority. The popular uprising, supported by the army, to overthrow President Mohammed Morsi—the first freely elected civilian president in Egypt's millennial history—exposes the complexity and tortuous dilemmas of assessing conflicting claims of legitimate rule. *Al-Gomhuria*, a government-owned newspaper, proclaimed that "the people's legitimacy was victorious." In supporting the coup d'état, *Al-Ahram* justified President Morsi's ouster as an act of "revolutionary legitimacy."[9] Two powerful movements—one anti- the other pro-Morsi—can't both be right, though both might well be wrong. Fundamentally conflicting rationales for legitimacy cannot occupy the same conceptual and moral space. That limitation poses the presently insoluble global challenge of discovering or creating a universally shared notion of legitimacy. Not only are value systems in fundamental conflict with each other, but they also generate incentives for partisans to use force to impose their preferred system on those of opposed beliefs.

The current deadly conflict between and among supporters of competing Egyptian conceptions of legitimacy arises from the fundamentally subjective, immaterial nature of legitimacy. For Egyptians, it lies deeply rooted in the value system of each Egyptian, as a claimant, both to define the legitimate authority of a regime and, consensually, to be subject to its rule. The struggle for ascendancy between and among rival notions of legitimacy is conditioned further by the particular parochial, personal, and community interests of those engaged in determining who or what is legitimate in the Egyptian context. The only clear and unequivocal point to draw from the contesting claims to authoritatively rule Egypt is that legitimacy remains the prize of governance, however achieved or rationalized. General Abdel Fattah el-Sisi was elected president of Egypt on June 4, 2014. He garnered an incredible 96 percent of the vote, attesting to the significance attached by Sisi to legitimacy despite the obvious mockery of the electoral count. The Sisi regime's solutions to the imperatives of Order and Welfare hinge on its capacity to sustain its dubious claim to legitimacy.

If gaining consensus on legitimacy at the nation-state level is freighted, as the Egyptian case illustrates, with insoluble disputing claims, how much more difficult then is the challenge of defining a conception of legitimacy compatible with the divergent value systems of the world's populations? Unlike past eras, which involved separate, often isolated and autonomous human societies, the search for legitimacy now encompasses the world's populations under the globalizing condition of widening, deepening, and cumulative webs of interdependence. Each exchange between the multiple actors of the global society implicitly joins the issue of legitimate government, as the metaphor of family governance in chapter 1 suggests. This comes as no surprise. What is at stake in governing these interrelations are the most profound values of different human communities, the meanings they infuse into the lives of their adherents, and the integrity and validity of their self-appreciation of these communities and of the moral worth of each member of the group.[10]

If the imperative of Legitimacy is treated as a negotiable object, it is emptied of its human value as well as of its social and individual worth. Its power to command is no less devalued. Why, for example, are India and Pakistan bitter nuclear opponents? As Stephen Cohen explains, bending to the demands of a rival over the disputed territory of Kashmir would undermine the legitimacy of the Indian and Pakistani states—one secular, the other religious and Muslim.[11] Political leaders in both states rely on mutual opposition over Kashmir to retain their authority and legitimacy. Why, too, did apartheid fall in South Africa? Exclusive rule by a white minority was doomed before the claims of majority rule and a biracial social compact to underpin the post-apartheid regime. Why is it impossible for Israel to renounce its formation as a Jewish state? Its raison d'etre would be eviscerated, even as it struggles to retain its democratic credentials, while ascribing second-class citizenship to its Arab minority and extending its rule over the occupied territories.[12] Why did the Eurocentric system of empires collapse before the claims of national self-determination? Legitimacy as a moral force and form of political power proved irresistible.

In the pursuit of legitimate rule, the American Civil War determined by force of arms whether the states of the United States would be half-slave and half-free or whether all citizens would be in principle free and equal.[13] There was no middle moral ground for rival contestants for legitimacy to mutually occupy as the central issue of the American Civil War. Abraham Lincoln grasped this moral truth. His electoral opponent for the US Senate, Stephen Douglas, who hewed to the divisive solution of state popular sovereignty to determine whether a state would be free or slave, did not. It would require another century for the nation to bury the notion of "separate but equal," which retained the seeds of the flawed moral doctrine of popular sovereignty. It would take that long for mature popular understanding of what legitimacy required before the Thirteenth, Fourteenth, and Fifteenth Amendments to the Constitution would be implemented through the courts, culminating in the rejection of "separate but equal" in *Brown v. Board of Education* in 1954 and in the Civil Rights Act of 1964.

These selected examples illustrate in principle that the multifaceted issue of global legitimacy is politically articulated largely within nation-states. The challenge confronting the world's populations, if their inescapable interdependencies are to be governed successfully, is to settle upon at least the rudiments of a coherent conception of legitimacy. The peoples of the world have been unable to agree upon a shared notion of legitimacy similar to Hedley Bull's notion of a society of states or Adam Smith's vision of a transnational market system supported by billions of economic actors who are heroically expected to suspend their national identities and clashing value systems in their economic exchanges presumably for their mutual (if differential) material benefit.

Several considerations, quite apart from constraints of space, warrant a focus on democratic regimes as the solution to legitimate rule.[14] First, as figure 7.1 suggests, the model of liberal democracy has been progressively adopted by an ever-enlarging number of states and of the world's populations as the basis for legitimate and authoritative rule of their particular states. Since 1900 there has been a steady upward climb in the number of states that are democratically ruled. Freedom House criteria report a rise from zero in states and populations as democratic in 1900[15] to approximately 60 percent,

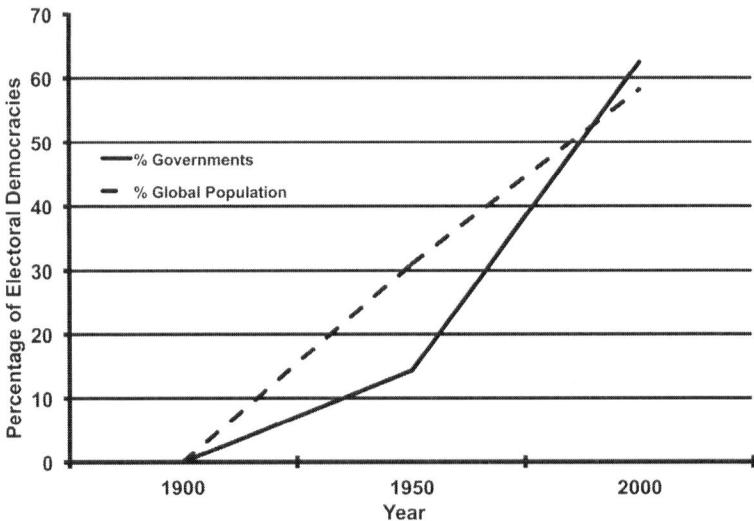

FIGURE 7.1

Growth in Democratic States (1900–2000) (governments elected on the principal of universal adult suffrage for competitive multiparty elections)

Source: Freedom House, *Democracy's Century: A Survey of Global Political Change in the 20th Century*, 2005, http://www.social-sciences-and-humanities.com/PDF/century_democracy.pdf.

respectively, for states and populations by the end of the twentieth century. By the end of the first decade of the twenty-first century, Freedom House categorized 129 states as electoral democracies.

Figure 7.2 displays the movement toward democratic rule by using a different set of metrics. In 2012 Freedom House divided the set of states it examined into 48 not-free countries (24 percent); 87 free (45 percent); and 60 partly free (31 percent). Translated into populations, approximately 3.0

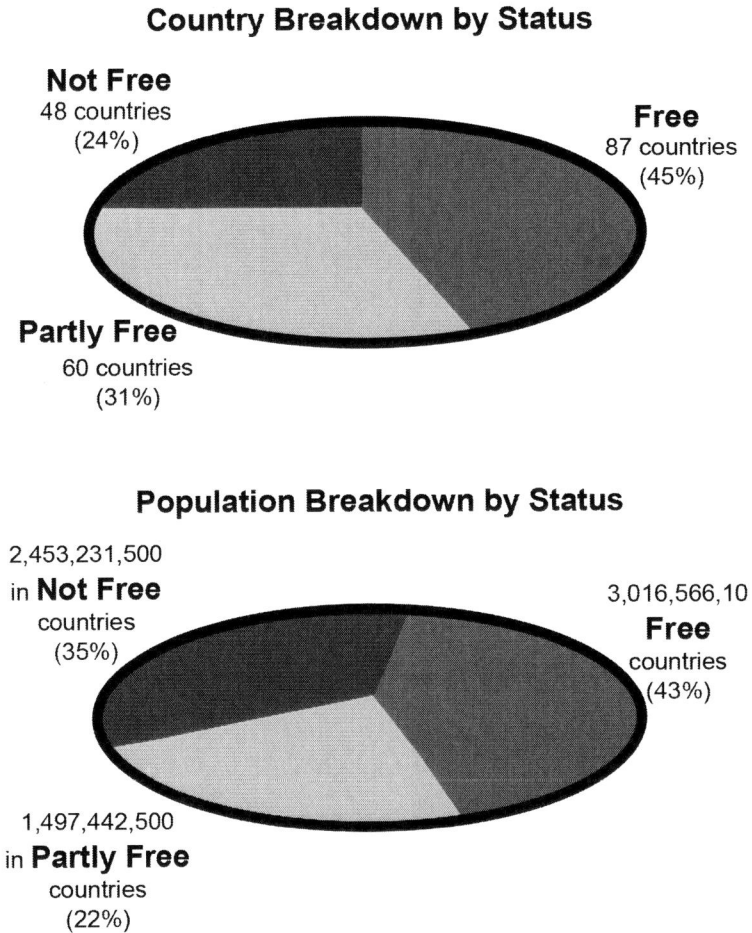

Country Breakdown by Status

Not Free
48 countries
(24%)

Free
87 countries
(45%)

Partly Free
60 countries
(31%)

Population Breakdown by Status

2,453,231,500
in **Not Free**
countries
(35%)

3,016,566,10
Free
countries
(43%)

1,497,442,500
in **Partly Free**
countries
(22%)

FIGURE 7.2
Freedom in the World 2012, Global Data
Source: Freedom House, *Freedom in the World 2012: The Arab Uprisings and Their Global Repercussions*, 24, https://freedomhouse.org/sites/default/files/inline_images/FIW%20 2012%20Booklet--Final.pdf.

billion were free (43 percent); 1.5 billion, partly free (22 percent); and 2.5 billion (35 percent), not free. These numbers, if assumed to be roughly accurate, indicate that the democratic model, despite its spread, is still actively and effectively rejected by large segments of the world's populations and, understandably, by all authoritarian regimes.

A state qualifies as democratically governed, according to annual Freedom House surveys of freedom, if it meets two tests. First, the governing regime must be subject to periodic elections. To meet this requirement, (1) a multiparty system must exist; (2) suffrage must be universal; (3) regularly contested elections must express the public will, conditioned by the absence of massive voter fraud, and by ballot secrecy and security; and (4) political parties must have access to the public through the media and be allowed to mount free and unfettered political campaigns.

Second, a state may meet the tests for an electoral democracy but still fall short of being registered as a liberal democracy. The latter sets the bar higher for a regime in evaluating its capacity for protecting and promoting what Freedom House defines as seven political and seven civil rights. Experts in the politics of the countries that are evaluated score each state's political regime on the two dimensions of political and civil rights. These evaluations cover 193 countries and 16 select territories. The lower the score, the greater freedom, political and civil, that is evaluated as flourishing in a state or territory. Political rights practices are encapsulated in several questions, divided into three subcategories: (1) electoral process (three questions); (2) political pluralism and participation (four); and (3) governmental functioning (three). Civil rights are, in turn, grouped into four subcategories: (1) freedom of expression and belief (four questions); (2) associational and organizations rights (three); (3) rule of law (four); and (4) personal autonomy and individual rights (four).

Countries with low scores for political rights enjoy a wide range of rights. These include free and fair elections, competitive parties, strong opposition parties, and space for self-government of minorities. Conversely, countries with high scores are characterized by governmental oppression in combination sometimes with civil war. Extreme coercion and violence dominates political practices. Countries with low civil rights scores enjoy wide freedom of expression, assembly, association, education, and religion. The rule of law prevails, and economic activity is free-market–based. Those with high scores enjoy few or none of these rights. Economic activity is also state-controlled, fusing economic and political power in the hands of a centralized authoritarian regime.

These measures of electoral practices and political and civil liberties rest on Freedom House definitions. They do not necessarily represent the belief of individuals in the legitimacy of the political and economic institutions that rule them. Freedom House measures are particularly apt in estimating those populations that have opted for Western-style governments. They are less relevant to countries where competing notions of legitimacy, notably those based on religion, culture, or tribal traditions, conflict with those animating Western liberal regimes.

What is unique to the evolution of the democratic experiment today is that, as Robert Dahl notes, "An important threshold of democracy has been attained by a significant number of modern countries, as evidenced by a specific set of political institutions which, taken together, distinguishes the political system of these countries from all 'democracies' . . . prior to the eighteenth century and from all 'nondemocracies' in the contemporary world."[16] These democratic polities, or polyarchies, to use Dahl's term, form an unprecedented grouping of peoples who affirm the principle of popular rule. It is that system of states that, collectively, asserts its principle of governance as the basis for legitimate rule of the global society.[17]

Second, there is more to the ascendancy of the liberal democratic model than the persuasiveness of its case in the ideational debates over utopian forms of competing regimes.[18] The greater power and wealth of the global democratic states goes a long way to explain its ascendancy so far versus its many rivals. Of no less importance in the struggle over global governance is the freedom enjoyed by global state citizens, which unleashes their creativity, resourcefulness, and energy to advance their cause. Their power has been further enhanced and extended through their erection of an open market system. The superiority of global markets to alternative economic systems induced the authoritarian Chinese regime to adapt to the market system or be progressively outdistanced by the liberal democracies. The Chinese Communist Party, like its Soviet counterpart, found itself increasingly incapable of meeting the demands of its growing population by relying solely on a centralized economic system to underwrite its claim to legitimacy.[19]

Driven by the material power of the coalition of democratic states, there is much to be said for the proposition, in light of the historical record, that this regime is what the French would call a *force profonde*. It is an "ideal" model, so to speak, working its way into the psyches of the world's populations across states, individually and collectively, as the preferred regime to adopt and support. That a liberal democratic government may assume a presidential (United States), prime ministerial (United Kingdom), mixed-system (France), federated (India), or centralized (Sweden) form is of less importance than the fact that the peoples supporting these regimes—differing widely in culture, history, and language—converge on key political and moral values as well as on institutions and processes of collective decision-making that register the regime as legitimate.[20]

The record of the spread of the democratic solution to the imperative of Legitimacy in a broken, nonlinear, and punctuated line, characterized by advances and retreats, but relentlessly expansive, provides prima facie evidence of the pervasive and persuasive force of this system of governance.[21] Founded on the Rousseauean conjecture of the personal freedom and equality of each human, the liberal democratic model has had, until now, an edge in the competition with other solutions to the imperative of Legitimacy. Competing systems—for example, Muslim autocracies (Iran and Saudi Arabia) or their secular counterparts (China, Vietnam, and Cuba)—offer no prospect of universal acceptance and require extensive coercive controls to govern their populations.

The freedom of the market system and the inherent vulnerability of the Soviet Union to ethnic and national divisions (in excess of one hundred) also played a major role in undermining the Soviet regime.[22] These communities, held together by the coercive power of the Soviet state, never relinquished their loyalty to a conception of legitimacy directly opposed to the ideal of the "Soviet man." The legitimating force of nationalism over Marxist ideology better explains why the Soviet Union imploded than references to neorealist theory that attributed the survival of the Soviet state to its enormous military, paramilitary, and secret police forces. This complex of awesome violence proved no match to the attractive power of national aspirations and for some peoples, notably those East European states within the Warsaw Pact, who also sought inclusion in the global market system and rule by democratic regimes. The military and police powers of the Soviet Union failed to preclude the demise of the Communist state and regime, the collapse of its imperial system embodied in the Warsaw Pact, Germany's reunification, and the ascendancy of the coalition of democratic states as the dominant collective power in the state system.

Contrary to a unifocal, neorealist conception of governmental rule and state system stability,[23] the Soviet Union was "opted out" as a nation-state. It failed not only despite but also because of its hypertrophied reliance on force to govern its clashing ethnic, religious, and national communities. The immaterial power of legitimacy, defined (one must concede) more by national and ethnic sentiment than adherence to democratic values and the material benefits of the market system, conspired to undo a Soviet order resting almost exclusively on force, coercive threats, intimidation, and fear. The Soviet Union can be credited for provisionally responding to the imperative of Order, but it failed to devise enduring responses to the imperatives of Welfare and Legitimacy either in governing its own subjects or in advancing a feasible solution to global governance. The regime (and realist theory) failed the OWL test. As of the beginning of 2016, whether the same fate awaits the authoritarian Russian regime of President Vladimir Putin remains to be seen.

Liberal democratic regimes currently include the states of the OECD and significant non-OECD members of the Group of 20 (G20).[24] The material means and muscle—political and economic—of the liberal democracies act as magnets, attracting aspiring peoples to associate with this loose and enlarging coalition. The European Union has been particularly successful in extending the reach of the democratic experiment. It requires a state and its regime to comply with liberal democratic norms to be admitted to the Union—hence the rapid accession of the Soviet Union's former satellite East European states as democracies within the European Union. Absent the draw of European economic and political power, the Balkan peoples might still be not only at war with each other but also subject to domestic authoritarian rule. Slovenia and Croatia have now acceded to EU criteria for admission. Serbia and Kosovo have yet to meet the tests for membership. The crisis in Ukraine is largely attributable to Russian objections to the popularly expressed Ukrainian determination to position Ukraine for EU membership and, presumably thereafter, for membership in NATO—a particularly disquieting prospect for the Kremlin leadership.

What is also noteworthy is that democratic regimes that lapsed into autocratic rule subsequently reverted to popular rule. Internal public demands for a return to democratic rule and external pressures from the members of the coalition of democratic states engineered the revival. Among these temporarily lapsed democratic regimes are India, Greece, South Korea, Taiwan, the Philippines, Chile, Argentina, Brazil, Spain, and Portugal. The tentative relaxation of dictatorial rule in Myanmar in 2013, tilted toward opening the regime to increased popular say in governance, can hardly be attributed solely to the normative values of liberal democratic government. Its glacial movement toward openness is explained to an appreciable degree by the power exercised by the liberal democratic states in isolating Myanmar and its ruling military clique and, especially, by the pressures exerted by the United States to open the regime. The experience of backsliding from democratic practices advises against assertions of the "end of history,"[25] as an envisioned inexorable march toward a fully democratic global government. Many peoples do not prize liberal democratic rule and vigorously oppose its spread. As the third section develops, mass democracies are prone, as Fareed Zakaria warns, to slide into "illiberal democracies,"[26] as the experiences of Venezuela under Hugo Chavez, Ukraine under Viktor Yanukovych, or Russia under Vladimir Putin suggest.[27]

Third, democratic regimes are also disposed and suited to adapt to the dynamic, changing forces at work in globalization. Popular governments, given their open processes of collective decision-making, rely on institutions amenable to reform. Revisions of governmental operations are embedded in the

written and unwritten social contracts of these regimes. They undergo continuous change in adapting to new challenges in their domestic or external
environments, such as terrorist threats. Or governmental power is reordered
in light of new thinking about the efficacy and justice of prevailing practices,
such as the end of separating the races in public schools in the United States
or extending the vote to women among the Western democratic states. However, on some collective issues—addressing the environmental challenges of
global warming—the democracies on the whole have not been more responsive than authoritarian regimes, notwithstanding the recent announcement
of President Xi Jinping of China that Beijing was prepared to accept a "cap
and trade" solution to combat climate change.[28] It remains to be seen whether
Beijing will actually enact a "cap and trade" policy absent a similar move by
the democracies.

Liberal democracies also draw on the support of populations socialized and
schooled over generations to reform their governments under changing circumstances through peaceful means. Norberto Bobbio strikes this note in his
pithy definition of democracy: "What is democracy other than a set of rules
for the solution of conflicts without bloodshed?"[29] Liberal democratic societies are acculturated to open debate, self-criticism, and frank assessment of the
defective workings of their governing arrangements.[30] This does not imply
that all of these regimes uniformly realize the normative ideals of this model
of democracy—far from it. The contradictions between democratic theory
and practice are still better managed within the framework of free and open
rule than within the rigidities of authoritarian rule. For the latter, deferring to
opponent preferences and interests risks dissolution of the regime. Tautologi-
cally, nondemocratic, dictatorial, authoritarian regimes resist reforms that
would provide for greater transparency, accountability, and the protection of
civil liberties and human rights. They likewise have no interest in submitting
to popular will through periodic free elections unless, as the lopsided victory
of President Sisi suggests, the election can be staged.

The fourth reason for limiting the evaluation of legitimacy to liberal democracies is embedded in the socio-ideational composition of the world's
populations. The world's populations are profoundly divided by religion, culture, sectarian communities, language, and history. Even within major civi-
lizational groupings of Muslims, Christians, or Hindus, factions within each
are as deeply opposed to each other as between adherents of rival cultures and
religions. Recall that Christian peoples were principally responsible for World
Wars I and II. Note, too, the profound and enduring conflicts today between
Catholics and Protestants, Protestants and Protestants, Sunnis and Shi'ites,
Hindus and Sikhs, or Buddhists and Muslims. The divergent social evolutionary paths taken by different Muslim communities, ranging from North Africa

to Southeast Asia, and the decentralized authority structure of the Muslim religion invite conflict between and among these communities and between them and non-Muslim populations.

Democratic regimes cannot be expected to bridge the animosities of warring communities or harmonize incompatible value systems intensively held by uncompromising loyalists. A liberal democratic model is not a comfortable fit for states socially torn by discord over values and legitimacy and preserved in the frozen historical memories and narratives of antagonistic communities (e.g., Iraq, Syria, Libya, Yemen, et al.). Democratic global states cannot claim that their notions of legitimacy will be adopted by these communities. Given the flood of refugees flocking to these states across the globe, voting with their feet, democracies can claim that open societies provide greater measures of security and material welfare, and accord their citizens greater freedom and a say in how they will be governed, than their rivals do.

A fifth reason for privileging the liberal democratic solution to legitimacy is that the democracies have been the principal engine for the continued expansion of global civil society. Open societies have been principally responsible for the creation of global markets, covering trade, investment, and technological innovations. The countless noneconomic human transactions across state boundaries, including, among others, sports, all forms of social media, or health, depend on a state system, drawing much of its support from democratic regimes that have created the global state.

The sixth and most compelling reason for focusing on popular rule is that, as the succeeding discussion argues, it is superior to its rivals in addressing the imperative of Legitimacy. In its ideal form it establishes better than its opponents the conditions for mutual consent to governance of ruled and rulers. The prospects for individual and group freedom and self-development under open regimes trump all alternative solutions to legitimacy. Popular rule fits the times despite the formidable powers resisting its expansion.

Democracy's superior normative ideals will not alone ensure its continued ascendancy. The degree to which the global society will be free and open will ultimately hinge on the power of the populations comprising the coalition of democratic states and peoples. They have a weapon in that struggle that is greater and more powerful than what is typically referred to as soft power, which is largely limited in scope to interstate bargaining and diplomacy.[31] The pull of democratic rule and norms is transformational, not simply tactical or strategic in the struggle for global governance. "Democracy," as Adam Przeworski observes, "is the only mechanism by which the people can implement their power and the only form of political freedom feasible in the world."[32] In less abstract and more telling terms, a young Ukrainian protester, refusing submission to Russian power, summarized the case for democratic rule: "She said she wanted a country 'where people are free to tell what they think; to do what they want; and to go where they dream.'"[33]

Bobbio, following Immanuel Kant,[34] has sententiously stated the case for open, free rule as the model for global rule: "Human rights, democracy, and peace are the three essential components of the same historic movement: if human rights are not recognized and protected, there is no democracy, and without democracy, the minimal conditions for a peaceful resolution of conflicts do not exist. In other words, democracy is a society of citizens, and subjects become citizens when they are recognized as having certain fundamental rights. There will be stable peace, a peace which does not have war as its alternative, only when there are citizens not of this or that particular state, but of the world."[35] Bobbio's vision extends to all peoples. Anything less falsifies the potentially limitless promise of democratic principles and practices as an attractive solution to the imperative of Legitimacy and global governance.

The evaluative criteria to be applied to the liberal democratic coalition will draw on Bobbio's insights. These are, however, insufficient to confirm the legitimacy of the democratic ideal. They fall short if open, free governments are unable also to adopt policies and provide public goods that address the shared challenges of the world's populations. These two criteria—norm achievement and effective policies—will form the critique of the final section of this discussion. Sir Henry Maine, no friend of popular rule, posed the challenge over a century ago: "There can be no grosser mistake," asserted Maine, "to have the impression that Democracy differs from Monarchy in essence. . . . The tests of success in the performance of the necessary and natural duties of a government are precisely the same in both cases."[36]

The demands on states and regimes, democratic or authoritarian, are unprecedented, largely as a consequence of the processes of globalization, which are weaving an entangling web of interdependencies across otherwise divided communities and states. Democratically governed populations are especially burdened, since they are obliged not only to consent to laws and policies to which they are subject but also to support laws and policies that address the issues confronting them and the world's populations. Interdependence makes that so. Reconciling these two requirements is vastly more difficult today than ever before in a globalizing world of billions of mutually dependent populations at sixes and sevens over values and interests. Echoing Abraham Lincoln's defense of his conduct of the Civil War, democratic global states are the last best hope for humanity. The global historian Ian Morris reminds us that there is an overriding question besetting the peoples of the world: "The question is not whether the West will continue to rule. It is whether humanity as a whole will break through to an entirely new kind of existence before disaster strikes us down—permanently."[37] A feasible strategy to avoid disaster is the spread of the democratic ideal across nations, religions, and cultures. The final chapter concludes on this note that the democracies—their preservation, extension, and enlarging power—are obliged to transform themselves into a concert of free peoples as a necessary, if not sufficient, response to the crisis of global governance.

The Superiority of Democratic Norms and Regimes

This section develops the superiority of democratic claims to legitimacy versus its rivals. It also assesses the prospects of exporting popular rule to peoples now subjected to nondemocratic regimes. Moral superiority does not translate into inevitable universal adoption of democratic norms and practices by the diverse communities into which the peoples of the global society are divided. The divergent religious, cultural, ethnic, and tribal paths taken by these communities preclude an unbiased hearing of the democratic message. Social identity trumps, inured to an open exchange of the rival claims of competing moral systems, much like those undertaken by the representatives of different Greek city-states in Plato's *Laws*.[38] A probing debate of rival regime claims is not in the cards within a fractious global society, riven by cultural and ideological clashes. Notwithstanding the multiple barriers to open and frank discourse, democracy, as a regime, is a defensible, if provisional, solution to the imperative of Legitimacy for the governance of the world's populations.

The magnetic pull of the democratic moral code—a dynamic force working over several centuries, eliciting popular consent across states and peoples—stems from its foundational moral principles: the *freedom* and *equality* of all humans. These properties are anterior and superior to any other moral qualities defining an individual as human. The democratic paradigm stipulates these properties to inhere in humans simply because they are human. However significant other properties of human identities may be in informing and in shaping the value systems of individuals—their religion, culture, ethnic and national affiliation, race, class, or gender—these qualities are necessarily particular to each person and discrete community. While obviously of great social and political importance in shaping the relations of human communities, these multiple properties lack the universality of the moral ideal of democratic rule. What makes these two properties so compelling are their mutual and reinforcing contingency: if all humans are free, all are also equal in moral stature and political status. Following Rousseau and all partisans of popular rule, these properties are renounced only at the expense of an individual's humanity.

Democratic regimes are necessarily dedicated to ensuring the realization of these properties in the laws and rules governing a democratic people. Realizing the expression of these properties in the thinking, behavior, and life chances of each individual is the promise of democratic rule, understood here (and it is crucial to underline) as an aspiration and normative ideal. As an ideal, democratic or popular rule rests squarely on each individual who is a citizen of a democratic government. The legitimacy of a democratic regime depends solely and exclusively on the consent of its citizens to be subject to its laws and to the authority of its freely and fairly elected officials and, reciprocally, for the latter to be no less bound by the rule of law than their subjects.[39]

All democratic regimes, as explained in more detail below, confront a dilemma. They can never achieve the realization of the democratic ideal. Freedom and equality are not fully reconcilable. A thoroughly democratized society and government will then in theory and practice remain elusive. These shortcomings in no way either depreciate the directing aim of popular government or negate the opportunities afforded by democratic rule for the continued advance toward the elusive ideal of reconciliation of these foundational principles of democratic rule. A pure model, pivoting on freedom and equality, is a touchstone in tracking progress toward the ideal. The political contexts that best approximate these two principles are open to limitless possibilities. In balancing the rival claims of freedom and equality, an evaluation of the democratic experience must take into account the spectrum of possible democratic outcomes across working democracies, the diverse socioeconomic and political composition of each democratically ruled people, and the trajectories of their discreet histories and public memories.

Nondemocratic regimes, whatever their success in addressing the demands and needs of their subjects, cannot afford to make the opportunities afforded by freedom and equality available to their subjects. The unprecedented success of the Chinese Communist Party in lifting hundreds of millions of Chinese from abject poverty comes readily to mind as a limiting case. The Chinese government can justly claim to have achieved greater progress in raising the material conditions of its citizens than many other states, including those ruled by democratic regimes. Over half its population, as chapter 6 notes, have been moved out of abject poverty. That is no small achievement in addressing a central criterion of democratic rule. Conversely, if authoritarian regimes were to fully embrace the principles of freedom and equality and the moral and political autonomy of each of its citizens as the foundational principles of legitimacy, their demise would be sealed, their successful economic performance notwithstanding.

Reconciling freedom and equality are provisionally realized within nation-states. Implied is a distinct political process and institutional framework, marked by the ceaseless exercise of power disposed by engaged actors keen to implant their preferences of how these two Rousseauean principles will be defined in practice. Rousseau's conjecture that humans are free is a powerful moral claim—simply that. Its impact remains profound and pervasive on human governance. Its compelling remonstrance against illegitimate constraints (social chains lacking consent) explains in no small part the progress that has been made toward the Rousseauean moral ideal of a social compact freely entered into by the members of a polity. That progress is fraught and freighted by continued and continuing struggle and conflict. Achieving a society based on freedom and equality is not free goods.

The real, if intangible, importance of Rousseau's conjecture is that it is forward-looking. Its significance is that humans are morally equipped and capable to creatively fashion the regimes, institutions, and rules to govern themselves. They are ever free to undo their inherited social coils—to escape their "social cages"[40]—and to redefine who they are. They can reconstruct their identities and the social bonds that will both constrain and open new opportunities for personal and group self-development, according to each community's lights, values, and preferences. They are able, potentially, by the sheer force of their will to sculpt a society and governing regime that better approximate their vision of the social dimensions of the moral ideal of freedom and equality than what they had before. Humans can reformulate their identities and values as they choose. If this is the real nature of the human condition—its fundamental indeterminacy—there is then presented a limitless horizon for human choice about what rules and regime they wish to obey. Raised, too, is the disquieting prospect of ceaseless social tumult and turmoil and personal psychological disorientation in the pursuit of boundless visions of what is viewed by them as the model or ideal society and polity.[41]

How, then, can the principles of freedom and equality be advanced in the face of formidable resistance? An indispensable requirement is popular agreement on the rules of the political process. Without public accord on the procedures for reaching decisions on collective choices, there is little prospect that a democracy can survive. Embedded in mass politics are incommensurate, incompatible, and irreconcilable differences over values, interests, and policy choices to pursue them. Where fleeting agreement on these dimensions might be achieved, discord over the burdens, personal and material, to implement collective choices will still impede cooperation. Free-riding, hiding, and buck-passing are common currency in policy-making within democracies.

Exacerbating the development of coherent and effective responses to shared issues is the very complexity of policy-making. Both democracies and their rivals confront the difficulty of surmounting the uncertainties of delivering on collective decisions. The rule of unintended consequences and the so-called Murphy's Law of unexpected outcomes render contemporary policy-making unalterably problematic. A particular strength of a democratic polis is its capacity to reevaluate its failures and to take compensatory and ameliorative initiatives to address these complexities. The prospects for adaptation still depend on public and elite understanding of the challenges confronting them. Acquiring relevant, empirically based knowledge and its absorption by a distracted, disinterested public or, worse, a public in denial about the issues it confronts, remain severe constraints on effective collective decision-making in a democracy. The inabilities of the democracies to address climate change or widening income inequality are cases in point.

Accord on rules in the face of profound differences within a population implies that those participating in the political process also accept sustained instability and political conflict as a consequence of persistent social divisions. Agreement on rules as the accepted form of democratic rule to respond to these dilemmas of collective choice by political rivals is indispensable to bridge and moderate substantive, deep down, differences within a fractious population. This fractured condition is endemic of mass societies. Where agreement on collective decisional rules does not exist, the supportive instruments of a working democracy—institutions, norms, and practices—cannot function. A social compact on rules can hold together a divided society comprised of partisans of divergent and clashing value systems that are not susceptible to compromise, yet potentially amenable to pragmatic compromises within the rules of the democratic game. Losers can always hope that in the next round of decision-making on a policy issue, their preferences will prevail. Adherence to a body of collective rules, themselves subject and open to popular redefinition, is much to ask or expect of any body of human beings. It is, paradoxically, a prerequisite of a working democracy.

Preserving the rule of law, resting on popular consent to bind both rulers and ruled, also depends on agreement, explicit or implicit, to a set of preexisting or constitutional rules of the political game. This is a *sine qua non* of legitimate democratic rule. As authoritarian regimes, like Nazi Germany and Mussolini's Italy, made abundantly clear, and as the Chinese Communist regime continues to exemplify, the rule of law, dictated by a regime bereft of means of registering popular consent, can rely on its stipulation of the rule of law to suppress basic democratic rights. There can be no legitimate rule of law unless there is a preceding popular agreement on the rules by which the rules of law are produced and administered. If rule-making can be arbitrarily changed by a charismatic leader, junta, self-appointed guardians, party elites, or a dictatorial majority, a vulnerability to which democratic rule is particularly exposed, laws flowing from such a process are capricious, illegal, and illegitimate.[42]

Another asset of a democracy resting on a general will committed to rules for collective choice is that it maps more accurately and responsively than rival regimes to human resourcefulness, creativity, and ingenuity. If individuals are afforded freedom to think and act, they will tend to strive to fashion a social setting congenial to their preferences and to reform and transform themselves to their social liking. Over the past two centuries, the number of those eligible to participate in collective decisions that affect them have been increasingly enlarged. At varying rates of implementation in each democratically ruled state, gender, race, property, and other restrictions on voting have been progressively modified or eliminated. Best economic, social, and political practices have also been progressively implemented through this process, although some democratic reforms, like the end of segregation in public schools in the United States, required more than a century before they were partially realized.

Some form of majority voting is generally relied upon to produce binding collective decisions. Since direct mass participation in collective decisions is impossible, some form of representative system is employed to reach collective decisions through majority voting. The ruling majority of these elected representatives is invested with authority to determine laws and public policy. These public officials are acknowledged as possessed of authority to legitimate their rule. Included in this rolling consensus on rules are those in the minority whose preferences may not have prevailed on a particular issue but who expect with changing circumstances that their will may eventually become law.[43]

For majority rule to be recognized as valid, elections must be free and fair. Fulfilling this normative requirement implies several rights to be fully available to all citizens. Two are especially important and must be unfettered: freedom of expression and what Robert Dahl terms "associational autonomy."[44] Citizens of a polity must be able to express their opinions over the full range of public concerns. These entail criticisms of public officials, prevailing policies and how they are applied, and the dominant ideological rationales driving collective decision-making. The right of free speech is coterminous with the principle of equality that prescribes that, as an ideal, the interests of all participants in the democratic process should be heard and considered.[45] This includes both the control of the public agenda and the decisions flowing from these public priorities.

Mass democracies also highly depend on an open, free civil society to pursue their moral and political imperatives.[46] Aristocratic or oligarchical regimes invest a small elite—self-appointed and unelected guardians—to rule over their more populous subjects. Without the right to form associations to foster their particular interests—labor unions, think tanks, gay rights advocates

and opponents, and so forth—individuals, separate and alone, would be no
match for a minority with greater material resources or privileged access to
state authority. Unlike single, powerless individuals, associations are able to
influence and inflect public decisions to reflect member preferences. Collectively, these associations comprise a civil society that undergirds and legiti-
mizes a democratic regime. "Associational autonomy" provides alternative
information and narratives about policy issues and other, competing solutions to those advanced by governmental officials.

Of equal significance for the success of democratic rule is the right to form
political parties. They are expected to perform central roles in fulfilling the
functions of democratic governance. Parties are expected to marshal public
will and support for the nation's political agenda and priorities. They also
organize public opinion and win elections to fill vital public offices for the governance of a state. Given the inherent limits afforded the members of mass democracies to effectively participate in their self-rule and to advance their preferences, party competition among elites, as many democratic theorists insist,[47]
is an indispensable vehicle to inform a population of the complexities and
plausible alternatives available for collective decisions. If working freely and
independently, absent their collusion, party and elite competition can potentially provide choices for the public for alternative policy agendas and for slates
of officials, who are expected to advance their party's programs, legitimated by
their victory in free and fair elections. Along with other democratic theorists,
Joseph Schumpeter counts on parties to provide these public goods.[48] He also
viewed them as an indispensable means for molding rather than responding to
the people's will.[49] For Schumpeter the role of parties and democratic "norms
were supposed to keep alive the liberal ethos in a realistic manner suited to the
new conditions of large-scale bureaucratic, mass societies."[50]

As chapter 6 recounts, Schumpeter's optimistic expectations about the
positive roles of parties in framing public policy have been seriously undermined by the influx of huge sums of money dispersed by billionaires, corporations, and Super PACs to buy influence, corrupt elections, and undermine
party cohesion.

It may well be that today, with so many avenues for information, thanks
to public and social media, a democratic people may be overwhelmed by
conflicting information and misinformation in making up its collective mind.
However much these avenues have a constraining impact on effective policy-
making in a democracy, the alternative of control by authoritarian regimes
of the media, of access to alternative information through the Internet and
social networks, and of a monopoly of the narrative to support their policies
and performance is worse. Nondemocratic regimes, like China, North Korea,
Cuba, or the Egyptian military, must rely on these instruments of control to

survive, but at the expense of their citizens' preferences and interests, which are precluded from entering the public space.

The final dimension of democratic rule concerns the distribution of power and authority accorded the institutions of government and the bureaucracies charged with administering public policy. Montesquieu's *The Spirit of the Laws* is the classic statement of the necessity of dispersing and decentralizing the government's power among its several branches to ensure liberty, the expected consequence of a separation of powers.[51] James Madison and the *Federalist* papers, as well as the American Constitution, draw on Montesquieu's prescriptions for republican governance.

The American system divides governmental power and authority between the states and the federal government, and once again between the executive, legislative, and judicial branches. Madison feared that a majority faction might impose its preferences, religious or economic, on a minority, extinguishing their rights to protect and promote their values and interests.[52] The majority poor might tax or expropriate the wealth of a rich minority. Liberty of expression and beliefs, as well as belief in the ownership and disposal of private property and the protection of contracts, would be fostered by frustrating majorities bent on realizing Madison's fears.[53] Madison relied on institutional roadblocks (federalism and the separation of powers) and, more decisively, on the social divisions within a mass democracy, comprised of countervailing values, sentiments, and interests, to hold a majority faction from permanently forming.

In the American system, government and society are permanently divided against themselves. The constitution and the federal system institute inequality in voting. This structure and other impediments, like the separation of powers, place formidable obstacles in the path of a determined majority. As long as the rules of constitutional practice were observed (a rebuttable assumption as discussed below), a passionate majority would be obliged, simultaneously, to gain control of three branches of the American government to impose its preferences on a minority. Overlapping but distinct electoral units with elections at two-, four-, and six-year intervals, respectively, for members of the House of Representatives, the presidency, and the Senate were expected to impede the formation of an enduring ruling majority before it could impose its will on a minority. The nonelection of a Supreme Court, the final arbiter of what laws and administrative practices were constitutional, placed another damper on majority rule and its possible excesses.[54]

Alexis de Tocqueville and John Stuart Mill had reservations about the likely ability of these institutions either to teach and engender a spirit of liberty in the populace or to block a majority from assuming despotic rule over a minority. Extending Montesquieu's theory of government, Tocqueville, no less a partisan of liberty than Montesquieu, "sought out the equivalent of Montesquieu's intermediate institutions within the society, finding local governments, voluntary associations, and religious and familial habits and practices (to shape) . . . free democratic politics."[55] In varying ways, all democratic regimes rely on the division of powers among the branches of government and trust to a host of intermediate private and public units to ensure space for the liberty of individuals and groups. Buttressing these institutional mechanisms is a civil democratic society, the larger the better with competing interests, checking each other, to preserve a precarious balance between and among rival groups to advance, if never fully to ensure, the liberty of all.[56]

Democracy as the Problem

Offsetting this optimistic appraisal of the moral and practical superiority of democratic rule and its potential exportability are deep structural flaws, embedded in the rationale for the liberal democratic experiment. There are irreconcilable contradictions underlying democratic theory, viewed as popular accord on rules. These defects are reinforced by manifold discrepancies in the performance of popular regimes in pursuing democratic imperatives. These flaws, theoretical and practical, weaken the case for the superiority of democratic rule. As Carl Schmitt, a prominent critic of liberal democracy, observes, "Often liberal democratic rhetoric is simply used to provide a spurious legitimacy to politicians and the institutions to which they owe their power. New Right liberals such as Hayek, on the one hand, and social democratic liberals, such as Rawls and Dworkin on the other, have both pointed to these discrepancies between theory and practice."[57] Democratic ideals are seriously at odds with reality.

Among the most intractable problems of democratic rule, theoretically and practically, are (1) the contradiction between the principles of majority rule and the claims of freedom and equality as irrevocable rights and, in turn (2), as suggested earlier, the abiding tension between freedom and equality. These disjunctures undermine both the coherence of democratic rule and the legitimacy of its authority. If a majority is constrained from violating human rights claims, rooted in Rousseau's conjecture of each individual's right to freedom and equality and individuals' full participation in constructing a general will to bind them, what, then, is the scope of majority rule as the touchstone of legitimate rule? It falls well short of Rousseau's heroic ideal. Where, too, is the line to be drawn that allows for the rule of the majority to invade and limit the range of choices and actions afforded by freedom and equality? And which rights should be privileged: freedom or equality? John Rawls would opt for equality under the "veil of ignorance"; Frederick Hayek and Tocqueville elect freedom as a priority.[58] Maintaining a theoretically flawed but tenuously stable compromise between these rival principles are prerequisites of the continued vitality of democratic rule. Whatever provisional balance is struck among them still reveals the problematic nature of democratic rule. There are no agreed-upon means or measures that can render definitive and universally acceptable responses to these conundrums to satisfy the complex divisions of value and interest comprising mass societies.

If the tension between the principles of freedom and equality are isolated for analytic purposes from their problematic relation to majority rule, the incoherence of democratic norms and practices is more clearly exposed. The principal explanation for this impasse between these foundational rights arises from the competing incentives that the principles of freedom and equality generate to induce individuals and their agents to attempt to realize these conflicting rights simultaneously. Tocqueville's *Democracy in America* foresaw the drive toward this elusive convergence as inherent in the democratic process once set in motion. Since that illusory ideal has never been reached, nor can be satisfactorily achieved, democratic populations are compelled to reach imperfect, but workable, solutions to relax, if not surmount, the dilemmas of choice embedded in democratic norms and in their address of the political issues confronting them. These contingent arrangements approximate progress toward that ideal, but the unfulfilled promises of freedom and equality are always just below the surface of daily democratic practices. The provisional legitimacy of laws and policies rests then on an uneasy, punctuated acceptance by affected populations of a moving and unstable balance between these clashing principles that is politically and pragmatically adjudged as reasonable and right, pending the next clash between these demanding but competing norms of democratic rule.[59]

If we probe these tensions further, two conflicting and irreconcilable visions of democracy emerge. On one hand, the partisans of freedom privilege the rights of free speech, association, religion, "associational autonomy," and unfettered voting. These are negative rights. They limit a ruling majority from restricting these rights. The political effectiveness of this prohibition depends for its exercise on an implicit or explicit preexisting agreement of most citizens to recognize these political rights as limitations on state power. There is always the possibility that a majority will ignore constraints on its right to rule. These rights are never, nor can they be, written in stone. A written constitution, as the history of American government illustrates, simply invites ceaseless disputes over the interpretation of the scope of these rights.[60] They are the evolving product of socioeconomic, political, and moral understandings of these rights and the assembling of sufficient public support to uphold them. This unsettling condition induces a permanent tension between those demanding recognition of hitherto unrecognized rights and those insisting on the status quo. Examples of this evolutionary process are illustrated by the right to vote for those previously disenfranchised, for gays to marry, for women to have legal abortions, or for a rising generation to demand global solutions for adverse climate change produced by the damaging anthropomorphic behavior of their elders.

Exercise of political rights implies that individuals also have the material means and time to deploy them. These freedoms are not automatically available to all citizens. As many have argued,[61] citizens must also have other substantive rights to exploit these negative freedoms. Lacking equality of means and time, their voices and their political rights are diminished or extinguished in the push and pull of democratic politics. Substantive or positive rights, as prerequisites for the exercise of negative political rights, require the public provision of education, fulsome and meaningful employment, access to adequate health services, leisure, and assistance for those who are young, lame, halt, old, infirm, or mentally challenged. If some democratic states, like those in Scandinavia, have made progress in closing the gaps between freedom and equality, most democratic states have not registered as much success either for their populations or in addressing these issues worldwide.[62]

If there is no agreement on what values and interests should animate a democratic society and only pragmatic rules are the least unstable common denominator, democracy threatens to undermine liberal claims to rights. Carl Schmitt joined the issue that democracy ironically risked undermining liberalism and its passel of rights. Going beyond the Madisonian fear of a "majority faction," threatening liberty and minority rights to practice one's religious beliefs or the freedom to own and dispose of private property, protected against invasion by a majority's possession of the state's coercive powers, Schmitt foresaw that a democracy resting uneasily on provisional rules, which are the product of contingent compromises, could be undone by a determined majority: "Once sovereignty becomes vested in the will of the people or (more realistically) its representatives, the notion of a constitutional order upheld by the state loses any meaning. In a situation where a putative popular will and the rule of law are one and the same, the latter offers no check on the former but is rather formulated by it. Consequently, it becomes constitutionally possible to undo the constitution."[63]

The election of Mohammed Morsi, a devoted member of the Muslim Brotherhood, illustrates Schmitt's concern. The losing minorities, principally Egypt's non-Muslim population, feared that its minority status would be permanently subject to Shari'a law, as it was interpreted by Morsi's coreligious. Conversely, the return to military rule in Egypt by way of what was justified speciously as a democratic coup created the paradoxical outcome of two opposed factions vying for power and legitimacy, each claiming to be democratic but neither meeting liberal democratic tests. These required not only electoral victory but also respect for minority rights, notably those associated with civil liberties and human rights. Neither warring group was prepared to compromise their notions of legitimacy or accord to each other assurances that minority rights would be honored as central elements of a social compact.

The tensions within democratic theory are further complicated by a continuing dispute among partisans of traditional or newly affirmed rights with respect to what institutions and political processes are best suited to guarantee and foster their competing notions of rights. Some, like Norberto Bobbio, who draws extensively on the European experience, insist on their social contingency and on a tolerant and open political process to ensure them.[64] Others prefer to rely on an unelected judiciary for their realization.[65] Both avenues, political or judicial, may also be blocked, as evidenced by the struggle for equal rights of African Americans in the United States. Paralysis of the political process and stagnation at all levels of the judicial decision-making up to the Supreme Court of the United States, stanched progress toward racial equality for a century.

Nor has that struggle ended. The case for political over judicial protection of civil liberties and human rights is reinforced by the five-to-four decision of the US Supreme Court in *Shelby County v. Holder.*[66] The Court held that a key provision of the Voting Rights Act of 1965 was invalid because it was based on data that were over forty years old. This provision provided for federal oversight of voting discrimination by principalities that could be shown to have historically violated the act. The slim majority of the Court was not deterred by the fact that both houses of Congress had voted overwhelmingly to reconfirm the Act and its provisions.

The Court's action immediately opened the way to state legislation in Texas and North Carolina to require voter identification cards, although there was no evidence of widespread voter fraud. These initiatives damaged the principle of one person, one vote, the legitimate basis of democratic rule. The burden of acquiring IDs also falls unequally on the elderly, disabled, students, African Americans, Latinos, and, generally, persons of low income. These and other groups lack the means or opportunity to acquire these IDs without incurring serious personal expense, including loss of paid work time and ID fees. Some simply are physically unable or overwhelmed by their personal and familial obligations to get to ID-issuing offices, all with limited hours of operation and some situated at inconvenient distances from voters. In limiting many from voting, ID laws effectively disenfranchise them. It may well be argued, too, that ID costs in time, pay loss, and fees are tantamount to a poll tax, which is prohibited under the Twenty-fourth Amendment to the American Constitution.

Pluralism, which is so essential to the working of democratic regimes, is also a major obstacle to the realization of the democratic ideal. Examination of the workings of pluralism at the levels of domestic politics and among the democracies raises serious reservations about the performance of democratic politics in reaching its announced norms. What is particularly at risk is the power of individual agency and citizen equality in the making of collective decisions. As critics of democracy have noted,[67] wealthy minorities and large, powerful corporations are better positioned than the more populous and economically disadvantaged to influence and shape public policy to suit their preferences. These well-endowed and entrenched minorities are able to buy time on TV, the principal means of communicating their preferences, or avail themselves of social media to get their messages out. Greater material resources also afford them the ability to mount lobbying and election campaigns that can only be matched by concerted, but difficult to achieve, cooperation between individuals.

Of particular concern is the 2009, five-to-four decision of the US Supreme Court in *Citizens United v. Federal Election Commission*. The split Court equated the political freedom of individuals with a corporation, a legally but fictitiously created entity. Ignored was the obvious imbalance in wealth and resources between the individual citizen and a large corporation to determine the outcomes of governmental decision-making and the implementation of public policy. The Court's ruling fundamentally redefined citizenship. In reducing the weight of each individual's vote, it accorded the few wealthy and powerful a privileged position in the collective decision-making of public policy and its administration.

From a Rousseaunean perspective, the Court implicitly conceived the formation of the general will as the joint product of real and artificially created persons. The assignation of equality and freedom to both without differentiation, wherein judicial fiat equates the moral status of individuals to corporations, fundamentally undermines the foundations on which the legitimacy of democratic rule rests. The Court decision in *Citizens United* provides grist for Richard Bellamy's mill that the court systems cannot be relied upon as the principal means to protect and promote individual freedoms and equality.[68]

The Madison expectation that a large, mass democracy was itself the best guarantor of democratic rule and the principle of majority rule is also raised into question. The revolution in social and public media and the increasingly unequal distribution of wealth and political influence favoring the super wealthy and corporations are among the most important factors reducing the prospects of majority will to get its way in public policy. These changed conditions turn Madison's fears upside down. The challenge now is to find ways to ensure that some measure of majority rule can offset the trend toward the institutionalization of an oligarchy in the guise of popular rule. Robert Dahl's notion of contemporary democracies as "polyarchies" also needs refinement. Actors along the hierarchies comprising democratic rule possess unequal amounts of political power. Individuals with amassed wealth and corporations have a greater say in determining pubic policy and in ensuring that their wealth and power will be amplified greater than their number at the ballot box. The aphorism of one person, one vote, scarcely applies today.

Chapter 5 exposes the power of corporations and special interests to capture the domain of public financial policy. Actors—ranging from banks, investment firms, mortgage entrepreneurs, and speculators, not to forget insolvent home buyers and overextended consumers purchasing credit beyond their means to repay loans—cooperated like oligopolists to undermine the global financial system and, ironically, their own economic solvency. Similarly, the gun lobby in the United States—thanks to gerrymandered House districts, Senate filibuster rules, extensive lobbying and advertising by gun supporters and the National Rifle Association, and disciplined one-issue voters—can block gun control legislation that polls indicate a majority of voters would favor.[69] Pluralism under these conditions affords a determined, well-organized, and financed minority to assume rule of those public domains of interest to it at the expense of the interests of the larger community of citizens and voters.

An open democracy is between Scylla and Charybdis. Like ancient mariners who had to navigate between the monsters, who occupied those rocks and guarded a narrow strait, if they were to survive—and many did not, as the Greek myth tells us—there is no democracy without a vibrant civil society. If civil society is weakened or suppressed, there is little opportunity for the proliferation of advocacy groups to influence public policy or for public opinion to be heard. Conversely, there may be too much of a good thing. What are the limits, if any, to this profusion? In 1971 there were only 175 registered lobbying firms in the United States. That number grew to 13,000 by 2009. Total spending to influence laws, the implementation of public policy, and judicial decisions favoring lobby interests topped $3.5 billion. When lobbyist activity is linked to congressional decision-making, which is responsive to these interest pressures, there results either what Francis Fukuyama describes as a "vetocracy"[70] to preclude public regulation or a host of special interest legislation at the expense of common purposes and the provision of public goods—education, health, infrastructure, environmental protection, or leisure.

If this specter of minority rule and fractured public domains under the control of special interests is a structural weakness in democratic practices, what, then, are the implications of this chronic flaw for the ability of democratic regimes to address the shared challenges confronting the world's populations? Notions of common good resolve themselves into discrete listings of private interests. These thrive in this system of the push and pull of plural and factious democratic politics. This failing threatens all democratic regimes in greater or lesser degree. What was not fully appreciated by the Madison model was the leveraged rule of the minority as a consequence of the decentralization of power and authority across a federal system and a central government divided against itself with the result of magnifying minority sentiment over rule of the majority and its preferences.

Under minority and special interest rule, notions of a common good resolve themselves into a mosaic of discrete private interests. Democratic politics degenerates into power struggles to advance parochial interests at the expense of majority preferences and rule. Fractured is any conception, much less collective address, of shared problems or public good.[71] Fissiparous democratic politics nurture these reductionist and self-defeating filings. Special interests, possessed of superior material means and access to media, can manipulate the preferences of a distracted, ill-informed, and weakly organized majority to their advantage. This is a perennial threat to legitimate democratic rule.

The failings of democratic rule are not confined to the United States or any one popular regime. It is a systemic problem. A close study of the French Third and Fourth Republics reveals the power of special interest and party politics at the expense of the capacity of the government to address national issues.[72] Among the driving forces contributing to the collapse of both French regimes—a fate also suffered by the Weimar Republic—was the fragmentation of power fostered by a democratic process at odds with itself. In proposing the constitution for the French Fifth Republic, Charles de Gaulle insisted on creating a national politics through the election of a president with the power to dissolve parliament under conditions of national emergency. "*Je suis le garant*" was de Gaulle's claim as president to respond to national crises if the legislature were to fail. This was his remedy for the failed history of the Fourth Republic.[73] The rise of a Nazi dictatorship, although voted into office with only a plurality of the public vote, raises concern that the functions of the state may be lost in the contest of private interests, or, worse, the failings of plural politics may bring to office a minority bent on undermining the will of the majority and bring to an end democratic practices and civil liberties.

From an opposite perspective, ideology can also be the ruin of a democracy. A majority or minority may be so ideologically obsessed that compromises on public policy may prove difficult, even impossible. Rigidities are then introduced into the politics of democracy and into the struggle for legitimate rule. In lieu of addressing issues on their own complex merits, governmental policies are filtered through the myopic perspectives of ideological prisms. Thomas Mann and Norman Ornstein, two close observers of the American Congress, reach this conclusion in their critique of congressional politics and practices, "However awkward it may be for the traditional press and nonpartisan analysts to acknowledge, one of the two major parties, the Republican Party, has become an insurgent outlier—ideologically extreme; contemptuous of the inherited social and economic policy regime; scornful of compromise; unpersuaded by conventional understanding of facts, evidence, and science; and dismissive of the legitimacy of its political opposition."[74] Even before the donnybrook of the fall of 2013 during which the Republican majority of the House of Representatives shut down the government, Mann and Ornstein presciently titled the first chapter of their volume, "The New Politics of Hostage Taking."

The American experience of stalemate between the two houses of Congress and between the legislative and executive branches evidences the toxicity of combining the infections of interest group excesses and uncompromising ideology. The complicity of these two vulnerabilities of democratic politics debilitates the capacity of party politics to make mass democracies work reasonably effectively. If parties are captured by special interests in league with immovable ideologues, the constructive attributes attributed by democratic theorists and practitioners to party competition to make democracies work are scarcely realized. The parties are emptied of their ability to inform and mobilize public sentiment to address national issues. In lieu of organizing public debates and collective policy-making by providing alternative solutions to national and global issues, parties become instead agents of special interests and ideologues. Their programs will reflect these mandated and incoherent perspectives. Party competition devolves into a struggle for power to pursue narrow interests or ideological obsessions, secular or religious, at the expense of policies in response to collective issues confronting a population as a whole.[75]

However well democratic regimes might succeed in fulfilling the promise of democratic government in faithfully observing its norms, they may still not be able to persuade many peoples to emulate their example. For a large and complex number of factors, democratic rule is not desirable or feasible for many peoples. Millions, particularly those dedicated to a religious ideology as the basis for legitimate rule, reject the secular orientations of developed democracies.[76] In those societies where Muslim populations are a majority, this inclination to impose prevailing religious beliefs on all citizens of a state is especially prevalent. Their religious convictions and cultural mores, rooted in diverse and competing interpretations of Shar'ia law, view the open processes and freedoms of democratic regimes and the libertine behavior of their popu-lations as morally corrupt. The permissiveness, openness, and tolerance of different and opposed beliefs and value systems, characterizing democratic societies, is scarcely inviting to these populations. Gender equality, abor-tion rights, the acceptance of GLBT sexual orientations, or gay marriage are abominations to these communities. If liberal, secular democratic regimes produce these outcomes, this solution to legitimate rule is to be resisted at all costs, even by force and repression.

Even in states where there is a large proportion of the population attracted to democratic rule, as in Egypt, the social composition of the state's popula-tion might be so rent by communal divisions that there is little or no oppor-tunity to develop agreement on a social compact acceptable to all groups. All of the Arab states of the Middle East and most of the states of Africa and Asia suffer from this debility. The state tends either toward implosion, becoming a failed state, much as Yemen appears to be, or toward unremitting civil war, as Syria, Iraq, the Congo Republic, and Libya evidence. There is the danger that the state will fall under the iron rule of a party or dictator—the fate of Iraq under Saddam Hussein, Libya under Muammar Khaddafi, and Egypt under Hosni Mubarak and currently under General Sisi.

To use Samuel Huntington's phrase, torn communal societies are ill dis-posed to democratic rule or to general accord on open, electorally determined rules of collective choice.[77] Under these divisive social conditions, transitions from nondemocratic rule to democratic regimes are highly problematic. The histories of Turkey under secular and now under an entrenched Muslim party majority offer tenuous support that these torn communities will be able to abide by democratic rules. At the end of 2013, Turkey, Iran, and China accounted for 211 incarcerations of journalists.[78] Of this number, Turkey under Prime Minister Recep Erdogan's regime incarcerated seventy-five journalists. Many others in the media or academia were intimidated into self-censorship.[79]

Globalization and a Permanent Democratic Deficit

Globalization has created a permanent democratic deficit. In an ideal, fric-tionless political world, a virtual, imagined homogeneous world population would by majority vote direct and control their representatives to pursue policies of their choosing. We know that such a world does not exist, nor, *ad nauseam*, is such a world in the offing. There exists no acceptable way for the world's population to confer universal legitimacy on international actors and organizations to meet a liberal democratic test. They would then have to conform to the electoral processes and social compacts of working democratic regimes. A nonexistent world community is defined by its divided peoples and fractured by the sprawling, decentralization of power of multiple contesting actors.

Democratic and nondemocratic states and their populations can agree on one matter: their resistance to any notion of investing a world government with power and authority to cope with the shared challenges they all confront or to provide those public goods needed by the world's populations to flourish and to ensure that the global society can replicate itself. The norms defining liberal democratic rule do not apply to the governance of the multiple, intertwined, and entangling interdependencies of the world's populations. The governance of these transnational interdependencies is not amenable to the prevailing norms and expected practices of liberal democratic regimes.

Democratic rule is largely limited to the practices, power, and authority of nation-state regimes. The nation-state is a closed system. It assumes a historically defined population, reproducing itself through time, bounded and integrated within a territorial state, and subject to a regime, which, through periodic elections, a majority is conceived to control. Democratic theory proceeds on the estimable, but highly dubious, assumption that all those affected by a decision should, and can, have a say—at least theoretically—in shaping and influencing the collective decisions of the laws and institutions governing them. Democratic theory implicitly assigns authority to elected representatives who are charged to make collective decisions for a population defined as citizens of the polity. This closed system is viewed in some sense as impermeable. Certainly it is vulnerable to outside influences, but these factors are largely marginalized in democratic theory-building from determining whether democratic practices are being observed. These comfortable assumptions are not applicable in explaining or understanding how interdependent populations, democratic and nondemocratic, govern their affairs across all of the policy domains in which they are implicated.

Globalization is an open system of multiple, overlapping processes of decision and action between and among millions, indeed billions, of interdependent agents. It can be pictured as a metaphor, more as a dynamically evolving marble cake than as a neat layer cake. Determining the boundaries of the policy domains of interdependence into which globalizing processes resolve themselves is among the most challenging conceptual and public policy issues, confronting theorists, policy-makers, analysts, and the attentive public. Globalizing processes comprise countless and growing domains of human dependencies. The significance, salience, and relevance of these numberless interdependent transactions over a wide, expanding, and interrelated range of policy domains will obviously vary in the impact across individuals and

discrete communities. Everyone is not affected equally all of the time by globalization. Some domain sets may be comparatively small; others, large; some
may encompass the entire population of the world, like the effects of global
warming on the world's environment.

Those engaged in the webs of interdependencies in one domain may not
necessarily be equally involved in another. Others may not be affected directly, say, by the plight of billions living in poverty or care about the unequal
distribution of income and wealth among the world's populations. Neither
the academy nor public debate has developed the analytic and conceptual
tools, much less a moral sense of identity, to fully recognize these entangle-
ments or to agree on the necessity to devise institutions and rules to govern
their relations in ways that are effective and universally viewed as legitimate.

The division between the study of comparative politics and government
and international relations enshrines the separation between domestic democratic theory and global politics and governance. This discussion, sotto voce,
seeks to efface that distinction in determining the OWL solutions to global
governance. Particularly lamentable is the isolation within the academy of
American politics and governance from both these areas of political theorizing and practice. Isolating the study of American (or any other state) politics
from the processes of globalization implies that the American (or any other)
nation-state system can control both its internal affairs and those of outside
actors. The permeability of the American (and every other state system) to
outside actors and their power to influence state policy as a permanent feature
of the conditions of rule is suspended from consideration, as if the progressive integration of states and their population into a global society was not a
permanent condition of expanding globalization. The result of this mental
legerdemain is a falsified conceptual map of how the global society is governed—or not—and an undue magnification of state autonomy and power.[80]

A central issue confronting democratic theory is determining what actors
should be included within different policy domains.[81] Who should count
as the relevant populations in coping with weapons of mass destruction?
Who should have a say on the passel of issues raised by the control of these
weapons? Who should be included in the making of global farm policies,
covering state subsidies and tariffs, genetically modified organisms, or associated health issues? If human rights are being violated by a state or group of
states, what is the membership of the political unit that should be mobilized,
democratically, to pursue strategies to protect these rights and to sanction
and punish violators?

Ian Shapiro aptly states the dilemma confronting democratic theory in
moving from thinking about domestic to global democratic rule: "An enduring embarrassment of democratic theory is that it seems impotent when

faced with questions about its scope. By its terms democracy seems to take the existence of units within which it operates for granted. It depends on a decision rule, usually some variant of majority rule, but the rule's operation assumes that the question 'majority of whom?' has already been settled. . . . A chicken-and-egg problem thus lurks at democracy's core. Questions related to boundaries and membership seem in an important sense prior to democratic decision-making, yet paradoxically they cry out for democratic resolution."[82]

There is no feasible political way around this chicken-egg dilemma. Admirable calls for global democracy or democratic cosmopolitanism to provide the communal foundation for global popular rule largely fail to confront, directly and simultaneously, the flaws of the state and market systems. How global democratic government, however conceived, can meet the tests of OWL imperatives as a singular, not decomposed, reductionist response to global governance is never fully addressed in the discussion of democratic theory.[83] The imaginative but unlikely scenarios generated by these discussions are highly useful in establishing the ideal endpoints of a global democratic order under the conditions of globalization. This literature uncovers many of the hidden problems associated with democratic theory at both domestic and global levels. This discussion has relied on these insights, while departing from them in developing a theory of global governance, grounded in the power exercised by the competing powers of the state and market systems and the conflicting sources of power arising from opposing and irreconcilable value systems which define legitimacy as a source of power across the divisions of the world's populations. The latter constraint in advancing global rule is the most daunting. Nondemocratic states and peoples pose formidable and, in many cases, insurmountable obstacles to any movement toward a more open, transparent, and accountable system of global governance approaching an ideal democratic system.[84]

In attempting to project current democratic theory to a global plane, a host of difficult issues arise. These include the vast differences in power of those states implicated in a particular issue domain, durable minority rights that cannot be accommodated by majority rule, the complexity of the issues to be resolved, and the widespread ignorance or indifference of voters. Given these and other constraints that can be readily identified, what may be projected at the outset as a possible global democratizing process risks being captured by elites who are situated to profit from this complex process with the rise of mass democracies. Max Weber was among the first to foresee the potential capture of the democratic process by bureaucratization: "The democratization of society in its totality, and in the modern sense of the term, whether actual or perhaps merely formal, is an especially favorable basis of bureaucratization. . . . After all, bureaucracy strives merely to level those powers that

stand in its way and in those areas that, in the individual case, it seeks to occupy. We must remember this fact . . . that 'democracy' as such is opposed to
the 'rule' of bureaucracy, in spite and perhaps because of its unavoidable yet
unintended promotion of bureaucratization."[85]

David Held suggests that one way out of this dilemma is to define con-
stituencies according to the scope of individual issues.[86] Emphasis on the
breakdown of the nation-state as an all-inclusive unit of analysis with which
to develop democratic theory, as one critic of democratic cosmopolitanism
observes, "rightly provokes us to rethink standard democratic categories in
the light of major events which have destabilized our notions of political community."[87] Yet the hard fact remains that the populations of the globe define
themselves as citizens of a nation-state, and not as members of some analyti-
cally conceived issue domain. Nor do they view themselves as members of
a global society, much less citizens of the world (those of a cosmopolitan
disposition to the contrary notwithstanding).

To his credit, Held concedes that "in a world where powerful states make
decisions not just for their people but for others as well, and where transnational actors and forces cut across the boundaries of national communities in
diverse ways, the questions of who should be accountable to whom, and on
what grounds, do not easily resolve themselves. Overlapping spheres of influence, interference, and interest create fundamental problems at the centre
of democratic thought, problems which ultimately concern the very basis of
democratic authority."[88]

So where does this leave us? Is democratic theory, even in circumscribed
form, still applicable in some way to providing a basis for legitimacy for global
democratic rule? If we cast the problem of global democratic rule within the
context of the coalition of democratic states and peoples, it can be argued
that this coalition has an objective, if neither fully recognized nor institutionalized, interest to advance its values and power in addressing global issues
within a global society populated by powerful rivals.

Some modest progress toward closing a permanent democratic deficit in
global governance is conceivable. Two possibilities suggest themselves. First,
international organizations can be made more inclusive as a partial down
payment toward their democratization. Currently excluded or marginalized states and populations within these organizations should be increasingly integrated into the decisions of these organizations with the support
of the democracies. Progress toward this goal would increase the say of the
world's populations over the decisions and material aid of these organizations that impact on their way of life. As John Glenn advises, inclusion would
strengthen both the input and the output legitimacy of these organizations.[89]

It is useful to recall why international organizations, which are largely the
creation of the democracies, are indispensable as instruments of global gov-

ernance, however defective their democratic credentials. States alone are no longer (if they ever were) capable of coping with the many issues posed by globalization. Through treaty accords they yield limited power and authority to these organizations to address issues beyond their capacity to master unilaterally. This attribution and orchestration of limited power and authority to international organizations for targeted purposes facilitates the search for ways to prevent war, to ameliorate its damaging human and material impacts, and to promote the conditions for peace between states and rival communities (United Nations and regional security organizations). International organizations are equipped to provide needed assistance for states in financial need (the International Monetary Fund [IMF]), to combat poverty and foster economic development (World Bank), to foster mutually advantageous trade and investment opportunities, and to protect property rights and enforce contracts (World Trade Organization [WTO]).

At a more general level of analysis, international organizations are expected to provide public goods not otherwise available through the anarchical process of discrete nation-state initiatives. They reduce transaction costs and orient otherwise distracted or resistant states to focus on common shared issues. In their ideal form, as Jean-Marc Coicaud notes, "They have attempted, through procedures and substance, to short-circuit the dividing and disrupting effects of bringing such diversity together. They have tried to sublimate and transform these in added value and to reach out for more international reciprocity, shared responsibility, and accountability."[90] As Michael Barnett and Martha Finnemore remind us, "Historically, liberal sentiments favored international organizations as champions of community interests over self-seeking states, and as clearly preferable to the alternative mode of conflict resolution, war, which was so painfully evident in the early twentieth century."[91]

State-based international organizations institutionalize interdependence among states and peoples. They also provide the framework for debate, negotiation, and bargaining among states in providing for public goods. In some measure, they afford voice, if not power, to the weak and underdeveloped states and thus keep inequality on the global agenda. They provide some additional accountability of deviant states, which fail to adhere to treaty obligations or observe at least minimal standards of human rights protections. They are necessarily equipped and oriented, "intellectually, normatively, and politically,"[92] to seek non-national approaches and solutions to global issues. While these organizations are unable to meet the demanding tests of domestic democratic rule, they can promote, as the European Union has demonstrated, the development of democratic practices in nation-states, as a condition for membership.

Composed of democratic and nondemocratic regimes, these organizations are obviously not governments. They are what Robert Dahl, echoing Max

Weber, characterizes as "bureaucratic bargaining systems," within which jostling states of varying power, relying on their bureaucratic capacities, attempt to influence the organization's decisions, policies, and behavior to suit their particular interests. Despite their many positive advantages, there is no reason, as Dahl argues, "to clothe international organizations in the mantle of democracy simply in order to provide them with greater legitimacy."[93] This does not imply that they cannot be progressively directed to relevant democratic norms (e.g., transparency and accountability) and aims (inclusiveness and increasing say for those affected by the organization's actions). As some scholars have argued, norms drawn from prevailing democratic theory can be modified and partially applied to these organizations.[94] The democratic states have, potentially, a major role in advancing these objectives.

The second strategy potentially available to the coalition of democratic states promises to be more determinative in moving global governance toward a democratic ideal in substance and form. It has two modes. The first is for each democratic state to improve its performance in adhering to the norms of popular rule. The second and the more exacting component obliges the democracies to meet the Sir Henry Maine test: to deliver on the public goods needed by their populations and by those living under nondemocratic regimes. This challenge is what Alexis de Tocqueville might have characterized as the pursuit of self-interest rightly understood. The current and future status of the democracies, as still the collective ascendant power in the global society, depends on meeting the challenges thrown down by Dahl and Maine. Doing so will strengthen their power and increase the impact of their influence on deciding global issues. Through the promotion of a virtuous circle, the democracies can conceivably draw more peoples within their ambit of power and authority as a function not only of the superiority of their norms and dedication to individual freedom and equality but also because democracy promises effective and just government for all. The concluding chapter addresses these promises.

Notes

1. Egyptian president Mohammed Morsi defying a military demand that he vacate his office. Reproduced by permission of the Australian Broadcasting Corporation—Library Sales © 2013 ABC. For additional references to Morsi's defiance on grounds of his legitimacy, won by free elections of the Egyptian people, consult the *New York Times*, July 1–4, 2013.

2. The quote is drawn from Reus-Smit's article, "International Crises of Legitimacy" (Reus-Smit [2007]) in an issue of *International Politics* devoted to the power and authority of legitimacy.

3. See Fukuyama (1992); Archibugi (2004); Archibugi et al. (2012); Buzan (2004) for more optimistic viewpoints.

4. Furniss (1960, 1964); Kolodziej (1974, 1992).

5. For a wide-ranging discussion of the relevance of democracy to global governance, consult David Held (1995, 2006).

6. For more optimistic views of the possibility of value system convergence across world populations, see Fukuyama (1992).

7. Dahl (1989, p. 319).

8. This is a path first delineated by the Greeks, who were the first to raise the question of what is the best or ideal polity to conscious deliberation. See, for example, Plato (2004) and Aristotle (1947). In Plato's *Laws* travelers from different Greek city-states debate which of their polities is morally superior. Aristotle specifically raises the question of the search for the ideal polity in the opening pages of the *Ethics*. Leo Strauss first introduced me to this issue as a graduate student at the University of Chicago. See Strauss (1953, 1975, 1979). Robert Dahl's comprehensive defense of the superiority of democracy, on which this discussion heavily relies, is consciously cast in this Greek tradition. See Dahl (1989).

9. Review of Egyptian newspapers on July 4, 2013, in the wake of the overthrow of President Morsi.

10. In greater or lesser measure, I have relied on the following, scarcely compatible works, to navigate through the turbulent waters of legitimacy: Besides Tocqueville's *Democracy in America* and the *Federalist Papers*, the following are relevant to my thinking about democracy: Bobbio (1987, 1988, 1996); Boulding (1989); Coicaud (2001, 2002); Dahl (1989); Held (1995, 2006); Holden (2000); Kant (1991 ["Idea," *Kant*]); Manin (1997); Mann (1986); Sandel (1996, 2012); Strauss (1979); Przeworski (2010); Bellamy (2007); Shapiro & Hacker-Cordon (1999).

11. Cohen (2013).

12. Ari Shavit's *My Promised Land: The Triumph and the Tragedy of Israel* makes this point at length. See Shavit (2013).

13. Burt (2013); Jaffa (2009).

14. The gradual spread of democratic regimes is traced in the following volumes: Bendix (1964 [*Nation-Building*], 1978, 1984); Bobbio (1987, 1988, 1996); S. P. Huntington (1991); Keane (2009); Manin (1997); Przeworski (2010); Schumpeter (1942).

15. Various barriers to voting in the United States, France, or the United Kingdom (e.g., excluding women, requiring property, or intimidating racial groups) preclude these states at the turn of the twentieth century from being categorized as democracies.

16. Dahl (1989, p. 117).

17. David Held develops models of democracy and relates them to his vision of human cosmopolitan development. See Held (1991, 1999, 2006). For a brief critique of cosmopolitanism, see Holden (2000) and, especially, Bellamy & Jones (2000).

18. The Greek dialogues revolved around a debate over what regime was ideal. See, for example, Aristotle (1947); Plato (2004, n.d.). Leo Strauss makes this point in his numerous writings about Greek moral philosophy; see Strauss (1979, 1989).

19. Micklethwait & Wooldridge (2014) make this point.

20. See Kolodziej (2003) for this proposition. The citations to Norberto Bobbio in note 14 parallel my view of ideas and values having a continuing impact on human populations. The causal force of human values on social change, viewed from the perspective of the global tension between traditional and modern society over time, was first developed in Ferdinand Tönnies's *Community and Society* (1957). Determining where cause and effect begins and ends is difficult to pinpoint precisely in adopting this methodological approach. See "A Brief Note on Method," in this volume.

21. Bendix (1964 [*Nation-Building, State and Society*], 1978, 1984); S. P. Huntington (1991); Keane (2009). This theme is echoed by Joseph Ellis in his Pulitzer Prize–winning history of the American Revolution and its global spread; see Ellis (2002).

22. Carrère d'Encausse (1993); Kolodziej (2005); Lebow & Risse-Kappen (1995).

23. See chapter 3 for a critique of the realist and neorealist position, and note 22.

24. While the G20 includes the leading economies, some clearly are not democracies, including China and Saudi Arabia. Non-OECD countries that meet a democratic test include South Africa, Brazil, Argentina, and India.

25. Fukuyama (1992).

26. Zakaria (1997). Along these lines of democratic vulnerability to authoritarian rule, see Diamond (2008 ["Democratic Rollback"]); Kurlantzick (2013). For the dark side of democracies, see Mann (2005).

27. Kurlantzick covers a larger spectrum of democratic backslidings besides Venezuela and Russia.

28. See *New York Times*, September 26, 2015.

29. Bobbio (1987, p. 156). This quote is suggested by Adam Przeworski in his defense of a minimalist conception of democracy. Sheldon Wolin (2008) despairs for the future of mass democracy even in a minimalist form.

30. This point is developed by Huntington (1981). The history of the European Union provides additional evidence of the openness of liberal democracies to reform themselves; see Dinan (2010).

31. Nye (2006).

32. Przeworski (2010, p. xii).

33. *New York Times*, November 27, 2013, p. A9.

34. Kant (1983, 1991 ["Idea," *Kant*]).

35. Bobbio (1996, pP. vii–viii).

36. Maine (1886, p. 60–61). The quotation from Maine is slightly revised, but its essential meaning remains the same.

37. Morris (2010, p. 36).

38. Plato (2004). Amartya Sen argues persuasively for reason over identity; see Sen (1999).

39. See citations to Bobbio in note 14.

40. Maryanski & Turner (1992).

41. Friedrich Nietzsche explores this frightening psychological and moral impasse in his grappling with modern rejection of natural law and the absence of certain and sure moral lodestars to guide human relations and governance. See Nietzsche (1905).

42. The film *Judgment at Nuremberg* dramatizes the Nazi regime's corruption of the judicial process.

43. Democratic populations rapidly abandoned any notion of elected office through lot, Rousseau's preferred procedure; they assigned authority to rule to elected representatives. See Manin (1997); Mill (1948).

44. See Dahl (1989), who makes the case for the superiority of democratic rule more comprehensively and convincingly than I can attempt here.

45. See Dahl (1989); Held (2000).

46. Tocqueville (1945).

47. Schumpeter (1942) is the traditional source of this position. For a skeptical view of the capacity of mass democracies to ensure majority rule, see Riker (1982). Consult Dahl's critique not only of Riker's position but also of other prominent theorists of democracy who reject the capacity of a majority to rule in a democracy, including Gaetano Mosca, Karl Marx, Vladimir Lenin, Vilfredo Pareto, Robert Michels, and Antonio Gramsci. See Dahl (1989, pp. 135–52 and 265–79). Relevant, too, is Wolin (2008).

48. For example, see Schattschneider (1960).

49. Bellamy (1993).

50. Ibid., p. 119.

51. Montesquieu (1989).

52. *Federalist* (n. d., especially nos. 10 and 51). The *Federalist Papers* provide a comprehensive argument for divided government to preclude the creation of a permanent majority faction to oppress a minority by imposing religious tests or expropriating the property of the rich. The public will would be fragmented in being mediated through the division of powers of a government based on popular will, but a will divided against itself.

53. Madison may well have overstated the fear of economic expropriation in a democracy. Cheibub and Przeworski show that democratic populations do not redistribute wealth to their advantage at the expense of the rich; see Cheibub & Przeworski (1999).

54. For a critique of courts as a barrier to rights violations, see Bellamy (2007).

55. Montesquieu (1989, p. xxvii). The commentary is by translator/editor Anne M. Cohler.

56. These societal and institutional supports for popular rule are explicitly developed in Madison's *Federalist* No. 10.

57. Quote in Bellamy & Baehr (1993, p. xx).

58. Rawls (1971). See Hayek (1948).

59. Michael Zurn (2005) implicitly operationalizes the notion of legitimacy, based on freedom and equality, as the pragmatic acceptance by populations of policy choices and the global order.

60. Ellis (2002); Pritchett (1981).

61. Sen (1980, 1992, 2000). For a more recent statement of the case for substantive rights, see Fukuyama, Diamond, & Plattner (2012).

62. The US Bureau of the Census reports in September 2013 that 15 percent of the nation's population lives below the poverty line for developed states and that in adjusting for inflation, the medium income of American households in 2013 was no higher than in the 1980s. *New York Times*, September 18, 2013.

63. Quoted in Bellamy & Baehr (1993, p. 176).

64. Bobbio (1987, 1996).

65. Bellamy & Baehr (1993) develop a detailed critique of relying on courts to protect civil liberties and human rights.

66. See *Shelby County v. Holder*.

67. See note 47 above and Dahl's critique of Mosca, Pareto, and Michels, on the Right, and Marx and Gramsci, on the Left, who view liberal democracies as prone to minority rule, in Dahl (1989, pp. 265–79).

68. Bellamy (2007).

69. See an extensive listing of polls regarding public attitudes toward gun control: http://www.pollingreport.com/guns.htm.

70. Francis Fukuyama, *American Interest*, http://www.the-american-interest.com/2013/12/08/the-decay-of-american-political-institutions/.

71. Walter Lippmann (1955) dwells on this issue.

72. Giles (1991).

73. See de Gaulle (1998) for his critique of the Third Republic. His rejection of Fourth Republic politics is developed at length in Furniss (1960); Kolodziej (1974).

74. Mann & Ornstein (2012, p. xiv). See their chapter 1, pp. 3–30, for an extensive analysis.

75. The long-running debate over the ideological role of political parties was brought to a head in the exchange between Austin Ranney and the Committee of the American Political Science Association over its call for a more ideologically coherent two-party system. See Ranney (1951) and Webb (2007).

76. Mark Juergensmeyer's numerous writings develop this point at length. See, for example, Juergensmeyer (2008).

77. Huntington (1996). Also see Diamond (2008 [*Spirit of Democracy*]).

78. *New York Times*, December 19, 2013, p. A10.

79. http://en.wikipedia.org/wiki/List_of_arrested_journalists_in_Turkey.

80. There are, of course, prominent exceptions. See the work of Norberto Bobbio and Robert Dahl, noted throughout this discussion.

81. The fertility of thought in attempts to extend democratic theory to the world society is evident in the burgeoning literature devoted to global democracy. See Archibugi, Koenig-Archibugi, & Marchetti (2012); Archibugi (2004); Archibugi & Held (1995); Archibugi, Held, & Kohler (1998); Christiano (2010, 2012); Glenn (2008); Moravcsik (2005). Especially important is the work of David Held (1991, 1995, 1999, 2000, 2006).

82. Shapiro & Hacker-Cordon (1999, p. 1). See also Shapiro's critique of democracy (2003) that complements the discussion in this chapter. He casts democracy within the context of power, whether democracy is viewed as a power itself in the form of legitimacy or as dependent on the use of power to ensure its creation, survival, and flourishing.

83. David Held has devoted much to the concept and proposal of democratic cosmopolitanism. See Held (1991, 1995, 1999, 2000, 2006); Held et al. (1999).

84. Thomas Christiano (2010) parses the weaknesses of the proposal for global democracy.

85. Weber (1958 [*From Max Weber*], p. 231). The entire section on bureaucracy can be read with profit and its challenge to democratization, especially in international organizations. See Michael Barnett and Martha Finnemore (2005) for reference to this tension.

86. Held (2000, p. 194).

87. Saward (2000, p. 45).

88. Held (2000, p. 194).

89. Glenn (2008).

90. Coicaud (2001, p. 524).

91. Barnett & Finnemore (2005, p. 181).

92. Coicaud (2001, p. 532).

93. Dahl (1999, p. 32).

94. Bobbio (1987, 1996); Dahl (1999); Held (1995); Scholte (2011 ["Civil Society," *Building Global Democracy?*]).

III

STRENGTHENING THE DEMOCRATIC SOLUTION TO OWL IMPERATIVES

8

From Coalition to Concert of Democratic States and Peoples

THIS VOLUME ENDS AT ITS BEGINNING. The world's populations have created a global society. It is defined by their growing interdependencies across all domains of significant value and interest to humans. To regulate these interdependencies, the democracies have created a model for global government, which serves as their standard-bearer for governance of the global society. For Order, they erected the global state to relax, if not surmount, the warfare proclivities of the WHW state; for Welfare, they constructed a global market system to confound the Malthusian prediction of perpetual misery; and for Legitimacy, they installed popular rule, animated by the moral vision of the universal freedom and equality of all humans.

These solutions to OWL imperatives defeated formidable antidemocratic opponents—the German Nazi regime, the Japanese imperial state, and the Soviet Union. What this volume has attempted to demonstrate is that these OWL responses no longer suffice to effectively frustrate or defeat their opponents. Absent their reform, the governing model of the democracies is placed at risk—and so are they.

From a Coalition to a Concert

How can the promise of democratic rule and its model of global governance be preserved, protected, and expanded? The currently parlous circumstances in which the democracies find themselves today loosely parallel those of the states of the American Articles of Confederation in the wake of their victory over the British Empire. Their divisions undermined their external security and generated incentives for internal conflict; their barriers to the free flow of trade, investment, and labor impeded economic development; and the absence of a strong central government imperiled popular rule, the protection of property, religious tolerance, and civil liberties. The democracies face a similar choice: to form a concert to enhance their collective power to deter and defeat their rivals and thus expand the circle of free peoples.

A concert of democratic states will strengthen the power of the democracies. It would expand the reach of the democratic states to nondemocratic peoples and contain the power of their adversaries. However urgent the move to a concert may be, it will not ensure the adoption of the democratic model for global governance. Two unassailable obstacles remain: (1) conflicting value systems, pitting the world's populations against themselves, are irreconcilable, and (2) the adherents of these contesting religious, cultural, and ideological communities have the power, singly or in convenient and timely league, to forestall any solution to governance at odds with their preferences.

The democracies currently lack the institutions capable of fully exploiting their technological, material, and value systems to expand their sphere of influence. A fully developed concert, a long-term goal, would provide a vehicle for the progressive integration of ad hoc arrangements, like NATO for security or the European Union for economic and political unification or the OECD for economic development. None of these otherwise indispensable, but piecemeal, institutions is sufficiently inclusive to advance cooperation among the democracies for their mutual advantage.

These institutions are still bounded by member state constraints and circumscribed by the national identities of their citizens. There is little recognition among democratic populations of their membership in a global society. Nor do the democracies share a consensus about the multiplying threats menacing both their discrete societies and the democracies themselves. Endangered are their hard-earned achievements in human governance. Hobbled, too, is the expansion of the global civil society to foster the unfettered movements of ideas, goods, services, and people across state boundaries.

Marshaling the OWL Power of the
Democracies: An Annual Concert Conference

For a start, the democratic states would hold an annual conference to assess their relative power positions in the struggle for governance. Initially, the conference would be devoted to acknowledging shared values and interests and the need to take common action to retain their currently ascendant position. The conference would pursue William McNeill's injunction "that every people and polity is forced to recognize its subordination to and participation in a global system."[1] More pointedly, the democracies would gradually realize that they must hang together or hang separately within a global society comprised of formidable opponents to democratic governance.

The conference would underline the transformative status of the human species as arbiter of the fate of the planet and of all other species. As William McNeill observes, "We will be, more than ever before, arbiters of our own fate. Our communication and cooperation skills have lately allowed us to join the editorial board of life on earth, deciding which species survive and which do not. . . . We will have biological evolution, as well as cultural evolution, in our own hands. A great deal will depend on just whose hands."[2] Either the democratic states will embrace these responsibilities or their rivals will fill this vacuum by default at the expense of humanity as a whole and, specifically, of the democratic promise.

The annual conference of the concert would be expected to develop joint strategies for the reform and strengthening of the concert of democratic states in support of their OWL solutions. This objective is likely to be best pursued through the cooperative policies that pool the human and material resources of the democracies to address the global issues that they confront. It makes a world of difference whether the democracies either frame their policy aims and interests in narrowly defined domestic political concerns, limiting themselves to self-regarding national perspectives, or cast them, more broadly, in terms of the challenges of pursuing the nation's values, interests, and aims with other like-minded democratic peoples within a resistant global society. It is also crucial that the democratic concert include all of the democracies, developed and developing, to create incentives for mutual assistance, since their several state interests will be conceived to depend on their mutual cooperation. Once this inclusive perspective is affirmed by the concert's members, they will be in a position to develop policies to attract potential nondemocratic inductees to join the democratic experiment.

Popular rule affords humans the capacity to surmount their self-created "iron cages" to enlarge and enrich their lives and knowledge of who they are, and what they want to be. Democratic rule is not an end in itself, but an endless discovery process. Extending the democratic reach eventuates in a model of governance whose attractive power promises to be compelling, evidenced, for example, by the hundreds of thousands crowding into Europe to escape civil wars in the Middle East, Africa, and Afghanistan and the depressing economic conditions of these regions. Open societies multiply new spaces for human liberty and creativity to find expression. Increasing numbers of people of different and diverging cultural, national, and ethnic backgrounds, if given a choice, can be reasonably expected to opt for free societies and to support their solutions to OWL imperatives and global governance.

The democratic OWL model is especially effective in addressing the imperative of Legitimacy, since it rests on the consent of the governed. What remains is Sir Henry Maine's challenge that the democracies, like other regimes, must still provide for the public order and welfare of their populations. The concert of democratic states is obliged to supply the public goods needed by their populations and those of the world society. An annual conference would be a significant institutionalized mechanism to address these issues and to strengthen the democracies in what is an enduring struggle against their rivals. The conference would debate and conceivably reach accord on a division of labor about how each would contribute to resolving the global issues besetting them.

How the annual conference might be organized would depend on the consensus that leading democratic states would be able to achieve. The United States, major European powers, Japan, and relevant developing states, like Brazil, India, and South Africa, might form a working executive committee. Subgroups could be created to focus on ways to cooperate to cover specific global issues—controlling weapons of mass destruction, global warming, sustainable growth, extending democratic rule and human rights, and so forth. The annual conference would eventually create a secretariat to prepare each annual conference.

In this vein, the democratic concert could evolve into a caucus within prevailing international organizations—the United Nations, the International Monetary Fund, the World Bank, and the World Trade Organization, among others—to advance the values and interests of open societies. In assuming an inclusive stance to include all states, democratic and nondemocratic, in developing global policies to combat, say, global warming or terrorism, the democratic concert would be enlarging the legitimacy of these organizations. As Michael Zurn has observed (a view seconded by Jean-Marc Coicaud),[3] "Without a strategy for increasing the democratic legitimacy of international organizations, internationalizing politics and multilateralism will be defeated by a lack of societal acceptance."[4]

The point to stress is the responsibility of the democratic states to tackle these reforms out of a concern for their own self-interest to retain their dominant power in the global society and their strong claim to legitimacy. It is naïve to believe that the peoples of the democracies will readily embrace the vision of this volume. The annual conference of stocktaking and policy cooperation is merely the first step on a long and uncertain road toward the institutionalization of the concert and the extension of the democratic governing model. As Jürgen Osterhammel observes, "Even today, in the age of the Internet and boundless telecommunications, billions of people live in narrowly local conditions from which they can escape neither in reality nor in their imagination."[5] That shift in identity, if it is ever to be realized, is a discovery process "in the longue durée of historical development."[6] The formation of the concert is a beginning, a long-term work in progress whose final end point, guided by the principles of human freedom and equality, is unknown.

The virtue of an annual conference of democratic states would be to reinforce both their shared identities and value systems. The conference would testify to the recognition that no one state or people has the power and resources to manage or resolve global challenges. The notion that the United States or a rising China could attain hegemonic status in a globalized world of decentralized power and proliferating ideologies relies on an outmoded rationale more appropriate to nineteenth- rather than twenty-first-century thinking and constraints. If this concert is to operate on democratic principles, then it must work to keep the global society open. Since the democratic promise crosses state boundaries, cultures, religions, and diverse human histories, it can serve as a promising step toward a breakthrough in governance. That breakthrough will require the gradual transformation of a loose and fractious coalition of democratic peoples into a concert in the service of the world's populations. Ian Morris projects the implications of this growing consciousness of humankind as a shared fate: "The great question for our times is not whether the West will continue to rule. It is whether humanity as a whole will break through to an entirely new kind of existence before disaster strikes us down—permanently."[7] That should be the siren call of the democratic concert. The guiding vision is a global society of democracies without borders.

What is projected here is not the utopian Kantian ideal of perpetual peace resting on a concert of democratic regimes.[8] The democracies will most certainly have to resort to arms to deter or to combat their opponents, whether an expansionist Russia or China, religious extremists, global terrorists, or criminal elements—and all simultaneously in pursuit of multiple strategies tailored to each threat. The democratic model and its stipulation of the freedom and equality of all humans threaten all regimes resting on the selective principles of religion, culture, nationalism, history, or custom. The universal breadth of the democratic promise directly challenges the problematic moral principles and legitimacy of all nondemocratic regimes.

There is no way to predict whether, as Morris warns, disaster—artificial, natural, or a conjuncture of both—will strike. Humans may still escape "by the skin of our teeth," as Thornton Wilder's play assures us. As mammals we are unique: we have boundless conceptual and linguistic capabilities to scientifically understand the universe, the planet, and our social condition, as well as an unmatched capacity to learn from experience and to adapt best social practices. We possess seemingly limitless curiosity and tool-making skills to help solve our shared problems. The democracies, armed with these instruments of power, are fully capable, if they can muster the will to act together, to reform their impaired OWL solutions. Democratic peoples are best suited to assume the challenge of governance for themselves and for all of humanity. They are "the core of World Order."[9] Abraham Lincoln's hope for Americans is now scaled to the global society to include all humanity. Only a concert of democracies holds out the promise that "government of the people, by the people, and for the people will not perish from the earth."

Notes

1. McNeill (1992, pp. xiv–xv).
2. McNeill & McNeill (2003, p. 323).
3. Coicaud (2001).
4. Zurn (2005). See also Zurn (2000).
5. Osterhammel (2014, p. xv).
6. Ibid.
7. Morris (2010, p. 36).
8. Kant (1970, 1991 ["Idea"], pp. 41–53).
9. Thomas L. Friedman, *New York Times*, April 29, 2015, p. A23.

A Brief Note on Method

IN THE INTEREST OF CLARITY and transparency, it may be useful to explain briefly the methodology I have chosen to lay some of the groundwork for a theory of governance and, specifically, to apply the concept of OWL (Order, Welfare, and Legitimacy) imperatives to global governance.

The method underlying this volume draws directly, and depends heavily, on the idealistic philosophical and sociological traditions of nineteenth-century theorists, notably German scholars and policy-makers. These ideational approaches to understand, explain, and predict how humans think, decide, and act are particularly relevant to globalization. Kant (and Hegel) set the philosophical basis for this approach. Max Weber, Karl Marx, and Ferdinand Tönnies followed the same route in developing their sociological theories, ranging from Weber's insights about bureaucracy to Tönnies's notions of *Gemeinschaft* and *Gesselschaft*. Marx's critique of capitalism adopts the Hegelian dialectic. This same methodological orientation also distinguishes the influential strategic thinking of Carl von Clausewitz, whose notions of pure and real war have influenced military planners for two centuries.

The three imperatives of Order, Welfare, and Legitimacy and their contemporary crystallization into the state and market systems and the continuing spread of democratic regimes and human rights are cast in this ideational approach. Social scientists and analysts who rely on this methodology have no expectation, and certainly I do not, that the "ideal" or pure end points posited by this method will actually ever be reached in practice. These pure end points provide a conceptual orientation for identifying tendencies in human thinking, decisions, and actions that systematize and rationalize large sets of significant human behavior, notably how societies are created and develop their particular personalities and how they are governed and why that is so. Obviously this method cannot predict much of what we would like to know in specific, concrete instances: how to stop wars, sustain economic development, or arrest global warming. Other methods, modeling, statistical analysis, psychological testing, and the like have to supplement the broad and high level of analysis chosen to identify the principal institutions, power structures, decisional processes, and incentives for actor choices that frame and guide human behavior in governing the behavior of the world's populations.

There is nothing archaic or strange about employing this approach. In a sense, contemporary economic theory, which posits a potentially omniscient rational actor—or all-knowing market where true prices are always displayed—owes much to this way of thinking about human behavior. Amendments to prevailing economic theory, for example, by way of the pioneering psychological research and theorizing of Herbert Simon, Daniel Kahneman, and Amos Tversky are important because they show deviations from rational economic expectation by essentially relying on these prevailing pure economic models to show variations from expected behavior.

In contrast to unifocal models of rational behavior, economic or military, this volume identifies three forms of competing and ultimately irreconcilable rational tendencies in the efforts of humans to construct the institutions they need to govern their interdependent transactions and relations. The modalities of each set of solutions to OWL imperatives will vary and differ wildly over time and circumstance as we move from one observed society to another, stretching from hunter-gatherers to our own modern ways and innumerable others in between. What does not change are the underlying constraints imposed on humans, as they have evolved as social animals, to respond to the dilemmas of choice imposed by OWL imperatives. Each society of each era is obliged to fashion relevant solutions to these imperatives, constrained by their human, biological, and material environments, if the members of that society are to survive, thrive, and ensure the replication of their society beyond the limited life span of any of its inhabitants.

The term "preferences" is used throughout this discussion. It refers more broadly to the fundamental values and interests, which define the outcomes sought by humans and all actors in their interdependent exchanges. These ceaseless unfolding exchanges form the warp and woof of all human societies.

Bibliography

Abbate, Janet. *Inventing the Internet*. Cambridge, MA: MIT Press, 1999.

Acharya, Vial V., and Matthew Richardson. "How Securitization Concentrated Risk in the Financial Sector." In *What Caused the Financial Crisis*, edited by Jeffrey Friedman, 183–99. Philadelphia: University of Pennsylvania Press, 2011.

Acheson, Dean. *Present at the Creation*. New York: W. W. Norton, 1969.

Adams, Richard H., Jr. "Economic Growth, Inequality and Poverty: Estimating the Growth of Poverty." *World Development* 32, no. 12 (2004): 1989–2014.

Agarwal, Bina, Jane Humphries, and Ingrid Robeyns, eds. *Amartya Sen's Work and Ideas: A Gender Perspective*. London and New York: Routledge, 2005.

Akerlof, George A., and Robert J. Shiller. *Animal Spirits: How Psychology Drives the Economy and Why It Matters for Global Capitalism*. Princeton, NJ: Princeton University Press, 2009.

———. *Phishing for Phools: The Economics of Manipulation & Deception*. Princeton, NJ: Princeton University Press, 2015.

Allan, Pierre, and Kjell Goldmann, eds. *The End of the Cold War: Evaluating Theories of International Relations*. Dordrecht, NL: Martinus Nijhoff, 1992.

Allison, Graham. *Nuclear Terrorism: The Ultimate Preventable Catastrophe*. New York: Times Books, 2004.

———. "Nuclear Disorder." *Foreign Affairs* 89, no. 1 (2010): 74–85.

Alvaredo, Facundo, Anthony B. Atkinson, Thomas Piketty, and Emmanuel Saez. "The Top 1 Percent in International and Historical Perspective." *Journal of Economic Perspectives* 27, no. 3 (Summer 2013): 3–29.

Anand, Sudhir, Paul Segal, and Joseph Stiglitz, eds. *Debates on the Measurement of Global Poverty*. Oxford: Oxford University Press, 2010.

Anderson, Benedict. *Imagined Communities: Reflections on the Origin and Spread of Nationalism*. New York: Verso, 1992.

Andrain, Charles F. *Political Power and Economic Inequality: A Comparative Approach.* New York: Rowman & Littlefield, 2014.

Angell, Norman. *War and the Essential Realities.* London: Watts, 2013.

Appelbaum, Richard, Rachel Parker, Cao Cong, and Gary Gereffi. "China (Not So Hidden) Developmental State: Becoming a Leading Nanotechnology Innovator." In *State of Innovation: The U.S. Government's Role in Technology Development*, edited by Fred Block and Matthew R. Keller, 217–35. Boulder, CO: Paradigm, 2011.

Archibugi, Danielle. "Cosmopolitan Democracy and Its Critics: A Review." *European Journal of International Relations* 10 (2004): 437–73.

Archibugi, Danielle, and David Held, eds. *Cosmopolitan Democracy: An Agenda for a New World Order.* Cambridge: Polity Press, 1995.

Archibugi, Danielle, David Held, and M. Kohler, eds. *Re-Imagining Political Community.* Cambridge: Polity Press, 1998.

Archibugi, Danielle, Mathias Koenig-Archibugi, and Raffaele Marchetti, eds. *Global Democracy; Normative and Empirical Perspectives.* Cambridge: Cambridge University Press, 2012.

Aristotle. *Introduction to Aristotle.* Translated by W. D. Ross. New York: Modern Library, 1947.

Arneson, Richard. "Equality and Equality of Opportunity for Welfare." *Philosophical Studies* 56 (1989): 77–93.

Ash, Timothy Garton. "1989—The Unwritten History." *New York Review of Books* 55, no. 17 (September 5, 2009).

Ashcraft, Adam B., and Til Schuermann. "Understanding the Securitization of Subprime Mortgage Credit." *Wharton Financial Institutions Center Working Paper No. 07–43*, March 2008. Available at http://ssrn.com/abstract=1071189.

Aslan, Reza. *No god but God: The Origins, Evolution, and Future of Islam.* New York: Random House, 2005.

Atkinson, Anthony B. *The Changing Distribution of Earnings in OECD Countries.* Oxford: Oxford University Press, 2008.

———. *Inequality: What Can Be Done?* Cambridge, MA: Harvard University Press, 2015.

Atkinson, Anthony B., and Thomas Piketty, eds. *Top Incomes over the Twentieth Century: A Contrast between Continental European and English-Speaking Countries.* Oxford: Oxford University Press, 2007.

Atkinson, Anthony B., Thomas Piketty, and Emmanuel Saez. *Top Incomes in the Long Run of History.* Berkeley: University of California Institute for Research on Labor and Employment, 2009. Retrieved from http://escholarship.org/uc/item/8fd8654h.

Avant, Deborah D., Martha Finnemore, and Susan K. Sell, eds. *Who Governs the Globe?* Cambridge: Cambridge University Press, 2010.

Bair, Sheila. *Bull by the Horns: Fighting to Save Main Street from Wall Street and Wall Street from Itself.* New York: Free Press, 2012.

Ball, Desmond. *Politics and Force Levels.* Berkeley: University of California Press, 1980.

Banerjee, Abhijit V., Roland Benabou, and Dilip Mookherjee, eds. *Understanding Poverty.* Oxford: Oxford University Press, 2006.

——. "Introduction and Review." In *Understanding Poverty*, edited by Abhijit V. Banerjee, Roland Benabou, and Dilip Mookherjee, xiii–lii. Oxford: Oxford University Press, 2006.

Barnes, Barry. *The Elements of Social Theory*. Princeton, NJ: Princeton University Press, 1995.

Barnett, Michael, and Martha Finnemore. "The Power of Liberal International Institutions." In *Power in Global Governance*, edited by Michael Barnett and Raymond Duvall, 161–84. Cambridge: Cambridge University Press, 2005.

Barofsky, Neil. *Bailout: An Inside Account of How Washington Abandoned Main Street While Rescuing Wall Street*. New York: Free Press, 2012.

Bartels, Larry. *Unequal Democracy: The Political Economy of the New Gilded Age*. New York: Russell Sage, 2008.

Beaud, Michel. *A History of Capitalism*. Translated by Tom Dickman and Anny Lefebvre. New York: Monthly Review Press, 2000.

Beck, Ulrich. *Cosmopolitan Vision*. Cambridge: Polity Press, 2006.

——. *World at Risk*. Cambridge: Polity Press, 2007.

Bellamy, Richard. "Joseph A. Schumpeter and His Contemporaries." *European Journal of Political Research* 23 (1993): 117–20.

——. *Political Constitutionalism*. Cambridge: Cambridge University Press, 2007.

Bellamy, Richard, and Peter Baehr. "Carl Schmitt and the Contradictions of Liberal Democracy." *European Journal of Political Research* 23 (1993): 163–85.

Bellamy, Richard, and R. J. Barry Jones. "Globalization and Democracy—An Afterword." In *Global Democracy: Key Debates*, edited by Barry Holden, 179–201. London: Routledge, 2000.

Bendix, Reinhard. *Nation-Building and Citizenship*. Berkeley: University of California Press, 1964.

——. *State and Society*. Boston: Little, Brown, 1964.

——. *Kings or People: Power and the Mandate to Rule*. Berkeley: University of California Press, 1978.

——. *Force, Fate, and Freedom*. Berkeley: University of California Press, 1984.

Berdal, Mats, and Monica Serrano, eds. *Transnational Organized Crime and International Security: Business As Usual?* Boulder, CO: Lynne Rienner, 2002.

Berg, Andrew G., and Jonathan D. Ostry. "Equality and Efficiency: Is There a Tradeoff between the Two or Do the Two Go Hand in Hand?" *Finance and Development* 48, no. 3 (2011): 12–15.

——. *Inequality and Unsustainable Growth: Two Sides of the Same Coin?* Washington, DC: International Monetary Fund, 2011.

Bernanke, Ben S. *The Courage to Act: A Memoir of a Crisis and Its Aftermath*. New York: W. W. Norton, 2015.

Bhagwati, Jagdish. *In Defense of Globalization*. Oxford: Oxford University Press, 2004.

Bhalla, Surjit S. *Imagine There's No Country: Poverty, Inequality, and Growth in the Era of Globalization*. Washington, DC: Institute for International Economics, 2002.

——. "Crying Wolf on Poverty: Or How the Millennium Development Goals on Poverty Reduction Have Already Been Reached." *Economic and Policy Weekly* (July 5, 2003): 2843–56.

———. "Raising the Standard: The War on Global Poverty." In *Debates on the Measurement of Global Poverty*, edited by Sudhir Anand, Paul Segal, and Joseph E. Stiglitz, 115–42. Oxford: Oxford University Press, 2010.

Bhaskar, Roy. *The Possibility of Naturalism: A Philosophical Critique of Contemporary Human Sciences.* 3rd ed. London: Routledge, 1998.

Bhide, Amar. "An Accident Waiting to Happen: Securities Regulation and Financial Regulation." In *What Caused the Financial Crisis*, edited by Jeffrey Friedman, 139–49. Philadelphia: University of Pennsylvania Press, 2011.

Blinder, Alan S. *After the Music Stopped: The Financial Crisis and Response and the Work Ahead.* New York: Penguin, 2013.

Block, Fred. "Swimming against the Current: The Rise of a Hidden Developmental State in the United States." *Politics and Society* 36, no. 2 (2008): 169–206.

Block, Fred, and Matthew R. Keller, eds. *State of Innovation: The U. S. Government's Role in Technology Development.* Boulder, CO: Paradigm, 2011.

———. "Where Do Innovations Come From? Transformations in the U.S. Economy, 1970–2006." In *State of Innovation: The U.S. Government's Role in Technology Development*, edited by Fred Block and Matthew R. Keller, 154–72. Boulder, CO: Paradigm, 2011.

Bloom, William. *National Identity and International Relations.* Cambridge: Cambridge University Press, 1993.

Boardman, Fon Wyman. *America and the Robber Barons, 1865–1913.* New York: H. Z. Walck, 1979.

Bobbio, Norberto. *The Future of Democracy: A Defence of the Rules of the Game.* Translated by Roger Griffin. Edited by Richard Bellamy. Minneapolis: University of Minnesota Press, 1987.

———. *Liberalism and Democracy.* Translated by Martin Ryle and Kate Soper. London: Verso, 1988.

———. *The Age of Rights.* Translated by Allan Cameron. Cambridge: Polity Press, 1996.

Boorman, Scott. *The Protracted Game.* New York: Oxford University Press, 1969.

Boulding, Kenneth. *Three Faces of Power.* Newbury Park, CA: Sage, 1989.

Bourguignon, François, Francisco Ferreira, and M. Menendez. "Inequality of Opportunity in Brazil." *Review of Income and Wealth* 53 (2007): 585–618.

Bourguignon, François, and Christian Morrison. "Inequality among World Citizens: 1820–1992." *American Economic Review* 92, no. 4 (2002): 727–44.

Bozeman, Adda. *Politics and Culture in International Politics.* Princeton, NJ: Princeton University Press, 1960.

———. "The International Order in a Multicultural World." In *The Expansion of International Society*, edited by Hedley Bull and Adam Watson, 387–406. New York: Oxford University Press, 1984.

Breen, Michael. *The Politics of IMF Lending.* London: Palgrave, 2013.

Breuilly, John. *Nationalism and the State.* 2nd ed. Chicago: University of Chicago Press, 1994.

Broad, Robin, ed. *Global Backlash: Citizen Initiatives for a Just World Economy.* Lanham, MD: Rowman & Littlefield, 2002.

Brock, Lothar, Hans-Henrik Holm, George Sorensen, and Michael Stohl. *Fragile States Violence and Failure of Intervention*. Cambridge: Polity Press, 2012.

Brzezinski, Zbigniew. *Out of Control: Global Turmoil on the Eve of the Twenty-First Century*. New York: Scribners, 1993.

Bull, Hedley. *The Anarchical Society: A Study of Order in World Politics*. London: Macmillan, 1977.

Burt, John. *Lincoln's Tragic Pragmatism*. Cambridge, MA: Belknap Press, 2013.

Buzan, Barry. *People, States and Fear: An Agenda for International Security Studies in the Post-Cold War Era*. 2nd ed. Boulder, CO: Lynne Rienner, 1991.

——. "From International System to International Society: Structural Realism and Regime Theory Meet the English School." *International Organization* 47, no. 3 (Summer 1993): 327–52.

——. *From International to World Society?* Cambridge: Cambridge University Press, 2004.

Buzan, Barry, Richard Little, and Charles Jones. *The Logic of Anarchy: Neorealism and Structural Realism*. New York: Columbia University Press, 1993.

Cameron, Rondo. *A Concise Economic History of the World*. Vol. 2. New York: Oxford University Press, 1993.

Cameron, Sally, and Edward Newman, eds. *Trafficking in Humans: Social, Cultural, and Political Dimensions*. New York: United Nations University Press, 2008.

Carrère d'Encausse, Hélène. *The End of the Soviet Empire: The Triumph of the Nations*. Translated by Franklin Philip. New York: Basic Books, 1993.

Cassidy, John. *How Markets Fail: The Logic of Economic Calamities*. New York: Farrar, Strauss and Giroux, 2009.

Central Intelligence Agency. *International Crime Threat Assessment*. Washington, DC: Central Intelligence Agency, 2002.

Cerny, Philip G. *Rethinking World Politics: A Theory of Transnational Neopluralism*. Oxford: Oxford University Press, 2010.

Chatfield, Charles. "Inter-Governmental and Non-Governmental Associations to 1945." In *Transnational Soviet Movements and Global Politics*, edited by Jackie Smith, Charles Chatfield, and Ron Pagnucco. Syracuse, NY: Syracuse University Press, 1997.

Cheibub, Jose Antonio, and Adam Przeworski. "Democracy, Elections, and Accountability for Economic Outcomes." In *Democracy, Accountability and Representation*, edited by Adam Przeworski, Susan C. Stokes, and Bernard Manin. Cambridge: Cambridge University Press, 1999.

Chen, Shaohua, and Martin Ravallion. "The Developing World Is Poorer Than We Thought, But No Less Successful in the Fight against Poverty." *Quarterly Journal of Economics* (2010): 1577–1625.

Christiano, Thomas. "Democratic Legitimacy and International Institutions." In *The Philosophy of International Law*, edited by Samantha Besson and John Tasioulas, 119–28. Oxford: Oxford University Press, 2010.

——. "Is Democratic Legitimacy Possible for International Institutions?" In *Global Democracy; Normative and Empirical Perspectives*, edited by Daniele Archibugi,

Mathias Koenig-Archibugi, and Raffaele Marchetti, 69–95. Cambridge: Cambridge University Press, 2012.

Clark, J. D., J. Fox, and K. Treakle. *Demanding Accountability: Civil-Society Claims and World Bank Inspection Panels*. New Delhi: Rainbow, 2003.

Clarke, Richard A. *Against All Enemies*. New York: Free Press, 2004.

Clausewitz, Carl von. *On War*. Translated by Michael Howard and Peter Paret. Princeton, NJ: Princeton University Press, 1976.

Coase, Ronald H. *The Firm, the Market, and the Law*. Chicago: University of Chicago Press, 1988.

Cohen, Avner. *Israel and the Bomb*. New York: Columbia University Press, 1998.

Cohen, Gary A. "Self-Ownership, World-Ownership, and Equality." In *Justice and Equality Here and Now*, edited by F. Lucash. Ithaca, NY: Cornell University Press, 1986.

——. "Equality of What? On Welfare, Goods, and Capabilities." *Recherches Economiques* 56 (1990): 3–4.

Cohen, Jessica, and William Easterly, eds. *What Works in Development?* Washington, DC: Brookings Institution Press, 2009.

Cohen, Stephen P. *Shooting for a Century*. Washington, DC: Brookings Institution Press, 2013.

Coicaud, Jean-Marc. "Reflections on International Organisations and International Legitimacy: Constraints, Pathologies, and Possibilities." *International Social Science Journal* 53, no. 170 (2001): 523–36.

——. *Legitimacy and Politics*. Cambridge: Cambridge University Press, 2002.

Collander, David, Michael Goldberg, Armin Haas, Katarina Juselius, Alan Kirman, Thomas Lux, and Brigitte Sloth. "The Financial Crisis and the Systemic Failure of the Economics Profession." In *What Caused the Financial Crisis*, edited by Jeffrey Friedman, 262–78. Philadelphia: University of Pennsylvania Press, 2010.

Cooper, Richard. *The Economics of Interdependence: Economic Policy in the Atlantic Community*. New York: McGraw-Hill, 1968.

Cox, W. Michael, and Richard Alm. "Creative Destruction." In *The Concise Encyclopedia of Economics*, edited by David R. Henderson, 1–6. Indianapolis, IN: Liberty Fund, 2007.

Craig, Paul, and John Jungerman. *Nuclear Arms Race: Technology and Society*. New York: McGraw-Hill, 1986.

Crenshaw, Martha, and John Pimlott, eds. *Encyclopedia of World Terrorism*. 3 vols. Armonk, NY: M. E. Sharpe, 1996.

Crocker, Chester A. "Engaging Failing States." *Foreign Affairs* 82, no. 5 (2003): 32–44.

Curtis, Glenn E., and Tara Karacan. *The Nexus among Terrorists, Narcotics, Traffickers, Weapons Proliferations, and Organized Crime Networks in Western Europe*. Washington, DC: Federal Research Division, Library of Congress, 2002.

Dahl, Robert A. *Who Governs? Democracy and Power in an American City*. New Haven, CT: Yale University Press, 1961.

——. *Democracy and Its Critics*. New Haven, CT: Yale University Press, 1989.

——. "Can International Organizations Be Democratic: A Skeptical View." In *Democracy's Edges*, edited by Ian Shapiro and Casiano Hacker-Cordon, 19–36. Cambridge: Cambridge University Press, 1999.

Danzinger, Sheldon H., and Robert H. Haveman, eds. *Understanding Poverty.* New York: Russell Sage, 2001.

Davies, James B. "Wealth and Economic Inequality." In *The Oxford Handbook of Economic Inequality,* edited by Wiemer Salverda, Brian Nolan, and Timothy Smeeding, 127–49. Oxford: Oxford University Press, 2009.

De Gaulle, Charles. *The Complete War Memoirs of Charles de Gaulle.* Translated by Jonathan Griffin and Howard Richard. New York: Carroll and Graf, 1998.

Deaton, Angus. "Measuring Poverty in a Growing World (or Measuring Growth in a Poor World)." In *Debates on the Measurement of Global Poverty,* edited by Sudhir Anand, Paul Segal, and Joseph E. Stiglitz, 187–224. Oxford: Oxford University Press, 2010.

Dehesa, Guillermo de la. *What Do We Know about Globalization? Issues of Poverty and Income Distribution.* Victoria, AU: Blackwell, 2007.

Dekmajian, Hrair. *Spectrum of Terror.* Washington, DC: CQ Press, 2007.

Dessler, David. "What's at Stake in the Agent-Structure Debate?" *International Organization* 43, no. 3 (Summer 1989): 441–73.

Deutsch, Karl. *An Interdisciplinary Bibliography on Nationalism 1935–1953.* Cambridge: MIT Press, 1956.

Deutsch, Karl, and Richard Merritt. *Nationalism and National Development: An Interdisciplinary Bibliography.* Cambridge, MA: MIT Press, 1970.

Diamond, Jared. *The Third Chimpanzee: The Evolution and Future of the Human Animal.* New York: HarperPerennial, 1992.

———. *Guns, Germs, and Steel: The Fates of Human Societies.* New York: W. W. Norton, 1997.

Diamond, Larry. "The Democratic Rollback: The Resurgence of the Predatory State." *Foreign Affairs* (March/April 2008).

———. *The Spirit of Democracy: The Struggle to Build Free Societies throughout the World.* New York: Times Books, 2008.

Dicicco, Jonathan M., and Jack S. Levy. "Power Shifts and Problem Shifts: The Evolution of the Power Transitions Research Program." *Journal of Conflict Resolution* 43 (1999): 675–704.

Diehl, Paul F. *Peace Operations.* Cambridge: Polity Press, 2008.

Dinan, Desmond. *Ever Closer Union: An Introduction to European Integration.* 4th ed. Boulder, CO: Lynne Rienner, 2010.

Donnelly, Jack. *The Concept of Human Rights.* London: Croom Helm, 1984.

———. *Universal Human Rights in Theory and Practice.* Ithaca, NY: Cornell University Press, 1989.

———. *International Human Rights.* Boulder, CO: Westview, 1993.

Drezner, Daniel W. *All Politics Is Global: Explaining International Regulatory Regimes.* Princeton, NJ: Princeton University Press, 2008.

Dworkin, Ronald. "What Is Equality? Part 1: Equality of Welfare." *Philosophy and Public Affairs* 10, no. 3 (1981): 185–246.

———. "What Is Equality? Part 2: Equality of Resources." *Philosophy and Public Affairs* 10, no. 3 (1981): 283–345.

Easterly, William. "Inequality Does Cause Underdevelopment: Insights from a New Instrument." *Quarterly Journal of Economics* 84, no. 2 (2007): 755–76.

Ebrahim, Alnoor, and Steven Herz. "The World Bank and Democratic Accountability: The Role of the Civil Society." In *Building Global Democracy? Civil Society and Accountable Global Governance*, edited by Jan Aart Scholte, 58–77. Cambridge: Cambridge University Press, 2011.

Edelheit, Abraham J., and Hershel Edelheit. *The Rise and Fall of the Soviet Union: A Selected Bibliography of Sources in English*. Westport, CT: Greenwood Press, 1992.

Eden, Lynn. "The End of the U.S. Cold War History? A Review Essay." *International Security* 18, no. 1 (Summer 1993): 174.

Edwards, Adam, and Peter Gill, eds. *Transnational Organized Crime: Perspective on Global Security*. New York: Routledge, 2003.

Eisinger, Peter K. *The Rise of the Entrepreneurial State: State and Local Economic Development Policy in the United States*. Madison: University of Wisconsin Press, 1988.

Elliott, John E. *Marx and Engels on Economics, Politics, and Society*. Santa Monica, CA: Goodyear, 1981.

Ellis, Joseph J. *Founding Brothers: The Revolutionary Generation*. New York: Vintage Books, 2002.

Elster, Jon. *Making Sense of Marx*. Cambridge: Cambridge University Press, 1985.

———. *The Cement of Society: A Study of Social Order*. Cambridge: Cambridge University Press, 1989.

Epstein, Paul R., and Dan Ferber. *Changing Planet, Changing Health: How the Climate Crisis Threatens Our Health and What We Can Do about It*. Berkeley: University of California Press, 2011.

Evans, Peter. *Embedded Autonomy: States and Industrial Transformation*. Princeton, NJ: Princeton University Press, 1995.

———. "The Eclipse of the State? Reflections on Stateness in an Era of Globalization." *World Politics* 50, no. 1 (October 1997): 62–87.

Evans, Peter, and James Rauch. "Bureaucracy and Growth: A Cross-National Analysis of the Effects of 'Weberian' State Structures on Economic Growth." *American Sociological Review* 64, no. 5 (1999): 748–65.

Evans, Peter, Dietrich Rueschemeyer, and Theda Skocpol, eds. *Bringing the State Back In*. Cambridge: Cambridge University Press, 1985.

The Federalist. Garden City, NY: Modern Library, n.d.

Ferguson, Niall. *The Ascent of Money*. New York: Penguin, 2008.

Ferreira, Francisco H. G., and Martin Ravallion. "Poverty and Inequality: The Global Context." In *The Oxford Handbook of Economic Inequality*, edited by Wiemer Salverda, Brian Nolan, and Timothy Smeeding, 598–636. Oxford: Oxford University Press, 2009.

Financial Crisis Inquiry Commission. *The Financial Crisis Inquiry Report: Final Report of the National Commission on the Causes of the Financial and Economic Crisis in the United States*. Washington, DC: Government Printing Office, 2011.

Findlay, Ronald, and Kevin H. O'Rourke. *Power and Plenty: Trade, War and the World Economy in the Second Millennium*. Princeton, NJ: Princeton University Press, 2007.

Finer, S. E. *The History of Government*. Oxford: Oxford University Press, 1999.

FitzGerald, Frances. *Fire in the Lake: The Vietnamese and Americans in Vietnam*. New York: Simon and Schuster, 1973.

Fox, Jonathan A., and David L. Brown, eds. *The Struggle for Accountability: The World Bank, NGOs, and Grassroots Movements*. Cambridge, MA: MIT Press, 1998.

Frank, Robert H. *The Darwin Economy: Liberty, Competition, and the Common Good*. Princeton, NJ: Princeton University Press, 2011.

Frank, Robert H., and Philip J. Cook. *The Winner-Take-All Society*. New York: Free Press, 1995.

Franz, Douglas, and Catherine Collins. *The Nuclear Jihadist*. New York: Twelve, 2007.

Freedman, Lawrence. *The Evolution of Nuclear Strategy*. 2nd ed. London: Macmillan, 1989.

Freeland, Chrystia. *Plutocrats: The Rise of the Super-Rich and the Fall of Everyone Else*. New York: Penguin, 2012.

Frieden, Jeffrey A. *Global Capitalism: Its Fall and Rise in the Twentieth Century*. New York: W. W. Norton, 2006.

Friedman, Benjamin M. *The Moral Consequences of Economic Growth*. New York: Knopf, 2005.

Friedman, Jeffrey, ed. *What Caused the Financial Crisis*. Philadelphia: University of Pennsylvania Press, 2011.

Friedman, Milton. *Capitalism and Freedom*. Chicago: University of Chicago Press, 1962.

Friedman, Milton, and Rose Friedman. *Free to Choose*. New York: Harcourt Brace Jovanovich, 1980.

Friedman, Milton, and Anna Jacobson Schwartz. *A Monetary History of the United States, 1867–1960*. Princeton, NJ: Princeton University Press, 1963.

Friedman, Thomas L. *The Lexus and the Olive Tree*. Rev. ed. New York: Farrar, Straus and Giroux, 2000.

———. *The World Is Flat: A Brief History of the Twenty-First Century*. New York: Farrar, Straus and Giroux, 2006.

Fukuyama, Francis. *The End of History and the Last Man*. New York: Free Press, 1992.

———. *The Origins of Political Order: From Prehuman Times to the French Evolution*. New York: Farrar, Straus and Giroux, 2011.

Fukuyama, Francis, Larry Jay Diamond, and Marc F. Plattner, eds. *Poverty, Inequality, and Democracy*. Baltimore: Johns Hopkins University Press, 2012.

Furniss, Edgar S. *France, Troubled Ally: De Gaulle's Heritage and Prospects*. New York: Harper, 1960.

———. *De Gaulle and the French Army*. New York: Twentieth Century Fund, 1964.

Gabel, Medard. *Global Inc*. New York: New Press, 2003.

Gellner, Ernest. *Nations and Nationalism*. Ithaca, NY: Cornell University Press, 1983.

———. *Encounters with Nationalism*. Cambridge: Blackwell, 1994.

Giddens, Anthony. *New Rules of Sociological Method: A Positive Critique of Interpretative Sociologies*. 2nd ed. Stanford, CA: Stanford University Press, 1993.

Gilens, Martin. *Affluence and Influence: Economic Inequality and Political Power in America*. Princeton, NJ: Princeton University Press, 2012.

Giles, Frank. *The Locust Years: The Story of the Fourth French Republic, 1945–1958.* London: Secker & Warburg, 1991.

Gill, Stephen, and David Law. "Global Hegemony and the Structural Power of Capital." In *Gramsci, Historical Materialism and International Relations*, edited by Stephen Gill. Cambridge: Cambridge University Press, 1993.

Gilpin, Robert. *The Political Economy of International Relations.* Princeton, NJ: Princeton University Press, 1987.

———. *The Challenge of Global Capitalism.* Princeton, NJ: Princeton University Press, 2000.

———. *Global Political Economy: Understanding the International Economic Order.* Princeton, NJ: Princeton University Press, 2001.

Glenn, John. "Global Governance and the Democratic Deficit: Stifling the Voice of the South." *Third World Quarterly* 29, no. 2 (2008): 217–38.

Godinot, Xavier, ed. *Eradicating Extreme Poverty.* London: Pluto, 2012.

Gordon, Michael R., and Bernard E. Trainor. *Cobra II: The Inside Story of the Invasion and Occupation of Iraq.* New York: Pantheon, 2005.

Greenspan, Alan. *The Age of Turbulence: Adventures in a New World.* New York: Penguin, 2007.

Guare, John. *Six Degrees of Separation.* 2nd ed. New York: Vintage, 2004.

Halberstam, David. *The Best and the Brightest.* New York: Random House, 1972.

Hall, Rodney Bruce, and Thomas J. Bierstecker, eds. *The Emergence of Private Authority in Global Governance.* Cambridge: Cambridge University Press, 2002.

Hassner, P. "Rousseau and the Theory and Practice of International Relations." In *The Legacy of Rousseau*, edited by Clifford Orwin and Nathan Tarvoc, 200–219. Chicago: University of Chicago Press, 1997.

Hayek, Friedrich von. *The Road to Serfdom.* Chicago: University of Chicago Press, 1944.

———. *Individual Freedom and Economic Order.* Chicago: University of Chicago Press, 1948.

———. *Capitalism and the Historians.* Chicago: University of Chicago Press, 1954.

———. *The Constitution of Liberty.* Chicago: University of Chicago Press, 1960.

———. *Studies in Philosophy, Politics and Economics.* Chicago: University of Chicago Press, 1967.

———. *Law, Legislation and Liberty: A New Statement of the Liberal Principles of Justice and Political Economy.* Chicago: University of Chicago Press, 1982.

———. *The Fatal Conceit: The Errors of Socialism.* London: Routledge, 1988.

———, ed. *Collectivist Economic Planning: Critical Studies on the Possibilities of Socialism.* New York: A. M. Kelley, 1967.

Hayes, Carlton J. H. *Essays on Nationalism.* New York: Macmillan, 1926.

———. *The Historical Evolution of Modern Nationalism.* New York: Russell and Russell, 1968.

Held, David. "Democracy, the Nation-State, and the Global System." In *Political Theory Today*, edited by David Held, 197–235. Stanford, CA: Stanford University Press, 1991.

———. *Democracy and the Global Order: From the Modern State to Cosmopolitan Governance*. Stanford, CA: Stanford University Press, 1995.

———. "The Transformation of Political Community: Rethinking Democracy in the Context of Globalization." In *Democracy's Edges*, edited by Ian Shapiro and Casiano Hacker-Cordon, 84–111. Cambridge: Cambridge University Press, 1999.

———. "The Changing Contours of Political Community: Rethinking Democracy in the Context of Globalization." In *Global Democracy: Key Debates*, edited by Barry Holden, 17–31. London: Routledge, 2000.

———. *Models of Democracy*. 3rd ed. Stanford, CA: Stanford University Press, 2006.

Held, David, and Matias Koenig-Archibugi, eds. *Global Governance and Public Accountability*. London: Blackwell, 2005.

Held, David, and Anthony McGrew, eds. *The Global Transformations Reader*. Cambridge: Polity Press, 2002.

Held, David, Anthony McGrew, David Goldblatt, and Jonathan Perraton. *Global Transformations: Politics, Economics, and Culture*. Stanford, CA: Stanford University Press, 1999.

Hillebrand, Evan. "The Global Distribution of Income in 2050." *World Development* 36, no. 5 (2008): 727–40.

Hirst, Paul, Grahame Thompson, and Simon Bromley. *Globalization in Question*. Vol. 3. 2nd ed. Cambridge: Polity Press, 2009.

Hobbes, Thomas. *Leviathan*. Edited by Richard Flathman. New York: W. W. Norton, 1997.

Hobsbawm, Eric J. *Industry and Empire*. New York: Pantheon, 1969.

———. *The Age of Capital, 1848–1875*. New York: Scribner, 1975.

———. *The Age of Empire 1875–1914*. New York: Vintage Books, 1989.

———. *Nations and Nationalism Since 1780: Programme, Myth, Reality*. New York: Cambridge University Press, 1990.

Hochschild, Adam. *King Leopold's Ghost*. New York: Houghton Mifflin, 1998.

Hoffman, Bruce. *Inside Terrorism*. New York: Columbia University Press, 1998.

———. *Re-Thinking Terrorism in Light of a War on Terrorism*. Santa Monica, CA: Rand, 2001.

Hoffmann, S., and D. Fidler, eds. *Rousseau on International Relations*. Oxford: Oxford University Press, 1991.

Holden, Barry. *Global Democracy*. New York: Routledge, 2000.

Hsiang, Solomon M., Kyle C. Meng, and Mark A. Cane. "Civil Conflicts Are Associated with the Global Climate." *Nature* 476 (2011): 438–41.

Hughes, Barry B., Mohammod T. Irfan, Haider Khan, Krishna B. Kumar, Dale S. Rothman, and Jose Roberto Solorzano, eds. *Reducing Global Poverty: Patterns of Potential Human Progress*. Boulder, CO: Paradigm, 2009.

Hulme, David, and John Toye, eds. *Understanding Poverty and Well-Being: Bridging the Disciplines*. London: Routledge, 2007.

Hunt, Elgin F., and David C. Colander. *Social Science: An Introduction to the Study of Society*. 13th ed. Boston: Pearson, 2008.

Huntington, Samuel P. *American Politics: The Promise of Disharmony*. Cambridge: Cambridge University Press, 1981.

——. *The Third Wave: Democratization in the Late Twentieth Century*. Norman: University of Oklahoma Press, 1991.

——. *The Clash of Civilizations*. New York: Simon and Schuster, 1996.

Hytek, Gary, and Kristine M. Zentgraf. *America Transformed: Globalization, Inequality, and Power*. New York: Oxford University Press, 2008.

Ignatieff, Michael. *The Rights Revolution*. Toronto: Anansi Press, 2000.

——. *The Lesser Evil: Political Ethics in the Age of Terror*. Princeton, NJ: Princeton University Press, 2004.

International Institute for Strategic Studies. *The Military Balance: 2007*. London: Routledge, 2007.

International Monetary Fund. *Global Financial Stability Report: Responding to the Financial Crisis and Measuring Systemic Risks*. Washington, DC: International Monetary Fund, 2009.

International Monetary Fund, Research Department. *World Economic Outlook: Globalization and Inequality*. Washington, DC: International Monetary Fund, 2007.

Jablecki, Juliusza, and Mateusz Machai. "The Regulated Meltdown: The Basel Rules and Banks' Leverage." In *What Caused the Financial Crisis*, edited by Jeffrey Friedman, 183–99. Philadelphia: University of Pennsylvania Press, 2011.

Jacobs, Lawrence, and Desmond King, eds. *The Unsustainable American State*. Oxford: Oxford University Press, 2008.

Jacobson, Harold K. *Networks of Interdependence: International Organizations and the Global Political System*. 2nd ed. New York: McGraw-Hill, 1993.

Jacques, Martin. *The End of the Western World and the Birth of a New Global Order*. New York: Penguin, 2009.

Jaffa, Harry V. *Crisis of the House Divided: An Interpretation of the Issues in the Lincoln-Douglas Debates*. Chicago: University of Chicago Press, 2009.

Janeway, William H. *Doing Capitalism in the Innovation Economy: Markets, Speculation and the State*. Cambridge: Cambridge University Press, 2014.

Jojarth, Christine. *Crime, War, and Global Trafficking: Designing International Cooperation*. Cambridge: Cambridge University Press, 2009.

Joll, James. *The Origins of the First World War*. New York: Longman, 1984.

Jones, Eric Lionel. *The European Miracle: Environments, Economies, and Geopolitics in the History of Europe and Asia*. 2nd ed. New York: Cambridge University Press, 1987.

——. *Recurring Growth*. Oxford: Oxford University Press, 1988.

Juergensmeyer, Mark. *Terror in the Mind of God: The Global Rise of Religious Violence*. Berkeley: University of California Press, 2003.

——. *Religion in Global Civil Society*. Oxford: Oxford University Press, 2005.

——. *Global Rebellion: Religious Challenges to the Secular State, from Christian Militias to Al Qaeda*. Berkeley: University of California Press, 2008.

Kagan, Donald. *The Peloponnesian War*. New York: Viking, 2003.

Kahn, Herman. *On Thermonuclear War*. Princeton, NJ: Princeton University Press, 1960.

Kahneman, Daniel. *Thinking Fast and Slow*. New York: Farrar, Straus and Giroux, 2011.

Kahneman, Daniel, and Alan B. Kreuger. "Developments in the Measurement of Subjective Well-Being." *Journal of Economic Perspectives* 20 (2006): 3–24.

Kahneman, Daniel, Alan B. Kreuger, David Schkade, Norbert Schwarz, and Arthur Stone. "Toward National Well-Being Accounts." *American Economic Review* 94, no. 2 (2004): 429–34. doi: 10.1257/0002828041301713.

———. "Would You Be Happier If You Were Richer? A Focusing Illusion." *Science* 312, no. 5782 (2006): 1908–10. Retrieved from http://www.sciencemag.org/cgi/content/abstract/312/5782/1908.

Kaiser, Robert J. *The Geography of Nationalism in Russia and the USSR.* Princeton, NJ: Princeton University Press, 1994.

Kaldor, Mary. *Global Civil Society: An Answer to War.* Cambridge: Polity Press, 2003.

———. *New and Old Wars.* London: Polity Press, 2006.

Kaldor, Mary, Marlies Glasius, and Helmut Anheier, eds. *Global Civil Society 2004/5.* London: Sage, 2005.

Kaldor, Mary, Terry Lynn Karl, and Yahia Said, eds. *Oil Wars.* London: Pluto, 2007.

Kanet, Roger E., and Edward A. Kolodziej, eds. *The Cold War as Cooperation.* Baltimore: Johns Hopkins University Press, 1991.

Kant, Immanuel. "Perpetual Peace: A Philosophical Essay." In *The Theory of International Relations,* edited by M. G. Forsyth, 200–244. New York: Atherton, 1970.

———. *Perpetual Peace and Other Essays on Politics, History, and Morals.* Translated by Ted Humphrey. Indianapolis, IN: Hackett, 1983.

———. "Idea for a Universal History with a Cosmopolitan Purpose." In *Kant: Political Writings,* translated by H. B. Nisbet, edited by Hans Reiss, 2nd ed., 41–53. Cambridge: Cambridge University Press, 1991.

———. *Kant: Political Writings.* 2nd ed. Translated by H. B. Nisbet. Cambridge: Cambridge University Press, 1991.

Kaplan, Steven N. "Are U.S. CEOs Overpaid?" *Academy of Management Perspectives* (May 2008): 5–20.

Kaplinsky, Raphael. *Globalization, Poverty, and Inequality.* Cambridge: Polity Press, 2005.

Karl, T. R., J. M. Melillo, and T. C. Paterson, eds. *Global Climate Change Impacts in the United States.* Cambridge: Cambridge University Press, 2009.

Karns, Margaret P., and Karen A. Mingst. *International Organizations: The Politics and Processes of Global Governance.* Boulder, CO: Lynne Rienner, 2004.

Kaufman, William W. *The McNamara Strategy.* New York: Harper & Row, 1964.

Keane, John. *Civil Society, New Visions.* Stanford, CA: Stanford University Press, 1998.

———. *Global Civil Society?* Cambridge: Cambridge University Press, 2003.

———. *The Life and Death of Democracy.* New York: W. W. Norton, 2009.

Keane, John, ed. *Civil Society and the State: New European Perspectives.* London: Verso, 1988.

Keck, Margaret E., and Kathryn Sikkink. *Activists beyond Borders: Advocacy Networks in International Politics.* Ithaca, NY: Cornell University Press, 1998.

Kehr, Eckart. *Battleship Building and Party Politics in Germany 1894–1901.* Translated by Pauline R. and Eugene N. Anderson. Chicago: University of Chicago Press, 1973.

Kelly, Robert J., Jess Maghan, and Joseph D. Serio. *Illicit Trafficking: A Reference Handbook*. Santa Barbara, CA: ABC-CLIO, 2005.

Kennedy, Paul M. *The Rise of the Anglo-German Antagonism 1860–1914*. London: George Allen & Unwin, 1980.

Kier, Elizabeth. "Culture and French Military Doctrine before World War II." In *The Culture of National Security*, edited by Peter J. Katzenstein, 186–215. New York: Columbia University Press, 1996.

Kindleberger, Charles P. "The Great Transformation." *Daedalus* 103 (Winter 1974).

———. "Dominance and Leadership in the International Economy: Exploitation, Public Goods, and Free Rides." *International Studies Quarterly* 25 (1981): 242–54.

———. "On the Rise and Decline of Nations." *International Studies Quarterly* 27, no. 1 (1983): 5–10.

———. *A Financial History of Western Europe*. New York: Oxford University Press, 1993.

Klare, Michael. *Resource Wars: The New Landscape of Global Conflict*. New York: Henry Holt, 2002.

———. *Blood and Oil*. New York: Metropolitan Books, 2004.

———. *Rising Powers, Shrinking Planet: The New Geopolitics of Energy*. New York: Henry Holt, 2009.

———. *The Race for What's Left: The Global Scramble for the World's Last Resources*. New York: Metropolitan Books, 2012.

Knight, Frank H. *Risk, Uncertainty and Profit*. New York: Houghton Mifflin, 1921.

Koch, H. W., ed. *The Origins of the First World War*. New York: Taplinger, 1972.

Kohl, Richard, ed. *Globalisation, Poverty and Inequality*. Paris: OECD, 2003.

Kolbert, Elizabeth. *The Sixth Extinction: An Unnatural History*. New York: Henry Holt, 2014.

Kolodziej, Edward A. *French International Policy under De Gaulle and Pompidou: The Politics of Grandeur*. Ithaca, NY: Cornell University Press, 1974.

———. "Arms Transfers in International Politics." In *Arms Transfers in the Modern World*, edited by Stephanie Neuman and Robert Harkavy. New York: Praeger, 1980.

———. *Making and Marketing Arms: The French Experience and Its Implications for the International System*. Princeton, NJ: Princeton University Press, 1987.

———. "Renaissance in Security Studies? Caveat Lector." *International Studies Quarterly* 36 (1992): 421–38.

———. "The Great Powers and Genocide: Lessons from Rwanda." *Pacific Review* 12, no. 2 (June 2000): 121–45.

———. *Security and International Relations*. Cambridge: Cambridge University Press, 2005.

———, ed. *A Force Profonde: The Power, Politics and Promise of Human Rights*. Philadelphia: University of Pennsylvania Press, 2003.

Kolodziej, Edward A., and Roger Kanet, eds. *From Superpower to Besieged Global Power: Restoring World Order after the Failure of the Bush Doctrine*. Athens: University of Georgia Press, 2008.

Kostovicova, Denisa, and Vesna Bojicic-Dzelilovic, eds. *Persistent State Weakness in the Global Age.* Burlington, NH: Ashgate, 2009.

Krause, Keith. "Small Arms and Light Weapons: Toward Global Public Policy." In *Coping with Crisis Working Papers.* New York: International Peace Academy, 2007. http://www.isn.ethz.ch/Digital-Library/Publications/Detail/?lang=en&id=126967.

Kremer, M., and E. Masking. "Globalization and Inequality, Working Paper 2008–2009." Cambridge, MA: Weatherhead Center for International Affairs, Harvard University, 2006.

Kreuger, Alan B., and D. A. Schkade. "The Reliability of Subjective Well-Being Measures." *Journal of Public Economics* 92 (2008): 1833–45.

Kriesberg, Louis. "Social Movements and Global Transformation." In *Transnational Social Movements and Global Politics: Solidarity beyond the State,* edited by Jackie Smith, Charles Chatfield, and Ron Pagnucco, 3–18. Syracuse, NY: Syracuse University Press, 1997.

Krugman, Paul R. *The Return of Depression Economics and the Crisis of 2008.* New York: W. W. Norton, 2009.

Kurlantzick, Joshua. *Democracy in Retreat: The Revolt of the Middle Class and the Worldwide Decline of Representative Government.* New Haven, CT: Yale University Press, 2013.

Landes, David S. *The Unbound Prometheus: Technological Change and the Development in Western Europe from 1750 to the Present.* Cambridge: Cambridge University Press, 1969.

———. *The Wealth and Poverty of Nations.* New York: W. W. Norton, 1998.

Lang, Graeme, and Bo Miao. "China's Emissions: Dangers and Responses." In *The Routledge Handbook of Climate Change and Society,* edited by Constance Lever-Tracy, 405–22. London: Routledge, 2010.

Langwith, Jacqueline. *Pandemics.* Farmington Hills, MI: Greenhaven Press, 2012.

Layne, Christopher. "The Unipolar Illusion: Why New Great Powers Will Arise." *International Security* 17, no. 4 (Spring 1993): 5–51.

Lazonick, W., and O. Tulum. "U.S. Biopharmaceutical Finance and the Sustainability of the Biotech Business Model." *Research Policy* 40, no. 9 (2011): 1170–87.

Lebow, Richard Ned, and Thomas Risse-Kappen, eds. *International Relations Theory and the End of the Cold War.* New York: Columbia University Press, 1995.

Leslie, S. W. "The Biggest 'Angel' of Them All: The Military and the Making of Silicon Valley." In *Understanding Silicon Valley: The Anatomy of an Entrepreneurial Region,* edited by Martin Kenney, 44–67. Stanford, CA: Stanford University Press, 2000.

Lewis, Bernard. *The Crisis of Islam: Holy War and Unholy Terror.* New York: Modern Library, 2003.

Lewis, Kevin N. "The Prompt and Delayed Effects of Nuclear War." *Scientific American* 241 (July 1979): 35–45.

Liddick, Don R., Jr. *The Global Underworld.* Westport, CT: Praeger, 2004.

Lindblom, Charles E. *Politics and Market: The World's Political-Economic Systems.* New York: Basic Books, 1977.

———. *Democracy and the Market System.* New York: Oxford University Press, 1988.

———. *The Market System: What It Is, How It Works, and What to Make of It.* New Haven, CT: Yale University Press, 2001.

Lippmann, Walter. *Essays in the Public Philosophy.* Boston: Little, Brown, 1955.

Logan, B. Ikubolajeh, ed. *Globalization, the Third World State and Poverty—Alleviation in the Twenty-First Century.* Burlington, VT: Ashgate, 2002.

Lumpe, Lora, ed. *Running Guns: The Global Black Market in Small Arms.* London: Zed Books, 2000.

Lybeck, Johan A. *A Global History of the Financial Crash of 2007–2010.* Cambridge: Cambridge University Press, 2011.

Maine, Sir Henry. *Popular Government.* New York: Henry Holt, 1886.

Malthus, Thomas R. *Principles of Political Economy.* 1836. Reprint, New York: A. M. Kelley, 1964.

Manin, Bernard. *The Principles of Representative Government.* Cambridge: Cambridge University Press, 1997.

Mann, Michael E. *The Sources of Social Power: A History of Power from the Beginning to A.D. 1760.* Vol. 1. Cambridge: Cambridge University Press, 1986.

———. *The Sources of Social Power: The Rise of Classes and Nation-States, 1760–1914.* Vol. 2. New York: Cambridge University Press, 1993.

———. *The Dark Side of Democracy: Explaining Ethnic Cleansing.* Cambridge: Cambridge University Press, 2005.

Mann, Michael, ed. *The Rise and Decline of the Nation State.* Oxford: Blackwell, 1990.

Mann, Thomas E., and Norman J. Ornstein. *It's Even Worse Than It Looks: How the American Constitutional System Collided with the New Politics of Extremism.* New York: Basic Books, 2012.

Marley, David. *Modern Piracy: A Reference Handbook.* Santa Barbara, CA: ABC-CLIO, 2011.

Marx, Karl. *A Contribution to the Critique of Political Economy.* Translated by S. W. Ryazanskaya. Moscow: Progress, 1970.

Maryanski, Alexandra, and Jonathan H. Turner. *The Social Cage: Human Nature and the Evolution of Society.* Stanford, CA: Stanford University Press, 1992.

Masters, Roger. "Rousseau and the Rediscovery of Human Nature." In *The Legacy of Rousseau,* edited by Clifford Orwin and Nathan Tarvoc, 110–42. Chicago: University of Chicago Press, 1997.

Mayer, Arno J. "Domestic Causes of the First World War." In *The Responsibility of Power,* edited by Leonard Krieger and Fritz Stern, 308–24. New York: Anchor Books, 1969.

Mazzucato, Mariana. *The Entrepreneurial State: Debunking Public vs. Private Sector Myths.* New York: Anthem Press, 2013.

Mazzucato, Mariana, and Giovanni Dosi, eds. *Knowledge Accumulation and Industry Evolution: The Case of Pharma-Biotech.* Cambridge: Cambridge University Press, 2006.

McCrary, W. Patrick. "From Lab to iPod: A Story of Discovery and Commercialization in the Post–Cold War Era." *Technology and Culture* 50 (January 2009): 58–81.

McDonald, Lawrence G. *A Colossal Failure of Common Sense: The Inside Story of the Collapse of Lehman Brothers.* New York: Crown Business, 2009.

McGrew, Anthony G., and Paul G. Lewis. *Global Politics: Globalization and the Nation-State*. Cambridge: Polity Press, 1992.

McLean, Bethany, and Joe Nocera. *All the Devils Are Here: The Hidden History of the Financial Crisis*. New York: Penguin, 2010.

McNeill, John R., and William H. McNeill. *The Human Web: A Bird's Eye View of Human History*. New York: W. W. Norton, 2003.

McNeill, William H. *The Rise of the West: A History of the Human Community*. New York: Mentor, 1963.

———. *The Pursuit of Power: Technology, Armed Force, and Society Since A.D. 1000*. Chicago: University of Chicago Press, 1983.

———. *Polyethnicity and National Unity in World History*. Toronto: University of Toronto Press, 1986.

———. *The Global Condition*. Princeton, NJ: Princeton University Press, 1992.

———. "World History and the Rise and Fall of the West." *Journal of World History* 9, no. 2 (Fall 1998): 215–36.

———. "Long-Term Process or New Era in Human Affairs?" In *Globalization: A Global Studies Reader*, edited by Manfred B. Steger. Boulder, CO: Paradigm, 2010.

Mearsheimer, John J. "The False Promise of International Institutions." *International Security* 19, no. 3 (Winter 1994): 5–49.

———. *The Tragedy of Great Power Politics*. New York: W. W. Norton, 2001.

Michels, Robert. *Political Parties: A Sociological Study of the Oligarchical Tendencies of Modern Democracy*. Translated by Eden and Cedar Paul. New York: Free Press, 1966.

Micklethwait, John, and Adrian Wooldridge. *The Fourth Revolution: The Global Race to Reinvent the State*. New York: Penguin, 2014.

Milanovic, Branko. "The Two Faces of Globalization: Against Globalization As We Know It." *World Development* 31, no. 4 (2003): 667–83.

———. "A Short History of Global Inequality: The Past Two Centuries." *Explorations in Economic History* 48, no. 4 (2011): 494–506.

Mill, John Stuart. *On Liberty and Considerations on Representative Government*. Oxford: Blackwell, 1948.

Mills, C. Wright. *The Sociological Imagination*. New York: Oxford University Press, 1959.

Modelski, George, Tessaleno Devezas, and William R. Thompson. "Introduction: A New Approach to Globalization." In *Globalization as Evolutionary Process: Modeling Global Change*, edited by George Modelski, 1–29. New York: Routledge, 2008.

Montesquieu. *The Spirit of the Laws*. Translated by Anne M. Cohler, Harold Stone, and Basia C. Miller. Cambridge: Cambridge University Press, 1989.

Moravcsik, Andrew. "Is There a 'Democratic Deficit' in World Politics? A Framework for Analysis." In *Global Governance and Public Accountability*, edited by David Held and Mathias Koenig-Archibugi, 212–39. Oxford: Blackwell, 2005.

Morgan, Patrick M. *Deterrence: A Conceptual Analysis*. 2nd ed. Beverly Hills, CA: Sage, 1983.

———. *Deterrence Now*. Cambridge: Cambridge University Press, 2003.

Morgenson, Gretchen. *Reckless Endangerment: How Outsized Ambition, Greed, and Corruption Led to Economic Armageddon*. New York: Times Books, 2011.

Morgenson, Gretchen, and Louise Story. "Banks Bundled Debt, Bet Against It and Won." *New York Times*, December 23, 2009, A1.

Morris, Ian. *Why the West Rules—For Now: The Patterns of History and What They Reveal about the Future*. New York: Farrar, Straus and Giroux, 2010.

Motoyama, Yasuyuki, Richard Appelbaum, and Rachel Parker. "The National Nanotechnology Initiative: Federal Support for Science and Technology, or Hidden Industrial Policy?" *Technology in Society* 33, nos. 1–2 (2011): 109–18.

Murphy, Martin N. *Contemporary Piracy and Maritime Terrorism: The Threat to International Security*. London: International Institute for Strategic Studies, 2007.

Naim, Moises. *Illicit: How Smugglers, Traffickers, and Copycats Are Hijacking the Global Economy*. New York: Doubleday, 2005.

Nayan, Chanda. *Bound Together: How Traders, Preachers, Adventurers, and Warriors Shaped Globalization*. New Haven, CT: Yale University Press, 2007.

Nietzsche, Friedrich Wilhelm. *Thus Spake Zarathustra*. New York: Boni and Liveright, 1905.

Noah, Timothy. *The Great Divergence: America's Growing Inequality Crisis and What We Can Do about It*. New York: Bloomsbury, 2012.

Nordhaus, William. *The Climate Casino: Risk, Uncertainty, and Economics for a Warming World*. New Haven, CT: Yale University Press, 2013.

North, Douglass C. *Institutions, Institutional Change, and Economic Performance*. Cambridge: Cambridge University Press, 1990.

Nye, Joseph S. *Soft Power: The Means to Success in World Politics*. New York: Public Affairs, 2006.

OECD. *Growing Unequal? Income Distribution and Poverty in OECD Countries*. Paris: OECD, 2008.

———. *Divided We Stand: Why Inequality Keeps Rising*. Paris: OECD, 2011.

Olson, Mancur. *The Rise and Decline of Nations: Economic Growth, Stagflation, and Social Rigidities*. New Haven, CT: Yale University Press, 1982.

Osborne, David, and Ted Gaebler. *Reinventing Government: How the Entrepreneurial Spirit Is Transforming the Public Sector*. New York: Addison-Wesley, 1992.

Osterhammel, Jurgen. *The Transformation of the World: A Global History of the Nineteenth Century*. Translated by Patrick Camiller. Princeton, NJ: Princeton University Press, 2014.

Pan, Jiahua, Jonathan Phillips, and Ying Chen. "China's Balance of Emissions Embodied in Trade: Approaches to Measurement and Allocating International Responsibility." In *The Economics and Politics of Climate Change*, edited by Dieter Helm and Cameron Hepburn, 142–66. Oxford: Oxford University Press, 2009.

Paolini, Albert J, Anthony P. Jarvis, and Christian Reus-Smit, eds. *Between Sovereignty and Global Governance: The United Nations, the State, and Civil Society*. Houndmills, Basingstoke, UK: Macmillan, 1998.

Pape, Robert A. *Dying to Win: The Strategic Logic of Suicide Terrorism*. New York: Random House, 2006.

Paulson, Henry M. *On the Brink*. London: Business Plus, 2010.

Peters, Michael Adrian. "The Changing Architecture of Global Science." *Policy Brief, No. 3*. Urbana-Champaign, IL: Center for Global Studies, 2009.

Peters, Michael Adrian, and T. Besley. *Building Knowledge Cultures.* Lanham, MD: Rowman & Littlefield, 2006.

Peters, Michael Adrian, Simon Marginson, and Peter Murphy. *Creativity and the Global Knowledge Economy.* New York: Peter Lang, 2009.

Phillips, Anne. "Dealing with Difference: The Politics of Ideas, or the Politics of Presence?" In *Democracy and Difference: Contesting the Boundaries of Politics*, edited by Seyla Benhabib, 139–52. Princeton, NJ: Princeton University Press, 1996.

Piketty, Thomas. *Capital in the Twenty-First Century.* Translated by Arthur Goldhammer. Cambridge, MA: Belknap Press, 2014.

Piketty, Thomas, and Emmanuel Saez. "Income Inequality in The United States, 1913–1998." *Quarterly Journal of Economics* 118, no. 1 (2003): 1–39. doi:10.1162/00335530360535135.

Pittock, Barrie. "The Science of Climate Change: Knowledge, Uncertainty, and Risk." In *The Routledge Handbook of Climate Change and Society*, edited by Constance Lever-Tracy, 13–33. London: Routledge, 2010.

Plato. *The Laws.* Translated by Trevor J. Saunders. London: Penguin, 2004.

———. *The Republic.* Translated by B. Jowett. New York: Modern Library, n.d.

Pogge, Thomas. "How Many Poor People Should There Be? A Rejoinder to Ravallion." In *Debates on the Measurement of Global Poverty*, edited by Sudhir Anand, Paul Segal, and Joseph E. Stiglitz. Oxford: Oxford University Press, 2010.

Polanyi, Karl. *The Great Transformation.* Boston: Beacon Press, 1944.

Posner, Richard A. *A Failure of Capitalism: The Crisis of '08 and the Descent into Depression.* Cambridge, MA: Harvard University Press, 2009.

———. *The Crisis of Capitalist Democracy.* Cambridge, MA: Harvard University Press, 2010.

Power, Samantha. *"A Problem from Hell": America and the Age of Genocide.* New York: Basic Books, 2002.

Pritchett, C. Herman. *The American Constitutional System.* 5th ed. New York: McGraw-Hill, 1981.

Przeworski, Adam. *Democracy and the Limits of Self-Government.* Cambridge: Cambridge University Press, 2010.

Putnam, Robert D. *Our Kids: The American Dream in Crisis.* New York: Simon and Schuster, 2015.

Quammen, David. *Spillover: Animal Infections and the Next Human Pandemic.* New York: W. W. Norton, 2012.

Rajan, Raghuram. *Fault Lines: How Hidden Fractures Still Threaten the World Economy.* Princeton, NJ: Princeton University Press, 2010.

Ranney, Austin. "Toward a More Responsible Party System: A Commentary." *American Political Science Review* 45, no. 2 (1951): 488–99.

Ravallion, Martin. "Why Measurement Matters." In *Debates on the Measurement of Global Poverty*, edited by Sudhir Anand, Paul Segal, and Joseph E. Bourguignon, 25–41. Oxford: Oxford University Press, 2010.

Rawls, John. *A Theory of Justice.* Cambridge, MA: Harvard University Press, 1971.

Reus-Smit, Christian. "International Crises of Legitimacy." *International Politics* 44 (2007): 157–74.

Richardson, Louise. *What Terrorists Want.* New York: Random House, 2006.

Ricks, Thomas E. *Fiasco: The American Military Adventure in Iraq.* New York: Penguin, 2006.

——. *The Gamble: General David Petraeus and the American Military Adventure in Iraq, 2006–2008.* New York: Penguin, 2009.

Riker, William H. *Liberalism against Populism.* Prospect Heights, IL: Waveland Press, 1982.

Risse-Kappen, Thomas. "Ideas Do Not Float Freely: Transnational Coalitions, Domestic Structures, and the End of the Cold War." *International Organization* 48, no. 2 (Spring 1994): 185–214.

——, ed. *Bringing Transnational Relations Back In: Non-State Actors, Domestic Structures, and International Institutions.* Cambridge: Cambridge University Press, 1995.

Rodrik, Dani. "Globalisation, Social Conflict and Economic Growth." *World Economy* 21, no. 4 (1998): 143–58.

——. *The Paradox of Globalization: Democracy and the Future of the World Economy.* New York: W.W. Norton, 2012.

Roemer, John. *Equality of Opportunity.* Cambridge, MA: Harvard University Press, 1998.

Roncaglia, Alessandro. *The Wealth of Ideas: A History of Economic Thought.* Cambridge: Cambridge University Press, 2001.

Rosecrance, Richard. *The Rise of the Trading State: Commerce and Conquest in the Modern World.* New York: Basic Books, 1986.

Rosenau, James N. *Turbulence in World Politics.* Princeton, NJ: Princeton University Press, 1990.

——. "Citizenship in a Changing Global Order." In *Governance without Government: Order and Change in World Politics,* edited by James Rosenau and Ernst-Otto Czempiel, 272–94. Cambridge: Cambridge University Press, 1992.

Rosenau, James N., and Ernst-Otto Czempiel, eds. *Governance without Government: Order and Change in World Politics.* Cambridge: Cambridge University Press, 1992.

Rosenberg, David Alan. "The Origins of Overkill." *International Security* 7, no. 4 (1983): 3–71.

Roubini, Nouriel, and Stephen Mihm. *Crisis Economics: A Crash Course in the Future of Finance.* New York: Penguin, 2010.

Rousseau, Jean-Jacques. *The Social Contract.* Translated by G. D. H. Cole. New York: E. P Dutton, 1950.

——. *On the Social Contract.* Translated by Judith R. Masters. New York: St. Martin's, 1978.

Ruggie, John G. *Globalization and the Embedded Liberalism Compromise: The End of an Era?* Bonn: Max Planck Institute for the Study of Societies, 1997.

Rummel, R. J. *Never Again,* 2005. http://www.hawaii.edu/powerkills/NH.HTM# SUPPLEMENT.

Russett, Bruce, and John R. Oneal. *Triangulating Peace.* New York: W. W. Norton, 2001.

Russett, Bruce, and Harvey Starr. "From Democratic Peace to Kantian Peace: Democracy and Conflict in International Relations." In *Handbook of War Studies II*, edited by Manus I. Midlarsky, 93–128. Ann Arbor: University of Michigan Press, 2000.

Sachs, Jeffrey D. *The End of Poverty: Economic Possibilities for Our Time*. New York: Penguin, 2005.

Sala-i-Martin, Xavier. "The World Distribution of Income: Falling Poverty and Convergence." *Quarterly Journal of Economics* 12, no. 2 (2006): 351–97.

Salverda, Wiemer, Brian Nolan, and Timothy M. Smeeding, eds. *The Oxford Handbook of Economic Inequality*. Oxford: Oxford University Press, 2009.

Sandel, Michael J. *Democracy's Discontents*. Cambridge, MA: Harvard University Press, 1996.

———. *What Money Can't Buy: The Moral Limits of Markets*. New York: Farrar, Straus and Giroux, 2012.

Santarelli, Enrico, and Paolo Figini. "Does Globalization Reduce Poverty? Some Empirical Evidence for the Developing Countries." In *Understanding Globalization, Employment, and Poverty Reduction*, edited by Eddy Lee and Marco Vivarelli, 309–26. London: Palgrave, 2004.

Sarkees, Meredith Reid. "The Correlates of War Data on War: An Update to 1997." *Conflict Management and Peace Science* 18, no. 1 (2000): 123–44.

Sarna, David E. Y. *History of Greed: Financial Fraud from Tulip Mania to Bernie Madoff*. New York: Wiley, 2010.

Sassen, Saskia. *Cities in the World Economy*. 3rd ed. Thousand Oaks, CA: Sage, 2006.

———. *Territory, Authority, Rights: From Medieval to Global Assemblages*. Princeton, NJ: Princeton University Press, 2006.

———. *A Sociology of Globalization*. New York: W. W. Norton, 2007.

———. *Cities in a World Economy*. Thousand Oaks, CA: Sage, 2012.

Saward, Michael. "A Critique of Held." In *Global Democracy: Key Debates*, edited by Barry Holden, 32–46. London: Routledge, 2000.

Schattschneider, E. E. *The Semi-Sovereign People*. New York: Holt, Rinehart & Winston, 1960.

Schelling, Thomas. *The Strategy of Conflict*. New York: Oxford University Press, 1960.

———. *Arms and Influence*. New Haven, CT: Yale University Press, 1966.

Schelling, Thomas, and Morton Halperin. *Strategy and Arms Control*. Washington, DC: Pergamon-Brassey's, 1958.

Schendel, Willem van, and Itty Abraham, eds. *Illicit Flows and Criminal Things: States, Borders, and the Other Side of Globalization*. Bloomington, IN: Indiana University Press, 2005.

Scholte, Jan Aart. "Civil Society and IMF Accountability." In *Building Global Democracy? Civil Society and Accountable Global Governance*, edited by Jan Aart Scholte, 78–104. Cambridge: Cambridge University Press, 2011.

———, ed. *Building Global Democracy? Civil Society and Accountable Global Governance*. Cambridge: Cambridge University Press, 2011.

Schroeder, Paul W. *The Transformation of European Politics: 1763–1848*. Oxford: Oxford University Press, 1994.

Schultz, George P., William J. Perry, Henry A. Kissinger, and Sam Nunn. *A World Free of Nuclear Weapons*. Santa Barbara, CA, 2007.

Schumpeter, Joseph A. *Capitalism, Socialism and Democracy*. 3rd ed. New York: Harper, 1942.

———. *History of Economic Analysis*. New York: Oxford University Press, 1954.

Sen, Amartya. "Equality of What?" In *The Tanner Lectures on Human Values*, edited by F. McMurrin. Salt Lake City: University of Utah Press, 1980.

———. *Commodities and Capabilities*. Amsterdam: North-Holland, 1985.

———. "Goals, Commitment, and Identity." *Journal of Law, Economics, and Organization* 1 (Fall 1985): 341–55.

———. *Inequality Reexamined*. Cambridge, MA: Harvard University Press, 1992.

———. *Reason before Identity*. Oxford: Oxford University Press, 1999.

———. "A Decade of Human Development." *Journal of Human Development* 1, no. 1 (2000): 17–23.

———. "Social Justice and the Distribution of Income." In *Handbook of Income Distribution*, edited by Anthony B. Atkinson and François Bourguignon, Vol. 1, 59–85. Amsterdam: Elsevier, 2000.

Shapiro, Ian. *The State of Democratic Theory*. Princeton, NJ: Princeton University Press, 2003.

Shapiro, Ian, and Casiano Hacker-Cordon, eds. *Democracy's Edges*. Cambridge: Cambridge University Press, 1999.

Shapiro, Ira. *The Flight from Reality in the Human Sciences*. Princeton, NJ: Princeton University Press, 2005.

Shavit, Ari. *My Promised Land: The Triumph and the Tragedy of Israel*. New York: Spiegel and Grau, 2013.

Shaw, Martin. *Global Society and International Relations*. Cambridge: Polity Press, 1994.

———. *Theory of the Global State: Globality as an Unfinished Revolution*. Cambridge: Cambridge University Press, 2000.

———. *What Is Genocide?* Cambridge: Polity Press, 2000.

Sheehan, Neil. *A Bright Shining Lie: John Paul Vann and America in Vietnam*. New York: Random House, 1988.

Shiller, Robert J. *Irrational Exuberance*. 2nd ed. Princeton, NJ: Princeton University Press, 2005.

———. *The Subprime Solution: How Today's Global Financial Crisis Happened, and What to Do about It*. Princeton, NJ: Princeton University Press, 2008.

Simon, Herbert. *Administrative Behavior*. New York: Free Press, 1975.

Singer, Peter. *Marx: A Very Short Introduction*. Oxford: Oxford University Press, 2000.

———. *One World: The Ethics of Globalization*. New Haven, CT: Yale University Press, 2002.

———. *The Expanding Circle: Ethics, Evolution, and Moral Progress*. Princeton, NJ: Princeton University Press, 2011.

Sinha, R. K. *Understanding Poverty*. New Delhi: Anamika, 2003.

Smeeding, Timothy M. *Globalization, Inequality, and the Rich Countries of the G-20: Evidence from the Luxembourg Income Study (LIS)*. Syracuse, NY: Syracuse University: Center for Policy Research, 2002.

Smelser, Neil J., and Richard Swedberg, eds. *The Handbook of Economic Sociology*. Princeton, NJ: Princeton University Press, 1994.

Smith, Adam. *An Inquiry into the Nature and Causes of the Wealth of Nations*. New York: Modern Library, 1937.

———. *The Wealth of Nations*. Oxford: Clarendon Press, 1976.

Smith, Anthony. *Theories of Nationalism*. London: Duckworth, 1971.

Smith, Jackie, Charles Chatfield, and Ron Pagnucco, eds. *Transnational Social Movements and Global Politics: Solidarity beyond the State*. Syracuse, NY: Syracuse University Press, 1997.

Solow, Andrew R. "Environmental Science: Climate for Conflict." *Nature* 476 (2011): 406–7.

Song, Ligang, and Wing Thye Woo, eds. *China's Dilemma: Economic Growth, the Environment, and Climate Change*. Washington, DC: Brookings Institution Press, 2008.

Soros, George. *Open Society: Reforming Global Capitalism*. New York: Public Affairs, 2000.

Speth, James Gustave. *Red Sky at Morning*. New Haven, CT: Yale University Press, 2004.

———. *The Bridge at the Edge of the World: Capitalism, the Environment, and Crossing from Crisis to Sustainability*. New Haven, CT: Yale University Press, 2008.

Spruyt, Hendrik. *The Sovereign State and Its Competitors*. Princeton, NJ: Princeton University Press, 1994.

Stewart, James B. "Eight Days: Behind the Scenes of the Financial Crisis." *New Yorker*, September 21, 2009, 58ff.

Stiglitz, Joseph E. "Markets, Market Failures, and Development." *American Economic Review* 79, no. 2 (May 1989): 197–203.

———. *Globalization and Its Discontents*. New York: W. W. Norton, 2002.

———. *Making Globalization Work*. New York: W. W. Norton, 2006.

———. *Freefall: America, Free Markets, and the Sinking of the World Economy*. New York: W. W. Norton, 2010.

———. *The Price of Inequality: How Today's Divided Society Endangers Our Future*. New York: W. W. Norton, 2012.

———. *The Great Divide*. New York: W. W. Norton, 2015.

Stiglitz, Joseph E., and Linda Bilmes. *The Three Trillion Dollar War: The True Cost of the Iraq Conflict*. New York: W. W. Norton, 2008.

Stinnett, Douglas M, Bryan R. Early, Cale Horne, and Johannes Karreth. "Complying by Denying: Explaining Why States Develop Nonproliferation Export Controls." *International Studies Perspectives* 12, no. 3 (2011): 308–26.

Strauss, Leo. *Natural Right and History*. Chicago: University of Chicago Press, 1953.

———. *The Political Philosophy of Hobbes: Its Basis and Its Genesis*. Translated by Elsa M. Sinclair. Chicago: University of Chicago Press, 1963.

———. *The Argument and the Action of Plato's Laws*. Chicago: University of Chicago Press, 1975.

——. *What Is Political Philosophy?* New York: Free Press, 1979.

——. *An Introduction to Political Philosophy: Ten Essays.* Detroit, MI: Wayne State University Press, 1989.

Strayer, Joseph. *On the Medieval Origins of the Modern State.* Princeton, NJ: Princeton University Press, 2005.

Taleb, Nassim Nicholas. *The Black Swan: The Impact of the Highly Improbable.* New York: Random House, 2007.

Tausch, Arno, and Almas Heshmati. *Globalization, the Human Condition and Sustainable Development in the Twenty-First Century.* London: Anthem Press, 2012.

Taylor, Andrew. *State Failure.* London: Palgrave, 2013.

Thachuk, Kimberley L., ed. *Transnational Threats: Smuggling and Trafficking in Arms, Drugs, and Human Life.* Westport, CT: Praeger, 2007.

Thucydides. *The Peloponnesian War.* Translated by Walter Blanco. New York: W. W. Norton, 1998.

Tilly, Charles. "Reflections on the History of European State-Making." In *The Formation of National States in Western Europe*, edited by Charles Tilly, 3–83. Princeton, NJ: Princeton University Press, 1975.

——. "War Making and State Making as Organized Crime." In *Bringing the State Back In*, edited by Peter Evans, Dietrich Rueschemeyer, and Theda Skocpol, 169–91. New York: Cambridge University Press, 1985.

——. *Coercion, Capital, and European States: A. D. 990–1990.* Cambridge: Blackwell, 1990.

——, ed. *The Formation of National States in Western Europe.* Princeton, NJ: Princeton University Press, 1975.

Tocqueville, Alexis de. *Democracy in America.* Translated by Henry Reeve and Francis Bowen. New York: Knopf, 1945.

Tönnies, Ferdinand. *Community and Society.* Translated by Charles P. Loomis. New York: Harper, 1957.

Townsend, Peter. *Poverty in the United Kingdom: A Survey of Household Resources and Standards of Living.* Berkeley: University of California Press, 1979.

UN Conference in Trade and Development. *World Investment Report 2002: Transnational Corporations and Export Competitiveness.* New York: United Nations, 2002.

UN Intergovernmental Panel on Climate Change. *Climate Change 2007: Synthesis Report.* New York: United Nations, 2007.

——. *Climate Change 2013: The Physical Science Basis; Summary for Policymakers.* New York: United Nations, 2013.

UN Office on Drugs and Crime. *World Drug Report 2008.* New York: United Nations, 2008.

——. *A Global Report on Trafficking in Persons.* New York: United Nations, 2009.

——. *Afghanistan Opium Survey: 2013.* New York: United Nations, 2013.

US Congress. *Trends in the Distribution of Household Income between 1979 and 2007.* Washington, DC: Congressional Budget Office, 2011.

US Department of Defense. *The Pentagon Papers: The Defense Department History of United States Decision Making on Vietnam.* Boston: Beacon Press, 1971.

US Department of State. *Ninth Annual Trafficking in Persons Report*. Washington, DC: US Government Publishing Office, 2009.

Van Evera, Stephen. "The Cult of the Offensive and the Origins of the First World War." *International Security* 9, no. 1 (Summer 1984): 58–107.

Voitchovsky, Sarah. "Inequality and Economic Growth." In *The Oxford Handbook of Economic Inequality*, edited by Wiemer Salverda, Brian Nolan, and Timothy Smeeding, 549–98. Oxford: Oxford University Press, 2009.

Wade, Robert. *Governing the Market: Economic Theory and the Role of Government in East Asian Industrialization*. Princeton, NJ: Princeton University Press, 1990.

———. "Is Globalization Reducing Poverty and Inequality?" *World Development* 32, no. 4 (2004): 567–89.

Wallerstein, Immanuel. *Unthinking Social Science: The Limits of Nineteenth-Century Paradigms*. Philadelphia: Temple University Press, 2001.

Wallison, Peter J. "Housing Initiatives and Other Policy Factors." In *What Caused the Financial Crisis*, edited by Jeffrey Friedman, 172–82. Philadelphia: University of Pennsylvania Press, 2011.

Walt, Stephen M. "The Renaissance of Security Studies." *International Studies Quarterly* 35 (1991): 211–39.

Waltz, Kenneth N. *Man, the State and War*. New York: Columbia University Press, 1959.

———. "The Stability of the Bipolar World." *Daedalus* 93 (Summer 1964): 881–909.

———. *Theory of International Politics*. Reading, MA: Addison-Wesley, 1979.

———. "Globalization and Governance." *PS: Political Science and Politics* 32, no. 4 (1999): 693–700.

Watson, Adam. "European International Society and Its Expansion." In *The Expansion of International Society*, edited by Adam Watson and Hedley Bull, 13–32. Oxford: Oxford University Press, 1984.

Watson, Adam. *The Evolution of International Society: A Comparative Historical Analysis*. London: Routledge, 1992.

Webb, Paul. "Political Parties and Democracy: The Ambiguous Crisis." In *The State of Democracy*, edited by Julio Faundez, 9–26. New York: Routledge, 2007.

Weber, Max. *From Max Weber: Essays in Sociology*. Edited and translated by H. H. Gerth and C. Wright Mills. New York: Galaxy Books, 1958.

———. "Politics as a Vocation." In *From Max Weber: Essays in Sociology*, edited and translated by H. H. Gerth and C. Wright Mills, 77–128. New York: Galaxy Books, 1958.

———. *The Protestant Ethic and the Spirit of Capitalism*. Translated by Talcott Parsons. New York: Charles Scribner's Sons, 1958.

———. *Economy and Society*. Vol. 2. Berkeley: University of California Press, 1968.

———. *General Economic History*. Translated by Frank H. Knight. New Brunswick, NJ: Transaction, 1992.

Weinberg, Gerhard L. *Germany, Hitler & World War II*. Cambridge: Cambridge University Press, 1995.

Welch, Finis. "In Defense of Inequality." *American Economic Review* 89, no. 2 (1999): 1–17.

Wendt, Alexander E. "The Agent-Structure Problem in International Relations Theory." *International Organization* 41, no. 3 (1987): 335–70.

———. "Anarchy Is What States Make Out of It: The Social Construction of Power Politics." *International Organization* 46, no. 2 (1992): 391–425.

———. "Collective Identity Formation and the International State." *American Political Science Review* 88, no. 2 (1994): 384–96.

———. "Constructing International Politics." *International Security* 95, no. 1 (Summer 1995): 71–81.

Wessel, David. *In Fed We Trust.* New York: Crown Business, 2009.

Williams, Phil. "Transnational Criminal Organisations and International Security." *Survival* 36 (Spring 1994): 96–113.

———. "Transnational Organized Crime and the State." In *The Emergence of Private Authority in Global Governance*, edited by Thomas J. Biersteker and Rodney Bruce Hall, 161–82. Cambridge: Cambridge University Press, 2002.

———. *Criminals, Militias, and Insurgencies: Organized Crime in Iraq.* Washington, DC: Strategic Studies Institute, 2009.

Winters, L. Alan, Neil McCulloch, and Andrew McKay. "Trade Liberalization and Poverty: The Evidence So Far." *Journal of Economic Literature* 42 (March 2004): 72–115.

Wolfe, Nathan. *The Viral Storm: The Dawn of a New Pandemic Age.* New York: Times Books, 2011.

Wolin, Sheldon. *Democracy Incorporate: Managed Democracy and the Specter of Invested Totalitarianism.* Princeton, NJ: Princeton University Press, 2008.

World Bank. *World Development Report for 2006: Equity and Development.* Oxford: Oxford University Press, 2006.

———. *Atlas of Global Development.* 3rd ed. Washington, DC: Collins, 2011.

Wright, Quincy. *A Study of War.* 2nd ed. Chicago: University of Chicago Press, 1965.

Yergin, Daniel, and Joseph Stanislaw. *The Commanding Heights: The Battle for the World Economy.* New York: Touchstone, 2002.

Zakaria, Fareed. "The Rise of Illiberal Democracy." *Foreign Affairs* (November/December 1997): 22–43.

Zurn, Michael. "Democratic Governance beyond the Nation-State." *European Journal of International Relations* 6, no. 2 (2000): 183–222.

———. "Global Governance and Legitimacy Problems." In *Global Governance and Public Accountability*, edited by David Held and Matias Koenig-Archibugi, 136–63. Oxford: Blackwell, 2005.

Index